CLAIMING
SACRED
GROUND

CLAIMING

Pilgrims and Politics at

SACRED

Glastonbury and Sedona

GROUND

Adrian J. Ivakhiv

INDIANA UNIVERSITY PRESS   BLOOMINGTON & INDIANAPOLIS

This book is a publication of

Indiana University Press
601 North Morton Street
Bloomington, Indiana 47404-3797 USA

www.indiana.edu/~iupress

Telephone orders 800-842-6796
Fax orders 812-855-7931
Orders by email iuporder@indiana.edu

The paper used in this publication meets the minimum
requirements of American National Standard for Information
Sciences—Permanence of Paper for Printed Library
Materials, ANSI Z39.48-1984.

Manufactured in the United States of America

Library of Congress Cataloging-in-Publication Data

Ivakhiv, Adrian J.
Claiming sacred ground : pilgrims and politics at Glastonbury
and Sedona / Adrian J. Ivakhiv.
p.   cm.
Includes bibliographical references and index.
ISBN 0-253-33899-9 (alk. paper)
1. Sacred space—England—Glastonbury. 2. New Age movement—
England—Glastonbury. 3. Glastonbury (England)—Religion. 4. Sacred
space—Arizona—Sedona. 5. New Age movement—Arizona—Sedona.
6. Sedona (Ariz.)—Religion.   I. Title.

BL980.G7 .I83 2001
291.3'5—dc21

00-050639

1 2 3 4 5   06 05 04 03 02 01

CONTENTS

ONE. DEPARTURES

TWO. GLASTONBURY

THREE. SEDONA

FOUR. ARRIVALS

ILLUSTRATIONS

FIGURES

(All photographs by Adrian Ivakhiv, except where noted.)

MAPS AND TABLES

PREFACE AND ACKNOWLEDGMENTS

Human history has been a rather episodic affair. Depending on where and when one was born into it, the world may have looked comfortingly—or oppressively—certain, stable, and secure; or it may have been dizzyingly open-ended and uncertain. Ours is one of the latter episodes. The certainties that had held together much of Euro-American modernity—stories about human progress, scientific rationality, and technical and social advance—seem to have lost much of their credibility of late, even in the West itself. Meanwhile, those that had held together non-Western or traditional cultures—certainties about God or gods, the cyclic and seasonal round of life, or a people's covenant with its landscape—have either long dissipated or are struggling to reassert themselves in exclusionary and often aggressive ways.

Our nascently global society exists in what could be called a metanarrative vacuum. For all the signs and symbols that increasingly fill this vacuum (internationally tradable currencies, the English language, T-shirts, Pepsi, Nike), there is no commonly accepted and genuinely credible grand narrative about who we are and what our purpose is on this Earth. So a bewildering array of competing tales are emerging to fill the gap. Among the more powerfully imposed are those of transnational capitalism and techno-science: respectively, the story that humans are wage laborers, entrepreneurial individualists, and cheerful consumers in a triumphantly global market economy, or that we are complex biocomputers driven forward by selfish genes, destined to advance evolution, through our technological proficiency, into realms of artificial intelligence, genetic engineering, and ultimately the colonization of other worlds.

But these are only two of the competing tales in the much contested arena of global culture. This book is about one of their less visible but rapidly spreading alternatives. Specifically, it is about a certain global-subcultural strand of ideas, an alternative narrative, according to which humans and our planet are in the midst of an epochal shift to a more enlightened and ecologically harmonious era. Within this alluring tale, specific sites on the Earth's surface are credited with extraordinary power, energy, sacredness, or even sentience—and are thought to play a catalytic role in this hoped-for global transformation. This book is about the spread, in the last thirty years or so, of these ideas about Earth's "power places" and about the people who have felt drawn to such places. It is about what they do when they arrive there, and the wider social and natural contexts and effects of their activities.

These alternative movements have come to be known by such terms as the "New Age movement," "earth spirituality," "Creation spirituality," "nature religion," and "neopaganism." My interest here is in examining the cultural and ecological politics (and geographics) of these movements in their struggles with the surrounding culture. I describe and analyze the circulation of ideas about the Earth and about nature as these make their way between science, popular culture, and these alternative cultural milieux. I examine the clashes that occur between contending interpretive communities at two specific places that have been identified by these movements as sacred sites, as well as the negotiations between these human communities and their nonhuman environments, as people attempt to anchor their ideas about nature in the landscape itself. And I critically discuss how their respective ideas and practices reflect, support, or resist the pressures of a "postmodernizing" global-capitalist culture.

As such, this work takes an interdisciplinary approach to a subject that, by its nature, slips and slides across disciplinary boundaries. It is therefore addressed to several audiences, of scholars and of the broader public. To scholars in cultural and religious studies, this work contributes an ethnographic and sociocultural analysis of the New Age and earth spirituality movements (in two of their local variants), interpreted in context of a larger set of global processes. My intent is to bring these movements within the purview of a range of ideas developed by geographers, sociologists, anthropologists, and other scholars—ideas about postmodernity, global cultural change, and the politics of space, place, and landscape. On a somewhat theoretical plane, I hope my thoughts will contribute to the ongoing work of theorizing the relationship between people, culture, and natural environments—an area that for some time has been characterized by, at one end, a social constructivism that ignores our (human) dependence on the natural world, and, at the other, an objectivist realism that reduces the human realm to the dimension of quantifiable causal relations. By focusing on imagination, interpretation, and the embodied experience of living in particular places over time, I hope to contribute to a growing movement of postconstructivist sociocultural and environmental theory.

To environmental theorists and activists, this book provides an examination and assessment of a set of ideas by which nature and the Earth are being conceived, discussed, represented, and defended. Sedona and Glastonbury share with many other nonurban places the environmental pressures imposed by a social and economic system that seems to gobble up the natural world in its quest for resources to extract, locations to commodify into real estate or tourist dollars, or empty space to pave over and "develop." As resource-extraction industries have declined, many such communities have turned to tourism—ecotourism and especially spiritual tourism, in the cases I examine—to carry them into the global economy. But this solution is fraught with risks and challenges, many of which I will identify and explore.

Finally, this book is also aimed at readers who are themselves drawn to landscapes and places they feel to be special, sacred, or powerful, and who wonder what this urge might mean in our time, and what, if anything, they can or should do about it. My hope is that this book can contribute to the forging of conversational links between these disparate audiences, and can help us think through a few of the environmental and cultural dilemmas of our day.

ACKNOWLEDGMENTS

This book began its life as a doctoral dissertation and, as such, my greatest debts are to its supervisory committee. Jody Berland provided invaluable supervision, mentoring, critical insight, and enthusiastic support, and has become a friend whose counsel I will continue to trust on all things scholarly and worldly. Roger Keil and Jordan Paper spent many hours reading my work and offering generous feedback, encouragement, and expertise, while Jennifer Daryl Slack provided extremely helpful advice and critique as its external examiner. Leesa Fawcett, Sam Mallin, Cate Sandilands, and Neil Evernden read, advised and assisted me at one point or another; John Livingston and Alejandro Rojas provided guidance and enthusiasm at the project's earliest stages. Of the many others who read portions of the work or offered their time, thoughts, or invaluable research materials, I would especially like to thank Sarah Pike, Rob Shields, Kevin Hetherington, Ruth Prince, Barbara Bender, and my friends and colleagues in the Environmental Studies program at York University, especially Anik Bay, Andy Fisher, Mark Meisner, Joan Steigerwald, and Elisabeth Abergel.

I also gratefully acknowledge the generous material support of a two-year doctoral fellowship from the Social Sciences and Humanities Research Council of Canada, and a G. A. P. Carrothers Scholarship from the Faculty of Environmental Studies at York University. Earlier versions of some chapters have been presented at conferences, and parts of chapters 6 and 7 have appeared in *Social Compass* 44 (3) (1997). Comments on these, and more recently those of an anonymous reviewer for Indiana University Press, have helped me immensely. I am also grateful to Marilyn Grobschmidt, Jane Lyle, Bob Sloan, Miki Bird, Carrie Jadud, and the others at Indiana University Press whose patience, perseverance, and general helpfulness have made this book possible; to Bob Furnish for his many insightful and sensitive editorial suggestions; and to Freya Godard for her perceptiveness up to the last minute.

My heartfelt thanks extend to those whose friendship, assistance and interest in the project carried me through months of fieldwork: in Glastonbury, these included Roy and Maddie Norris, Caroline Woolley, Jaana

Hakala, Taras Kosikowsky, Angela Henderson, Bruce Garrard, Ann Morgan, Keith Mitchell, Frances Howard-Gordon, Palden Jenkins, and Kathy Jones; in Sedona, Bennie Blake, Max Licher, John Armbruster, Paul Fried, Dove, and Mary; and elsewhere (namely, at the original third site of this research, which disappeared somewhere along the way), Cecilia Honisch, Judy Perry, Ken Treusdell, Bill McKay, Guujaaw, and Simon Davies. Nor can I forget the treasured chance encounters, resonant moments, and friendships inadequately explored along the way: Batya, Ben, Andrew, Mary Anna, J'net and Ocean, Dawn and Morgan, Thea and Carter, Vratya, Maria and family, Michelle, Emiko, Karen and Wale, the monks of Mount Tabor, Kathleen, Sandy. From all these and others who have lived much closer than I to the sites described in this book, I beg forgiveness for any inaccuracies, misperceptions, hasty judgments or outright errors that have crept into my account, and I alone take responsibility for them. To Yuri, many thanks for your flaming red truck, which kept me moving through the North American leg of my fieldwork. And to all my friends and loved ones who kept me anchored at different points in my journey (Gillian, Kat, the whole extended family of Vapniak frères et soeurs), my deepest love and gratitude. I am most grateful to Sherilyn MacGregor, without whose loving companionship, encouragement, and wise and critical counsel, the last few years would have been unthinkable; and to my parents, Peter and Irene, whose love for me knows no bounds.

In a book about place and landscape, I feel a need to also thank and remember those places that have shaped me and formed my understanding of place and our (human) place in the world: enchanted pockets of wood in Toronto's extensive and remarkable network of ravines, especially the Humber River, which taught me how a landscape can become an intimate and familiar guide to one's own psychic geography; the Credit River in the vicinity of Terra Cotta, Ontario, where I spent my childhood summers; certain stretches of the Niagara Escarpment, of southern Ontario's remaining Carolinian forests, and of the mixed forests, rocks, and lakes of the Canadian Shield of south-central Ontario and the province's parks system; the mountains and forests of western Canada and the United States; the Carpathian Mountains of southern Poland and western Ukraine (a wished-for "second home" which taught me how desire and landscape can commingle) and the middle Dnipro (Dnepr) basin in central Ukraine; the west of Ireland; the deserts of Egypt and Israel; and all their inhabitants, human and otherwise, who have forced me to reckon with the fluidity, yet compelling perplexity, of those boundaries that separate and connect us all.

This book is especially dedicated to the memory of my beloved brother, the Reverend Marian Iwachiw, whose respect for and faith in my own abilities supported me, especially, and all the more paradoxically, since his premature death midway through my wanderings. May his passion for truth, his tremendously kind (and, in the end, overextended) heart, and his bearlike, loving embraces continue to nourish all those who knew him as they have nourished me.

PART ONE

DEPARTURES

A landscape is a series of named locales, a set of relational places linked by paths, movements, and narratives. It is a cultural code for living, an anonymous "text" to be read and interpreted, a writing pad for inscription, a scape of and for human praxis, a mode of dwelling and a mode of experiencing. It is invested with powers, capable of being organized and choreographed . . . and is always sedimented with human significances. It is story and telling, temporality and remembrance.

—CHRISTOPHER TILLEY, *A Phenomenology of Landscape*

Pilgrimage is born of desire and belief. The desire is for solution to problems of all kinds that arise within the human situation. The belief is that somewhere beyond the known world there exists a power that can make right the difficulties that appear so insoluble and intractable here and now. All one must do is journey.

—E. ALAN MORINIS, *Sacred Journeys*

The correlate of the migratory condition of [modern humans'] experience of society and self has been what might be called a metaphysical loss of "home." It goes without saying that this condition is psychologically hard to bear. It has therefore engendered its own nostalgias—nostalgias, that is, for a condition of "being at home" in society, with oneself and, ultimately, in the universe.

—PETER BERGER ET AL., *The Homeless Mind*

Perhaps the world resists being reduced to mere resource because it is—not mother/matter/mutter—but coyote, a figure for the always problematic, always potent tie of meaning and bodies. . . . Perhaps our hopes for accountability, for politics, for ecofeminism, turn on revisioning the world as coding trickster with whom we must learn to converse.

—DONNA HARAWAY, *Simians, Cyborgs, and Women*

ONE

Power and Desire in Earth's Tangled Web

One of the defining narratives of Western culture has been a story of power and of knowledge: that science and technology—the disinterested pursuit of knowledge and its technical application toward human welfare—have established humanity as the reigning power on this Earth. Though this power might not always be equitably shared nor wisely deployed, it is a power, so the story goes, that has been harnessed by human ingenuity from the forces of nature. It is the power of the steam engine, the turbine, the atom, and the silicon chip (and, aiding in the circulation of all of these, the power of the dollar, pound, or yen).

It seems paradoxical that some of those more privileged within this economy of power—relatively educated and, on a global scale, well-off Westerners—betray doubts about this techno-humanist project. Millennial times encourage such doubts: from wide-screen tornadoes, earthbound asteroids, and extraterrestrial invasions, to the real-life escap(ad)es of sects like Heaven's Gate, to the more common lament over the loss of "that old-time religion," the idea that humans are subject to the whims of a higher power, or that we must answer to it for the misuse of our own power, is widespread.

In one of its more recent guises, this power takes on the form of the Earth itself, the body of a being increasingly known by its feminized, ancient Greek name Gaia. This book is about one of the responses to this particular form of power, and about those people who seek out places where one might reconnect with it, feel the pulse of its energy, and allow it to guide one's actions in the direction of some sort of reconcordance of a world gone askew. Many of these people consider themselves part of an emerging New Age of spiritual and ecological awareness. They share a desire to communicate with a numinous, extrahuman Other—a realm of power, meaning, and intelligence found somewhere beyond the boundaries of the ego, and beyond the confines of a rationalist modern worldview. This desire is felt to be part of a broader societal imperative—a refusal of the disenchanting consequences of secular, scientific-industrial modernity, and an attempt to develop a culture of reenchantment, a new planetary culture that would dwell in harmony with the spirit of the Earth.

This desire for contact with an extrahuman Other, if it is taken seriously, raises a series of questions: about the *reality* of the Other, the different *kinds* of Others imagined or experienced to be real (such as gods and goddesses, spirits, angels, or extraterrestrials), and the possible forms of relationship between human individuals and such nonhuman intelligences. In their most stark formulation, these concerns revolve around the question: is the Other encountered by these Gaian pilgrims *real*, or is it simply an empty screen onto which they project their own fantasies and unconscious desires? A religious believer would typically answer this question by affirming the first possibility—that these Others are *quite* real (and may proceed to make significant distinctions between them, for instance, between benevolent and maleficent ones), while the majority of secular intellectuals would likely deny their reality as such, explaining them instead as wish-fulfillment fantasies or useful social constructs at best.

I will stake out a third position in this book, one that avoids the sterile, as I see it, dichotomies that underlie the terms of the question—dichotomies which separate the *human* from the *nonhuman*, and the *real* from the *illusory*. My premise, rather, is that both of the opposite poles of these paired dichotomies emerge out of an interactive web that is tangled and blurred at its very origins. This is a tangled web within which the world is ever being created—shaped and constituted through the imaginative, discursive, spatial, and material practices of humans reflectively immersed within an active and animate, more-than-human world. It is a tangled web of selfhood and otherness, identities and differences, relations both natural and cultural; a web through which circulate meanings, images, desires, and power itself (the power to act, to imagine, to define, impose, and resist). I will argue and try to demonstrate that the Earth—actual places, landscapes, and geographies—and imagination—the ways we conceive, narrate, and "image" the world—are thoroughly intertwined within this tangled web of power- and desire-laden relations. And I will suggest a few ways in which we might begin to reimagine our lives, and the landscapes which surround us, from within a recognition of this messy entanglement.[1]

In a sense, the question that underlies all of what follows, is this: If the Earth speaks to us, as Donna Haraway suggests in one of the epigraphs that opens this study—if it speaks to us not in any language familiar to linguists, but as a kind of "coding trickster with whom we must learn [once again?] to converse"—how are we to interpret what it says? How, amid the tangled politics of living in places where the Earth seems to speak *louder* and *clearer* than elsewhere, are we to make sense of its speech?

INTERPRETING CONTESTED LANDSCAPES

Making sense of the world, and of the places and landscapes in which we live, is basic to human experience. Philosophers call the art and science of making sense hermeneutics—an allusion to the messages delivered by the Greek god Hermes, the meanings of which were never self-evident but had to be carefully unpacked and interpreted. This study aims to make sense of two landscapes, distinct and unique places on the surface of this Earth, by providing hermeneutic readings of the social, cultural, material, and ecological forces which interact to shape them, and by burrowing into the cultural images and discourses produced by those groups of people who live in close interaction with those landscapes.[2] Much of my focus will be on the *interpretive* moment in their production: their cultural construction through stories and place-myths, symbols and representations, images and tropes, all of which emerge out of and, in turn, shape the practical and repeated encounters of residents and visitors with the features of the given landscapes. To this task I bring the tools of the social scientist: specifically, those of participant-observer ethnography, hermeneutic phenomenology, social and environmental history, and cultural-constructivist discourse analysis.

At the same time, this book provides a study of the geographics of the sacred in the New Age and earth spirituality movements. By *geographics* I mean the ways the surface of the Earth (*geo*) is "written" (*graphein*), inscribed, and constituted, in discourse, imagination, and practice, and how in turn the Earth constitutes or inscribes *itself* into the ideas and activities of people. The two places on which I focus, Glastonbury and Sedona, are among the most widely celebrated of sites believed to be sacred by followers of New Age and earth spirituality. As a result of their popularity they have become vigorously contested between competing interpretive communities. These local struggles, in my view, represent intensified versions of broader cultural clashes—struggles between competing worldviews and notions of nature, land, place, and relations between humans and nature. As large numbers of people perceive society to be in the midst of a thoroughgoing crisis, an ecological, cultural, spiritual, and political crisis of an unprecedentedly global scale, attempts are made to reconceive the myths or master stories of society to respond to this crisis. New Agers and ecospiritualists reach out *beyond* modernity's dominant metanarratives in their efforts to make sense of the world and to facilitate its transformation. They invoke seemingly nonmodern sources, which range from the creatively anachronistic (pagan folk traditions, premodern ethnocultural identities, re-creations of ancient Goddess-worshipping cultures) to the more audaciously speculative, prophetic, and fantastic (alleged extraterrestrial contacts, freewheeling decipherments of Mayan codices, psychic revelations of ancient civilizations like Atlantis, and so on). They attempt to ground themselves within real or imagined "traditions" thought to be older than, deeper than, and thus more universally rooted than those of the modern world.

This search for new or *a*modern (Latour 1990) stories with which to build an alternative metanarrative, casts its net closer to home as well in its quest for interpretive resources. In particular, it draws upon scientific ideas that are thought to be compatible, such as Gaia theory and organismic or holographic conceptions of nature. All of these are brought to bear on the actual places and landscapes where the "culture of reenchantment" attempts to take root. As New Agers and earth spiritualists move to such pilgrimage centers, these various representations and beliefs about nature, landscape, and history clash with those of other people living there, and struggles develop over what to do and how to live at these sites.

Ultimately, however, the newcomers' values come up against the two predominant, legitimizing value imperatives of our time: the epistemological imperatives of *science*, and the economic imperatives of *transnational capitalism*. The latter, in particular, imposes a monetarization and rationalization onto space and time which is antithetical to certain of the values of New Age and ecospiritual culture. As I will show, the responses which emerge out of the tensions and clashes between these are predominantly the following. With the first (science), there is a range of interactions and negotiations which take place between science and its popular consumption: these include New Age challenges to science, which may take the form of outright rejection, but more frequently involve the selective appropriation of science, or at least of its language and its aura, combined with calls for an alternative or new-paradigm science. With the second (capitalism), there may be attempts to develop an alternative economy of sorts, but more frequently—and usually more successfully—there is the development of a tourist-based service industry catering to the needs of tourists, pilgrims, and spiritual seekers. These attempts in turn affect the nonhuman landscape.

The questions I will raise and try to answer in the process include the following. (1) What accounts for the attraction, or spiritual magnetism (Preston 1992), these specific landscapes hold for believers and practitioners of New Age and ecospirituality? In what lies their charisma or potency? (2) How do these landscapes become so highly charged with a richness of conflicting cultural meanings? Specifically, how are the landscapes themselves—their component features, numinous qualities, and active ecological agents—woven into the activities of diverse groups of people? (3) What are the differences and similarities between the alternative values and interpretations of these landscapes represented by New Age and ecospiritual beliefs and, on the other hand, the values and interpretations held by the other cultural communities connected to them (for instance, evangelical Christians, real estate developers, and others)? How do these differences and conflicts play themselves out in the practice and politics of everyday life? (4) And finally, to what extent do these subcultural conceptions present a viable alternative to contemporary Western society's dominant ideology of nature—nature seen primarily as resource, property, and commodity? Do these ideas and practices facilitate or enable possibilities for developing counterpractices and spaces of resistance to the commodification of the Earth? Or do they merely reflect and perpetuate processes within the dominant society, such as the globalization of consumer capitalism, the replacement of resource extraction industries by tourism and "disneyfication," and the commodification of spirituality or of environmental concern?

THE NEW AGE AND EARTH SPIRITUALITY MOVEMENTS

The concept of the New Age arises from the belief or hope that the present time constitutes a historical turning point inaugurating an era of ecological harmony, personal and planetary integration, and spiritual fulfillment. Over the last thirty years, the term has been used to describe a heterogeneous spectrum of ideas, beliefs, organizations, personalities, and practices, many explicitly religious, others less so, all of which together make up a large and decentralized subculture. Without stretching the term too far, New Age spirituality or, more broadly, New Age *culture* as a whole, can be seen to include the ideas and practices of several million North Americans and Europeans, affecting many others less directly.[3] While drawing its principal inspiration largely from sources outside the Judeo-Christian tradition, New Age spirituality reworks mainstream ideas into new forms. Its defining characteristics include belief in the primacy of personal transformation; an optimistic and evolutionary (though millenarian) outlook on the future; a monistic and immanent notion of the divine (which brings it closer to Hinduism, Christian Science, or belief in a Star Wars–like universal "force," than to mainstream Western traditions); and a do-it-yourself form of epistemological individualism, whereby personal experience, drawn upon an eclectic and syncretic array of sources, serves as a more important locus for determining what is true than the authority of custom, scripture, or ecclesiastical power.

New Age culture, however, is neither easily identified nor circumscribed. It includes people who identify themselves with a variety of specific religious or spiritual traditions, as well as tens of thousands of more eclectic seekers and dabblers, self-styled gurus, and conspicuous consumers drifting through the contemporary spiritual marketplace. Though my gaze will be limited to the North American and British contexts, New Age culture has increasingly become international, affecting local traditions and giving rise to hybrid forms of religious and spiritual practice and identity.[4] Moreover, the new and alternative spiritualities which emerged in the 1960s and 1970s have proliferated and diversified to the point where significant differences have developed between their related streams. Among these streams are two which will figure prominently within these pages. The first is a broad and loose grouping of orientations which I will be calling *earth spirituality* or *ecospirituality* (I will use these terms more or less interchangeably, though they are not, strictly speaking, identical). Earth spirituality overlaps with, but is in some ways quite distinct from, the mainstream of the New Age movement.[5] In this category I would include the women's spirituality movement, the ecopaganism and pantheistic nature mysticism of many radical environmentalists, the whole-earth beliefs of the neotribal "Rainbow family," feminist and environmentalist revisionings of mainstream religious traditions (such as Matthew Fox's and Thomas Berry's Creation-centered Christianity), and various forms of neopaganism and Native reconstructionism and revivalism, such as Wicca, Celtic and Druidic paganism, neoshamanic and Native American forms of spirituality, and syncretistic Afro-Caribbean religions.[6] Proponents of contemporary earth spirituality understand the divine or sacred to be *immanent* within the natural world, not transcendent and separate from it, and speak of the Earth itself as being an embodiment, if not *the* embodiment, of divinity.

Markedly different in its emphases is the second stream which will figure prominently here, and which I will call *New Age millenarianism* or *ascensionism*. This more otherworldly stream has been more closely identified with the term "New Age" in recent years, and has become particularly well known through the growing body of literature by authors who allegedly "channel" information from "discarnate" and highly evolved spirits of supposedly ancient or extraterrestrial origin.[7] Ascensionism reflects a more dualistic (or neognostic) cosmology, identifying "forces of Light" aligned against those forces which would constrain humanity's spiritual potential. This evolutionary potential of humanity is often modeled on the motif of "ascension" to higher levels or dimensions of existence; and ascensionist literature makes frequent use of quasi-scientific language to describe the "higher frequencies," "vibrations," "light quotients" and "energy bodies," energy shifts and DNA changes, that are said to be associated with this epochal shift.[8]

Earth spirituality and ascensionism can be seen as two sides of a loosely unified spiritual-cultural movement: one seeks to rekindle the connection with Earth's power directly, while the other looks for wisdom beyond our planet's weakened frame, but both aim to challenge, largely through spiritual means, the status quo of late modernity. Despite their differences (which may be very significant for believers), the two streams overlap and blend, in practice, within the amorphous culture of New Age and alternative spirituality. Sharing roots in the countercultural movements of the 1960s and the spiritual experiences of the Baby Boom generation, they draw on a common language shaped by, among other things, the importation of Eastern thought in the 1960s (notions of karma, reincarnation, and so on), the personal-growth orientation of humanistic and transpersonal psychology and of the holistic health movement, the popular ecological imagery of the last thirty years, especially that of Gaia and "earth mysteries," and a propensity to absorb, reshape, and reinvent traditions to suit individual spiritual needs. The latter characteristic has led many scholars to speculate that New Age spirituality may, in large part, be a response to the increasingly globalized and polyglot culture of postmodern capitalism (e.g., Lyon 1993; Ross 1991; Mills 1994; P. Johnson 1995; Bruce 1996; Heelas 1993, 1996; Kubiak 1999).

HETEROTOPIC SPACES OF POSTMODERN CAPITALISM

The idea that the modern era has shifted or is mutating into a postmodern one has been much debated. *Postmodernity* is said to signify a new historical epoch marked by an exhaustion of the metanarratives of Euro-American modernity—the belief in the linear forward march of objective Reason, technological and social Progress, and their unified subject, Humanity—and by corresponding shifts in historical consciousness, artistic sensibility, and individual and collective identity. The Eurocentric modernist worldview, it is claimed, has been decentered by a babel of alternative discourses, at the same time as capitalism, the world's reigning economic force, has mutated into much more flexible and transnational, decentralized and post-Fordist forms.[9] Whether these changes warrant the label *postmodernity* or are better captured by such terms as *late modernity, reflexive modernity,* or *advanced* or *transnational consumer capitalism,* is a point that is much debated by sociologists; however, it could be said that processes of postmodernization are occurring all around us, at different rates in different places.[10]

Postmodernization involves changes in political economy (the decline of state authority, the transnationalization of economic and financial capital, a new international division of labor and gentrification on a global scale), in culture and identity (globalization, fragmentation, and the compression of time and space), and an ever greater saturation of social space by communications and information technologies. The latter developments result, some argue, in a decreasing ability to distinguish the "real" world from the "hyperreality" of image and spectacle, simulation and model (Baudrillard 1983). They also lead to a "society of generalized communication" in which cultural differences have become much more visible (Vattimo 1992). Internationally, relations between once colonial or imperial societies and former colonies, or, more generally, between the global rich and poor, have altered. Tourism, for instance, has become a generalized mode of being, whereby the world's rich consume the Earth's cultures, landscapes, and monuments, while the poor rush to package and market themselves for the tourist's gaze (MacCannell 1992; Urry 1992). At the same time, the growth of far-flung diasporas, the flight of refugee groups, and the nomadic circulation of migrant workers has contributed to a "reverse movement of peoples from formerly remote regions of the world into the centers of wealth and power" (MacCannell 1992:1), with all this movement resulting in an increasingly hybridized and polyglot world culture.

Meanwhile, class, nationality, and other markers of identity have been fragmented, and, in their place, social relations have become saturated with shifting cultural signs and symbols (Lash and Urry 1994). Among these are the markers of ethnicity, race, and religion, but their meanings are at once eroding, mutating, and melding, as "human ways of life increasingly influence, dominate, parody, translate and subvert one another" (Clifford 1988:22). The cultural style of postmodernity becomes that of a global eclecticism, with the "whole of mankind," in philosopher Paul Ricoeur's words, becoming "an imaginary museum: where shall we go this weekend — visit the Angkor ruins or take a stroll in Tivoli of Copenhagen?" (in P. Johnson 1995:163). Or as Jean-François Lyotard puts it, "one listens to reggae, watches a western, eats McDonald's food for lunch and local cuisine for dinner, wears Paris perfume in Tokyo and 'retro' clothes in Hong Kong; knowledge is a matter for TV games" (1993:42). Postmodern lifestyles in turn produce postmodern personalities: fragmented, multiple and contradictory identities pursuing schizoid intensities. If in modernity, as Marx and Engels described it, "all that is solid melts into air," then in postmodernity even the individual self becomes, in Lukács's words, "kaleidoscopic and changeable," "nefarious and evasive," "transcendentally homeless" (1971). For neoconservatives nostalgic over the (real or imagined) meanings of an earlier age, postmodernity represents the *intensification* of modernity accompanied by the unleashing, to the furthest extents, of narcissism, desire, instinct, impulse, hyperindividualism, and hedonism (e.g., Bell 1976). For the traditional left, meanwhile, this latest phase of capitalist expansion only intensifies the gap between a wealthy global elite and a growing and increasingly marginalized and powerless underclass.

Neither celebrating nor bemoaning these developments, sociologists Philip Mellor and Chris Schilling argue that the centuries following the Protestant Reformation have been "accompanied by a shrinkage in the social spaces filled by transpersonal meaning systems." As natural and social worlds have become emptied of their previous meanings — as, for instance, a "sky empty of angels becomes open to the intervention of the astronomer and ultimately the astronaut" — privatized values take over, leading to a growing sense of "ontological insecurity," a sense of disorder and discontinuity in the events and experiences of everyday life (1994:34). Understandably, there are countermovements — fundamentalist religious groups, ethnic nationalisms, new religious and ecological movements — all expressing a cultural desire to reestablish a sense of communal and universal foundations. Proponents of New Age and earth spirituality respond to modernity's perceived failure by seeking some sort of reconnection with the Earth: they feel compelled to look beyond the images and commodities of popular culture in search of the *real* nature, the *real* sacred, for hints that the Earth speaks and that gods are in our midst. But these hoped-for new foundations are proposed in an arena which is increasingly that of the marketplace, a realm in which "tradition," the "sacred," "nature," the "good life," have all become signs in a play of "staged authenticities" (MacCannell 1992). Privileged tourists may set out from their safe abodes to explore the world of their perceived others, seeking signs of some sort of authenticity, but those others learn to resist the categories imposed on them, or play them with a nod and a wink. Postmodernity reflects this mirror play of images and desires, this fragmented and deterritorialized landscape within which new identities and places are being constructed and contested, and where the very notion of authenticity has become a sales pitch, a joke, or a site of cultural or ethnic strife.

In this globalized and polyglot, spatially and temporally compressed world, physical landscapes have themselves become more fragmented, contradictory, contested, and indeterminate in their meanings. Michel Foucault's notion of *heterotopia* offers an apt metaphor for conceptualizing the kinds of spaces I will be describing and interpreting in this book. Heterotopias, for Foucault, are spaces which exist in relation to other social spaces "in such a way as to suspend, neutralize or invert the set of relationships designed, reflected or mirrored by themselves" (1986:24). They are spaces of discontinuity and heterogeneity, bringing together meanings from incommensurable cultural worlds. Carnivals, brothels, prisons, gardens, museums, cemeteries, shopping malls, amusement parks, cruise ships, festival sites—such heterotopic spaces simultaneously mirror, challenge, and overturn the meanings of those features to which they refer in the surrounding society.[11] In a more optimistic reading of Foucault's argument, heterotopias constitute spaces of resistance, insofar as they resist and undermine any attempts to encompass or dominate them within totalizing forms of "power/ knowledge." In heterotopic space, "the common ground on which [. . .] meetings are possible has itself been destroyed" (Foucault 1973:xvi). Inasmuch as the dominant formations at present are those which serve a capitalist economy, heterotopic "counterspaces" can be defined as those spaces and spatial practices which resist or disrupt the nexus of commodification, resourcification, and privatization. The sacralization of Sedona and Glastonbury can, in this sense, be seen as attempts to create such heterotopias of resistance.

On the other hand, with the blurring of such dichotomies as sacred-profane, nature-culture, urban-rural, private-public, and commercial-noncommercial, heterotopic space is that which is neither mere commodity nor noncommodity—it is both of these and none, including as it does a surplus of contradictory meanings and practices which cannot be brought into a unifying synthesis. Heterotopic space, in this sense, is "the geography that bears the stamp of our age and our thought—that is to say it is pluralistic, chaotic, designed in detail yet lacking universal foundations or principles, continually changing, linked by centerless flows of information; it is artificial, and marked by deep social inequalities" (Relph 1991:104–5). As argued by Baudrillard (1983), Jameson (1991), Hannigan (1998), and others, the heterotopic space par excellence of postmodernity may in this sense be the theme park (Disneyland), the fantasy city (Las Vegas), or the shopping-entertainment complex (West Edmonton Mall). Neither the red rocks of Sedona nor the green hills and waters of Glastonbury are quite as artificial and commodified as these kinds of spaces. Indeed, their construction as sacred, natural, and authentic would seem to pit them in opposition to the consumer-entertainment mythology of Hollywood and popular culture which is embodied by places like Disneyland and Las Vegas. Yet, as I will show, the sacralization of Glastonbury and Sedona—the attempt to shape them into sacred land haunted by the noble spirits of Indians, Celts, and mysterious others—has itself depended on a history of far-from-sacred pursuits: in Glastonbury, the machinations of power-hungry monarchs and competing ecclesiastical estates, the imaginative forgeries of monks, and the political agendas of romantic nationalists; and, in Sedona, the removal and extermination of Indians, the profiteering of agriculture, energy, and real estate industries, and the image machinery of Hollywood itself. The resulting mixture of desires and power plays has turned both into multivalent and conflict-ridden heterotopias. Far from being merely the emblems of a marginal but idyllic rurality surrounded by natural power, they are both firmly entwined within the cultural and political-economic circulations of advanced, postmodernizing capitalism.

Beneath the shifting flux of images which characterizes postmodernity, however, there are signs that "invented communities" based on shared meanings may still be possible. Scott Lash and John Urry (1994) argue that the transformations accompanying post-Fordism and transnational "disorganized capitalism" involve not only an increased mobility of circulating objects such as money, productive capital, and commodities; they also allow for an increasing reflexivity in social relations and identities. This reflexivity, they posit, could lead to the development of an informed society full of "new sociations," not only the electronically mediated communities of like-minded Netizens, but also cosmopolitan communities centered around refashioned or reimagined places (such as the two which I will examine in this book). Within an increasingly homogenized global culture, then, there is a concurrent heterogenization (Appadurai 1990) and localization—ongoing attempts to redefine and reinvent specific places and to reposition them within contested and contradictory geographies of space. Places are remade for a variety of reasons: to attract flows of tourists and entrepreneurs, or to repel migrants and low-wage capital, but also to make them more livable and meaningful, however tenuous these meanings. Within this context of postmodernization and "glocalization" (Robertson 1995), New Age and earth spiritualities play a complex and ambivalent role in the places where they have grown. My intent will be to shed some light on the role they play, exploring their potential to contribute to an ecologically sensitized differentiation of places, spaces, landscapes, and communities.

PERSONAL STARTING POINTS

A Travel Tale

The long hot summer of 1988, when record-breaking temperatures across North America convinced many on that side of the Atlantic that global warming was real, I was a graduate student hitchhiking along the back roads of the British Isles. I had spent several weeks trekking across Ireland and Scotland and had turned in, tired and ill, for a few days' rest at a friend's home in London. When I set out again with only a vague idea of heading west, I hadn't expected it would turn into a sleepless, forty-hour zigzag across such a strange countryside. I say *strange* not because there is anything particularly unusual about south-central England. But these two days, the eve and the day of the summer solstice, introduced me to a different kind of landscape, a more diffuse and nomadic sort of subcultural geography which congealed according to its own curious logic.

I was picked up by a carload of young men heading for Stonehenge, the most celebrated and, at the same time, most commercially defiled ancient stone monument in Britain. But getting to "the stones" was not going to be easy this time of year. Since the early 1970s Stonehenge had been the scene for a People's Free Festival held every June, but by the mid-1980s this annual gathering of countercultural forces had somehow turned into a pitched battle between well-armed police troops and unarmed "hippies"—as they were still called by locals and the press—and the festival was officially banned. With a strong police presence surrounding the megalithic site this year, our vehicle joined what was to become a nearly mile-long convoy of semi-dilapidated cars and colorfully painted vans and buses snaking along the Wiltshire countryside. The convoy of self-styled travelers finally settled for the night on a country lane outside the town of Amesbury, then proceeded to party the way they imagined that their ancient forebears may once have done—with bonfires, music, diverse intoxicants, and general revelry.

In the hazy morning I set out again, accepting an unexpected lift to the larger but less popular stone circle at nearby Avebury. By evening I had arrived in the small town of Glastonbury, or, as its devotees would have it, the sacred Isle of Avalon. A Christian pilgrimage site of great repute in medieval times, Glastonbury has been rumored to be the burial place of King Arthur, the final destination and repository of the Holy Grail of Christ's blood, carried there allegedly by Joseph of Arimathea, and an ancient pre-Christian holy place. For some, it is even thought to be the center of a giant zodiacal earthwork carved thousands of years ago into the surrounding countryside, as well as a long-time pit stop for UFOs; and, with its famous Tor and its numerous springs, one can easily see how it might be taken for a place that was sacred to an ancient Earth Goddess.

On this night, a palpable energy filled the town's narrow streets and pubs, as locals and visitors alike gathered to celebrate the solstice and to climb the Tor, the 520-foot conical hill that rises quixotically above the town and marks it as *a place apart* from the otherwise flat lowlands of central Somerset. Making my way up the windy hill, I passed by scattered bonfires resounding with the strumming of guitars and beating of bongos. Partway up, in a large clearing on one side of the Tor, a solemn ritual was being performed by a couple dozen berobed members of a contemporary Essene order. Finally I reached the broad, gently sloping summit, where well over a hundred people were gathered. The atmosphere was festive: guitars, drums, chanting, dancing, and several dogs running around, until, at a certain point, a large circle of bodies took shape and voices led its participants in a solstice rite. (All this appeared spontaneous enough to me, but not to a few of the more anarchistic revelers present, whose quirkily satirical sheep bleats —*maa-aaa, maa-aaa*—though ignored by the more devoted celebrants, indicated to me some of the diversity of this gathering.)

By dawn, a mist had surrounded the now quiet Tor and separated it from the town below, leaving the unmistakable impression that this was indeed a "blessed isle" located somewhere between the mundane world below and some mysterious Otherworld. Still drowsy, I sat and gazed out into the ocean of gray all around, the town far below, and the idea dawned on me that here—on this hill that may have been sacred to Christians, pagan Celts, and their more mysterious predecessors—the transcendentally sky-directed religiosity of my own Greek Catholic upbringing was somehow being reconciled with the earthy and more pagan orientation of my subsequent intellectual searches. Here, it seemed to me, Earth and sky meet, and pagan and Christian, ancient and modern worlds, intermingle in some strange harmony. Nothing at all seemed out of place here: in the middle of my hitchhiker's whirlwind, this was the eye of the storm.

Over a decade has passed since this event, but it has remained in my memory as a kind of anchor point within my travels. And this feeling has been reinforced by the repeated references I've heard since from numerous pilgrims and travelers who have followed their urge to visit such reputed places of power or "energy points" on the Earth's surface. Though their experiences have inevitably differed from mine and from each other's, their stories demonstrate a common thread: the thread of *desire*, a personal and cultural desire for a reinvigorated relationship with the Earth, in the sheer physicality of its more distinctive geographic formations, and with the forces that are imagined to be allied with it in a time of resistance and renewal.

Critical Sympathy

During the three years in which I conducted this research, in the mid-1990s, I was a participant-observer of this increasingly global subculture. I attended meditation retreats and psychic fairs, group visualizations and ritual circles. I watched the mediumistic performances of psychic channelers, and dowsed with copper rods the invisible energies believed to circulate within the enigmatic crop formations of southern England. Along the way, I visited several of the sites that have become gathering places and travel stops for New Age and ecospiritual pilgrims, from Britain's megalithic monuments to the remains of the so-called Anasazi culture in the U.S. Southwest, from California's Mount Shasta to intentional communities and "centers of light" like Scotland's Findhorn Community. In each of these activities, I could, and often did, fit into the role of participant. This role came easily to me, as I had had contact with certain streams of these alternative cultural movements for well over a decade prior to taking on this research, and I remain sympathetic to the urge infusing the quests of many of their participants. I am buoyed by the diversity of expressive styles and the pluralistic democratization of spirituality that can be found in these movements (particularly in the more creative and self-reflexive branches of neopagan ecospirituality), and I see these as a healthy postmodern antidote to the various resurgent fundamentalisms at large in the world. In the current intellectual sparring between a modernist and scientific rationalism and a postmodernist or multiculturalist identity politics, I find the more intellectually sophisticated contributions of New Age or "New Paradigm" thought—the idea of "planetary consciousness" and the quest for personal liberation, psychological healing, and ecological renewal—to provide a potentially useful counterpoint.

At the same time, I have been dismayed by the depoliticization and privatization of New Age values and ideas since their emergence in the countercultural brew of the 1960s and 1970s. The general lack of political analysis in the New Age movement extends not only to its engagement with the general culture, but also to relations of power and authority within New Age groups and organizations, and to its problematic relations with other disempowered groups, such as contemporary Native communities. I am disturbed by the speed by which New Age ideas have been commercialized and sold, turned into commodities, marketable fads, and individual lifestyle options —and by the way many New Agers uncritically devour, regurgitate, for a price, and otherwise appropriate the symbols and practices of other traditions. My interest, therefore, is marked by a critical and skeptical perspective which sees New Age and ecospiritual beliefs as potentially *dis*empowering and *dis*enlightening as much as they may facilitate personal empowerment and enlightenment.

My observant participation, therefore, has always been tempered by my own personal commitments: to the practice of a critical social science, and to the project of a democratic ecological politics and philosophy. As a scholar and activist, I place myself among those who believe that engaged, critical, and reflexive sociocultural research has much to contribute—not so much to knowledge for its own sake, but to the development of a wise, just, intelligent, and ecologically sensible and sustainable society. In contrast to many New Agers and other spiritual seekers, I have maintained a healthy skepticism toward anyone's "revealed truth." But mine is a skepticism rooted in an anthropologist's sympathy for human imagination and creativity in all its forms—an appreciation of the multiple and varied ways humans have come to culturally construct their worlds. This "sympathetic skepticism," as anthropologist David Hess describes it, brackets out questions about the objective truth of people's beliefs, and instead tries to see them "from the perspective of the people who hold them" and "by situating these beliefs in their historical, social, and cultural contexts" (1993:159). Such a view makes it easier for the cultural analyst to see the effects of these beliefs and how they play themselves out in the broader cultural arena. This approach also rejects the oversimplified view that these movements are part of a growing "irrationalism" which threatens to topple the edifice of scientific rationality (e.g., Kurtz 1985a; M. Gardner 1991; Faber 1996). Rather, I see them as representing *alternative* rationalities, more or less coherent within themselves, vying with each other and with the dominant rationality (scientifico-positivist, utilitarian, and instrumental) for epistemological status and recognition.[12] I see New Age and ecospirituality as responses—as lucid or confused, coherent or incoherent as their practitioners—to the challenge that Chellis Glendinning has called the need "to re-invent an Earth-honoring way of living" (1995:84). Whatever the shortcomings of the responses described herein, I believe the task itself requires our utmost attention.

OUTLINE

Of the seven chapters which follow, the first two provide the background and context for the empirical work of the next four, while the final chapter presents my conclusions. Chapter 2, "Reimagining Earth," introduces the main New Age and ecospiritual ideas about Earth and landscape, and describes the historical evolution of these ideas, their reception, and frequently rejection, by the scientific community, and their relation to broader cultural discourses about nature. Chapter 3, "Orchestrating Sacred Space," focuses in turn on the practices and activities of "Gaia's pilgrims." I contextualize their activities within the larger geographical context of the post-sixties counterculture and the growth of spiritual tourism, and I examine the things they do (or claim to do) at places they consider sacred, interpreting these as spatial practices which themselves sacralize the landscape, and which, by repositioning peripheral places into a sacred geography in which they are taken to be central, articulate an *alternative geography* to that of industrial modernity. And yet, the landscape is hardly a tabula rasa to be shaped like putty into whatever people desire; so I present a model for interpreting places and landscapes as *heterogeneous productions*, shaped or orchestrated not only by the activities of human social groups, but also by nonhuman biological and material others, the actions of which resist as well as accommodate human impositions on the land.

Chapters 4 through 7 consist of empirically detailed, interpretive readings of Glastonbury and Sedona. The first is a town marked by a significant and focal landscape feature, Glastonbury Tor, which together with an ensemble of other landscape features is soaked within a complex, many-layered, and much-contested history (or geology) of cultural myths and meanings. The second is in some ways a more obviously *natural* landscape; the layers of cultural myths and meanings on which I will be focusing here range from those of Native Americans to present-day New Age pilgrims, evangelical Christians, and a high-stakes real estate industry. These four chapters constitute the substantive core of this book; and readers more interested in either of the two sites than in broader theoretical or sociological questions may wish to proceed directly to the relevant chapters (4 or 6), returning to chapters 2 and 3 afterwards.

Following these place-readings, I attempt, in the final chapter, to pull together the theoretical and empirical strands making up this work. Drawing on some of the specific place-stories of my interview subjects—stories about how they came to their destinations, and how they have been changed by them—and on the representational discourses and imaginal languages that circulate around these places, I develop a hermeneutic phenomenology of such ecospiritual heterotopias. The model I present involves recognizing three active constituents in the making of such places: (1) the creative imagination, desire and intentionality of the place-pilgrims; (2) the landscape or place itself, with its specific environmental features and agents or "actants" (entities that can be said to *do* things)[13] and the various interpretive possibilities these afford to people; and (3) the cultural lore that builds up around these places, which includes stories, symbols, place-images and representations, and various expectations derived from these. These three factors interact with each other, but also with the outside world, with competing interpretive communities, and with broader sociocultural realities. I attempt, finally, to arrive at some conclusions about what the *place* of such heterotopic places, and of New Age and ecospiritual *place-practices*, might be in today's world. I end with a few tentative suggestions which I hope might encourage and facilitate dialogue between New Agers and ecospiritualists, their skeptical detractors, and others involved in the social life of the places they share.

TWO

Reimagining Earth

There was a general understanding, prior to the brief centuries of our present culture, that the earth was alive, with subtle but powerful forces flowing through its body, the land. These concentrated at various points that came to be regarded as totemic spots, sacred areas, power places, or temples. . . . Each of these locations had its own quality, tutelary deity or "spirit of place"—*genius loci*. They were points of *geographical sanctity*.

—PAUL DEVEREUX, *Places of Power*
(italics in original)

. . . if Gaia is the living planet and is literally the *body* of some kind of intelligence, then that intelligence must have energy centres, and often these coincide with holy places, whether they're Mecca, or Ayers Rock, or Glastonbury.

—informant interviewed by Marion Bowman,
"Drawn to Glastonbury" (italics in original)

The axis around which New Age and ecospiritual beliefs about the Earth revolve is the idea that modernity has alienated humans from the natural world, but that this alienation can be dissolved or cured. Three themes predominate in the expanding body of New Age and ecospiritual literature. First, there is the idea that the Earth is a living organism or being of which we are a part: most commonly, this is not just *any* being, but a Goddess whose relationship to humans is like that of a mother. Second, we find the notion that there are "energies" of some sort, as yet poorly understood by science, which circulate within the Earth, arranging themselves in fluid or possibly geometric patterns, lines, grids, or currents, and meeting or accumulating at particular places. Finally, there is the widespread belief that premodern, ancient, or indigenous cultures have been more attuned and sensitive to, and more knowledgeable about, these energies and "mysteries" of the Earth, mysteries which our modern culture has denied or forgotten but which are being rediscovered today.

In this chapter I will examine these three sets of ideas and trace their growth and contestation within the ranks of their supporters as well as scholarly detractors. The literature in these areas is vast and wildly varying in merit, so my overview will focus on a selection of key figures, ideas, and moments, which I will contextualize within broader debates over prehistory and over the natural environment and our relationship to it. In chapter 3, I will focus on the *practices* by which these ideas and models are actualized in specific places. Ideas and practices can hardly be understood in separation from each other, however; and the place-readings that make up the remainder of the book will make clear that it is the *interaction* between the two that is most important for us to understand and critically analyze.

GODDESS GAIA, PAST AND PRESENT

> Our modern culture is a little like a person suffering from amnesia. Something happened to cause a significant—but not total—loss of memory. . . . While virtually all modern cultures consider the Earth to be deaf, dumb and inanimate, the people who lived on our planet for tens of thousands of years, from the dawn of the Paleolithic some 40,000 years ago, experienced it as a great living being that was responsive, intelligent and nurturing.
>
> —PAUL DEVEREUX, *Earthmind:*
> *A Modern Adventure in Ancient Wisdom*

> Gaia, God's wife. God, Gaia's husband. The great G-words paired and recoupled like recombinant DNA in the murky, high-nutrient soup of the New Age subconscious. Try as [scientists James] Lovelock and [Lynn] Margulis might to bring their living Earth brainchild up as a proper scientific theory, their budding princess, like most any other beauty, did not care a fig to be understood when she could be adored.
>
> —LAWRENCE JOSEPH,
> *Gaia: The Growth of an Idea*

In the early 1970s, biochemist James Lovelock and microbiologist Lynn Margulis advanced the "Gaia hypothesis"—the notion that the biogeochemical components of the Earth behave as if they constituted a single, dynamically self-regulating organism. Following a suggestion by novelist William Golding, Lovelock named the hypothesis after an ancient Greek goddess. Since then, the speed at which the idea has been taken up outside the academy has been astonishing. Analogous to the spread of the whole-earth photographic image (which originally triggered the insight for Lovelock's hypothesis) in its uses for advertising, marketing, and environmental consciousness raising, the *idea* of Gaia seems to respond to a widespread desire for a life-affirming, mythic, or symbolic connection to the Earth. It provides an apparently scientifically credible and up-to-date version of "mother nature," and has been taken up as such by many proponents of a New Age or ecological worldview. Indeed, Lovelock has mused that "Gaia may turn out to be the first religion to have a testable scientific theory within it" (L. Joseph 1990:70).[1] The reason for this rapid spread of the idea must be sought in its resemblance to similar ideas that have been brewing elsewhere and that have, in a sense, paved its way: ideas of biospheric holism, of the Earth as a Goddess, and of ancient Goddess-worshipping civilizations. I will briefly deal with each of these and with their interrelationships.

Ideas of biospheric holism are not new. Some idea of an *anima mundi*, a "soul of the world" or "Earth spirit," has persisted for centuries, and has been an undercurrent within the mystical and occult traditions of the West. Within science, organismic conceptions of the biosphere have been proposed by James Hutton, Jean-Baptiste Lamarck, Alexander von Humboldt, geologist Eduard Suess, who coined the term *biosphere*, and Russian earth scientist Vladimir Vernadsky, who developed it most fully (Grinevald 1988). Of greater popular impact have been the ideas of Jesuit priest and geologist Pierre Teilhard de Chardin. Together with Eduard Le Roy and Vernadsky, and influenced by the vitalism of Henri Bergson, Teilhard developed the idea of the Biosphere as the organic totality of living beings; but he couched it within a far-flung philosophy of cosmic evolution that was to strongly influence a number of New Age thinkers of the 1970s and 1980s.[2] A similar line of thought, inspired by the systems theories of Buckminster Fuller and Gregory Bateson, has informed the whole-earth counterculturalism that emerged in the 1960s and which has been documented by the long-running publication of the *Whole Earth Catalog* and its offspring (*CoEvolution Quarterly*, *Whole Earth Review*), with their heady mixture of anarcho-decentralism, soft-tech and high-tech, esoteric mysticism, and do-it-yourself pragmatism.

Parallel sources for the Gaia idea can be traced to the neopagan and Goddess spirituality movements. The notion of the Earth as a living organism and deity, one of whose names is Gaea, was proposed as early as 1971 by Tim Zell (1971) of the neopagan Church of All Worlds. "Literally, we are *all* 'One,'" Zell exhorted. "The blue whale and the redwood tree are *not* the largest living organisms on Earth; the entire planetary biosphere is," with "all sentient life function[ing] collectively as the nervous system of the planet" (in Adler 1986:300; italics in original). The women's spirituality movement, however, has been more widely influential in spreading the Earth Goddess idea. In a study of this movement, Naomi Summer (1992) summarizes the movement's "mega-myth" in this way:

In the beginning there was a state of paradise in which the whole world lived in harmony—men with women, humans with the natural world. No-one had dominion over anyone else. Society was matriarchal and the goddess was worshipped. Then men began to take power for themselves and to replace the goddess with a male god. They exploited women and the natural order. Their rule has been characterized by war, injustice, and rationalism. But a New Age is dawning in which people are returning to the goddess and realising their connectedness with all Being. Soon patriarchy will be overturned and peace will come to the earth once more. (in Woodhead 1993:176)

This idea that tribal cultures and ancient civilizations—Paleolithic hunter-gatherers, or later Neolithic farming communities, or both—worshipped a single Goddess or Earth Mother, and that they organized their societies along matriarchal or matricentric lines, has become rather widely held in the last twenty years. It is, like that of Gaia, not a new idea (cf. Georgoudi 1992; Hutton 1997); but its recent spread can be accounted for by two main factors: (1) the archaeological work on ancient civilizations, and primarily—in fact, almost single-handedly—the scholarly and polemical writings of archaeologist Marija Gimbutas and her popularizers; and (2) the apparent cultural *desire* to believe in this idea, most obviously among radical and cultural feminists, but also among other critics of modernity.

Controversial and hotly contested by scholars (a point I will discuss later in this chapter), the writings of Marija Gimbutas have popularized the idea of an "Old European civilization," which she situates in east-central Europe and the Balkans in the seventh to fourth millennia B.C. In a nutshell, Gimbutas proposes that Neolithic Old Europe was a peaceful, egalitarian, gylanic (woman-centered), Goddess-worshipping culture that spread from western Ukraine in the east and the Aegean peninsula in the south, to beyond the Carpathian Mountains into central Europe. Its end, according to Gimbutas, came through a series of invasions by horse- and chariot-riding, patriarchal Indo-European pastoralist warriors. Gimbutas has assembled a voluminous amount of evidence to support her theory, and presented it in a series of widely read and lavishly produced books (1982, 1989, 1991). For her eager and growing audience Gimbutas, as Meskell puts it, plays "the role of translator (channeller?) for a symbolic language stretching back millennia into the Neolithic mindset" (1995:79). Rapidly disseminated by sympathetic authors, her ideas have become a kind of alternative orthodoxy in many feminist, environmentalist and New Age/New Paradigm circles (cf. Stone 1976; Sjöö and Mor 1987; Eisler 1987; Gadon 1989; Orenstein 1990; Spretnak 1978; Sheldrake 1991:17–18; Campbell 1989:xiii–xiv; McKenna 1991). They have served as the groundwork for a burgeoning Goddess industry, which includes the growing Goddess spirituality movement (Eller 1995; Griffin 2000), Goddess-inspired art (Gadon 1989, Lippard 1983, Chicago 1979), travel guides to "Goddess sites" (e.g., Rufus and Lawson 1991), and works by "alternative archaeologists" who set out to find and decipher the signs of the Goddess in the cultural and natural landscapes of the world

(e.g., Dames 1976, 1977; Jones 1990, 1991; Meaden 1991). Taking their
cue from Gimbutas herself, such speculative prehistorians draw liberally
from archaeology, folklore, etymology, place-names, freewheeling recon-
structions of megalithic science and astronomy, and leaps of intuition, to
weave a spell of narrative associations. Each of these may or may not be
individually plausible, but their combined impact enchants and compels
their followers to believe that the Earth indeed is and has been enchanted,
a numinous presence, and that our present-day efforts to reenchant it will
allow "her" to throw off the shackles of the patriarchal and industrial era.

LEY LINES, EARTH ENERGIES, AND OTHER MYSTERIES

> I understood the power points on Mother Earth
> to be similar to the acupuncture points on the
> human body. The power points are precise
> geographic locations where there is a unique
> energetic dynamic which allows for a mutually
> beneficial relationship between the planet and
> humans. Humans may assist in the energy
> balancing and thereby the healing of Earth by
> visiting the power points. They may also benefit
> from the various Earth spirit energies emanating
> from those sites.
>
> —MARTIN GRAY, "Sacred Sites and Power
> Points: A Pilgrim's Journey for Planetary
> Healing," describing a vision he received at
> the Izumo Taisha shrine on Honshu Island
> off Japan, during a Shinto religious festival

Related to the discourse of Gaia has been the rapidly growing literary, artistic, and tourist industry dedicated to so-called earth mysteries. Whereas the
Gaia myth has served to articulate possible relationships between people
and the Earth as a whole, much of the earth mysteries discourse focuses in
on specific places and on energies believed to be present and accessible at
these places. It thus serves to support New Age and ecospiritual efforts to
resacralize landscapes and to protect them from practices that would deny
their sacredness, such as industrial development. These ideas constitute the
largest source of material informing the Gaian landscape politics to be examined in the later chapters of this book.

The beginning of the earth mysteries movement is usually traced back
to the English businessman, magistrate, and field naturalist Alfred Watkins. Though research on the geometrical alignments of ancient sites had
been undertaken sporadically since the mid-nineteenth century (Heselton
1991:17ff.), it wasn't until Watkins proposed that ancient sites were aligned
in straight lines called *leys* that the idea began to attract significant popular
attention. The legendary beginnings of "ley hunting" go back to a fateful day
on the summer solstice of 1921, when Watkins "stood on a hilltop in Here-

fordshire and suddenly perceived the beautiful English landscape spread out before him as newly laid out in a web of lines linking together all the holy sites of antiquity" (Leviton 1991:246). These were invisible straight lines making up what he called an "Old Straight Track" or "fairy chain stretched from mountain peak to mountain peak" (cited in Leviton:246), and marked by stone circles, standing stones, holy wells, old churches, castles, hilltop beacons, crosses, and old crossroads, among other markers. In his 1925 book *The Old Straight Track*, Watkins presented the complete case for a network of completely straight roads used by traders and travelers in early England and aligned through a variety of prehistoric, Roman, and medieval monuments. He portrayed Britain as a vast archaeological relic, a meaningfully organized structure of lines and centers, the ancient meanings of which were far more advanced than archaeologists of the day acknowledged. To pursue the new field, Watkins founded the Old Straight Track Club, a group of ley aficionados, which flourished between the wars and inspired thousands of other enthusiasts. Ley hunting became a favorite pastime for numerous clubs, for whose members it was as good an excuse as any for an outing in the countryside.

In Watkins's original formulation, leys were simply convenient ancient transport routes marked in straight lines over the terrain. As Hutton explains, however, "the logical and practical difficulties of imagining medieval traders trundling through swamps, rivers and a host of other obstacles, and a natural weariness with a spent enthusiasm, brought about a virtual demise of 'ley-hunting' by the 1950s" (1993b:121). Between the wars, it was in Germany that ley line theorizing was taken up and developed. In 1939, Josef Heinsch made the connection between the ley networks and ancient *geomancy*, "the sacred layout of the landscape" or "divination of the earth." German ley hunting, by the likes of Wilhelm Teudt's Society of Friends of German Prehistory, was a more politically motivated pursuit, intended to praise the intelligence of ancient Germanic peoples. In fact, the search for "holy lines" and astrological orientations was encouraged as a pro-party act by the Nazis before and during World War II (Screeton 1993:11). Teudt claimed that the Teutoburger Wald district in Lower Saxony—with its astronomical lines linking sacred places, all centered around the dramatic rock formation called Die Externsteine—was the sacred heartland of Germany (Michell 1989:58–65).

By the 1960s, analogous ideas about ancient civilizations were being advanced in other quarters. Among these was an increasing fascination with *archaeoastronomy* (or astro-archaeology), the study of the relationship between prehistoric and megalithic sites and the observed positions of the heavenly bodies at the time of the sites' construction. Earlier studies in this area, such as Sir Norman Lockyer's turn-of-the-century studies of Stonehenge, had remained speculative and marginal in their impact, but with the publication of Boston University astronomer Gerald Hawkins's "decoding" of Stonehenge (1963, 1965), archaeoastronomy exploded onto the scene.

Hawkins analyzed the positions of the stones on Salisbury Plain using a modern computer, and related them to the positions of the rising and setting midsummer and midwinter sun, and to the moon and other celestial bodies. Positive results for the sun and moon led Hawkins (1965:vii, 177, 181) to tout Stonehenge as an "observatory" and an "ingenious computing machine," a prehistoric ancestor of his own Harvard-Smithsonian IBM 7090 digital computer, whose genealogy he traced in the pivotal chapter ("The Machine") of his 1965 book *Stonehenge Decoded*.[3]

At around the same time, mechanical engineer and Oxford professor Alexander Thom was carrying out extensive investigations and detailed surveys of British stone circles. Thom's vision of a "megalithic science," complete with precise measuring units and detailed astronomical alignments, provoked much discussion among scientists and led to a further growth in amateur "megalithomania" (Michell 1982). Further encouragement for such speculative prehistory was provided by the theories of Euan MacKie, according to whom the ancient Britons were part of an international prehistoric intelligentsia possessing an intellectual and religious elite like that of the ancient Mayas.[4] Studies undertaken in the 1970s supported the growing view that some prehistoric civilizations were more sophisticated than had been thought previously; and the much more speculative work of "alternative archaeologists" has continued to fuel a growing popular fascination with "ancient sciences" and "earth mysteries" to this day. Besides the hundreds of European megaliths, foci of attention have included Mayan temples and cities, networks of straight lines at Nazca ("rediscovered" by English explorer Tony Morrison in 1967) and Cuzco (where a system of straight lines linked sacred places around the capital) in the Bolivian Andes, sites of the pre-Columbian Anasazi in the U.S. Southwest, and many other places (e.g., Mavor and Dix 1989).

From "Megalithic Science" to "Energy Currents"

Buoyed by a growing interest in unexplained phenomena, ley hunting has undergone a dramatic revival and expansion since the early 1960s. In 1965 a group of ley aficionados, including Philip Heselton and Allen Watkins (son of Alfred), founded *The Ley Hunter*, a magazine which was to become the longest-running publication devoted to earth mysteries (it is still publishing today). The new journal soon attracted the attention of others who were to become household names in the field, including John Michell, Paul Devereux, Anthony Roberts, Nigel Pennick, and Paul Screeton.[5] Michell's 1969 publication *The View over Atlantis* helped to crystallize the movement, and single-handedly transformed an obscure underground writer into a literary and mystical luminary. Michell brought together previously disparate fields such as sacred geometry and ancient architecture, numerology, gematria, pyramids, Chinese geomancy, and ley lines into an alluring narrative of a glorious past whose fragments remain to haunt and inspire us:

A great scientific instrument lies sprawled over the entire surface of the globe. At some period, perhaps it was about 4000 years ago, almost every corner of the world was visited by a group of men who came with a particular task to accomplish. With the help of some remarkable power, by which they could cut and raise enormous blocks of stone, these men erected vast astronomical instruments, circles of erect pillars, pyramids, underground tunnels, cyclopean stone platforms, all linked together by a network of tracks and alignments, whose course from horizon to horizon was marked by stones, mounds and earthworks. . . . Whether this enormous surge of energy, which within a few hundred years covered the whole earth with stone circles and earthworks, was released from one group or race, or whether it flowed spontaneously as a wave of universal inspiration is not yet clear. . . . [yet commonalities and local variations indicate that] every race made its own contribution towards a universal civilization. (1969:69–70)[6]

Michell at once portrayed ancient megalith builders as priests, astronomers, engineers, and pagan mystics attuned to the spirits or to the psychic and emotional body of the Earth Goddess herself. Alongside other proponents of sacred geometry (Pennick 1980; Critchlow 1982; Lawlor 1982), Michell proposed that there are correspondences between geometrical shapes, mathematical principles, natural energies, and cosmic harmonies; and that these principles, relating to form, shape, proportion, number, measure, and materials, were utilized in the design and construction of sacred monuments and their placement within the landscape. Heselton explains that sacred geometry is "expressed within the fabric of some architectural structure so as to cause the structure to 'resonate' when permeated by earth energies" and to perceptibly affect those people within the structure (1991:116).[7] By associating leys with Chinese "dragon-paths" or *lung mei*, Michell made geomancy a central concern of the earth mysteries movement in Britain and America: "Like the energies of the human body, the spirit of the earth flows through the surface in channels or veins, and between the two energy currents of man and earth there exists a natural affinity that enables men to divine the presence and local character of the earth spirit, to intuit how best to bring human ways into harmony with it, and even, by the exercise of will and imagination, to influence its flow" (Michell 1975:12). Responding to the criticism that Chinese dragon lines are not straight, but "spiral and undulate like surface rivers or currents of air" (Leviton 1991:251), while Britain's leys are straight, Michell suggested the straight leys might be of human construction, and the present pattern of earth currents in Britain must itself therefore be of artificial origin (Leviton 1991:251). To support this far-flung theory, he produced a detailed local case study of West Penwith in Cornwall, *The Old Stones of Land's End* (1974), which, to date, is considered by ley aficionados as one of the strongest demonstrations of the ley phenomenon.

From Alfred Watkins's original "straight track" notion of leys, then, we have arrived at a view which sees invisible but perceptible energies circulating in currents through the landscape—"etheric" or "subtle" energies which can be directed and manipulated for good or ill like the *qi* or *prana* of Eastern medicine. One of the ways in which these energies can be perceived is through dowsing, that is, divining with metal rods, twigs, or other aids. Dowsers have, over the decades, enthusiastically mapped out not only the underground water sources for which they are better known, but countless other purported energies in the vicinity of ancient sites.[8] "Once alight in the USA," ley researchers Pennick and Devereux note with some ambivalence, the "energy ley" theory "knew no bounds. Before long there were concepts of leys as cosmic *yang* energies, entering the ground as 'downshoots,' turning at right angles and moving through the earth and exiting as 'upshoots'; there were past, present and future leys, all dowsable; there were energy lines not marked by sites, and lines of sites with no dowsing energies. Depending on the dowser . . . leys had different widths, and were made up of various dowsable linear components. Crystals placed on them could stop, reduce or deflect leys. The use of leys for healing, the avoidance of 'black' or noxious leys, was developed by certain dowsers" (1989:241).

Amid this potpourri of ideas, one of the more coherent and sophisticated accounts of energy leys was dowser Tom Graves's *Needles of Stone* (1978, 1986b). Graves's underlying thesis was the idea "that the earth itself is alive and aware" (1986b:1), and that magic and "earth-acupuncture" are appropriate responses to the ecological crisis. According to Graves's acupuncture analogy, megaliths are great "earth needles" for regulating "overground" leys, perceivable energy pathways "living, breathing, pulsing" and circulating through ancient stone sites. Different leys—equivalent to the Chinese yang white tiger and yin blue dragon lines (respectively, those flowing through higher areas and those in lower-lying valleys)—supposedly meet at nodes or concentrated power points. For Graves, "the pivot around which all of the 'earth mysteries' begin to make sense" (70) is the "pagan" notion that the earth itself *chooses* the organization of sacred sites. Such sites "connect up all the earth-fields of a given area, and at the same time connect them with the over-grounds of the ley-system" (121). This system of energy, he claims, is "activated" through ritual and ceremonial activity, and the energy is real and perceptible: "High energy levels at a place like Glastonbury can make the whole area surrounding it unstable, at an emotional level and beyond. . . . In a personal sense, sacred sites can be mirrors that pick out your flaws, amplify them, and then throw them back at you in a way that forces you to do something about those flaws or go insane" (125). Graves notes as well the negative effects of highways, pylon lines, mining and quarrying, and so forth on the energy system of a landscape.

A pivotal idea for Graves is the positing of a subtle, imaginal realm of existence which mediates between humans and nature, but which has been displaced by the hegemony of Cartesian body-mind dualism. "One of the side-effects of the so-called 'Age of Reason,'" Graves argues, "has been to destroy most of the experiential meanings . . . of all the key words we need to describe the phenomena we're dealing with" (154). These key words included the animist and religious terminology of "angels and demons . . . fairies, goblins, elves, dragons, devas, dwarves, nature spirits and the rest of the mystical menagerie," all of which are "personifications of obscure and ephemeral forces that are every bit as abstract as, say, gravity or radiation" (144).[9] Graves contrasts his theory with that of Michell, who posits a complex system of geomancy by which the siting of stone circles would have to have taken into account underground and overground energy matrices, astronomical alignments, geometrical and numerological structure, musical resonance, and other factors, all of which would have required the analytical skills of an elite brotherhood of ancient astronomer-priests. Lacking the evidence for such a sophisticated elite, Graves instead suggests the "pagan solution"

> that nature is intelligent, and is using people, through the forms that people in those siting-legends described as fairies, angels, the Devil or just "something," to help it maintain its energy-matrix, its nervous system, its veins and arteries. The sacred sites, as we have seen, are on node-points of the energy-matrix: and the structures at those sites were built where and how they are, and with the extraordinary properties they show, not through analysis and logical systems, but because the builders understood and obeyed that "something" beyond them, through dreams, through divination, through "coincidence," through feelings. (172–73)

Graves is effectively proposing a localized version of Gaia theory and an innate human ability to access this broader web of nonhuman intelligence.[10]

Two British dowsers, Hamish Miller and Paul Broadhurst (1989) have pushed this energy-ley line of research forward with a work documenting their pilgrimage-odyssey following the so-called St. Michael ley line: from the west coast of Cornwall through Glastonbury and Avebury, there discovering a second, companion line with a "gentler, more female quality," which they called the St. Mary line (and which tends to move through lower-lying areas including holy wells), and on to the East Anglian coast. According to Miller and Broadhurst, dragon lines on this path pass through many churches and mounds dedicated to St. Michael and St. Mary. Where the two (Michael and Mary) currents cross, the authors claim to have discovered energetic "node points." They speculate that stone circles are "the nerve centres of the landscape," where streaming terrestrial energy currents meet and interact with deeper, more subterranean forces (125). Miller and Broadhurst's work, like that of Michell and Graves, appeals to readers through its combination of environmental bad news—expressed in a critique of modernity's forgetfulness of the Earth spirit and a we-must-listen-to-the-Earth rhetoric—and an affirmative and reconstructive vision. For instance, the apparent opposition between the Christian archangel St. Michael, the "dragonslayer," and the earth's pagan "dragon energy" they reinterpret in positive terms: the Archangel Michael, they claim, is the equivalent of Apollo, the Celtic Bel, and Mercury/Hermes, each supposedly the guardian of earth energies; he was not a sword-wielding dragonslayer, but a healer who holds the caduceus, the serpent-entwined healing rod (and now the emblem of modern medicine). No less attractive in their writing is the palpable sense of excitement they convey in the process of discovering, in the course of their on-the-land pilgrimage, hitherto unknown or forgotten secrets of the Earth spirit itself.

Measurements and Speculations:
Groping toward a Science of Sacred Place

Sensing a need to establish scientific credibility for earth mysteries research, *Ley Hunter* editor Paul Devereux in 1977 launched the Dragon Project (now the Dragon Project Trust), an interdisciplinary research effort to document and measure unusual energy phenomena, such as magnetic or radiation anomalies, ultrasonic emissions, and light phenomena, at stone circles in Britain. The project would use scientific instrumentation and methodology, and would draw on the combined energies of dowsers, psychics, electronics engineers, and archaeologists, among others. A shoestring operation, the project has lumbered along since then in fits and starts, making slow and generally ambiguous progress and resulting in occasional articles, reports, and radio and television interviews. By 1989, Devereux had admitted that the Dragon Project's psychic archaeological work (using dowsers and psychics for archaeological purposes) had produced "so far unclear results," and that "'energy dowsing' . . . has not yet developed much beyond belief-system status, and awaits the spirit of genuine research" (Devereux 1989b:105). The project's work on measuring energy anomalies of ancient sites had, however, produced some intriguing and suggestive, if inconclusive, evidence of magnetic, ultrasound, and radiation oddities (105–23; Devereux 1990). Devereux surmises that widely reported light phenomena at megalithic sites may be related to the natural radiation of the stone used, usually granite (Devereux 1989b:115ff.). This hypothesis parallels the claims of North American researchers regarding the apparent association between sacred sites and underground uranium deposits (e.g., in the U.S. Southwest), a connection that has also been supported by the work of a few neurophysiologists (Persinger 1987, 1989; Derr and Persinger 1990; Persinger and Derr 1985, 1986; Regush 1995).

In line with this more pragmatic approach, Devereux and his colleague Nigel Pennick (1989:13) have more recently rejected the energy ley theory entirely and disassociated themselves from the "'New Age' cultists, would-be gurus, 'soft' or popular theoreticians and journalistic hacks," whom they see as straining the credibility of the field.[11] Devereux argues that the term "earth energy" is too vague: "the planet teems with countless forms of energies: gravity, geomagnetism, natural radiations, infra-red emissions, natural microwaves and other radio emissions, electrical telluric currents, ultraviolet light" (1992b:48). Instead, he proposes his own, perhaps no less adventurous hypothesis of leys as collective mental constructs or "shamanic spirit paths." "Landscape lines, leys, alignments," he writes, "are *traces* . . . of an effect of the human central nervous system transferred to the land," the effect being "the remarkable ability of the human mind to roam experientially, if not actually, beyond the body." Devereux proposes that "our minds carry the blueprint of the spiritual earth," an inner geography visited for millennia by shamans in altered states of consciousness. Actual straight-line tracks, such as those found in the South American Andes, are, in his view, representations of the shaman's trance-state travels; and Devereux urges his readers to set out likewise into the "Spirit Earth" where we might "rediscover the perennial protocols for inhabiting the physical earth" and "for correcting our worldview" (219–20).

Another line of research descending from Watkins's straight track theory has been that taken up by "energy grid" theorists. In the 1970s, Cambridge mathematician Michael Behrend began detecting vast networks of ancient site alignments across southern Britain, plotting them with the aid of computers, and finding that churches and megalithic sites were set out in vast geometrical formations (such as heptagons and decagons) and according to multiples of fixed distances. Other researchers have since projected such geometrical patterns over the entire Earth, portraying the planet as a crystalline structure made up of regular geometrical patterns based on Platonic solids (Childress 1987; Becker and Hagens 1991), or, following New Zealander Bruce Cathie's (1977) speculations, as including a "planetary energy grid" whose power could conceivably be tapped by extraterrestrial craft.[12] Inspired by Buckminster Fuller's mapping of the world's surface as a series of squares and equilateral triangles, Becker and Hagens propose a planetary grid model according to which the Earth's energy field is comprised of great circles on the surface of the Earth—so-called "Rings of Gaia," whose intersections may mark energy points or "planetary chakras" (1991:273). Manfred Curry hypothesizes that such a grid pattern could consist of magma radiation and earth magnetism, and may be influenced or created by the Earth's rotation on its axis. All these theories leave far too many question marks to attract much scientific attention, yet, all fit comfortably within the worldview captured by Richard Leviton's argument that "[t]he emergence of the perception of ley lines as light or energy pathways arranged in a purposeful, geometrical order over the surface of the planet is part of a larger perception of the earth herself as a living, evolving, conscious and sacred being—Gaia" (1991:254).

Places where the Earth's "energy" is thought to be more concentrated are commonly referred to as power places, vortexes (or vortices), or Earth chakras. In her popular book *Terravision: A Traveler's Guide to the Living Planet Earth* (1991), psychic Page Bryant cites the Gaia hypothesis and theoretical physicist David Bohm's holographic universe theory to support her arguments about Earth vortices. She proposes intuition as the method of arriving at knowledge of Gaia's "power spots," and suggests that pilgrimages to sacred sites serve as a means of attuning to "Life Energy" and developing "ecological consciousness." Bryant classifies vortices into three types: *electrical* vortices, which include areas of high elevation and sacred mountains (Shasta, Kilauea, Denali/McKinley, and the San Francisco Peaks) and are said to be physically charging and stimulating; *magnetic* vortices, which are lower lying and include wells and springs (Lourdes, Glastonbury's Chalice Well), lakes (Titicaca in Peru), and caves (the Pyrennean and Dardogne caves), and are said to be conducive to quiet meditation, healing, past-life recall, and intuitive guidance; and *electromagnetic* vortexes, which combine the two types of features, and include waterfalls such as Niagara Falls and Yellowstone Falls. As a special type of "electrical" vortex she mentions "beacon" vortexes such as Sedona's Bell Rock, Mount Sinai, Devil's Tower in Wyoming, and Glastonbury Tor. She also identifies larger "grids," where energy is spread out over a broader area. *Magnetic* grids, for instance, include the Everglades and Venice, Italy, while *electromagnetic* grids include Maui and Kauai in Hawaii, much of Alaska and the Pacific Northwest of North America, and the Blue Ridge, Smoky, and Rocky mountain ranges. Finally, the volcanic Ring of Fire that stretches across the Pacific is, for Bryant, an "electrical" and potentially very destructive vortex (and earthquake and volcano zone) which she calls one of the Earth's seven "chakra" locations, specifically, the channel for the Earth's "kundalini" energy (75–76). (In Hindu and Buddhist spiritual and physico-medical traditions, the *chakras* are thought to be energy centers which run along the body's central axis, and along which flows the spiritual or "life energy" known as kundalini.)[13]

Mixed in with much of this literature on earth energy is frequent reference to UFO sightings, mysterious crop formations, the geophysical phenomenon known as Earth lights, and other anomalous phenomena. Earth mysteries researchers join ranks with parapsychologists and transpersonal psychologists, citing scientific research supporting a correlation between ancient and traditional sacred places, areas with frequent UFO sightings or unusual psychospiritual experiences, and geophysical landscape characteristics.[14] Dean Holden and Paul Scott (1991:98), for instance, surmise that the "Wessex Triangle" in Britain, the Sedona area in Arizona, and the island of Maui, are places "where legend and phenomena abound on the interdimensional comings and goings of supernatural beings," and that for some people such places are "gateways into global grid configurations." Crop circle researchers speculate that these formations—thousands of which have appeared (some mysteriously, others less so) carved into grain fields since the early 1980s—may be "a spilling over of the etheric into physical manifestation" or even "a manifestation of an attempt at self-healing by nature itself" (Messenger 1991:187).

Many of the authors discussed here conceive of their work as a form of *geomancy*—the reading or "divining" of a landscape through a variety of methods.[15] Nicholas Mann defines geomancy as the divination of the spirit of the place—the "Earth Spirit." Geomantic knowledge embraces the geography, the natural and the human history and the geometric and spiritual dimensions of a particular place or an area of the earth. It includes the study of the flora and fauna, the climate and the local magnetic and electrical fields. It attempts to explain their relationship to adjacent natural features, to heavenly bodies, to underground currents and to the nature invested in the place by human activities. (1991:17)

For ecopsychologist James Swan, geomancy is "the art of reading the subtle qualities of a place to discern what actions might best be conducted there" (1990:31). Devereux (1992) advocates an approach to sacred sites that combines conventional archaeology, systematic observation, archaeoastronomy, folkloristics, sacred geometry, scientific measurement, and monitoring of energetic properties, clairvoyant techniques (such as dowsing, direct sensing, and remote viewing), geomancy strictly speaking (the attempt to read the orientation and relationship of sites with one another and with topographical and astronomical factors), and speculative forays into previous worldviews. For those active in this multidisciplinary field, this work is exciting and explicitly responds to a cultural need; there is a feeling that such geomancy is crucial in the much-espoused reorientation of relations between humans and the rest of nature. Proponents of such a paradigm shift, however, forward their ideas within a broader interdiscursive arena; and, in the debates over earth energies, Gaia, Goddess civilization, and the like, their work brings them into inevitable tension with mainstream archaeologists and prehistorians, physical scientists and psychologists, and other specialists. The boundary conflicts that result constitute highly charged sites for the cultural contestation of ideas about the Earth. In what remains of this chapter, I will examine the boundary conflicts surrounding New Age and ecospiritual interpretations of prehistory and the broader context of contemporary environmental discourse, within which New Age and New Paradigm ideas are shaped and contested.

CONTESTING PREHISTORY:
BLOWS AGAINST THE ESTABLISHMENT?

The past is and has always been contested territory, and the more distant the past, the wilder and more varying the claims made about it. Scientific archaeologists and prehistorians have carved out the intellectual authority to speak on behalf of this distant past, but this authority has always been subject to challenges from within as well as outside the scholarly world. Moreover, paradigms do change, and even challenges from the fringes can provoke insights or raise important questions. At those times when social or cultural movements attempt to appropriate scientific support for their claims, however, the relationship between them and the scholarly establishment can become quite strained. In the case of more specific theories, such as Lovelock's Gaia hypothesis or Gimbutas's interpretation of Old European civilization, there has been a fluid passage of ideas between scientists and other discourse communities, with the latter often finding allies on the other side of the fence. Yet in the dissemination of these ideas, popularizers have tended to abandon all but the most tenuous connection to their scholarly foundations. Most of the popular writing on ancient Goddess civilizations, for instance, has relied almost exclusively on the work of Gimbutas, without even hinting at its tendentious position within the field (e.g., Eisler 1987; Campbell 1989).

Gimbutas herself has been heavily criticized by other archaeologists, among them feminists, for her artistic license and unwarranted overinterpretations of data.[16] Recent archaeology has been revealing a much more complex image of the past than has been assumed up to now. Contrary to the idea of a peaceful and ecologically benign Neolithic in Britain, for instance, some present-day archaeologists argue that it was crowded, warfare was endemic, environments were disrupted on a large scale (with forests burned and wastelands created), and yet, that ritual monuments were everywhere. The latter, it seems, served more as territorial and visual, impact-oriented statements than as astronomical observatories or "ancient computers" (Griffith and Hutton 1990; Hutton 1993b). Regarding Goddess imagery, critics also contest Gimbutas's argument that a plenitude of feminine imagery in art reflects gender equality or matricentrism in society. Hutton (1993) points out that remorselessly androcentric societies like that of ancient Rome, or cities like Babylon and Athens, created remarkable poetry, art, and a plenitude of female goddesses. In Hawaii, the goddess Pele seemed in charge, but the actual society was very male dominated. In contrast, early Christianity had an overwhelmingly female membership and appealed to women, despite its lack of obvious female imagery.[17]

In the anything-goes realm of earth mysteries speculation, relations between the scholarly establishment and alternative researchers have tended to be especially poor, if not downright hostile. Earth mysteries researchers, like other researchers of the paranormal, have suffered regular attacks at the hands of popular defenders of science, "scientific skeptics" and professional debunkers such as Martin Gardner, James ("The Amazing") Randi, Christopher Evans, and members of the Committee for the Scientific Investigation of Claims of the Paranormal (CSICOP).[18] The archaeological establishment, meanwhile, has largely ignored or cursorily dismissed the ley line hypothesis, though it featured as the subject of a series of scathing editorials by Glyn Daniel in *Antiquity* in the early 1970s.[19] Alternative archaeologists, for their part, have generally considered orthodox archaeologists to be not only wrong, but dangerous—they are, as William Thompson puts it, the "unconscious apologists for industrial civilization" (1978:54–58). Earth mysteries proponents generally define their project in opposition to that of the scientific establishment: theirs, in their view, is a sacred project, not the profane one of modern science, and they perceive themselves to be "the conscious initiators of a new sacred and mythopoeic world view" (Screeton 1993:40).

In recent years this antagonism has abated somewhat, as archaeologists have more openly embraced dialogue with their extra-academic counterparts.[20] Some earth mysteries researchers have taken this as an indication that scientists are beginning to accept their theories (e.g., Screeton 1993:54), but the evidence for this remains meager. Few academic prehistorians are well informed about "alternative archaeological" theorizing; and the one notable exception—in fact, the only extended treatment of the ley line hypothesis by scholars, English rural historians Tom Williamson and Liz Bellamy's book *Ley Lines in Question* (1983)—supports the opposite conclusion. Calling the study of leys "one of the biggest red herrings in the history of popular thought" (11), Williamson and Bellamy undertake a rigorous and thorough appraisal of the theory of ley lines, and in the end demolish it, on the whole, fairly convincingly. They find holes and inconsistencies in many of the arguments used by ley hunters, including their choice and selectivity of evidence,[21] the statistical arguments they have at times claimed for themselves (most of which have been, as they show, variously flawed), their use of evidence from folklore and from place-names (all somewhat dubious),[22] and their argument by "site evolution" or "site continuity," according to which different cultural groups, separated from each other by many centuries, are said to have recognized the sanctity of a place, erecting a variety of structures, from stone circles to tumuli to churches, to mark it out.[23] They are particularly critical of ley hunters' "telescoped" view of prehistory, which sees "all grass covered mounds and all prehistoric earthworks [as] roughly contemporaneous, all being 'ancient.'" Williamson and Bellamy point out, rather, that different prehistoric structures were "built for different purposes at different periods of time" (141). The common claim that the ley network was established back in the Neolithic, they argue, is contradicted by the fact that most purported leys require the use of Bronze Age, Iron Age, Roman, and medieval sites, as well as ill-defined "mark points" (such as moats, ponds, lanes, crosses, castle mounds, holy wells, and even trees) to "confirm" their veracity as leys.[24]

Williamson and Bellamy conclude that all supposed ley alignments "connect sites and features which are quite unrelated in any other respect," and that the claim that such alignments occur more often than chance would predict is a spurious and unproven one (132). As regards the "mysterious ley energy," variously called "telluric energy," "geodetic force," and so on, they sarcastically jibe: "It is hardly surprising that ley hunters are 'baffled' by this force. It is a strange kind of force that has preference for Scots pines above other trees, that can be conducted by ponds and hilltops, that runs to a mark stone the size of a football because it is on alignment and avoids similar stones that are not, and is totally undetectable by scientific instruments" (128).[25] The authors acknowledge, however, that in several respects "ley hunters seem to have been right for the wrong reasons" (214). They single out, as ley hunters' possibly accurate insights, the notion of "a past [that was] very different from the ethnographic present" (213); the idea that the pre-historic, and specifically neolithic, landscape was widely cleared and set-tled; the view that "continuity of development" is a keynote to European history (in contrast to early archaeologists' emphasis on invasions and mi-grations); and, most important, the fact that "we have underestimated the complexity of prehistoric social organization" (214). It has only been since the radiocarbon-dating revolution that archaeologists have conceded that megalith building did not arrive in western Europe from the more "civi-lized" East, but in fact preceded the building of the Egyptian pyramids. As the authors write, we now know that "from as early as the early Bronze Age, Europe was inhabited by communities of farmers whose numbers and ac-tivities were comparable with those of the Middle Ages" (215). So, if the dreamers were obviously wrong on details, it is the archaeologists who have been struggling to catch up with the generalities.[26]

Historian Ronald Hutton summarizes the situation well. The current archaeological picture of British prehistory, he writes, one of "intense lo-cal regionalism, profound changes in tradition over time and rough-and-ready surveying methods, suggests a world in which the great ley system would have had no place" (1993b:128).[27] Hutton himself sympathetically addresses the ideas of modern pagans and earth mysteries writers, even ap-pearing at New Age and pagan gatherings to discuss and debate historical and spiritual matters. But he admits that any rapprochement between the camps is made difficult by the religious motivations of earth mysteries pro-ponents, and by their frequent antipathy toward orthodox institutions. He claims that this antipathy results in an overreliance on outdated archaeo-logical ideas, and a critique of a model of archaeology that is at least twenty years out of date (119ff.). More crucially, the "elements of the past" which earth mysteries researchers and academic archaeologists have in common "are precisely those of which modern academics are most ashamed and which they are most eager to reject." When alternative researchers quote scholars, they tend to prefer those—like James G. Frazer, Carl Jung, Mircea Eliade, Joseph Campbell, and Marija Gimbutas—who have been judged guilty by their peers of skimming over details in their quest for vast, glo-bal generalizations. Recent archaeology, in contrast, has tended to focus on the "separate and distinct nature of peoples, places and periods" (124–25) (though one could, of course, argue that this itself is a temporary scholarly trend). Hutton also chides the earth mysteries researchers for failing "as mystics" as well. "During the last twenty years," he writes, "thousands of hitherto unsuspected prehistoric monuments have been rediscovered by means of geophysical surveys and aerial photography," yet "not one has been found by all the psychics and dowsers who abound in 'alternative' archaeol-ogy" (130).

Myths about an earlier Golden Age, a Fall into modern industrial society, and a sentient Earth with which we can communicate in order to restore that Golden Age, carry a particular resonance in our time. The activity of imagining and "re-mything" the past is and has always been part of the effort to make sense of the present, whether through science or by other means. An interesting example of the syncretistically creative way in which a contemporary myth emerges is that of the association of "dragons" with earth energy and with the "sacred feminine." Hutton neatly summarizes this development, and it is worth quoting here in full:

> The English word dragon is a translation of a Latin term, used in the Middle Ages to describe the fire-breathing, flying reptilian monster of Scandinavian and Germanic myth. In that myth, these creatures feature as threats to humankind, to be slain by heroes, and they entered the pan-European medieval imagination in that guise. They did not exist in ancient Celtic, or Roman or Greek mythology, although human-eating serpent-like monsters (often dwelling in water) did. Nor were they found in ancient Egypt, where the closest equivalent, the crocodile, had positive sacred associations. But in the Babylonian creation myth, the earth goddess Tiamat assumed the form of a mighty lizard (usually translated as "dragon" by English writers) and in that guise was killed by the hero Marduk. The Chinese, by contrast, have always believed in great lizard-like winged beasts very similar in form to the north European dragon and therefore described as "dragons" by English-speakers. Their legendary function, however, is quite different, for they are viewed as vessels of great spiritual power, very often beneficial to humanity. When John Michell transplanted the tradition of *lung mei*, "dragon-paths," to the English landscape, he had to reckon with the fact that in English tradition dragons were regarded as destructive monsters. He did so by superimposing Chinese upon English myth so that the English dragon-slaying heroes were turned into villains, striking symbolically at the sacred forces represented by the *lung mei* or leys. Feminist writers and artists among the earth mystics brought in the myth of Tiamat and Marduk to suggest that both Babylonian and Germanic dragon-slaying stories were folk-memories of the destruction of matriarchal religions and societies by militaristic patriarchal brutes. By the mid-1970s it was a widespread creed among "alternative" archaeologists that wherever dragons were mentioned, across the world, they were the symbol of the Earth Mother and her energies. This well-rounded picture draws upon Scandinavian, Germanic, Chinese and Babylonian myth. But it would not have been recognizable to the Vikings, or the Germans, or the Chinese, or the Babylonians, let alone to other ancient peoples. It is a modern mythology, constructed by a process which may be compared to the looting of stonework from ruined buildings of several different kinds and ages in order to put up a brand new cathedral. (Hutton 1993b:125–26)

Hutton's allusion to looting is helpful in understanding the mythic imagination, which, as Lévi-Strauss (1966) pointed out, works by way of *bricolage*: the new dragon mythos represents a *bricoleur*'s attempt to make sense of today's world, a world that is perceived to be undergoing an environmental crisis as well as a crisis of meaning. The task of making sense of the world necessarily appropriates the past for its purposes, using it to justify, explain, or critique the present. But in the process, those representatives of the present culture whose officially sanctioned task it is to study and represent the past (i.e., scholarly historians and archaeologists) begin to appear threatening to the revisionists, while the latter appear no better than looters to the scholarly establishment.

At stake is the authority to speak for the past, a past whose physical remnants consist of little more than scattered artifacts—shards of pottery, ruins of stone, and fragments of bone—to which are added layers upon layers of historical conjecture and (mis)interpretation. The interpretive debate today is often considered to be one that pits scholars who see the past either in terms familiar to our present culture or who attempt their utmost to let the remnants speak for themselves, adding little of their own imaginings, against critics of modernity who idealize the past, seeing in its remnants, for instance, a vast "scientific instrument" lying "sprawled over the entire surface of the globe" (Michell 1969:69), its ruins haunting the modern imagination like the dim memory of an amnesiac. Depending on one's chosen perspective, the contest is either over whose story is the more *credible* one (as scientists would claim) or whose is the more useful and desirable (as New Age and ecospiritual radicals might sooner acknowledge). Many archaeologists today share some of the ley hunters' criticisms of modern industrial society; and Williamson and Bellamy rightly point out that ley hunting has been "at least a praiseworthy attempt to give the study of the past a vital role in the present" (1983:211). Yet, they argue, the ley hunters' conception of a Fall from a Golden Age is "an ideological non-starter": "It shows us an ideal to strive for, but it gives us no clue about how to get there because it never shows us how we got here." "To change the present," they conclude, "and the competitive, industrial and technological society in which we live, we need to understand its origins" (211). My implicit argument in the remainder of this book will be that we also need to understand how *ideas* about the past shape our actions and relations with others, including nonhuman, *natural* others, in the present.

CONTESTING ENVIRONMENTAL DISCOURSE:
NATURE IN THE NEW AGE

A variety of ideas about nature float about in science and popular culture today. Taking the word as a categorical stand-in for the nonhuman and non-artifactual world which surrounds and interpenetrates with human social communities, it is possible to identify a diverse range of meanings and cultural representations of nature. A partial inventory could include: nature as a divinely ordained system of norms and rules, rights and obligations; a book to be read, interpreted, and studied; a motherly female, nurturing and providing for the needs of her children; a bodylike organism, whose features mirror those of the human body; a clocklike object or machine, to be studied dispassionately, taken apart, and manipulated for human benefit; a ruthless and harsh kingdom, "red in tooth and claw," from which humans should distance ourselves through the social contract of civilization; a flour-

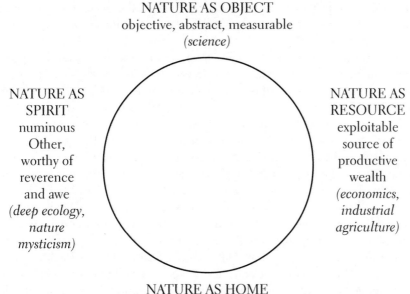

NATURE AS OBJECT
objective, abstract, measurable
(science)

NATURE AS
SPIRIT
numinous
Other,
worthy of
reverence
and awe
(deep ecology,
nature
mysticism)

NATURE AS
RESOURCE
exploitable
source of
productive
wealth
(economics,
industrial
agriculture)

NATURE AS HOME
source of emotional identification, relationship, tradition
(social ecology, traditional agriculture)

Figure 2.1. Contemporary discourses of nature

ishing web of life; a storehouse of resources; an Edenic Garden that should be set aside in protected areas, to be visited periodically for the replenishment of one's soul; a museum or theme park for curiosity seekers, or an open-air gymnasium for trials of masculinity; a cybernetic system or data bank of circulating information; a spirit or divinity, or a locus for the residence of many spirits; and an avenging angel, capriciously and unpredictably meting out its inhuman justice to a humanity that has transgressed its natural order (cf. Glacken 1967; Gold 1984; Horigan 1988; Evernden 1992; Simmons 1993; Cronon 1995; Soper 1995; Macnaghten and Urry 1998). Each of these images suggests different actions as appropriate in relation to nature: these range from subjugation and domination, classification, measurement, prediction, and management, to aesthetic appreciation and contemplation, segregation, and protection (through the formulation of appropriate land use policy, for instance), active defense using the tactics of civil disobedience, and reverence or worship.

For typological and comparative purposes, the main concepts of nature found in present-day environmental discourse can be mapped into a fourfold schema of typical models or "root metaphors" (see fig. 2.1):[28] Contemporary environmental discourse has been dominated by the top-right quadrant of this diagram, that is, by resourcism and objectivism, the respective dominant languages of economics and of mainstream science.[29] Environmental activists and theorists have promoted alternative models built primarily around nature-as-spirit (for instance, in the deep ecology movement), nature-as-home (social ecology), or combinations of the above (cf. Killingsworth and Palmer 1992).

New Age and ecospiritual models of nature intersect with scientific, popular, and environmentalist discourses in various ways. Much New Age writing is anthropocentric, understanding the human role to be that of a "global brain" or "Gaia's nervous system" (Russell 1984) and emphasizing our divine potentials and our technological capacities to take control over evolution (W. Anderson 1987), not only on Earth but even on other planets (e.g., Marx Hubbard 1994:79). Other New Age voices are less technocentric, and neopagans and ecospiritualists generally lean toward a biocentric view of the human-nature relationship (e.g., Oates 1989). Sociologist Michael York observes that "at best, New Age flourishes as an unresolved dialectic between the idea of *Nature as Real* and *Nature as Illusion*, between the immanentist pagan concept of pantheism and the transcendental gnostic concept of theism, between a numinous materialism and a world-denying idealism" (1994:16). Where nature is considered "real," it is frequently seen as an underlying source of commonality which founds and grounds human values, identities, or biologically built-in "drives" and desires; or it is seen as an idealized and largely presocial Other with which we can and should attempt to harmonize. At the Findhorn community in Scotland, widely acknowledged to be an incubator of New Age ideas, nature is seen as humanity's partner—the community's "vision statements" stress "co-creation" and cooperation between humans and nature, with humans acting as "stewards," not as "overlords"—but it is also seen as a realm inhabited by a diversity of elusive spiritual entities, "elemental kingdoms" with whom we are encouraged to converse so as to obtain "instructions" on how to work on the land (A. Walker 1994; Spangler 1994:105–7).[30]

On the other hand, much New Age discourse employs a terminology drawn from twentieth-century science, especially from ecology and a variety of systems theories in biology, theoretical physics, and other fields (see Hanegraaff 1998). The relations between New Age culture, scientific culture, and other intellectual and popular discourses can be usefully viewed, as Andrew Ross (1991) suggests, through an analogy with "taste cultures." In the spectrum of scientific and popular explanations for things, the official scientific culture constitutes a "highbrow" culture; popular scientific gadget-fetishism represents its "lowbrow" analogue; while "the components of New Age culture are both *middlebrow* and *alternative*, a composite that can probably be found in any counterculture that has found some kind of breathing space, however marginal, within the dominant culture" (26; italics added). Ross explains,

> On the one hand, the devotion to alternative, non-rationalist belief systems
> places New Age thought outside the hierarchical structure of cultural capital

observed by the legitimate scientific culture. On the other hand, the New Age commitment to transforming science into a more humanistic and holistic enterprise involves taking on, to some degree, the structure of deference to authority that governs the institutional system of rationalist cultural capital. As a middlebrow scientific culture, New Age wants to be fiercely self-determining, but the path to establishing that authority leads through the obstacle course of accreditation that underpins scientific authority and marks non-institutionalized options as illegitimate. (1991:26–27)

New Age thinkers have therefore sought alliances with respected scientists, and it is out of this intercourse that so-called New Paradigm thought has developed.[31] In this milieu one finds a mixture of scientific and religious ideas applied to the task of countering the ecological crisis and providing a bold intellectual vision capable of thrusting humanity into an era of "planetary culture." Following from Fritjof Capra's 1976 bestseller *The Tao of Physics*, a string of popular authors and intellectuals have drawn on the findings of quantum physics, nonlinear thermodynamics, complex and self-organizing systems theories, Gaia theory, holographic models of mind, and other twentieth-century scientific developments, to articulate a new and "constructive postmodern" cosmology.[32] New Paradigm thinkers can be seen as appropriating the glamour and respectability of science while critiquing its modernist foundations: its Cartesian rationalism (founded on a mind-body and spirit-matter dualism), its mechanistic materialism (which denies spirit altogether), and its complicity with medical, political, and military establishments. In their calls for a "constructive postmodern" worldview (e.g., Griffin 1988a, 1988b, 1990, 1993), many of these authors align themselves with a growing movement critiquing modernity *tout court*, while distancing themselves from the more "pessimistic" or antimetaphysical proponents of cultural and philosophical postmodernism.[33]

New Age and New Paradigm thinkers, then, invoke the authority of science—though theirs is a highly selective version of "new" or "leading edge" science—at the same time as they invoke the authority of spiritual traditions (in the guise of a "perennial philosophy") and of "inner," intuitive and holistic bodily wisdom.[34] They have developed a distinctive nonreligious vocabulary which draws on scientific and otherwise "neutral" terms such as "holistic, holographic, synergistic, unity, oneness, transformation, personal growth, human potential, awakening, networking, energy, consciousness" (Basil 1988:10–11). At the more popular and millenarian end of New Age discourse, quasi-scientific and technophilic lingo is mixed together with environmentalist sentiments and metaphysical references. José Argüelles's "Open Letter" announcing the Harmonic Convergence (discussed in the next chapter) calls its readers to travel to sacred sites and meditatively "surrender" to "the planet and to the higher galactic intelligences which guide and monitor" it during this "window of galactic synchronization" (Buenfil 1991:178). Meanwhile, workshops on "How to achieve ascension in this lifetime" hold out a zesty pastiche of promises, including

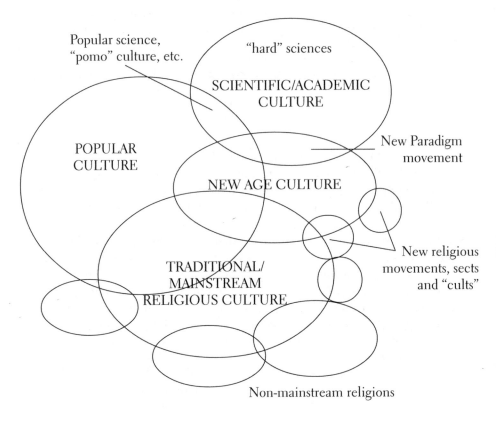

Figure 2.2. Interdiscursive relations between New Age culture,
scientific/academic culture, and popular culture

- Building of light quotient at a speed never dreamed possible;
- Removal of implants, elementals and parasites;
- Cutting edge Arcturian/Ashtar spiritual light technology;
- Cosmic cellular clearing & rewiring—anchor 50 chakra grid;
- Ascension seats in the Golden Chamber of Melchizedek, Metatron, Lord Maitreya and other ascended masters. (*Common Ground Magazine*, Winter 1995/96:57)

Between the New Paradigm intellectuals and the grassroots spiritual fringes, there is a broad discursive arena within which ideas about reality, and about the respective authorities of science, the "new sciences," and spiritual traditions or "inner wisdom," are articulated and contested. (Fig. 2.2 presents a general mapping of this cultural terrain.) Hard-nosed scientific skeptics may try hard to defend the citadel of science from any New Age inroads, writing the latter off as products of an irresponsible media and a gullible public (e.g., Kurtz 1985a, M. Gardner 1991), but a cultural-hermeneutic perspective suggests that these can also be seen as attempts to reframe societal metanarratives by selectively appropriating from present-day sources of discursive authority, including science and religion. New discursive alliances emerge at the boundaries of accepted science and spiritual traditions and practices: the traffic between Eastern philosophy and Western science, for instance, has increased since Capra's initial formulations, resulting in increasingly sophisticated work in fields as varying as cognitive science and the psychology of consciousness, parapsychology, anthropology, and medicine.[35]

Taking into account, then, the literature on earth mysteries, Gaian consciousness, and sacred sites, as well as more general inspirational New Age and New Paradigm writings, several additional ideas of nature can be distinguished. Developing an interpretive typology of these will be helpful in understanding their relative roles in the interpretive dynamics surrounding Glastonbury and Sedona. Using the above mapping of models of nature as a template, the dominant New Age and ecospiritual ideas can be mapped on a similar circular continuum in figure 2.3.[36]

This diagram is intended as an echo of my previous mapping: thus, Nature as Object, in New Age and ecospiritual discourses, becomes Nature as Sacred Mathematics; Resource becomes Organism, Home becomes Mother, and Spirit becomes Trickster-Teacher. In each case the second mapping adds a quality of immanence, personification, or *meaningfulness:* nature as sacred mathematics may be an object, but it is one that is interpreted as inherently meaningful (i.e., sacred); a trickster-teacher is not merely a spirit, but is one which interacts with the observer directly; and so on. I have also included additional suggestions for models of nature that are transitional between the four. The crossover between the Organism and Mathematics models results in an emphasis on *earth energy sciences*, which might include attempts to measure life energies scientifically, and the assumption that the math involved might be reflective of natural laws or cosmic harmonies. Mother and Organism, in turn, combine in the model of *Gaia* as a living (though not necessarily conscious) body; while the terrain between the Mother and Trickster-Teacher models suggests a less monolithic, more polytheistic image of a sentient divinity within nature—one according to which the Goddess has many aspects (such as the maiden-mother-crone trinity, as found in Wicca) or, conversely, according to which a variety of gods, goddesses, or spirits, are included within a larger unified whole (Gaia). The Mother and Sacred Geometry models do not easily combine with each other into a single model, since the abstraction of one is in principle incompatible with the personal and emotional nature of the other; perhaps not surprisingly, the former is favored by proponents of women's spirituality, while the adherents of the latter tend to be male practitioners of Euro-American geomancy and "esoteric science." Finally, in the area between Sacred Geometry and Trickster-Teacher I have included Donna Haraway's notion of nature as a *coding trickster*. Though this idea is not prominent within New Age or ecospiritual discourse, the term captures the combina-

NATURE AS SACRED MATHEMATICS

ordered according to the harmonies of number, geometric form, proportion, Platonic essences

Evidence: "megalithic science" of ancient astronomer-priests, ley lines and geometrical alignments ("scientific instrument . . . sprawled over the entire surface of the globe" (Michell 1969:69)), Hermetic and magical traditions

Appropriate relationship with nature: "harmonization" by design according to principles of the esoteric and spiritual sciences

NATURE AS TRICKSTER-TEACHER

"coding trickster sciences"

unpredictable, changeable, ultimately unknowable, but highly responsive

Evidence: experience of spirits and devas, "dragon paths," UFOs, crop formations and "earth lights"

Approp. relationship with nature: listening, attunement, "going with the flow" (*wu wei*)

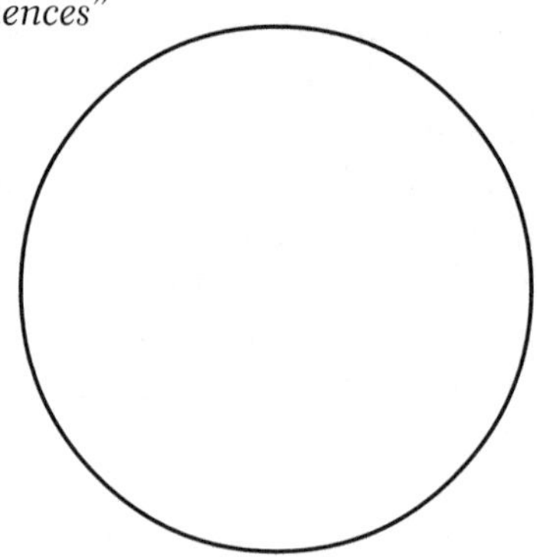

pagan animism

NATURE AS LIVING ORGANISM

"earth energy"

biologically alive, pulsating with circulating life-energies

Evidence: traditional/folk geomancy, "earth energy sciences," dowsing and intuition

Approp. relationship with nature: "attunement" with natural energies through divination, intuitive, psychic, and physical means

unconscious Gaia

NATURE AS MOTHER

female Goddess

Evidence: indigenous cultures, archaeology (ancient Goddess civilization), Gaia theory, intuition, women's experience

Appropriate relationship with nature: worship, emotional and intuitive communication

Figure 2.3. New Age and ecospiritual discourses of nature

tion of chaotic elusiveness and unrepresentability with an ordered mathematical rationality (an idea to which I will return in my concluding chapter).

All these ideas of nature and the Earth are articulated as part of broader historical narratives which can be seen, in part, as responses to a perceived crisis of modernity, a crisis centered around the uneasy relationship between humans and the Earth. From a cultural-hermeneutic perspective, the efforts of these alternative discursive communities, like those of scientists, are attempts to make sense of the world by appropriating available interpretive resources and weaving them into coherent and livable narrative. By seeing the differences between scientists and scholars on the one hand, and New Agers and ecospiritualists on the other, as *interpretive* differences—that is, by taking a cultural-hermeneutic approach to the interdiscursive arena within which these different views are articulated—I will attempt to foreground some of the commonalities between them. And by relating these interpretive differences to two specific landscapes or places, I will attempt, in the remainder of this book, to weave the broader-than-human ecological world into this transepistemic cultural arena.

THREE
Orchestrating Sacred Space

Every sacred space implies a hierophany, an irruption of the sacred that results in detaching a territory from the surrounding cosmic milieu and making it qualitatively different.

—Mircea Eliade, *The Sacred and the Profane*

Sacrality is, above all, a category of emplacement.

—Jonathan Z. Smith, *To Take Place: Toward Theory in Ritual*

Most societies distinguish places that are deemed especially significant, sacred or powerful, imbued with authority or prestige, or reserved for special uses, from those which lack such significance.[1] The idea that sacredness inheres in a place, emanating from it of its own accord, is frequently taken for granted by believers in that place's sacred status. The distinguished scholar of religion Mircea Eliade characterized all religious behavior as concerned with one's relationship with a sacred realm. Sacred places, in his view, are manifestations or "irruptions" of inherent power and numinosity, exuding potent meanings and significances for the religious practitioner, who is able to shed everyday constraints of socially conditioned time and space by "entering into" or "partaking of" their sacred power. In Eliade's words, "For religious man, space is not homogeneous"; rather, "some parts of space are qualitatively different from others" (1959:20) and these qualitative differences are given by the sacred itself: sacred sites are the places where divine or supernatural power breaks through into the human world, manifesting in the form of specific *theophanies* or *hierophanies*.[2]

In contrast to this view, which sees the sacred as a sui generis force whose action *precedes* the activities of social groups, much recent scholarship by cultural geographers and others has demonstrated that spaces, places, and landscapes—including sacred places and landscapes—are actively produced by a myriad of social activities, and that this "social production of space" is dynamic and highly contested, imbued with cultural presuppositions and marked by social differences.[3] As Kay Anderson and Fay Gale put it, "In the course of generating new meanings and decoding existing ones, people construct spaces, places, landscapes, regions and environments. In short, they construct geographies. . . . They arrange spaces in distinctive ways; they fashion certain types of landscape, townscape and streetscape; they erect monuments and destroy others; they evaluate spaces and places and adapt them accordingly; they organise the relations between territories at a range of scales from the local to the international" (1992:4). The carving out of particular kinds of places and spaces, endowed with specific meanings, is an activity sociologist Rob Shields calls *social spatialization.* "Partly through ongoing interaction," he writes, "a site acquires its own history; partly through its relation with other sites, it acquires connotations and symbolic meanings" (1991:60). These meanings, or "place-myths," are integrated within larger systems by which places are contrasted against each other and differentiated into, for instance, the sacred and the profane, or the central and the peripheral. Sacred space, in other words, is produced through the spatial, material, and discursive practices of social groups. As such, it does not exist apart from the human meanings, sedimented over time in actual landscapes and places, which imbue them with their "sanctity" and which are always subject to reinterpretation and contestation.

The sacred geographies of the New Age and earth spirituality movements can be viewed through both of these lenses: that of the insider or believer, who sees the sacred as really existing in particular places (or the scholar who empathetically assumes the believer's stance in order to better understand the belief), and that of the outsider who skeptically scrutinizes or deconstructs the sacred to show how it is socially produced and contested. In the latter view, a hermeneutics of *suspicion* rather than one of *trust,* sacred space is seen as a kind of "religious void," "a vessel into which pilgrims devoutly pour their hopes, prayers, and aspirations," and which accommodates "the meanings and ideas which officials, pilgrims, and locals invest" in it (Eade and Sallnow 1991:15).

Sacred places, however, like all places, are *not* empty vessels or voids, and, like literary texts, they cannot *equally* accommodate all possible interpretations.[4] Rather, places and landscapes are constituted in and through histories of human-nonhuman interaction in specific biophysical and material topographies and ecologies. Meanings, in other words, are not simply imposed onto preexisting environmental *tabulae rasae;* they emerge reciprocally with landscapes, cultures, and activities. To the above two perspectives, then—sacred space as inherently given, and as socially constructed and contested—we can add a third one: sacred space as shaped through interaction, over time, between humans and specific extrahuman environments. As people live in particular places, their activities, including their attempts to "anchor" their own views of the world in the landscape, "orches-trate" those places in particular ways.[5] But the orchestration includes play-ers with very different agendas—among them, nonhuman inhabitants and environmental "forces" or "actants." Agency, in other words, is complex and multiple, and it is always shaped and influenced by larger social, institu-tional, and historical structures and processes. The interaction between the local and the global, and between *agency* and *structure* (as these are conven-tionally called by sociologists and human geographers) is mediated by signs and symbols, images and narratives, and by circulating meanings, desires, and power. In this chapter, I will introduce some of the ways New Age and ecospiritual geographies are shaped, while suggesting a conceptual means for interpreting the dynamic, dialectical, and historical interaction between human cultural groups and extrahuman landscapes.

The production of New Age and ecospiritual geographies involves a vari-ety of activities taking place at a range of scales. My analysis in this and later chapters will focus especially on four interconnected moments in this pro-cess: (1) the production of broad geographical and territorial spatializations, "imagined geographies" which demarcate between centers and peripher-ies, and are molded around ideas about the Earth as a whole (such as those examined in chapter 2); (2) the interpretive labor involved in identifying specific places and landscapes as sacred, producing appropriate "place-im-ages" and "place-myths" (Shields 1991), articulating and contesting claims to the legitimate ownership or control of such spaces and competing for the authority to speak for them; (3) the ritualization, consecration, and venera-tion of specific spaces through the discrete and local activities of individuals and groups, primarily the activities of worship, prayer, meditation, and cer-emonial ritual; and (4) physical and material practices of movement, em-bodied encounter with others (humans and nonhumans), and productive appropriation of the features of these landscapes over time. The geographi-cal practices associated with the New Age and ecospirituality movements can hardly be understood apart from the cultural changes of the last three decades, however; so I will begin by identifying some of the forms of geo-graphical mobility which have spawned and encouraged their growth.

ALTERNATIVE GEOGRAPHIES OF THE
SPIRITUAL COUNTERCULTURE

As a phenomenon that began largely within Western metropolitan centers, the sixties' counterculture was conspicuous in its tendency to move *away* from those urban centers, a movement which took place in two main forms: as a conscious relocation "back to the land," and as a more ephemeral drift to places of exotic allure or spiritual import.[6] Emerging from the idealism of the sixties' youth culture and its many experiments in urban communal living, the exodus of back-to-the-landers who fled to rural areas in the late 1960s and early 1970s constituted a reaction against the power and authority embodied, as many communards saw it, in urban industrial cities. Most large metropolitan centers had their preferred geographical routes outward, with such favored destination regions as, in North America, the Pacific Northwest and the Southwest; and, in Britain, the southwest counties, Wales, and parts of the north. Though many of the rural communards eventually returned to the cities, others stayed on and dug their heels into the land.[7] For some, the rural communes and intentional communities which emerged and grew in the 1970s were seen as places in which the practical implications of the new consciousness could be worked out; and, over the years, surviving communities have organized themselves into networks, such as the Federation of Egalitarian Communities, the Fellowship of Intentional Communities, the Alternatives Communities Network in Britain, and the International Communes Network.

As early as the mid-1970s, the more explicitly spiritual or New Age communities, such as Scotland's Findhorn Community and India's Auroville, had begun expressing the vision of a neomonastic communitarianism, consisting of "centers of light" linked in a network that would provide the infrastructure for a "new planetary culture" (Spangler 1977; W. Thompson 1974). Countercultural historian Theodore Roszak compared the present period with the waning decades of the Roman Empire, and saw this new communitarian "monasticism" as a tested historical model for the "creative disintegration of industrial society," a model which "illuminates the way in which the top-heavy and toxic institutions of an exhausted empire were sifted down into civilized, durable communities where a vital, new sense of human identity and destiny could take root" (1978:289). To this day, Findhorn, Auroville, Tennessee's The Farm, and numerous other intentional communities interact with the broader culture in a dialectic which helps to sustain New Age and alternative spirituality.[8] At the same time, both North America and Britain have witnessed a much broader movement of counterurbanization (Champion 1989; Halfacree 1997; Dahms and McComb 1999), consisting largely of urban expatriates seeking the quiet, safety, and access to nature associated with the "rural idyll" (Mingay 1989). The growth of amenity towns like Santa Fe and Taos (New Mexico), Aspen and Telluride (Colorado), Jackson Hole (Wyoming), Park City (Utah), Asheville (North Carolina), and their many analogues in other regions, shows the effects, both positive and negative, of this broadly postindustrial trend. The overlap between this broader counterstream of ex-urban migrants and the New Age and ecospirituality movements can be seen in the disproportionate presence of New Age and popular environmentalist imagery and values to be found in many of these towns.

A second line of geographic mobility within the countercultural and New Age milieu has been that centered around those sites which have been privileged within the spiritual seeker's global itinerary: faraway places like India, Bali, and parts of South and Central America, as well as those closer to home. Travel to sacred places became a staple of the Western hippie seeker's itinerary in the late 1960s and early 1970s. Already in the late 1960s one can find the idea that a network of "power places" is spread out across the planet (e.g., Michell 1969), and by the mid-1970s, a variety of guidebooks had appeared for the growing number of New Age pilgrims.[9] The "power place" idea fermented for two decades within the hippie and New Age countercul-ture, but it finally launched itself into popular consciousness with the Har-monic Convergence of August 1987.

Projected to be the largest simultaneously coordinated act of prayer, meditation, and ceremony ever to take place at sacred sites throughout the world, the Harmonic Convergence was an overt manifestation of the New Age movement's millenarianism. According to its primary instigator, art his-torian José Argüelles, the dates August 16–17 were supposed to mark the synchronous occurrence of several significant events: the beginning of the final twenty-six-year period of the Mayan calendar's 5,200-year Great Cycle, the return of Quetzalcoatl, the Mayan god of peace, and the culmination of the Aztec calendar;[10] the "dancing awake" of 144,000 Sun Dance en-lightened teachers (according to the Rainbow People of the Intertribal Med-icine Societies); the return of the Hopi Indians' lost white brother Poha'na; a "grand trine" in the astrological fire signs and the first time since the ear-ly 1940s that the seven planets have been so closely aligned; an anchoring of divine energy into the power points of the planet for their subsequent transmission through the "planetary grid system"; and "the precise calibra-tion point in a galactic and planetary harmonic scale" (Dame-Glerum 1987b:A3). Consonant with his calculations, Argüelles called for 144,000 people to meditate, pray, chant and visualize at sacred sites and power spots throughout the world, in order to launch the final twenty-five-year transi-tion into a New Age of peace and harmony. Convergers, including celebri-ties like Shirley MacLaine, John Denver, and Timothy Leary, gathered at places as varied as Sedona, California's Mount Shasta, Chaco Canyon in New Mexico, the Black Hills of South Dakota, New York's Central Park, Glastonbury and Stonehenge, Machu Picchu in Peru, the Great Pyra-mid in Egypt, and Mount Olympus in Greece, to celebrate the event and to "create a complete field of trust by surrendering themselves to the plan-et and to the higher galactic intelligences which guide and monitor the planet."[11]

In the growing body of popular literature on sacred places and power spots, such sites are seen as places of personal transformation, and pilgrim-ages to them are considered a tool of such transformation. Photographer Courtney Milne's *The Sacred Earth* (1991a) is emblematic of the genre. It is a stunningly photographed and lavishly produced coffee-table book docu-menting Milne's five-year odyssey to sacred sites on seven continents. Milne writes that he was set off on his pilgrimage by a "mysterious-looking docu-ment" by Robert Coon called *Revelations from the Melchisadek Priesthood.* Specifically, he was enticed by a section of the book describing "The Twelve Sacred Places of the Earth," a list which included Glastonbury, Ayers Rock

(Uluru) in central Australia, Haleakala Crater in Hawaii, Bolivia's Islands of the Sun and Moon, Palenque in Mexico, the Great Pyramid of Giza and Jerusalem's Mount of Olives (a "combination power spot"), and the mountains Tongariro (New Zealand), Shasta (California), Kailas (Tibet), Fuji (Japan), Table Mountain (South Africa), and the Four Sacred Mountains of Bali. "My heart pounding with excitement," he writes, "I said, 'I'm going'" (Milne 1991a:41).[12]

The New Age and earth spirituality literature projects a geography of nonhomogeneous space, marked by special places which stand out as especially important, meaningful, or powerful. Given the eclecticism and inclusiveness of New Age culture, it is not surprising that pilgrimage guidebooks include reference to many human-built structures, monuments, and temples of the world's religious traditions, in addition to natural locations associated with the mysterious powers of the Earth. According to New Age and ecospiritual beliefs, Earth's energies have been known and appreciated by previous civilizations. Thus, ancient cultures, such as the temple-building civilizations of Mesoamerica and the Near East, prehistoric "Goddess cultures," or the legendary civilizations of Atlantis and Lemuria (the remains of which are popularly believed to exist in various places) are thought to have constructed their own monuments on powerful "energy points" and to have, in turn, influenced Earth's energy currents.[13] Conversely, outstanding natural sites—mountains, unusual rock formations, spectacular lakes and canyons, falls and hot springs—are imagined to have been revered by indigenous or ancient cultures, even where evidence for this is lacking. Such natural "sacred sites" tend to share a common characteristic: they are somehow outstanding, and are places where the power, vitality, or sheer otherness of nonhuman nature seems obviously present. They are, in other words, places where the Earth *speaks*, relatively unobscured by the din of modern civilization. For ecospiritual pilgrims, who consider the Earth itself a potent and divine being, such places are the Earth's theophanies, and pilgrimage offers access to the power and spiritual secrets they hold. As in the perspective of Mircea Eliade, whose writings are sometimes cited as influential by New Agers and ecospiritualists, the power of the pilgrimage shrine is considered to be internally generated, its meanings largely predetermined; and the pilgrimage journey constitutes a quest to the sacred Center, which may represent divinity, the "true Self," or some other valued and transcendent ideal.

Liminality, Orientalism, and the New Age Pilgrim-Tourist

In partial contrast to Eliade's "substantive" (or essentialist) view of sacred space is the more "functional" or "situational" understanding of pilgrimage elaborated by anthropologist Victor Turner.[14] Turner (1969, 1974) contended that religious pilgrimage, festival, and ritual serve "anti-structural" and "liminal" (marginal or "in-between") functions within societies, and that these activities are motivated by a desire for what he called *communi-tas*, the temporary shedding of social roles and the experience of unmediated and liberatory relations between people. Elaborating on Arnold van Gennep's theories of ritual, Turner saw ritual as involving three successive phases: separation from everyday social life, transition (the liminal state), and reincorporation. Religious pilgrimage, which involves the ritual expedition to a sacred site or shrine, by activating the feelings associated with liminality and communitas, serves to sacralize the site and create a sacred geography for the religious practitioner. Turner writes:

> [In] the pilgrim's movement toward the "holy of holies," the central shrine, as he progresses, the route becomes increasingly sacralized. At first, it is his subjective mood of penitence that is important while the many long miles he covers are mainly secular, everyday miles, then sacred symbols begin to invest the route, while in the final stages, the route itself becomes a sacred, sometimes mythical journey till almost every landmark and ultimately every step is a condensed, multivocal symbol capable of arousing much affect and desire. . . . the pilgrim's journey becomes a paradigm for other kinds of behavior — ethical, political, and other. (V. Turner 1974:197–98)

According to Turner, the geographic distribution of pilgrimage sites is frequently polarized in relation to a society's political topography, with shrines being located in peripheral areas, well outside the main administrative centers of church or state (184). Liminality, however, is also *central* within the experience of religious conversion, which normally involves displacement and transition, a radical disorientation from the devotee's previous sense of order, values, and meanings, and the sudden influx or gradual acceptance of new values and meanings. To the extent that the preconversion reality was rooted in a particular geography, the event of conversion may replace it with a new sacred geography. This is clearly what occurs in much New Age experience of sacred place; and it is in this sense that New Age and eco-spiritual geographies can be seen as constituting an alternative geography to that of urban-industrial modernity. Valorizing these peripheral spaces and linking them together, in discourse and in practice, provides these pilgrims with a spatial anchor for the forging of their identities as part of an alternative culture.

Travel to the peripheries is, of course, in itself hardly a radical act.[15] Reincorporated into the broader cultural logic of capitalist and neocolonialist social relations, travel becomes global tourism, a consumption of countries and places by privileged and mobile members of the (largely Western) developed world. The construction of a global tourist imaginary contributes to a geopolitical discourse which, in Edward Said's (1979) terms, "orientalizes" other parts of the world, turning them into the modern West's Other, to be desired at the same time as they are dominated and denigrated. The aim of tourism, as Dean MacCannell puts it, has always been "to set up sedentary housekeeping in the entire world" and to make local peoples "the 'household' staff of global capitalists" (1992:5). In the New Age variant of "romantic Orientalism" (Lopez 1995:261), places like India, Bali, Tibet, or the Peruvian Andes are imagined to be more "authentic," representative of timeless tradition, sacredness, and spiritual wisdom; they offer restoration and salvation to the progressive, rational, but despirited West. But in the romantic veneration of non-Western Others, they (native peoples, Indians, Balians, etc.) are always expected to conform to the images we have created for them (Noble Savages, wise men, mysterious sensualists)—which is no less a form of colonialism than any other.[16]

MacCannell contrasts tourists with "neo-nomads," who "cross boundaries, not as invaders conquering territory, but as passersby accumulating nothing, and collecting nothing but perishables—impressions and stories," and who recognize the true character of the ground as shifting ceaselessly underfoot (4). Erik Cohen articulates the distinction between tourists and pilgrims in terms of the Center and the Other: pilgrimage is a culturally sanctioned movement from the mundane and profane everyday world to the Center of a religious group's or culture's sanctified cosmos, while tourist travel is "a movement in the opposite direction, toward the Other, located beyond the boundaries of the cosmos, in the surrounding chaos" of a culture's periphery (1992:50). Tourism, as John Urry suggests, always presupposes its opposite, "regulated and organised work," and includes a clear intent to return home within a relatively short period of time (1992:2–3). Many New Age sacred site travelers clearly do not fit this category: some have left behind jobs or domestic situations and are simply "drifting" or "searching" with no particular goal in mind, while others are genuine pilgrims embarked on spiritual quests. "For those most alienated from modernity," Cohen writes, "the search is crowned by the discovery of a new, personal or 'elective' Center [. . .] and the Other, encountered in the periphery of the modern world, is transformed [into] a Center for the escaping modern individual" (1992:52).

The movement of New Age and ecospiritual pilgrims and tourists has also given rise to an international network of healing and retreat centers. For many who travel the sacred-site circuit, personal desire combines with a perceived sense of mission or "planetary service"; and many themselves begin to lead tours, pilgrimages, workshops, and retreats, or to do whatever else may be necessary to support their travels. In the context of post-Fordist production and consumption patterns, this is likely to contribute to the commodification of such places.[17] As they become popular travel destinations, these sites are marketed and packaged, turned into spectacle and display, and a particular type of New Age "tourist gaze" is given shape through guidebooks, postcards, and sacred site tours led by recognized or self-proclaimed spiritual authorities.

In many ways, the postmodern context has made it increasingly difficult to distinguish between the pilgrim and the tourist: paying tribute to Elvis at Graceland can be as much a religious experience for his fans as paying homage to Muhammad in Medina for a Muslim (cf. Reader and Walter 1993;

Graburn 1989). MacCannell argues that most tourist sites undergo a process akin to sacralization (1976:42–48), through a series of stages which
include "naming the sight, framing and elevation, enshrinement, mechanical reproduction of the sacred object, and social reproduction as new sights
(or 'sites') name themselves after the famous" (Urry 1992:10).[18] This mixture of spiritual desire with tourist trade and consumption, identity construction, and cultural contestation, has been the focus of recent poststructuralist analyses, according to which sacred places and landscapes constitute
domains of competing social relations, claims and counterclaims, meanings and discourses (e.g., Eade and Sallnow 1991; Chidester and Linenthal
1995a; Crain 1997; Graham and Murray 1997). Eade and Sallnow, for instance, argue that "pilgrimage is above all an arena for competing religious
and secular discourses, for both the official co-optation and the non-official
recovery of religious meanings, for conflict between orthodoxies, sects, and
confessional groups, for drives towards consensus and communitas, *and* for
counter-movements towards separateness and division" (1991:2; italics in
original). In the case of an alternative cultural formation such as New Age
culture, sacred places would constitute sites where social and individual
identities are forged, where group solidarities as well as differences (say, between New Agers and fundamentalist Christians) are defined and elaborated, and where the tension between New Age ideals and the practical
necessities imposed by the surrounding culture (those of commerce, professional careers, and so on) make themselves evident. In the next section, I
will focus on those *ideals*, as expressed in manuals for visiting sacred sites;
afterward I will return to the task of theorizing the tensions between the
ideals and the practical social and ecological realities.

Ritualization: How to Visit a Sacred Site

> Tuning into power point energies is analogous to
> using a radio—you have to both turn on your
> receiver and tune in to an appropriate station. If
> you wish to derive the fullest possible benefit from
> the energies, you must also concentrate your
> awareness, quiet your mind, and tune your entire
> being to the energy broadcast of the power point.
>
> —MARTIN GRAY, "Sacred Sites
> and Power Points"

Sacred sites and power points, as Martin Gray suggests, hold the promise of
some sort of beneficial "energy connection" with the Earth, a connection
that is activated in part by the pilgrim, who travels to the sacred site purpose-
fully. Recent books on New Age and earth pilgrimage suggest a characteristic list of activities to be performed by the pilgrim: visualization, meditation
or prayer, ceremonial ritual, dreaming or perhaps "channeling" the spirit(s)

of the given place, and so on. All these activities are intended to facilitate an intuitive or nonrational "attunement" to the place itself (or its spirits), either as a goal in itself and as a way of healing our relationship to the earth, or for the purpose of individual spiritual growth.[19]

The better pilgrim guidebooks warn that the process of visiting a sacred site should not be performed hastily, but rather that it requires preparation and demands a certain etiquette. Preparing for a pilgrimage might involve a period of "purification" or "clearing," assessment of one's motivation, and "self-evaluation" or "personal inventory" (Corbett 1988:93). Philip Heselton recommends a cautious and gradual approach to a sacred place so to allow the area to "reveal itself as a living teacher" to you. This requires asking "permission of the spirit of the site," and then giving of oneself by establishing a practice of "tending," which might "involve clearing out the clogged-up holy well, weeding round the mark stone so that it can be seen, or encouraging the old tree species and companion plants where a clump is threatened," as well as "picking up litter on a regular basis." Heselton continues, "You will realize by such actions that you have 'adopted' the site and, if you act rightly, honestly, and with good intentions . . . the site will respond by allowing you to share in its store of wisdom" (1991:98). The process of "adoption" should involve regular visits, "at different times of the day, such as dawn, moon, sunset and midnight, at times of the full moon, perhaps, or the eight traditional festivals," which are the equinoxes, solstices, and cross-quarter days. "The important thing is to be open to the place: let it speak to you until you become aware of its spiritual essence. Then make that place special to *you*" by conducting a "non-invasive" ritual. This may mean "sitting out" or meditating overnight at the site. He concludes: "There can be no precise directions on how to approach sites. All we can do is to follow our inner guidance, realize we are a part of the Earth, and we will know" (98–100; italics in original).

Like Heselton, Jim Swan urges, "A person must go to the place with humility, perform his or her acts of respect, and then see what happens. Surrender, not control is the bottom line" (1990:224).[20] Since many sacred sites, particularly in North America, have a long-standing history of indigenous use, Swan recommends inquiring into whether indigenous people still use the site for ceremonial purposes, and, if so, steering clear of any ceremonies or rituals unless one is specifically invited to them (219). He continues,

> When you park your car and first set foot on the earth at this special place, stop and look around. . . . Get a sense of the place. Let its ambiance sink into your mind so you can walk gently on your pilgrimage.
>
> As you set off in the direction that feels correct, stop, say a prayer, and leave a little food like cornmeal. It doesn't have to be much, but the gesture of sacrifice is essential to demonstrate your attitude and purpose for being there.
>
> Move slowly as you walk along the trail. Watch for animals and plants which seem to stand out, not by their beauty necessarily, but because they feel like nodes of power.

> . . . If you feel moved to say prayers at some place, do what feels right to
> you; don't just copy what the Indians have done. If you want to conduct some
> kind of ceremony, let it be one that honors the place.
>
> If you plan to stay . . . you may want to mark off a special area for yourself.
> . . . Many people mark off each direction of the compass with an object or
> stone. The purpose of this is to create a microcosm of the macrocosm, and to
> draw in power during this special time of unity. If you use anything from the
> place, like rocks, return them to their original places when you finish. . . .
> (220–21)

Page Bryant similarly urges pilgrims to prepare for visits by engaging in dialogue with the site's spirits or "guardians" and asking their permission "to
partake of the powers" (1991:64). She provides a detailed guide to "ceremonial etiquette" in a checklist of "Ten Easy Steps," which include "ground-
ing" (sitting on the earth, relaxing the body and stilling the mind in order to
become receptive); "smudging," a traditional Native American practice of
purifying "the aura and body of any negative thought forms" by fanning
burning sage, sweetgrass, or tobacco over one's body; making an offering of
herbs, a small crystal, a chant, song, dance, or prayer; honoring the site by
performing a ritual or ceremony specifically chosen for its appropriateness;
and leaving "something of yourself behind," whether it be "a few of your
hairs" or the thought of "a stream of pure light flowing forth from your heart
to the Earth," but nothing that will deface the site or be distracting to visitors
(219–23, 64).

Some writers advocate specific methods of altering one's consciousness
in order to facilitate "attunement" or "interfacing" with the Earth. Devereux
suggests fasting, meditation, ritual drumming and movement, dreamwork
(paying attention to dreams and cultivating the ability to engage in conscious or lucid dreams), induction of out-of-body trance experiences, or the
use of psychoactive plants (Devereux 1989b).[21] Sacred sites, another auth-
or relates, have an energy "that we could term a 'deva' or 'guardian'" who
can give or deny access to the site (GC 5:18–19). This being is contacted
through a meditative trance state (a "Lower World journey") aided by drumming or some other trance-induction technique, with the particular "energy" of the place then revealing itself in symbolic and intuitive imagery.
Following the work of attunement and the gaining of whatever insights obtained, most authors suggest some expression of gratitude before leaving the
site. Frank Joseph lists the following as appropriate offerings: "A pinched
offering of tobacco or sage, a few drops of blessed or pure water, a seed or
flower from your garden, a crystal or attractive stone." These "serve as a
physiological link between the pilgrim and the sacred center" (1992, xiii).

The two central ideas in most of this literature are those of *ceremony* and
of *attunement* to the energies or spirits which are present at the particular
site. Ceremony reflects an attitude—a ritualistic appreciation of the sacred
—and attunement reflects the general goal of connection, wholeness, and
resacralization of the world. The act of traveling to sacred sites and perform-

ing rituals there is sometimes said to have tangible results on the sites themselves. As one earth mysteries theorist told me, the activity of visiting ancient sites, praying or channeling at them, conducting Full Moon meditations, and the like, is "creating dowsable and perceptible differences" at the sites: the number of active energy lines increases, and energy pathways which have remained dormant are being reopened (Jenkins, int.).

As many of these writings make clear, however, much of the desire motivating such pilgrimage is a personal one: the desire for experience, "personal transformation," or "self-actualization" (e.g., Swan 1990:224). Self-actualization can mean different things: it can refer to a psychologically and spiritually transformative, healing process, or simply to the experience of a feeling of personal power—the sort of power that pilgrims have otherwise not found in their everyday lives. Visiting sacred sites is for many New Agers and ecospiritualists only a beginning, or else a punctuation mark in a more extended life-pilgrimage. There are those for whom such places become so important that they leave behind their former places of residence and re-settle closer to their "elective Center." The activities of visiting and of relocation, however, both produce tangible effects on the sites themselves and on their social and economic surroundings. In the remainder of this chapter I will articulate a conceptual model for understanding the interaction between people, loosely organized into (mutable) interpretive communities, and nonhuman environments.

SPATIALIZATION, ORCHESTRATION, CONTESTATION

At the broadest scale, then, New Age and ecospiritual discourses organize space into a particular geography, one in which there are places, usually located at some remove from major urban centers, which are considered especially sacred and powerful. The flow of travelers to and between these places, supplemented by the flow of ideas and information through books, media, and word of mouth, facilitates the creation of an infrastructure— New Age bookstores, healing and retreat centers, vegetarian cafes, and so on—which attracts more migrants and relocatees and, in the process, solidifies the position of these centers within the alternative geography of New Age/ecospiritual culture.

Sacred places are further produced through the articulation and contestation of claims to the legitimate ownership or control of such spaces, and through the competition for the authority to speak for them. Those who attempt to dominate such space employ strategies of appropriation and exclusion, which may include discourses and claims of ownership, property rights, land use regulations, and so on. Those who resist such domination, in turn, may invert or reverse, alter or hybridize symbolic meanings and spatial relations. Through ritual actions and spatial and interpretive practices, social groups "anchor" their own claims and worldviews in the material landscape. This effort is never entirely successful: it is resisted both by other social groups' attempts to enlist the landscape to their own purposes, and by the nonhuman organisms and processes that make it up.[22] If, as Simon Coleman and John Elsner (1995:209, 202) suggest, sacred space is "orchestrated" through the organization of persons, texts, and places, there are numerous orchestral players who may not always play along with a particular score. Furthermore, the effort always occurs within broader social, institutional, and ecological structures which shape and influence the "orchestration." To theorize this interaction between culture and environment, I will draw on a range of approaches—including ecological psychology, environmental hermeneutics and the phenomenology of landscape, actor-network theory, and a poststructuralist understanding of agency and space—which variously contribute to a postconstructivist (or co-constructive) socio-environmental theory.[23]

A Relational, Co-Constructive, Multiscalar Model

In the "ecological psychology" first articulated by perceptual psychologist J. J. Gibson, ecosystems are conceived in terms of the interaction between *subjects*, effective agents equipped with particular action-capabilities or "effectivities," and *objects*, whose inherent potentials and properties render them apt for the actions and projects of subjects (Ingold 1992:42). The environment of a given subject-organism is made up of objects which present particular "affordances" to that organism. A rock, for instance, affords the possibilities of serving as a projectile to be thrown, a tool with which to crush a shell, a shield behind which to hide, a structural component of a larger construction, and so on.[24] Subjects can also be objects for other subjects. Social animals, including but not limited to humans, live in shared environments which consist of inanimate, animate, and *socialized* objects or actors: inanimate objects afford possible actions, animate objects afford interactions, and socialized objects or "persons" (i.e., other humans or socially recognized animals) afford *proper* actions and interactions—that is, interactions constrained or mediated by the "perceived need to present proper affordances to the other" (Reed 1988:121). Socialization is thus "a natural consequence of our living in a populated, animate environment, full of affordances" (117). Human language and conceptual thought, by this token, are also "natural," since, like tools, language transforms the perception of the environment and expands (or contracts) the effectivities of its users in specific ways (Ingold 1992:46). As the world offers affordances for various possible actions, interactions, and proper actions, so it also presents socially sustained *interpretive* affordances, which are taken up through and within linguistic and discursive practices and traditions that develop over time, and which in turn transform their environments. Both perception and language, in this view, emerge from an engagement and immersion in a world of affordances and effectivities, not in a disengaged mental representation and cognitive organization of data *from* the world by a subject who stands *apart* from it.

In anthropologist Tim Ingold's (1992) words, this engagement between persons and environments involves a mutual process of "production" or "bringing forth," and "consumption" or "taking up": people create their environments "in the sense that the environment is the embodiment of past activity" (50), shaped by the ways it has been appropriated and negotiated within the lifeworlds of its inhabitants. As production is a "becoming of the environment" through the active labor of social beings, so consumption is a "becoming of persons." For humans, Christopher Tilley suggests, a landscape is not simply a backdrop for action but, rather, "a cognized form redolent with place names, associations and memories . . . linking together topographical features, trees, rocks, rivers, birds and animals with patterns of human intentionality" (1994:24). The various affordances which are taken up by an interpretive community become interwoven within a spatial, narrative, and discursive nexus which guides action and further interaction with the landscape. The process of dwelling in a landscape, traversing, encompassing and appropriating its spaces and affordances, continually reshapes that landscape, inscribing meaningful spatializations deeper into its surface. The act of walking, for instance, is "a process of appropriation of the topographical system, as speaking is an appropriation of language" (Tilley 1994:28–29), with "pedestrian speech acts" (Certeau 1984) inscribing the ground with paths and tracks. Places, in turn, become emplotted within narratives, which organize space and place "by means of the displacements" they describe (Tilley 1994:32–33).

Seen in this perspective, a landscape can be defined as an interactive and dynamic, spatially, materially, and temporally linked assemblage of effective subjects (organized in collectivities) and affordant objects. The interpretive affordances of a landscape are taken up in various ways by different interpretive communities which appropriate them into their cultural practices, selectively thematizing certain affordances from out of the total array of interpretive possibilities. Nonhuman organisms and environmental affordances become "enrolled" to various degrees within the resultant networks, contributing to more or less stable or sustainable relations between the various actants.[25]

Human spatial and interpretive practices, in turn, arise within the historical unfoldment of interpretive communities, which construct themselves in relation to other communities and in interaction with larger, more global discourses and practices. Interpretive communities are never clearly bounded and pre-given; they are cultural achievements, always in process, produced through the labor of place-making and identity construction. Identity and alterity, as Akhil Gupta and James Ferguson put it, "are produced simultaneously in the formation of 'locality' and 'community'" (1997:13). Interpretive communities can be thought of as relatively *local* in their scale and location, while broader discourses (such as science) and structures (such as the transnational political economy) are more *global.* In actuality, however, neither is exclusively local or global (nor is the difference between the local and the global a self-evident and unchanging one). Science and economics are played out in specific locations, rather than in some supra-local realm apart from real places; and even the most local interpretive com-munities are connected to larger such communities elsewhere. In many cases, communities of belief (such as Sedona's New Age community) have more in common with similar communities some distance away (e.g., with Glastonbury's alternative community) than with other communities with whom they may share a particular geographic location (e.g., Sedona's Evan-gelical Christians). New Age culture has, in this sense, become a global cultural phenomenon: it is disseminated through the circulation of ideas and practices by way of a vast publishing industry, electronic media, and an international seminar circuit, as well as through networks connecting to-gether spiritual groups and communities, healing centers and other institu-tions, larger-scale gatherings, and specific physical sites.

Interpretive communities also diverge in their placement within social orders: some are more centrally aligned within spatially rooted hierarchical social relations than others, whose relatively deterritorialized movement they aim to control or dominate. Gilles Deleuze and Felix Guattari (1987) distinguish such communities in terms of the difference between "striated," "gridded," or "sedentary" space — characterized by closed boundaries, walls, and roads between enclosures — and the open-ended "smooth space" of de-territorialized and nomadic groups. The former is the "state space" created by "arborescent" systems — centered and sedentary, segmented, hierarchi-cally structured unities, which, for Deleuze and Guattari, include empires as well as logocentric philosophical systems (e.g., those centered around such founding concepts as the Logos, the philosopher-king, or the republic of minds). Opposed to "State thought," which aims to "root man" within a "world order," is "rhizomatic" thought, which moves laterally like bulbs or tubers along "lines of flight," always in the process of becoming, "a stream without beginning or end that undermines its banks and picks up speed in the middle" (24–25). In geographic terms, the State-form is expressed in the enclosure of land, the "forest-clearing of fields; agriculture-grid laying; animal raising subordinated to agricultural work and sedentary food pro-duction; commerce based on a constellation of town-country (*polis-nomos*) communications" (384). Nomadic movement, on the other hand, inhabits the smooth space of deserts, back countries, mountainsides, and the vague expanse around cities (380–81). And though "the nomadic trajectory may follow trails or customary routes, it does not fulfill the function of the seden-tary road, which is to *parcel out a closed space to people*, assigning each per-son a share and regulating the communication between shares"; rather, it "distributes people (or animals) in an open space" (380; italics in original), redistributing sociospatial relations by challenging the property system, for instance, through squatting (Shields 1991:53; cf. Benterrak, Muecke, and Roe 1984; MacCannell 1992).

Bringing these ideas together, we arrive at an understanding of humans as individually and collectively immersed in more-than-human environments, with relations between them always in process, characterized by conflicts, processes of alliance building and network formation (involving humans and nonhumans), and the ongoing production of identities and subjectivities. Interpretive communities, understood as temporary and fluid social configurations, selectively appropriate the affordances of their environments through the technical and material means at their disposal. Each constructs accounts about a place or landscape—historical narratives consisting of meaningful signs and representations, place-images, and place-myths,[26] "ways of seeing" (Berger 1972) and "structures of feeling" (R. Williams 1977, 1985). These narratives can be analyzed in terms of their social and discursive contexts and their sociopolitical and ecological investments and effects: that is, in terms of what they say about a place, who speaks them, to whom they appeal and whom they exclude, which groups they privilege or align together and which they marginalize or delegitimize, and the forms of human-nonhuman interaction which they make possible, authorize, or prohibit. It is this last dynamic, that between humans and their extrahuman environments, which serves as a focus for much of what follows here, and therefore requires a few further comments.

Intimations of the Other: Theorizing Nonhuman Agency

Apart from the human activities that make up this spatialization of landscapes, there is always the extrahuman landscape, with its specific environmental features, processes, actors, or agents, which must be accounted for, responded to, appropriated, or transformed in the process of dwelling. My concern in this book is focused around landscapes which are commonly considered to be more or less natural and therefore pregiven by such an extrahuman reality. For preliminary purposes, they share several characteristics. They include striking topographical features, or combinations of such features, which contrast markedly with their surroundings (visually or in some other way). They tend to involve an aspect of uncanniness, unknown or mysterious elements, or the presence of unanswered questions in their histories: features, for instance, which provoke questions such as, Who designed this place, and why? or Who has been here before and what did they do? Ready answers are not often available for such questions, and so the landscape features present themselves as underdetermined in their meanings and therefore highly open to interpretation. At the same time, they tend to be associated with some sort of history of sacred status (quite obviously in the case of Glastonbury, more latent or implicit in the case of Sedona). Finally, such places are usually geographically marginal or peripher-

al in relation to dominant socioeconomic geographies. (In this latter quality, New Age/ecospiritual sacred sites exist on a continuum with other kinds
of places, notably those which have been explicitly designated as ecological
refuges, wilderness areas, or national parks.)

On the most material level, then, there is *something* — a place, object, or
landscape feature — at the center of the spatialized sacred landscape, which
attracts and accumulates discourses of sacrality in the form of lore, tales,
pilgrimages, and ritual practices. But it would be a mistake to identify that
something too early in our interpretive effort, if only because all our understandings of the place are always already enmeshed within interpretive
traditions. Consider Mount Shasta in northern California, for instance: a
mountain which had been considered sacred by several Native tribes long
before Europeans arrived, and which in the past two centuries has become
a magnet for a multitude of mystical and metaphysical groups. To say that
the essence which lies behind this particular phenomenon, underlying all
its cultural interpretations, is a *mountain* is, in effect, saying very little. It is,
on the one hand, a *particular* mountain, whose appearance dominates the
horizon of a large part of northern California, whose broad, snow-covered
peak takes on particular qualities at particular times of day and year (e.g., a
hovering "ghost" overlooking a green summer landscape, a "benevolent
presence," etc.). But on the other hand, even the supposedly neutral term
mountain already privileges a reading of it as a physical thing-in-itself, something which speakers of English (and European languages) recognize as
sharing in the quality of *mountainness* — not a social or spiritual being whom
one might fear or revere, nor a pillar of the world whose presence is axial to
the well-being of all things, but simply a large mass of rock, formed through
the blind action of geological forces for no reason in particular. The language we use to describe the world, in other words, projects an epistemic
grasp over that world, encompassing it into a particular formation of power/
knowledge; and in the epistemic world picture embodied within this ostensibly neutral physicalist language of mountains and other objects, sacredness would seem to be ruled out, except as a quirk of cultural perception.

To understand the sacredness and the mystical allure of such a site, then,
it is important that we attempt to bracket out the unspoken metaphysical
presuppositions encoded in our language, with its assumptions of neutrality
and objectivity in describing a world of human subjects and nonhuman
objects or things-out-there. These sites are, at one and the same time, spatially organized *physical landscapes*, culturally meaningful *places* and regions (e.g., "homelands," "wastelands," etc.), *sites* for the working out of various cultural, economic, political, and ecological processes and struggles,
and *heterotopic openings* onto a dimension of genuine otherness, but whose
openness is threatened in every attempt to specify and identify what "it"
might be. In what follows, my strategy will be to probe into the interactive
geology and ecology of images, representations, myths, and practices that
has congealed around each site, to deconstructively tug at these threads so

as to unveil their contexts, their contestation and appropriation by different interpretive communities, their histories or genealogies, and the contested geographies, human and nonhuman, within which they are enmeshed. But this analytic and interpretive probing will be tempered by a recognition that there is always an elusive, tricksterlike otherness to these places, a never-encompassable remainder, the traces of which contribute to the distinct character, spirit, or sense of place that mixes and meshes with their culturally specific interpretive histories. I will take these interpretive histories and contests, then, as clues, openings onto a possible (and always only possible) otherness which makes its presence felt but eludes the grasp of systematic and objective knowledge. That is not to suggest that this extradiscursive reality is *prediscursive*, nor indeed that we can ever come to know it *apart* from our own discursive, linguistic, and conceptual labors; it is simply to recognize that there is always an ever elusive *more* which those categories cannot capture. Ultimately, then, I will try to leave these openings *open*, not to close them off by way of a reification to some pregiven essence, or of a reduction to ideology, social relations, or some other explanatory principle. My hope, in the end, is that such a method can produce insights into the interconnected political, cultural, and ecological investments that have woven themselves into the texture of two contemporary sacred sites—nodes in the productive circuits of an alternative, New Age, or Gaian ecospiritual geography.

PART TWO

GLASTONBURY

There are many Glastonburys, and though her ancient walls have never been cast down like the walls of Troy, her spirit has hidden levels, depth below depth, like the rocks of a mountain range, and in different places these come to the surface. The ancient courts and low-browed doors of her old houses are of the Middle Ages, and the spirit of the medieval Church broods over the centre of the town. The hand of the abbot ruled all the country around. . . .

—DION FORTUNE, *Glastonbury: Avalon of the Heart*

There was a time, when a traveller, if he had the will . . . could send his barge out into the Summer Sea and arrive not at Glastonbury of the monks, but at the Holy Isle of Avalon; for at that time the gates between worlds drifted within the mists, and were open. . . .

—LADY MORGAINE, in Marion Zimmer Bradley, *The Mists of Avalon*

Glastonbury has something to suit every taste. There are ancient fertility rituals and a Neolithic spiral maze; the Cauldron of Inspiration, the Holy Grail and the elixir of Life; a fairy castle, a magic mountain and flying saucers; King Arthur, the Round Table of the Zodiac, and the story of Creation; the Oldest Church, the coming of the Saints, and the Chalice of the Last Supper; secret passages, running water and inexplicable shafts of light; a megalithic moon-observatory, the ancient science of gematria, and a sacred egg stone. . . .

People come to celebrate solstices and equinoxes, to set up alternative or spiritual communities and to make magic. There are self-styled magicians, wandering witches, weirdo warlocks, masochistic meditators and reincarnations of everything from Queen Guinevere to the latest version of the New Christ. It's all good fun, a bit of a circus and living here, especially during the summer months, has been aptly described as living in the middle of a pack of tarot cards.

—FRANCES HOWARD-GORDON, *Glastonbury: Maker of Myths*

If you can't have Hippies at Glastonbury where on earth can you have them?

—SHEILA, a Rainbow Fields Villager at Molesworth cruise missile base, writing at Greenlands Farm outside Glastonbury

FOUR

Stage, Props, and Players of Avalon

Britain in recent decades has been a nation struggling to redefine itself amid a congeries of apparently irresolvable factions and tendencies: among them, long-standing English pride in a history glorified as the source of democratic ideals, of industrial and technological revolutions, and of a romantic, chivalrous, and royal past; a composite British identity, dominated by an English majority but fractured by Scottish and Welsh nationalisms and the perpetual "Irish problem"; an intensified multiculturalism brought about by the postcolonial return of the colonized to the home of the colonizer; and a characteristic aloofness and hesitancy to enter the fray of European politics. In England itself, a further divide separates the industrialized and working-class North from the rural and conservative South, with the bustling megalopolis of London mediating (politically) and dominating (culturally) the whole.

Within this conventional topography, the southwest is traditionally seen as a land of quiet, typically English landscapes, rural market towns, farming villages, and areas of tourist and historical interest, including resort towns, artistically tended gardens, and sparsely populated moors. The small West Country town of Glastonbury is, on the surface, an unspectacular and not even particularly attractive market town. But on closer inspection, it reveals itself to be a bustling and colorful enclave of unusual activities, a haven for New Agers, counterculturalists (or, as some locals still call them, hippies), and spiritually inclined pilgrims of various stripes, attracted to Glastonbury for its history, myths, and legends, and its undefinable "energy" and mystique.

On the further unraveling of its semiotic layers, the onion of Glastonbury becomes a kaleidoscope of images, stories, and visions, and it becomes clear that there are not one, but, as Dion Fortune says, many Glastonburys, and many "Avalons." The following two chapters will present a tableau of these competing place-tales and images, which mix and mesh across interpretive communities ranging from believers in Glastonbury's once or future glories to skeptical local residents and bemused outsiders. I will focus especially on the self-identified alternative community, the motley collection of

Figure 4.1. View of the "island" from Joseph of Arimathea's alleged resting spot

recent settlers—with pilgrims and nomads circulating on its peripheries—who have taken up the cause of Glastonbury's distinctness, and on its relations with other local residents and its troubled but increasingly successful integration within the town. I will situate their alternative vision of Glastonbury within the phenomenology of their encounters with the landscape, and within the struggle to define, control, and enact place and space in the town and its environs. This is a struggle that takes place predominantly in the tensions between (and within) the alternative community, mainstream and more conservative Glastonburyans, the broader mainstream of British society, and the counterstream (or understream) of nomadic "New Age travelers." Each of these is several in itself; the present chapter will focus primarily on the first and the last.

Finally, there is the *landscape* of Glastonbury, which serves not only as stage and props to the various tableaux that unfold against its backdrop, but which also actively shapes and participates in those plots. Before delving too deeply into these plots, I will introduce the town as it appears to a first-time visitor, an idealized and abstracted visitor who knows little about the town except what she sees on her first arrival, by motor vehicle over the rolling lowlands of Somerset.

A FIRST ENCOUNTER

No matter which direction a visitor arrives from, there is a certain point, sometimes up to twenty miles away, at which the strangely shaped Tor comes into one's field of vision. Shaped (depending on one's direction and one's interpretive predilections) like a breast, a humpback whale, or a sleeping dragon, with uncharacteristically steep upper slopes and a single tower on top, the Tor is cradled by three smaller, more rounded hills: the green, dome-shaped Chalice Hill; Wirral or Wearyall Hill, a ridge flung out like an extended limb to the southwest; and Windmill Hill. Together this cluster makes up a kind of island that rises prominently above the surrounding meadows of the otherwise flat Somerset landscape. Jungian analyst Jean Shinoda Bolen, in her midlife travelogue *Crossing to Avalon*, portrays this moment of arrival: "Suddenly the road changed—it could have been a shift in angle or elevation, or a gap in the hedgerow—and there was Glastonbury Tor! I say this with an exclamation point, because that is the impact; it is something to behold. . . . From any angle, the Tor emanates power and mystery. There is something unnatural and sculptural about its shape, with its spiral terraces that appear to wind around its sides and the tower on the top that looks like a Stonehenge-sized megalith" (1994:89).

Driving toward Glastonbury from every direction, visitors are greeted by a sign informing them that they are approaching the "Ancient Isle of Avalon." With its population of some 8,000 (and many more in the summer), the town is built around a square formation of four streets, two of which converge at what was once the Market Cross, the focal point of the town's social, economic, and agricultural life. As English market towns go, Glastonbury is relatively unimpressive; what may strike the perceptive visitor, in fact, is the constant stream of vehicular traffic down the town's High Street, the main road leading between the neighboring town of Street, a couple of miles southwest of Glastonbury, and the slightly larger cathedral and market town of Wells, some six miles to the northeast. (A bypass was built in the winter of 1994–95, cutting Glastonbury's previous traffic load perhaps by half.)

Stopping to take in some of the town on foot, our visitor discovers that the slope of the 400-meter-long High Street naturally edges her on from its upper end, where it is met by the Wells Road, to its lower ("downtown") end at the market square. Partway down, the street is punctuated by the pointed spire and long body and courtyard of St. John's Church, in front of which sit a group of disheveled, dyed-hair youths with their dogs. Questioning a local shopkeeper, our visitor learns that this courtyard had been open to the street until the early 1990s, and was the site of frequent summertime congregations of visiting "travelers," homeless young hippies ("drongos" or "crusties," as they are known locally), but the protests of townspeople led to its enclosure behind a wrought-iron fence. Some of the itinerants still pass their time on the benches in front of the fence.

Continuing toward the bottom of High Street, past historic buildings such as the Abbot's Tribunal (now the town museum) and the George and Pilgrims' Inn, our visitor can't help noticing an unlikely proliferation of unusual shops and amenities: no less than three New Age bookstores, a cafe that doubles as a gallery for Goddess and Green Man[1] sculptures, and sev-

Figure 4.2. Amid the ruins: Glastonbury Abbey

eral shops specializing in crystals, candles, New Age music, and rainbow-styled clothing. Through an archway at the bottom of High Street one can enter the Glastonbury Experience, a courtyard surrounded by storefronts with names like the Goddess and the Green Man, Pendragon, and Star

Child, alongside a vegetarian cafe, the Bridget Chapel, and stairs leading up to the Isle of Avalon Foundation, with its Brigit Healing Wing and Library of Avalon.

Similar storefronts present themselves on all sides of the Market Cross. Car parks line the sides of Northload Street, while, around the corner on Magdalene Street, next to the Town Hall, is the main entrance to the ruins of Glastonbury Abbey. The ruins lie in the center of town, literally and figuratively enclosed by it; except for this main gate and a less visible side gate, they are separated from the town by a rock wall. Owned and managed by the Church of England, which charges a £2 admission fee, the Abbey ruins constitute a large and quiet oasis in the town's bustling heart. Our visitor learns that since the Abbey grounds were bought for £30,000 on behalf of the Church of England in 1907, they have been cleared up and preserved, and today the Abbey plays host to some 150,000 visitors annually, a figure which includes tens of thousands of overseas visitors—many of them Americans interested in seeing Arthur's grave—as well as local and regional pilgrims attending the yearly Anglican, Catholic, and other Christian pilgrimages (McIlwain 1992:26; Bowman 1993:33–35; Rahtz 1993:128). Little remains of the Abbey except the restored Edgar Chapel and St. Mary's Chapel, and fragments of walls and markings on the ground to indicate where the remaining buildings stood. These mute remains are surrounded by mowed grass, some trees, a pond, a small wildlife haven established in 1984, and camera-toting tourists strolling about in the midst of it all. An impressive museum and interpretive center, opened in 1993, have ensured the Abbey's status as the town's primary tourist draw.

If the Abbey ruins constitute the heart of the town, the ever-present Tor hovers at its liminal edges. Foregoing the shuttle that connects the Tor to the Abbey, our visitor decides to take the leisurely twenty-minute stroll which takes her up and around the other side of the town center, past old stone buildings and newer housing clusters, to narrow Chilkwell Street, hemmed in on both sides by medieval stone walls and centuries-old residential blocks. On the way, she passes the entrance to the Chalice Well Gardens, another of the town's tourist attractions. Inquiring within, she discovers that these gardens are fed by a natural spring whose precise source is unknown (it is likely beneath the Mendip Hills) but which flows out between the Tor and Chalice Hill, giving an abundant and regular flow of about 25,000 British gallons (30,000 U.S. gallons) a day of clear and drinkable water. Its supply has never been known to fail, even in severe drought, and it reportedly saved the town from drought in the dry years of 1921 and 1922. Its high chalybeate iron content gives a reddish tinge to the rocks it passes over, accounting in part for its alternative names of Red Spring and Blood Spring.

The history of the Chalice Well, it turns out, prefigures a bit of the recent history of Glastonbury itself. In 1750 an apparent cure for asthma brought thousands of pilgrims to the Chalice Well, and its waters were reputed to have cured everything from deafness and blindness to ulcers. The crowds peaked at 10,000 in May 1751, then subsided soon after when someone reportedly drank too much and died (Ashe 1982:117). By the 1830s its reputation as a healing spa had ended (Dunning 1994:70). In 1888 the Chalice Well was bought along with the adjacent Anchor Inn property by a Catholic order; then, some twenty years later, came into the possession of writer Alice Buckton, who formed a craft center and theatre and concert space there. Its reputation spread as John Cowper Powys featured it in his *Glastonbury Romance* as a scene of faith healing. In 1959 the entire property was purchased by a charitable organization called the Chalice Well Trust, and it now receives some 50,000 visitors a year, a figure that has grown steadily from 10,000 in 1982.[2] Among the claims our visitor is likely to hear, sooner or later, about the Well are that it "was a centre of Druid ritual; Joseph of Arimathea lived near it; the Grail is or was at the bottom (hence the colour of the water and, despite etymology, the name 'Chalice'). A bowl, found in obscure circumstances, is credited with a most unlikely antiquity. Miracles of healing are claimed. Spiritual presences are discerned in the garden. Lines of mystic force emanate from the Well itself" (Ashe 1982:118). Today, the Chalice Well is a series of well-tended gardens, sloping up from street level to partway up Chalice Hill, where the well is located. A series of conduits and springs carry the well water through several pools and fountains and out into the street and underground. The actual well is several feet beneath the ground, and is covered with a lid made of wrought iron, designed by Frederick Bligh Bond, featuring two interlocking circles forming an oval known as the Vesica Piscis. (This symbol was supposedly adopted by early Christians to represent Christ, who is both the sacrificial "sacred fish" and the fisherman of souls. It has since accrued a reputation as a kind of Western yin-yang symbol, denoting the interlocking of the visible and invisible worlds, conscious and unconscious, masculine and feminine.) On any given day in the summer, the gardens can be humming with activity, but still retain the peaceful ambience so carefully cultivated by Chalice Well's guardians. On this particular weekday afternoon in July, our visitor finds two harpists tinkling away in the lower part of the gardens; farther up, several people huddled together performing a group healing; and at the gardens' upper end, two people spending several moments bent over the Chalice Well itself, contemplatively dropping coin offerings into the water. Elsewhere, people walk leisurely or lie on the grass. The sound of drumming comes in over the fence from the street, but no one appears at all disturbed by it.

Adjacent to the Chalice Well, on the other side of Well House Lane, is what has become known as the White Spring, an artesian spring which, according to the local Water Board, rises in the Midford sands overlying the upper Liassic beds of the Tor (N. Mann 1993:56). Its water is highly calciferous and perennial, though its rate of flow varies from as little as 5,000 to as much as 70,000 gallons a day. The reservoir is enclosed within a cavern-

Figure 4.3. By the Goddess Tree outside the White Spring Café

like cafe and crystal shop, its water flowing out into an altarlike setting, decorated with candles and Goddess figurines, and continuing along an open duct down the middle of the cavernous enclosure. Outside, a fountain spring pours down a wall stained reddish brown, yellow, green, and gray, and over vines and leaves, and collects in a little pool at the bottom, in which one can see coins, bracelets, and other objects. The branches of a tree that stands against the rock wall are decorated with knotted ribbons and kerchiefs, poems and prayers written on scraps of paper, feathers and makeshift dreamcatchers, and similar offerings and mementos left behind by pilgrims. The entire space has a gently sparkling, refreshing, and pagan shrinelike ambience. On this summer day, several people sit beneath or beside these waters, and on the street with guitars or children outside the cafe's entrance. Others come to refill their plastic jugs, pails, and bottles with water from the spring. While some of the loiterers resemble the "crusties" of High Street, sitting on the ground or on the rocks with their dogs, the atmosphere here is noticeably more relaxed.[3]

Continuing on, our visitor arrives at the base of the Tor. The most prominent landmark of central Somerset, the Tor overlooks the town from its eastern side. With its dramatically steep slopes and sculptured appearance, products of its geology and land use, the Tor appears uncanny. Its shape is rounded, but more steep at one end than the other, with a thousand-foot-long whaleback ridge sloping away to the southwest. The dominant visual features of the Tor are the tower of St. Michael's Church—the only remaining segment of the fourteenth-century structure (considerably repaired

Figure 4.4. Climbing the Tor

since then)—and the artificially cut terraces lying in concentric rings over every flank. There was once a Monastery of St. Michael on the Tor, dating possibly from the ninth century, but nothing remains of it since an earthquake destroyed it in the thirteenth century.

The Tor is approached by one of two routes. The first, the so-called Pilgrim's Path, leads from a path that begins near the White Spring up through a gate and into the old Fair Field and finally up the Tor's western spine. The second, a shorter but steeper climb, leads from a small parking area further up the narrow Wellhouse Lane on the Tor's south side. (In the summer, Well House Lane usually features a row of parked cars and vans, some of which appear to double as their owners' temporary or perhaps permanent residences.) A concrete footpath has been carved out at either entry point for Tor climbers, and the National Trust has kindly provided a couple of benches on both upward climbs for "stagers." There are trees at the Tor's base, but otherwise it is bare and grass covered, marked only by round, oval, or egg-shaped boulders known as burrs. Sheep or cows may be seen grazing the lower slopes of the Tor, while erosion and an uncontrolled rabbit population have exposed the underlying soil and rock of some of its steeper levels.

As one approaches it, the Tor and its summit take on different appearances depending on the angle of approach and the height of one's climb. From in front (on the path up from Well House Lane and Chilkwell), the Tor appears as a weirdly shaped sleeping dragon, with various folds, creases or humps which hide its summit from visibility from just above its base to about two-thirds of the way up the dragon's spine. "At first the perfect cone (as it is seen from half the county) seems suddenly to have sprouted an ungainly green hump, which conceals the tower during the earlier part of the venture" (Tarbat 1988:10). On the way up the climber is generally greeted by an increasing breeze and cooler air; and by the time one reaches the top, there may be a more forceful wind. At the Tor's summit is a broad flat area, sunken on one side, with the open tower standing closer to one end. Extensive views are presented in all directions: into Wiltshire to the east, Dorset to the south, the Quantock Hills and Exmoor to the west, the Bristol Channel to the northwest, and with good views of Wells and other surrounding towns. What can be seen of the Somerset landscape here, except for its general shapes and contours, is the human history of this part of England: farms, hedges, rhynes and ditches, and cows and sheep grazing on the grasses. Visitors frequently comment on the quality of light in the landscape surrounding the Tor. The light changes with the time of day and year; on a summer evening about half an hour before sunset it may appear hazy, slightly misty, with gentle light fading off into a wispy gray-blue toward the horizon. Dawn, with low-lying mists rising from the rivers and wetlands, and sunset are particularly evocative times to be up on the Tor. On summer evenings there may be dozens of people gathered at or near the top of the Tor watching the sun's golden-orange globe hovering over the horizon.

With its single tower the Tor calls out like a beacon to those for whom Glastonbury means sanctuary or holy ground. Along with its associated myths, the Tor has drawn visitors for centuries; but once they arrive and settle, there are any number of other sites which take on a special meaning: the springs, the rounded Chalice Hill, the protruding Wirral (or Wearyall) Hill, "Bride's Mound" at the Beckery, the "sacred trees" known as Gog and Magog, and others. Our weary visitor is confident that time will allow her to discover more of the wonders this landscape holds.

A LANDSCAPE HISTORY

> There was within the realm of King Aethelstan a certain royal island known locally from ancient times as Glastonbury. It spread wide with numerous inlets, surrounded by lakes, full of fish and by rivers, suitable for human use and, what is more important, endowed by God with sacred gifts. . . .
>
> —*The Life of St. Dunstan*, circa 1000 A.D.
> (quoted on the opening panel of the interpretive display at Glastonbury Abbey Visitor Centre)

> The early legends and poetic traditions, which hover around those grey old ruins, are like the November mists and fogs which sweep silently

over the moorlands up to the Isle of Avalon,
blotting out the landscape, save here and there,
leaving us in a world of ghostly mystery. . . .

The stern historian analyses and discards the
tradition and legendary lore . . . . But most of us
have an innate, it may be childlike, faith in that
hidden landscape, and we shall continue to
believe, in spite of our stern historian's warnings
and rebukes, that in Glastonbury we have a link
with the earliest history of the British church of
today.

—A. FOWNES SOMERVILLE, in his presidential
address to the Somerset Archaeological and
Natural History Society, June 1907, following
the sale of the Abbey grounds to the
Church of England

Digging into Glastonbury, one could do worse than to begin by investigat-
ing its history as it has been written by historians, archaeologists, geologists,
and other scholars, and so the first tale told will be theirs: a tale of islands
and marshes, struggles to tame and reclaim a watery landscape, monastic
intrigues and power struggles, and the long and slow denouement of a post-
Reformation market town in a peripherally industrialized but largely agricultural part of England.

Islands and Marshes

Glastonbury is located in the center of Somerset county, at the eastern edge
of the Sedgmoor plain, which stretches to the Bristol Channel in the west
and is bounded by the Mendip Hills to the northeast and the Quantock
Hills to the southwest. The small Polden Hills divide the plain from east to
west, and the River Brue runs from the east past (and to the south of) Glastonbury to the sea, fifteen miles away, draining the northern floodplain of
the low-lying Somerset Levels and Moors, today the largest wetland area in
the west of Britain. Some eight thousand years ago, these levels and moors
were a sea inlet. The glacial ice sheets had reached down to the Mendip
Hills, and with their melting, ten to twelve thousand years ago, the sea levels
had risen. As the waters receded, they were replaced by salt marsh, fen, and
bog, with thick peat deposits building up from the sedge vegetation in the
wetland valleys. Higher areas, once covered in wildwood forests, like most
of Britain, were largely cleared during the Neolithic and transformed into
farmland, moorland, woods, and hedges.

Glastonbury, the most prominent of the "islands" rising from the marshy
levels and moors, is based on strata of blue Liassic limestone beds of Jurassic
age, alternating with clay; the Tor, rising 520 feet above sea level, is capped
by hard sandstone that has largely resisted erosion. In historical times, during periods of river flooding or sea transgressions, Glastonbury had retained

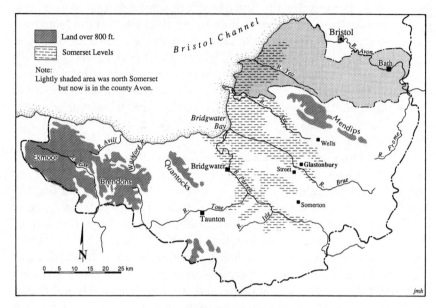

Map 4.1. Somerset County

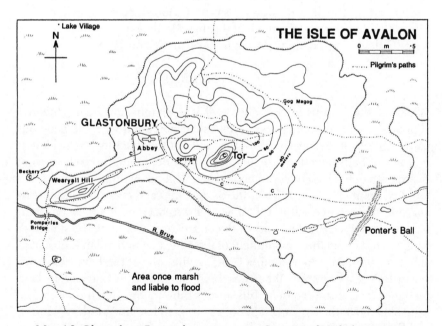

Map 4.2. Glastonbury Peninsula contour map. Courtesy of Nicholas R. Mann

its identity as a peninsula surrounded by swampy marshes (except for a neck of land connecting it to higher ground in the east). Most of the levels and moors remain below or just barely above the sea's high tide level. They are protected from flooding by a slightly higher ridge of coastal clay and by the results of past centuries' reclamation efforts: the building of extensive sea walls, the cutting of water channels, or rhynes, modification of river courses, and pumping and drainage schemes. As recently as 1607, however, seawater reached the foot of Glastonbury, and spring flooding or heavy rainfall continue to remind Somersetians of this watery heritage to this day.

In ancient times, the marsh edges provided a wealth of economic opportunities: fish, fowl, and mammals in the watery moors, rich pasturelands and timber stands farther up. Trade, by the end of the first millennium B.C., had already extended as far as the Mediterranean. The first attempts to control flooding are thought to have been made in Roman times. Not a great deal is known about settlements on the "island" of Glastonbury itself until early Saxon times, around the sixth or seventh century A.D., by which time there was a Christian community located on or near the Tor. Miles surmises that "the waterlogged areas of marsh and fen with the islands and ridges rising above them were most attractive to the early Christians, and for that matter anyone wanting solitude and security from others" (n.d.:7). Others have noted, however, that in early Saxon times the moor would have been considered practically worthless—a swampy morass, covered with areas of impenetrable alder woods, much of it subject to flooding, and whose rivers were shallow, clogged, and difficult to navigate (Moon 1978:8).

Glastonbury of the Monks

Whatever the reasons for the choice of its location—and many theories abound—a Christian abbey was established here, and with the generous patronage of the Saxon kings, it grew and consolidated its power base as a center of both sacred and secular authority. Beginning from the area of the so-called Twelve Hides, an area of semilegendary origin around Glastonbury, granted to the Abbey by the Saxon kings and given an entirely tax- and interference-free status, the Abbey grew to become the most powerful landowner in the area. The mid-tenth-century revival of monasticism under King Edmund and the appointment of the educated nobleman Dunstan as abbot continued this development, and by the time of the Domesday Survey in 1086, Glastonbury Abbey was the richest house in England. Its land included most of the Polden Hills, most of the moors, much of the more valuable land to the east, and additional pieces of land in Wiltshire, Dorset, and Berkshire (Moon 1978:9). The power of the Church in medieval England can hardly be underestimated. It dominated not only spiritual life, but economic life, as the major landowner, employer of labor, purchaser of services and goods, and patron and founder of markets and fairs; and it dominated social life, by providing "church houses" or parish meeting places for social gatherings, ales, feasts, and plays. In Somerset the church initiated land reclamation and drainage projects, promoted and financed mining schemes, founded towns and ports, and built farms, granges, and barns. Ecclesiastical estates in Somerset comprised more than one-third of the county (Bettey 1988:55).

Then, in 1184, a disastrous fire gutted the Glastonbury monastery, destroying most of its buildings, including its priceless library and the so-called Old Church. Further setbacks, resulting from an ongoing and sometimes violent rivalry between the Abbey and the bishop of Bath and Wells and from the death of the Abbey's most important patron, Henry II, led to a series of attempts by the Abbey to retain its position and authority. The twelfth and thirteenth centuries were a particularly creative period in the Abbey's historiographic mythmaking. During this period, the writings of William of Malmesbury, Caradog of Llancarfan, Giraldus Cambrensis, and others began to proclaim a supposedly ancient history tracing the Abbey's founding as far back as to the second century A.D. and connecting it to such figures as St. Patrick and King Arthur. Most historians today concur that these legends of the Abbey's founding, its association with various saints and their relics, and particularly the "discovery" of Arthur's and Guinevere's tombs buried on the Abbey grounds in 1191, were largely promotional strategies used by the monks to bolster the prestige of the Abbey and reassert its importance in the minds of the medieval populace. The establishment of an Arthurian cult at Glastonbury is thought also to have been used by the English kings in their efforts to subdue the Welsh, who rightfully claimed Arthur for their (Celtic) own. The initiative for Arthur's exhumation, for instance, came from Henry II, and nearly a century later, Edward I and Queen Eleanor visited Glastonbury to witness the opening of the tombs of their mythical predecessors (Crick 1991:218–19).

An alternative view on the alleged Arthurian connection to Glastonbury is presented by Geoffrey Ashe, one of the leading voices in Glastonbury's late-twentieth-century revival as a pilgrimage center. According to Ashe, the context behind the "discovery" of Arthur's grave in Glastonbury had less to do with the Abbey's need for money, or with its inmates' penchant for falsification, "real though these were," as it was "the revival in England of the lore of a Britain which preceded the English. At Glastonbury," he writes, "a piece of that Britain had survived, if forgetfully, without a break" (1982:75). In this view, Glastonbury may well have been the isle of Avalon, where the Britons' leader known as Arthur may have been buried; and memory of this might well have been preserved among the Celtic-speaking peoples, only later to be appropriated by the English.

In any case, the Abbey in the late Middle Ages became the prime pilgrimage center in British Christendom. Pilgrims were encouraged to come by the offer of indulgences issued by the Church, which gave days of remission from the time to be spent in Purgatory after one's death. Glastonbury was associated, in the popular mind, with numerous saints, and it was claimed that some of their relics were housed at the Abbey. The cult of St. Joseph of Arimathea, who was thought to have brought two vials containing Christ's blood to England and to have founded the first Christian church there, emerged in the mid-thirteenth century and reached its height by the early sixteenth century. Glastonbury also claimed roots in the Celtic Church of Ireland, Wales, and the southwest: the names of saints David, Bridget, Columba, Patrick, and Benignus all became associated with the monastery. The relics of several northern saints as well (Aidan, Hilda, Paulinus, the Venerable Bede) were reputedly brought here to protect them from the Viking raids of the eighth and ninth centuries. Glastonbury's own St. Dunstan, the tenth-century Saxon abbot, revived England's monastic movement and established the Abbey as a political and educational force.

The creation of the modern landscape of Somerset thus begins with the activities of the powerful ecclesiastical estates of Glastonbury and Wells. The landowners enclosed common grounds, regulated people's rights within specific boundaries, and undertook the work of draining the levels. Extensive reclamation work carried out throughout the twelfth to the fourteenth centuries, including the construction of seawalls and skillfully engineered drainage systems, resulted in the now familiar moorland landscape, with its fertile pastures and drainage rhynes (artificial watercourses) lined with pollarded willows and occasional flood control banks. Much of Somerset was made up of ordinary farmland, rented by small farmers, and common land, free pastureland for the stock of the village; the latter included the wild and untamed moorlands that were up for grabs to whoever would reclaim them. Rivalry between the bishopric of Wells and the abbey of Glastonbury (and sometimes the abbey of Athelney), however, led to a history of ownership disputes and, on occasion, open warfare. Disputes also occurred among landowners, freeholders, and commoners over pasture, peat-cutting, and timber rights, and between fishermen and millers who made weirs in the rivers, blocking them, and the drainers and navigators who wanted a free and uninterrupted flow to the sea. Eventually these disputes led to agreements and compromises between the landowning estates, including the formation of proper boundaries around their lands, and the division, enclosure, and further reclamation of peatlands (cf. Miles n.d.; Moon 1978; Bonham 1986).

The fourteenth century saw the onset of the Black Death and worsening economic conditions. It was Henry VIII's vicious dissolution of monasteries, however, that finally brought an end to the golden age of Glastonbury Abbey, then the second richest ecclesiastical house in Britain.[4] In 1539 its last abbot, Richard Whiting, was brutally executed on the Tor, his body dismembered, and its parts sent off to be displayed at the neighboring towns of Wells, Bath, Ilchester, and Bridgwater. The Abbey Church was smashed and blown up. Dom David Knowles described Abbot Whiting's execution: "No other landscape in all England carried so great a weight of legend. To the island valley at his feet the dying Arthur had been ferried. Through sedges from the Parrett had come Joseph of Arimathea bearing the Grail. On the pleasant pastures of Mendip had shone the countenance of the Child Jesus. Below him lay the now majestic pile of his abbey, desolate, solitary, and about to crumble into ruins" (in Rahtz 1993:40).

After the Dissolution

The end of the Abbey's reign left a power vacuum in Somerset. The Abbey and its estate passed from owner to owner, its riches divvied up, plundered, or looted. Much of the stone from the Abbey was taken and used for build- ing or sold by local residents (which some historians take as indication that attitudes to the Abbey's earlier absolute rule of the area were rather mixed). Somerset, in fact, was to become the county with the lowest population of Roman Catholics and the highest numbers of Protestant radicals and re- formers (Hutton 1993a). As the spatial regime of medieval Catholicism was dismantled in Glastonbury, the town itself, which had been built up around the Abbey's precincts and largely to serve its pilgrim market, was left cra- dling its ruins, and its economy rapidly declined.

By the late eighteenth century, enclosure and agricultural improvement in the moorlands resumed on a large scale. Between 1770 and 1840, all re- maining areas of wasteland were enclosed, drained, and divided into rectan- gular fields, bordered by artificial watercourses, and a pattern of roads and farms was created that largely continues to this day. A series of Parliamen- tary Enclosure Awards was used to effect drainage improvements; when drained, the land could be sold to anyone. Commoners agreed to reclama- tion in exchange for their own small plots. The resulting complicated own- ership pattern, of small fields, ditches and rhynes, pumps and drainage sys- tems, has existed until the present day.

In the late nineteenth and early twentieth centuries, the area's good sum- mer grazing conditions led to the creation of an extensive dairy industry, with numerous milk factories (the area is famous for its Cheddar cheese). The willow of the levels was used to develop a basketry and wickerwork industry. In the eighteenth and nineteenth centuries, tanneries and sheep- skin-processing industries became established in the area; this led to the development of footwear manufacturing, which remained the main indus- try of the Glastonbury-Street area until recently. In addition, demand for peat from the Brue Valley as agricultural fertilizer (it was formerly cut for fuel) grew dramatically in the latter half of twentieth century, becoming a major industry that strained the wetlands.[5] More recently, agro-industrial overproduction (with its reliance on a heavy water management regime), accompanied by the effects of the Common Agricultural Policy of the EU, and the rise of environmental concerns, have led to the "belated realization that the continued expansionist policies of agricultural growth could not . . . continue to be justified" (Brown, Croft, and Lillford 1988:114). Conser- vationists have been cautiously hoping that the moors and levels can be returned to a landscape of open water, reedbeds, and woodland. The 1986 designation of the Somerset Levels as an Environmentally Sensitive Area brought enhanced recognition of its ecological uniqueness; and the recent Avalon Marshes project has marshaled the cooperation of conservation bodies, local government, and the peat industry to restore large parts of the Somerset peatland to its wetland state by the year 2010. The project has included the creation of three new nature reserves; and there are plans for an Eco-Museum and a network of boating and off-road cycle routes along the Brue, with Glastonbury serving as a "strategic gateway" to the marshes (Humphreys 1995b:12; CSG, April 6, 1995:3).

The town itself has survived as a local market center. Its commercial viability was improved by the building of a canal and later a railway in the mid-nineteenth century (both have since been abandoned). Its prestige as a site of antiquarian interest had ebbed and flowed over the years, reviving considerably in the late nineteenth century through the writings of Tennyson and others. The first step toward Glastonbury's modern renewal as a Christian center was taken in 1888 by a Catholic religious order which purchased some property at the foot of the Tor and built a school for novices in the town. Following a contentious auction, the Church of England purchased the Abbey ruins in 1907, and began preservation work along with archaeological excavation in the years following. The valley above the Chalice Well, so named by the Catholic order that owned it in the nineteenth century, was the site of an open-air theatre festival in the early years of the twentieth century; and for a time a burgeoning artistic and "alternative" community, led by composer Rutland Boughton and a coterie of others, grew around it, leading some to celebrate the town as a potential English Bayreuth or Oberammergau (Bonham 1986:23).

In 1934 occultist and depth psychologist Dion Fortune wrote, "If any place could become the English Lourdes it is our Avalon" (1989:122). Since the end of the 1960s—and partly as a result of another arts festival, the Glastonbury Fayre free festival, begun in 1971 a few miles outside the town —Glastonbury has, for many, become that Lourdes. Its reputation now outscales by far the friendly, if insular and conservative, small-town vision preferred by many of its residents, who remain unimpressed by all the mythologizing and, instead, lament the disappearance of the area's traditional industries and basic amenities. The town has had little industrial growth since the late Victorian era. Its leather and sheepskin industries, once primary to the town's wealth, have declined significantly; and in material wealth Glastonbury has been surpassed by the neighboring town of Street (which was given a jolt of economic energy with the opening of a Clark's shopping complex in 1993).[6] The result, as one observer describes it, is "a traditional small provincial town . . . coexist[ing] with an international 'Disneyland'" (Nicholson 1992:13). Archaeologist Philip Rahtz, in perhaps the definitive scholarly book on the subject,[7] summarizes the conflicting interests vying over the future of Glastonbury:

the struggle of the rational against the draw of the irrational; pilgrimages for Christians and those of a more secular if mystic character; "ordinary, decent townspeople" who want to live in a quiet world unworried by drug-abuse, armed beggars and violence; academics and conservationists who want a quiet, historic, preserved Glastonbury, rather than a modernized town cluttered by tourists, cars, unnecessary shops and supermarkets; archaeologists witnessing the buried heritage being destroyed by developments sponsored by building and peat-extracting giants. (1993:132)

THE "ALTERNATIVE COMMUNITY"

Glastonbury's rich history of conflicts has provided numerous opportunities for the emergence of alternative visions of the town, but in recent decades the term *alternative community* has become the moniker used by some Glastonbury residents, self-identified members of this community, to make a distinction between themselves and the town's more conservative, longer-standing residential population. (Less frequent terms used include "Glastafarians," as opposed to "Glastonians," and the "New Age community.") The alternative community includes intellectuals, artists, unconventional scholars, spiritual devotees, and business people, the vast majority of whom (with the exception of children) moved to Glastonbury from elsewhere.

Predecessors and Early Growth

The first to have made this type of distinction between the townsfolk seems to have been Dion Fortune, who in the 1920s distinguished "Avalonians" from "Glastonburians." The former included artists, intellectuals, and spiritual explorers who had gathered around Rutland Boughton, Alice Buckton, archaeologist Frederick Bligh Bond, and Fortune herself. With the support of such luminaries as George Bernard Shaw, these "Avalonians" turned the town into a thriving artistic hub for a short period. Boughton's vision of Glastonbury as an English Bayreuth was propelled by his Glastonbury Festivals of music and drama, begun in 1912, and by his own Arthurian opera cycle (not completed until the 1940s and never performed in full). As if foreshadowing more recent decades, however, local puritans objected to Boughton, first for his unmarried companionship with Christina Walshe as well as to the stage presentations themselves, then for rumored adultery, and finally for his left-wing political views (cf. Benham 1993; Hurd 1993). Likewise with Bond, who, serving as diocesan architect at the Abbey from 1909 to 1922, catalyzed a great deal of interest in the still partly undiscovered remains of the Abbey: he, too, fell out of favor with locals as well as Church authorities for employing psychic mediums to carry out his otherwise lauded archaeological work.

Dion Fortune was the individual who provided the historical link between Glastonbury and the spiritual explorers of late Victorian England — Romantics, Rosicrucians and Freemasons, Theosophists, and the Order of the Golden Dawn (which itself has shaped the face of contemporary occultism and neopaganism more than any other single organization). Settling in Glastonbury in 1924, Fortune opened a hostel and pilgrimage center, and, with her Fraternity of the Inner Light, began espousing the vision of Glastonbury as a center for the reconciliation of a native paganism with established Christianity. The publication of her *Avalon of the Heart*, alongside the more popular novels of John Cowper Powys and the Romantic poetry of Tennyson, popularized the idea of Glastonbury as the legendary Isle of Avalon and, later, as a "heart chakra" of the earth.

For some twenty years following Fortune's death in 1946, the Avalonian vision lay fallow. But by the early 1960s, popular writer Geoffrey Ashe's book *King Arthur's Avalon* (1973 [1957]) had been out for a few years, the Chalice Well Trust had been reconvened to reestablish the Chalice Well as a pilgrimage sanctuary, and interest in "earth mysteries" was beginning to grow. By 1967 the *Bristol Evening Post* had reported a gypsy caravan of "hippies" living near the Tor (Benham 1993:269), and, soon afterward, countercultural journals like *International Times* and *Gandalf's Garden* were promoting the idea of Glastonbury as a "power center," a center of the Glastonbury Zodiac (a planisphere of landscape effigies of the twelve signs of the Zodiac, first delineated on a map by Canadian artist Katherine Maltwood in the 1930s), and a key to the spiritual rebirth of the Aquarian Age. In an article in *Gandalf's Garden*, Geoffrey Ashe wrote, "Britain will begin to be reborn when Glastonbury is. The Giant Albion will begin to wake when his sons and daughters gather inside the enchanted boundary, and summon him with the right words, the right actions, a different life" (cited in Benham 1993:271). Similarly, in 1972, John Michell proclaimed in *The Ley Hunter*:

> Glastonbury, formerly a centre of the ancient cosmic religion that last flourished in Britain among the Druids and, to some extent, among their successors the Celtic saints, is also distinguished in prophecy as the place where the true science and philosophy that sustained the harmonious world order of antiquity will again be revealed. The promise of the great return, expressed in such images as the descent of the New Jerusalem, the restoration of the Grail and the reconstruction of the Temple, is also written on a document recently discovered in the Glastonbury area. *This document is nothing less than the landscape itself*, inscribed with a number of leys, that form together a significant pattern, repeating in the most vivid and enduring manner the ancient promise of St. John's New Jerusalem. (in Screeton 1993:31; italics added)

Michell's writing (1969, 1972) typified the new genre of writing about Glastonbury, drawing on the growing fascination with Neolithic science and ancient knowledge, numerology, gematria, earth energies, and ley lines. Meanwhile, in 1971, the first noncommercial, genuinely "free festival" in Britain—the now legendary Glastonbury Fayre—took place in nearby Pilton, some four miles outside Glastonbury, in 1971.

The growing population of "floral, long-haired youngsters, encouraged by a few older mystics" (Garrard 1989:4) was initially greeted with disdain by many locals: sewage was dumped by council lorries near hippie camp sites, No Hippies Allowed signs appeared in local restaurants and shops, and there were public exhortations for local police to "get rid of them" (most of which the police politely ignored) (*Time Out,* August 10, 1972).[8] The new settlers, however, managed to organize themselves into the "New Glaston Community," with an information center in the Abbey Cafe, where they offered lectures and courses on organic gardening, esoteric traditions, and the like, and with a communications organ, *Torc,* of which fifteen issues eventually appeared. As *Torc* editor Patrick Benham (1993) later reflected, Glastonbury was felt to be just the place where the "alternative dream" of small-is-beautiful, human-scale community might achieve a measure of realization. The pages of *Torc* featured a characteristic mix of articles on astrology and the Glastonbury Zodiac, pagan, Arthurian, and mystical lore, ley lines and earth mysteries, esoteric and prophetic Christian content, health and vegetarianism. One member of the "new Glastonites" found himself feeling alienated after setting up a jewelry, antiques, and crafts business. "On one hand," he lamented, "it's ''e's mixed up with they Hippo's an such' and on the other hand it's 'Rip off Capitulate!'. . . I have it on authority that making money within the boundary of Glaston is sacrilege" (*Torc* 14 [1974]:21). For a few years in the mid-1970s, another center, the Dove Centre, served as Glastonbury's prototypical alternative community—a complex of crafts workshops, living accommodations, vegetable garden, restaurant, and gallery and exhibition space, with a constant flow of people "from the most respectable to the most bizarre" (*Torc* 15 [1975]).

By 1979 a Glastonbury women's group had also formed; it produced a journal, ironically titled *The Glastonbury Thorn*—a reference to a legendary thorn said to be brought by Joseph of Arimathea to Glastonbury, though also suggesting the intended role of the women's group, with its call for the "liberation of wimin," in the fabric of the town. Despite the hostility of local conservatives—for whom the women were a "coven of witches" intent on sabotaging Glastonbury's Christian heritage—ecofeminism and Green activism, antinuclear protests, natural childbirth, breast cancer, and ancient matriarchy had all, by the early 1980s, made their way onto the Glastonbury alternative community's agenda. With connections to the Greenham Common women's peace camp and to the ecofeminist journal *Women for Life on Earth* (produced for a time by American expatriate Stephanie Leland in Glastonbury), the women's group played an important role in shaping Glastonbury's burgeoning Green movement.

By the mid-1980s, Glastonbury was being inundated with travelers, hippies, and peace activists, many of them evicted from the Rainbow Village at the Molesworth peace camp or refugees from the clashes with police at Stonehenge (described below). A controversy developed around Greenlands Farm, a Christian-based community whose elderly but energetic owner, Alison Collyer, offered a haven and temporary refuge for pilgrims and transients in exchange for help on the farm. A couple of hundred travelers lived there at its peak, and in the summer of 1985, some 500 passed through it, staying for various lengths of time. By this time, local complaints and a sensationalistic campaign by the local press highlighting the supposed "hippie threat" of drugs, disease, and so on, had led to a police surveillance operation and, ultimately, a court decision requiring Ms. Collyer to close the farm and evict its tenants.[9]

Crystallization of the Community

The alternative community grew and learned through these trials and by the mid-1980s had developed an increased self-consciousness and confidence about its own identity as a more permanent fixture within the town. Regular Community Gatherings grappled with questions of power and leadership, and with the community's role in local politics as well as the broader social change and personal growth movements. Contrasting Glastonbury with the intentional communities at Findhorn and Machynlleth (an alternative-technology-based community in Wales), activist Ann Morgan wrote, "In Glastonbury, we're learning and demonstrating something special, which, amongst other things, is how to live in a conventional community and transform our lives" (GC 7:17). Among the developments which served as the media and the evidence for this new self-confidence, the following stand out.

(1) The Assembly Rooms and The Glastonbury Experience. Originally built in 1864, the Assembly Rooms had their historical heyday as the site of Rutland Boughton's festivals. After World War Two, during which the Assembly Rooms were occupied by the armed forces, gradual decay set in; but in 1977 the High Street building was revived by the founding of the Assembly Rooms Trust, and the Assembly Rooms were gradually turned into an arts and community center, the site of lectures and workshops, theatrical and musical performances, festivals and gatherings, and a vegetarian cafe. Meanwhile, in the mid-1980s, when the more grassroots wing of the alternative community was involved in reviving the Assembly Rooms, a more explicitly spiritual wing broke away to pursue their vision of creating a learning and craft center. Restoring a set of dilapidated buildings at the foot of High Street, they built a community complex called the Glastonbury Experience, which by 1984 included a vibrant courtyard, thriving cafe, whole foods shop, natural health clinic, bookstore, candle-making and crafts workshop, and more. Both venues have weathered severe financial crises and periods of restructuring, but today they remain at the heart of the alternative community, with the Assembly Rooms, now a cooperative trust, serving as a community center and gathering place, and the Glastonbury Experience as a thriving hub of commercial, creative, and intellectual activity.

(2) The Glastonbury Communicator. This more-or-less quarterly journal, published between 1984 and 1989, presented a striking range of views that reflected the changing and diverse nature of the alternative community. With a rotating editorship and up to sixty pages per issue of densely packed

material, the *Communicator* featured reports and analysis of local events and controversies; news about developments within or related to the alternative community; personal reflections on the meaning of Glastonbury and its role in the New Age and social change movements; radical critiques of police violence, drug laws, nuclear power, and the British establishment; writings on esoteric and mystical topics (ranging from Eastern philosophies to UFOs and earth mysteries, but also including incisive critiques of the pitfalls of New Age and personal growth philosophy and debates about the gender politics of spirituality);[10] interviews and profiles of local and visiting celebrities; poetry, stories, mystical prose, comics, recipes, and satire (including humorous jibes at Glastonbury personalities and trends in columns on "Glastonbury Speek," "Opening the Anal Portal," and the "Cosmic Wankers' Liberation Front"). The *Communicator* revealed its readership to be a tightly knit but eclectically minded and rambunctious assembly marked by tensions and barely concealed schisms, for instance, between Goddess spirituality feminists and male, New Age "Immortalist" philosophers, and between 1960s hippies and 1980s anarchist punks and "chaos magicians."

(3) High-profile local events, such as the 1987 Harmonic Convergence, the 1990 Earth Week events, and various arts and dance festivals. For the Harmonic Convergence, a group called the Hope Foundation (formed by an American expatriate) organized a four-day program of public events at various locations. Several hundred people gathered on the Tor before dawn on August 16, and many stayed to participate in a twenty-four-hour "Consciousness Vigil," involving the "activation" of sacred sites around the world. Earth Week in 1990 featured a week-long program of talks, workshops, exhibitions, music, theatre, outdoor events and celebrations, and a major ceremony on the Tor; and its participants included One Earth Arts, an organization devoted to presenting world music events, Phoenix Wholefoods (Glastonbury's oldest established "green" business), a handful of Church figures, the Glastonbury Conservation Society, and the Safe Energy Road Show. The ceremony involved the bringing of a golden cross from Jerusalem to the "sacred ground of Glastonbury Tor" (considered by some to be the New Jerusalem). The organizers' explicit aim was to "draw together the 'New Age' harmonic convergence movement with the more political greens and ecologists" (Garrard and Lepchani 1990:3).[11]

(4) Participation at the Glastonbury Festival. For many Britons, Glastonbury is synonymous with the largest and most prestigious rock and popular music festival in the country today. Originally called Glastonbury Fayre, the festival was begun by a Methodist dairy farmer, Michael Eavis, in 1969. Its original and now legendary Pyramid Stage, built in 1971, and constructed in this shape because of the alleged energetic benefits of the pyramid structure, was built "close to the Glastonbury Abbey/Stonehenge ley line and over the site of a blind spring . . . as it was believed that at such a place ancient earth forces could be harnessed and the earth revitalized during the Fayre" (Elstob and Howes 1987:16). Since 1981 the festival has been a ben-

efit for the Campaign for Nuclear Disarmament and, more recently, for Greenpeace and Oxfam; and it has featured speakers such as the peace movement's E. P. Thompson, the New Age movement's Sir George Tre- velyan, and the "establishment's" own bishop of Bath and Wells. Though the actual festival has always been held in the nearby town of Pilton, its influence on Glastonbury (and vice versa) has been enormous. The festi- val contributes significantly to the area's economy; this has gained it sup- porters from among local farmers and other residents,[12] and allows cer- tain individuals, including many from Glastonbury's alternative commu- nity, to survive for a large part of the year. It also contributes to the town's summer transient population—raising the ire of those who do not benefit from the festival economically—and it cements Glastonbury's reputation among British youth and the counterculture. Finally, the festival's proxim- ity to Glastonbury has stamped it with an unmistakable flavor—a consis- tent component of countercultural, green, ecological, and spiritual themes, which continues to this day despite its growth from a small free festival to a four-day virtual town of over 100,000 ticket buyers. Since the early 1980s, the festival has included an area devoted to environmental ideas and exhib- its (the Green Field), and, more recently, it has featured a Field of Avalon, a Healing Field (for alternative healing and spirituality), a Rainbow Field (with its grassroots eco-multiculturalism), and a Sacred Space (a large hill with a specially designed stone circle for meditation and quiet activities)— all making it unique among rock and pop festivals.

Following the demise of the *Communicator,* a few short-lived newspapers —the *Times,* the *Gazette,* and most recently the *Free State*—have attempted to take its place presenting an alternative perspective on events, while ex- plicitly shedding some of the *Communicator's* mysticism in favor of a more mainstream, "newsy" appearance. Meanwhile, the size of the alternative community has slowly increased, and its boundaries have become more permeable. Informal estimates for its size range from a few hundred living in the town itself to a couple of thousand in the Glastonbury area (Bowman 1993; Howard-Gordon 1982; personal interviews). As numbers grow and New Age ideas find larger audiences, the community has generated ambi- tious ideas and visions, among them the University of Avalon, the Avalon temple project (sanctuary), and the Morlands Village postindustrial devel- opment. The university, since renamed the Isle of Avalon Foundation, was formed in 1991 on the premises of the Glastonbury Experience, as an "edu- cational establishment concerned with exploring the whole of creation, en- compassing spiritual as well as material values and systems" (University of Avalon, Fall 1994 prospectus).[13] The foundation was an outgrowth of the Library of Avalon, which was originally founded in 1988 as a Library of British Mythology, but now includes a reference and lending library of sev- eral thousand books on various topics, in addition to organizing writing competitions, symposia, and conferences (including, since 1996, an annu- al multiday Goddess Conference). Also part of the foundation is its Brigit

Figure 4.5. Hare Krishna, Hare Rama: celebrants wind their way through Glastonbury

Healing Wing, the Isle of Avalon Press, and Isle of Avalon Tours; and these were more recently joined by the ambitious Avalon Project, whose objective is to create a large-scale spiritual and educational "temple complex," for which architectural plans are being developed and funds sought. The building of the temple is to use "sacred design techniques" and will have "minimum impact on the environment"; gardens around the temple "will use organic gardening and permaculture techniques, and land around the Temple will be acquired for planting with apple orchards to recreate the earlier environment of Somerset." Development of the project is to "take place in full consultation with the local community" and is intended to "reinvigorate the local economy."[14] The latter goals are also among the objectives of the Morlands Village project, a proposed community-led "sustainable redevelopment" of the derelict Morlands/Baileys factory site, which had provided Glastonbury and Street with their industrial base for nearly a century.

Ambitious ideas aside, many attempts at organizing community structures and institutions have faced difficulties and frequent failure. The alternative community has in fact been notorious for its practical and organizational inefficiencies. In part this is a result of the community's loose and relatively transient nature, and in part, as Ruth Prince (1991) argues in her ethnography of the alternative community,[15] it reflects the characteristics and ideology of the community's members: a strong valuing of individual freedom, an ambivalence toward money and business, an emphasis on process rather than practical results, and a need to feel good about how things are going and a propensity to lose interest if they don't.[16] Prince contends that the alternative community is in a perpetual state of flux: it is unified "by the style in which [it is] imagined" (44), but divides along changing intracommunity affiliations (based on shifting interests in specific spiritual and therapeutic practices, etc.), with much diversity in age, occupation, and specifics of belief.[17]

In the midst of these not-always-successful attempts at community building, spiritual groups and gurus, healing and retreat centers come and go, and their high turnover rate is interpreted by some as a sign that "[i]f you come to Glastonbury intending to throw your own trip on the place, Glastonbury will spit you out. You'll be able to stay here only if you are willing to learn, be humble, and attune yourself to the spirit of Glastonbury."[18] What exactly this "spirit" (or "angel," as it is sometimes called) represents depends on one's specific beliefs, and these fall into many variants. Many of Glastonbury's alternative settlers continue to frame their own personal and group identities in relation to two other groups: on one side, the mainstream community of Glastonburyans and, on the other, the more nomadic ranks of "travelers," with whom the alternative community shares a distinct spiritual affinity, but also from whose numbers many of them originally emerged. Though the travelers remain somewhat peripheral to the everyday life of Glastonbury, this relationship with the alternative community requires that we take a closer look at it.[19]

The Traveling Counterculture

... they sound as if they just have to be good people. Partly it's the rotten treatment they got from the police at Stonehenge last year—nobody deserves that. Partly it's the romance (however ill-founded) of their life on the road, under the stars, free from authority. Partly it's the sense that they are in some however absurd way, the lost tribe of the deserted village, the resurrected victims of the enclosure of the common land that devastated the lives of uncountable numbers of all our fore-bearers [sic], the spiritual heirs and witnesses of Gerrard Winstanley and all the deluded and humiliated utopians and millenians through our history who have tried to show by example—and in the teeth of derision and persecution—that there is a life that can be lived free from the State, money and the nuclear family.

—letter to *The Guardian*, June 30, 1986

You will have seen the pictures on television or in the newspapers . . . . If you live in the West Country and Wales you may have seen it on your own doorstep. Farmers powerless. Crops ruined and livestock killed by people who say they

commune with nature, but who have no respect
for it when it belongs to others. *New age travellers.
Not in this age. Not in any age.*

—Prime Minister JOHN MAJOR,
addressing a Conservative Party convention
in autumn 1992 (italics added)

Traveling culture in Britain has a long history that includes religious pilgrims and journeymen, showmen, itinerant traders, and Romany Gypsies.
Since the passing of the 1968 Caravan Sites Act (until its rescindment in
1994), town and district councils had been obligated to provide temporary
caravan sites for such travelers. With the growth of the posthippie movement of "New Age travelers"—so called in order to distinguish them from
traditional Romany Gypsies—relations between this mobile population and
settled townsfolk and farmers have, however, been frequently strained. Britain's traveling population has been among the largest in Western Europe,
and with the rise of unemployment, homelessness, and working-class hope-
lessness in the Thatcherite 1980s, the ranks of New Age travelers grew to
some fifteen or twenty thousand.[20]

The history of the new, non-Romany traveling culture begins in the late
1960s, with the emergence of hippie back-to-the-landers and the evictions
of squatters and anarchists from such countercultural havens as London's
Free City of Camden. Thousands of the suddenly homeless took to the road
and, merging with the back-to-the-landers, began organizing their own gatherings and summertime festivals, of which the annual Summer Solstice
People's Free Festival at Stonehenge became the largest and best known.[21]
By 1976 a network of reconditioned buses, vans, and trucks, and makeshift
nomadic dwellings—tipis, domes, and tentlike "benders"—was scattered
throughout Britain, and a full summer program of free festivals had evolved.
Festivals provided the opportunity not only for free entertainment and par-
tying, a carnivalesque atmosphere at which anything was allowed; it also
allowed for the exchange of goods, services, styles, ideas, and the forging of
collective identities (cf. Hetherington 1992, 1993, 1994).

In the late 1970s and early 1980s, the need to move around sound equipment, stages, tents, and other belongings meant that travelers' vehicles tended to get larger and more identifiable, and by 1983 the so-called hippie
convoy had achieved media notoriety. In the early 1980s the travelers had
mixed with peace, environmental, feminist, and antinuclear activists at the
antinuclear peace camps at Molesworth, Faslane, and Greenham Common, and the "hippie peace convoy" (or, as the media preferred, "the *so-
called* peace convoy") found itself under increasing verbal and sometimes
physical assault by police, county councils, local press, landowners, English
Heritage, and the National Trust. An estimated 40,000 attended the last
official Stonehenge free festival in 1984 (Bender et al. 1994). The following
year the festival was banned. In the same year that was to see police violence

against striking miners at the "Battle of Orgreave," the Rainbow Village
Peace Camp at Molesworth nuclear base was evicted by thousands of police
and troops. Following weeks of repeated evictions, arrests, surveillance by
police in cars and helicopters, and even fighter jets roaring overhead, many
of the activists ended up joining a larger convoy of travelers headed for
Stonehenge. A cat-and-mouse game ensued between police and the peace
convoy, unfolding over much of the summer and climaxing in an excessive
display of police brutality. In the now legendary "Battle of the Beanfield,"
over a thousand police officers in helmets and riot gear and carrying trun-
cheons chased and beat about five hundred travelers, including pregnant
women and children, trashed and looted and, in a few cases, burned their
vehicles, killed several dogs, and arrested some 500 people.[22] The travelers,
now genuinely homeless, ended up retreating to the only refuges they knew;
and for many the most obvious one was Glastonbury, "the only place," as
one of the travelers later wrote, "that seemed to offer any kind of sanctuary
at all" (Garrard 1989:5).

The Tor may have been the beacon, the clearest visual image beaming
out the signal of Glastonbury-as-sanctuary, but in practice it was Greenlands
Farm which ended up serving this function for several months in 1985–86.
Of the hundreds who passed through Greenlands, no more than ten to
twenty ended up staying in Glastonbury, though others kept in touch and,
in time, returned; but their effect on the town was unmistakable.[23] Among
more conservative residents, the presence of this newer generation of "hippies" was a threat worse than that of the original hippies, who by now had
become grudgingly accepted. In contrast to the earlier, largely middle-class
generation of societal dropouts, the newcomers were materially poorer, less
dreamy and optimistic, and more aggressive and rough-edged in their rejection of mainstream social mores.

After the Greenlands episode, the situation abated somewhat for the
town. But the late 1980s were not an easy time for the homeless and job-
less in Britain. With clampdowns on social security payments for young
people and Poll Tax demands, an increasing number of young people took
up the nomadic lifestyle. In his analysis of traveling culture, Hetherington (1993:164–65) identifies two predominant identity and clothing styles
among the new travelers: those he calls "authentic" styles, including "ethnic" styles of clothing and jewelry, New Age accoutrements, tipis, and so
on; and "grotesque" styles, characterized by a punk antiaesthetic of "resistance through dirt." It was the latter, especially those disparagingly known as
crusties or drongos—with their old combat fatigues, unlaced boots, long
matted dreadlocks, and dogs—who caused the strongest reactions among
"Glastonians." Repeatedly characterized by local media and residents in
terms of "dirt," contamination, pollution, and disease, their greatest offense
was probably their disrespect for private property and for "civilized" behav-
ioral norms.[24] The number of travelers in the Glastonbury area reached its
peak around 1989 and 1990 (Morgan 1990), as did the debate around what
to do with them, leaving the district council caught between their legal re-

quirement to provide short-term off-street parking facilities for their vehicles, and the anger of local residents who demanded that the authorities just "get rid of them." Quieter voices tended to get lost in the mix; though some members of Glastonbury's alternative community attempted to develop constructive solutions to the problem.[25]

Two developments have marked the last decade for Britain's traveling counterculture. On the one hand, a fertile cross-breeding occurred between travelers and other countercultural groups—urban squatters, anti-road and animal hunt protesters, and the acid-house inspired rave dance culture—consolidating into a broadly political movement dubbed "DIY culture" (McKay 1996, 1998; Malyon 1994). On the other hand, the Conservative government that dominated the earlier years of the decade responded to this movement by persecuting it through police efforts like Operation Snapshot (intended to establish the numbers and whereabouts of New Age travelers) and the draconian Criminal Justice and Public Order Act (CJA) of 1994. Repealing the 1968 Caravan Sites Act, the CJA aimed to effectively remove travelers' rights to authorized sites, to make camping on unauthorized sites a criminal offense (even if the campers have the landowner's permission to stay), and to make it difficult or impossible for large groups of people to meet outdoors for almost any purpose, but especially for free festivals, unlicensed outdoor raves, and environmental protests. The CJA specifically targeted "unauthorized campers" (travelers), squatters and "aggravated trespassers" (hunt saboteurs and environmental protesters), "raves" and unauthorized outdoor gatherings for the purposes of dancing or listening to "amplified music" (defined, in ludicrously broad terms, as "sounds wholly or predominantly characterised by the emission of a succession of repetitive beats").[26]

As I write, part-way into Tony Blair's New Labour government, it is still unclear what the long-term effects of the Criminal Justice Act will be. Resistance to the CJA has served as a unifying, rallying factor for DIY culture. Acts of collective defiance, protests, and mass trespasses have dominated the response, but a consensus has also been building on more proactive forms of direct action, including a broad-based land rights agenda aimed at developing alternative modes of survival.[27] In rural counties like Somerset, there have typically been endless debates over the provision of legal travelers' sites and the eviction of travelers from unofficial or illegal sites; the most frequent "policy" appears to be one of stalling and passing the buck. Some local residents have worried that the CJA will result in more travelers settling in Somerset. Local farmers have, with some success, attempted to have travelers evicted from sites at Middlezoy, Dommet Wood, Buckland St. Mary, and Somerton Moor; in one move, forty farmers supported by the National Farmers Union and by a reluctant county council successfully evicted an estimated 300 travelers at a site in Somerton Moor (*Squall* 7 [1994]: 12).

On the other hand, a possible solution has emerged as groups of travelers have purchased land and set up "traveler settlements." At a site in south

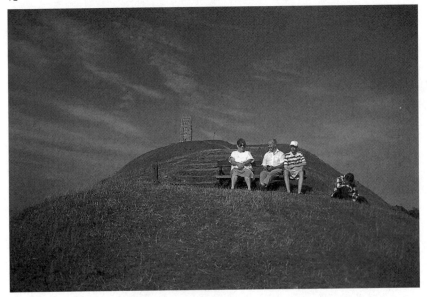

Figure 4.6. Glastonbury Tor: a nice place to rest

Somerset, such a group formed the Tinker's Bubble Trust; they bought forty acres of land for £50,000 and joined the National Farmers Union, despite strong opposition from some locals (*CSG*, June 30 1994:13). The trust's plan to create an Environmental Low Impact Dwelling Site—an Iron Age–style "minimum-technology" site of temporary or semipermanent dwellings —has had difficulties, however, in part because it flouts the canons of British planning policy with its strict demarcations "between development land and agricultural land; between dwelling and workplace; between where one lives and where one makes a living—or, put in fiscal terms, between council-tax and business rate" (*Guardian*, June 10 1994:16–17).[28] As of the mid-1990s, however, the vast majority of similar cases have been denied planning permission (Goodwin 1995:22–23). Local resistance to such new "settlers" remains strong, partly due to the ongoing campaign by authorities and media to portray the travelers in stereotypical terms, rather than facilitating dialogue and understanding (local complaints include "they're filthy" and "they'll spread disease," and vows that "we won't allow their kids in our schools"). In Glastonbury, where locals are more accustomed to unusual visitors and fellow residents, the situation is better than in much of the county, but local politicians make much use of residents' fears in pressing forward their agendas. As a result, the future of the traveling population in southwest England (and, by extension, in the rest of the country)— and the question of whether there will remain any travelers at all—remains uncertain. In the midst of such uncertainties, the politics of place and of landscape asserts itself all the more strongly; and to that I turn in the next chapter.

FIVE

Many Glastonburys:
Place-Myths and Contested Spaces

The task of living in a place requires the elaboration of myths and historical narratives around and about it. I have introduced two of Glastonbury's histories already: that told by scholarly historians (which figures its way into all the others to greater or lesser degrees), and that of the recently established alternative community. In the struggles between these and other interpretive communities to define and represent Glastonbury, one of the primary terrains for struggle is the notion of *tradition*, a notion reflecting the desire to stake a claim for historical authority and continuity. The struggle for this authority takes place through the generation of competing place-myths, each of which grounds itself in divergent interpretations of history, its mainstreams and its alternatives.

Certain of Glastonbury's place-myths have been more widely accepted in the recent history of the town than others, and these more "traditional" place-myths—with the quote marks indicating the contingent and constructed nature of that status—can be distinguished into several distinct types: those which focus on economic and subsistence values and recent history (Glastonbury as a "normal" English market town defined by its agricultural and light-industrial regional history), those which focus on the historical value of the landscape as heritage (though also as economic boon), and those identifying the town in its historically Christian context. Others, like the Arthurian and Celtic place-myths, spill across any possible boundaries demarcating the traditional from the alternative; while the Goddess-feminist, New Age, and countercultural Glastonburys are more obviously alternative. My movement in what follows, therefore, begins with the more traditional or mainstream and proceeds to the outer fringes (with a brief circling back to the scholarly and media-established mainstream), then focuses on the spatial conflicts between the different place-myths and respective interpretive communities, and finally concludes with an analysis of the alternative community's place within today's Glastonbury.

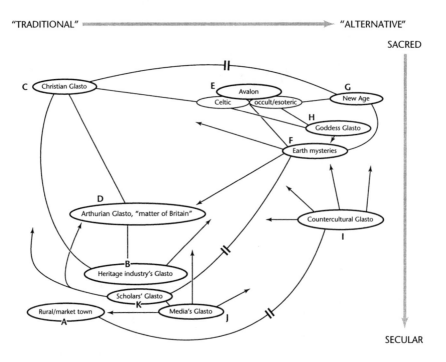

Figure 5.1. Mapping of Glastonbury place-images and -myths

PLACE-MYTHS OF GLASTONBURY/AVALON

Business as Usual: Glastonbury as a Rural Market Town

For much of the town's population, Glastonbury's spiritual significance is
little more than a curiosity. Its history is, for them, that of a market town,
and a center of leather and sheepskin production and tanneries. This heritage continues with a weekly market day, and shoes and leather remain a
mainstay of the central Somerset economy, particularly so in the neighboring village of Street. On the whole, however, this aspect of the town has
declined. Though some "traditional" shops and businesses remain in town,
many have departed High Street and been replaced by those catering to the
alternative and tourist market. Some residents are unhappy about this situation, and under the organizational leadership of the Glastonbury Residents Association, have tried to resist or reverse this process. (I discuss the
conflict over the town center in detail below.) Others, including the town's
commercial and property developers (among them GR Holdings, P and O
Properties, and B and I Partnership, which gave the town its Safeway, B and
Q Warehouse, and Little Chef, and submitted plans to the Mendip dis-

Table 5.1. Glastonbury place-images and -myths

Place-myth/ representation	Representatives	Narratives & claims	Spatial practices, socio-economic activities	Group constructs, "others"
(A) Rural market town in Protestant Somerset	local residents, Glast. Residents Association	Glastonbury's history as a market town, etc.	live, work	"we" are the "true Glastonians"
	"traditional" industries (wool, sheepskin, etc.)	relative prosperity of Street & other neighboring towns		Glasto. is threatened by outsiders, especially "filthy hippies," "drongos," "crusties," & other "urban refuse"
	"traditional" shops			
	local skinheads			
(B) Historical heritage site	local heritage & tourist industries (National Trust, Abbey Trust, Tourist Information Centre, historical museums, shopkeepers, etc.)	history of town and Abbey	specific places set apart as tourist sites (to which tourist info. center directs visitors)	
			coach tours, visits to the Abbey Grounds & Museum, etc.	
(C) Birthplace of Christianity, "Holieste erthe of England"	various Christian churches & groups	site of first church in Britain	annual pilgrimages	interdenominational differences
		Abbey's history	Abbey retreats	various views of "New Agers": misguided but well-meaning seekers; competitors; compatible/ complementary; or demonically inspired
		legends & traditions (Joseph, Jesus, saints)	church & ministry services	
			Catholic procession up Tor	

Place-myth/ representation	Representatives	Narratives & claims	Spatial practices, socio-economic activities	Group constructs, "others"
(D) Arthurian center, "Sancta Sanctorum of Britain"	(historically: 12–13th C. English kings; 19th C. Romantic movement) some "Avalonians" and New Agers some Arthurian scholars	burial place of Arthur and Guinevere	tours, etc.	Britain's important "role" and "destiny" in world affairs
(E) Avalon:				
(a) center of Celtic (Druidic + Christian) spirituality	Avalonians and New Agers "Celtic Christianity" proponents	lake villages Gog and Magog ("Druidic" trees) Tor legends (e.g. Gwyn ap Nudd story)	tours, etc. meditations on Tor, etc. Druidic seasonal celebrations	"Celts" Celtic Christianity as alternative to other Christian traditions, & as unique fusion of earth-centered Druid wisdom & Christianity
(b) (occult/esoteric interpretation): center of Celtic-Christian-pagan (solar-lunar, etc.) reconciliation				
(F) Center of earth mysteries (earth energies, ley lines, etc.)	earth mysteries researchers, "Avalonians," New Agers New Age tourist industry	sacred geometry in Abbey's construction Michael and Mary line etc.	dowsing & attunement practices, seasonal festivals, etc. sacred design, art, etc. (e.g. Vesica Piscis in Chalice Well Gardens) tours	see modern science & industrial civilization as deviation from centuries-old traditions, and as having forgotten the ancient earth wisdom

(G) New Age "center of light" and "heart chakra" of the earth	New Agers Isle of Avalon Foundation Companions of the Glastonbury Zodiac New Age tourist industry	Glastonbury Zodiac earth energies, UFO reports, crop circle formations in area, etc.	group meditations & events on Tor, gatherings (e.g. Harmonic Convergence) Zodiac walks proposed Temple/Sanctuary workshops, classes, talks, tours	Glasto.'s role in "network of light," connection with other sacred sites in Britain (Iona, Findhorn) and around world (Shasta et al.)
(H) Ancient pagan, Goddess worshipping site	women's/Goddess spirituality ecofeminists women's groups (in 1980s)	Tor as Neolithic or Bronze Age ritual maze/labyrinth serpent lines "Underworld" energies	maze walks, tours, etc. Tor meditations, etc. art	Christian churches seen as historical oppressors & appropriators of "Avalon" some New Agers seen as patriarchal
(I) Countercultural festival site	countercultural "travelers," free-festival goers & "DIY culture"	Glastonbury Festival history vague references to the spiritual history of the Tor Tor has "always" been a safe, free, sacred zone	hanging out (or camping) on/near Tor, drumming, etc. seasonal festivals occupying benches on High Street, "hanging out" near White Spring	"establishment" seen as oppressive New Agers seen as middle-class

Place-myth/ representation	Representatives	Narratives & claims	Spatial practices, socio-economic activities	Group constructs, "others"
(J) Media curiosity, magnet for weirdos	national media		news coverage of Glastonbury Festival (including references to Arthurian lore, etc.)	New Agers et al. seen as "weirdos" & eccentrics
(K) Anti-intellectual haven, scholarly contested zone	"establishment" scholars and historians	lack of hard evidence about most "alternative" claims the Abbey's medieval forgeries	archaeological digs, etc.	New Agers, occultists et al. seen as gullible, superstitious & irrational
(L) All of the above— a high-energy "pressure cooker," weird, uncanny, magical place whose weirdness & uncanniness cannot be pinned down	Avalonians, New Age/ alternative tourist industry	all of the above inability of alternative community to develop stable organizational structures (yet it persists)		

trict council for an Arthurian theme park and a massive garden center) are equally interested in maintaining the face of business as usual in Glastonbury; and local government organs, including the Glastonbury town council, Mendip district council, and Somerset county council, have frequently responded to their demands.[1]

The Heritage Industry's Glastonbury

In the growing global tourist market, where different countries specialize in different types of tourist expectations—Thailand for "exotic" holidays, Switzerland for skiing and mountaineering—Britain, notes John Urry, "has come to specialise in holidays that emphasise the historical and the quaint" (1992:108). Britain in effect manufactures heritage (Hewison 1987); heritage has become central to Britain's own definition of itself, as well as its definition in the eyes of the global tourist. The heritage marketed in Glastonbury includes that of the Christian past (the Abbey ruins and the historic churches of St. John's, St. Mary's, and St. Benedict's), the agricultural and architectural past (Somerset Rural Life Museum, on the site of the Abbey tithe barn, and several historic buildings in town), the more ancient past (Glastonbury Lake Village, an Iron Age village in the Somerset Levels outside the present town), the area's natural heritage (the Peat Moors Centre outside town), and, of course, the mysterious legends and myths associated with the Tor and the other hills and springs, among them that centered around the legendary figure of Arthur, which still rates highly in the popular imagination as the central icon of a glorious, if mysterious, ancient Britain.[2] Tourist brochures commonly refer to Glastonbury as "an ancient place of pilgrimage," "a place of history and mystery," and "the first Christian Sanctuary in the British Isles, so ancient that only legend can recall its origin" (as evidence apparently fails) (Glastonbury Tribunal Ltd. 1993; "Glastonbury" tourist pamphlet; McIlwain 1992; and other sources).

The centrality of the Abbey in the geography of the town underscores Glastonbury's importance as a Christian center, an importance supported by a wealth of legends and myths. Yet, the opening panel of the interpretive display (opened June 1993) at Glastonbury Abbey's Visitor Centre introduces the town as "hold[ing] a special place in the Christian Church and in the beliefs of many mystical cults," indicating a certain legitimacy to the non-Christian (or heterodox Christian) claims on the town, though it is a legitimacy rendered ambivalent by the word *cults*. Most other tourist-oriented publications by now make some reference to the New Age mysticism of the town. The official heritage industry thereby nods in the direction of the town's latest bringer of wealth: the alternative tourism offered by Gothic Image Tours, the Isle of Avalon Foundation, and the numerous guesthouses, healing centers, and bed-and-breakfasts of the alternative community. The diverse coalition of interests represented here draws local shopkeepers into alliance with writers and amateur historians, tour guides and guesthouse operators, the local tourist board and the managers of England's heritage (such as the National Trust, which owns and manages the Tor).[3] As such, this coalition of interests draws freely on many of the place-images described here for its construction of a touristically viable Glastonbury.

Christian Glastonbury: England's "Holyest Erthe"

Glastonbury's claim to being the cradle and fountainhead of British Christianity finds oft-quoted support in William Blake's *Jerusalem*:

> And did those feet in ancient time
> Walk upon England's mountains green?
> And was the Holy Lamb of God
> On England's pleasant pastures seen?

"According to tradition," it is always said, Glastonbury is the site of the first Christian church in Britain, and, some claim, in all of Europe. Commonly repeated legends include those of Joseph of Arimathea coming to Glastonbury and founding the first church shortly after the Crucifixion, or, even earlier, bringing the young Jesus (and possibly Mary) with him; of Mary Magdalene, Arthur and Guinevere, and numerous saints. Joseph is said to have arrived by water and come ashore at what is now Wirral Hill, or Wearyall Hill, as believers prefer; he is supposed to have placed his staff in the ground, saying something akin to "Friends, we are weary all," presumably in whatever language he would have spoken. From that staff a thorn tree sprang to life, whose descendants still bloom twice a year, and which has been known since medieval times as the Holy Thorn.[4]

Past partisans of the various legends have included mystical nationalists, British Israelites, Druid revivalists, and Protestant reformers. In the twentieth century, it has been largely Anglican clergymen such as Rev. Lionel Smithett Lewis, vicar of Glastonbury in the 1920s and 1930s, H. A. Lewis, and Cyril Dobson who compiled and further elaborated the legends, drawing on place-names, folklore, and even old Cornish miners' traditions in their support. A variety of Christian denominations is found in Glastonbury today, including Anglicans, Catholics, Orthodox believers, Methodists, Quakers, Evangelicals, and other Protestants. For many of those who stake claims on the town, the high point of the year is the weekend of the Glastonbury pilgrimages, commencing on the last Saturday in June (which frequently falls on the same weekend as the Glastonbury Festival in nearby Pilton). Since their revival around the turn of the century, the pilgrimages have grown to involve some seven or eight thousand participants annually for the Anglican pilgrimage, which takes place on the Saturday in the Abbey grounds and in the streets of the town, complete with a procession, prayer services and rosaries, choral concerts, and theatrical presentations; and a few thousand more during the Catholic pilgrimage up to the Tor and in the Abbey ruins on the following day (McIlwain 1992:27–28).[5] The historical figure of Dunstan continues to generate respect for the historical legacy, and Christian pilgrims come to Glastonbury from nearly all of the eighty countries in which there is a church dedicated to St. Dunstan (Dunning 1994:92–93).

The Church of England is naturally the largest of the Christian denominations in Glastonbury, represented by two parishes, and it manages the Abbey grounds and the Abbey House retreat center. The Catholic connection remains strong, however, since the Abbey had historically been loyal to the papacy until its decimation by Henry VIII. Catholics emphasize the Marian and saintly cults associated with the town. As Oliver Reiser notes, Glastonbury's monks "established a prototype for Maryology by enshrining the Virgin at the very heart of the Glastonbury traditions" (1974:43). A statue of Our Lady St. Mary of Glastonbury was blessed by the apostolic delegate in 1955, in the presence of the bishop of Clifton and 18,000 Catholics, and was crowned and venerated as a major Marian shrine in 1965 (the other major one in Britain is at Walsingham). A "Glastonbury tapestry" found at the Our Lady shrine features figures of various saints, including Joseph of Arimathea, Patrick, Bridget, David, Dunstan, Blessed Richard Bere, and Blessed Richard Whiting.

Glastonbury is also thought by many to have been the center of a Celtic Christianity that differed significantly from the Roman brand. Specifically, it is thought that Celtic Christianity, in the sixth through ninth centuries or so, combined the best features of the old (pagan) and new (Christian) religions and tolerated both, until it was replaced by metropolitan, Catholic Christianity. Though Glastonbury's Christianity was, by the seventh century, a Saxon phenomenon, the many legends of Saints Patrick, Bridget, Indracht, and others, are offered in support of the "Celtic thesis";[6] and they have attracted Irish pilgrims to the town since at least the twelfth century. More recently, this Celtic connection has attracted pilgrim-activists like Marjorie Milne, an ecumenical pioneer who lived in Glastonbury in the 1960s and 1970s, involving herself with the problems of homeless youth, mediating in conflicts between hippies and townsfolk, and taking on the role of guru and elder for some.[7] Milne took her task to be that of "articulating from Glastonbury a vision of a new world, drawing on the old roots, but roots where forgiveness had sprinkled the dust of combats long ago with a sweet aroma for the future" (quoted in Frost 1986:125–26). Seeing the Grail myth as a eucharistic cup of fellowship, Milne envisioned a future "forest cathedral" for the town (161). Others inspired by such a vision have included the Rev. James Turnbull, a one-time traveling preacher and journalist, who, with Milne, saw that the U.K. was "facing a major crisis which was part of a world crisis" and believed Glastonbury should become Britain's "spiritual capital" (McKay 1988:17). Today, the nondenominational Quest Community sees itself as following in Milne's footsteps; this small ecumenical community considers itself "called by God specifically to work amongst the many and varied visitors to Glastonbury," which they envision as becoming "a centre of renewal and Christian unity" (Frost 1986:133). In addition, at such places as Chalice Well, one finds an even more unorthodox form of mystical Christianity—a "sort of Christianity" as Ashe (1982:118) calls it—which overlaps with the theosophical occultism of the New Age movement and speaks of "the Christ" as a kind of impersonal, universal force.

Arthurian Glastonbury and the Matter of Britain

> Glastonbury is a spiritual volcano wherein the fire that is at the heart of the British race breaks through and flames to heaven. . . .
>
> —DION FORTUNE, *Glastonbury: Avalon of the Heart*

However far back the people who call themselves British peer into their national past, the figure of Arthur stands there somewhere near its misty origins. Arthur's legacy and the so-called matter of Britain have long been points of contention: between the Welsh and Breton Celts, for whom Arthur was a great leader and defender against the Saxon invaders, and one who will yet return, and the Saxon and Anglo-Norman kings, with their attempts to appropriate his legacy for themselves; between English monarchs and the Roman church; and, most recently, between skeptical scholars and a myth-hungry populace.

Outside of myth, folktale, and purported histories of events written down centuries after they were said to have occurred, Arthur's appearance as the legendary "once and future" hero-king of Britain enters the political fray of Anglo-Norman Britain in the twelfth century. As Ashe (1971:3) argues, Henry II's monarchy at the time had a desperate need for a "fortifying mythos," and the twelfth-century historian William of Malmesbury provided one with his reworking of the Celtic literary revival that had been developing in Wales, Cornwall, and Brittany at the time. The writing down of the lives of saints and of Arthurian tales and prophecies provided William with raw material for his accomplishment, which, argues Ashe, was that by "disclosing" the Celtic past and presenting "the English and Normans as legitimate successors to the Britons and Romans, William laid the foundation for a mature national dignity" (Ashe 1973:175). He was in turn followed by Geoffrey of Monmouth, whose account of Arthur in his *History of the Kings of Britain* became the "fountainhead of Arthurian romance" (176). By the end of the twelfth century, Geoffrey's account had spread across the then-extensive French-speaking elites of the Continent, and the "matter of Britain" took its place alongside the "matter of France" (of Charlemagne and his peers battling the Saracens) and the "matter of Rome" (Aeneas, the siege of Troy, and the fortunes of Rome) as a source for romantic fiction (Ashe 1973:178; 1971:3; MacColl 1999).

At the time, the Bretons on the mainland had been boasting that Arthur vanished somewhere in Brittany, so when Henry II conquered that country and decided that Arthur must be buried in England, the monks of Glastonbury came up with what was for Henry a most convenient solution: "he is buried here, on English soil." But was this soil English (Anglo-Saxon), or was it Welsh (Celtic)? If Henry's claim of an English home for Arthur's body was meant to stifle Welsh claims, the Welsh could claim, in turn, that Glastonbury was theirs. Whether or not there was any previous connection between Glastonbury and the legendary Ynis-witrin ("Glass Isle") or Avalon, with the monks' announcement of Arthur's exhumation in 1190, Glastonbury was publicly equated with the legendary isle. With the Arthurian tales weaving their way through the literary networks of aristocratic Europe, the "visionary themes of romance," as Ashe notes (1973:195), "acquired, for the first time, a local habitation. Also for the first time, they came squarely into contact with Christian tradition"—specifically, that of Glastonbury Abbey, where it was now possible to claim that disciples of Christ, bringing along with them a sacred object (the Grail), had founded the "earliest Christian church in all of western Europe" (195). By the time of a series of fifteenth-century Synodal Councils, the English used this latter assertion to support their claim to a Christianity which was equal and parallel to that of the Roman church (Britannia 1996). Historical accuracy aside, Glastonbury's contribution, in Ashe's assessment, was therefore crucial in three areas: the ascent of the Church of England to a high level of authority; the growth of the island monarchy as an institution with its distinctive mythos; and the later exploitation of the Abbey's legends in the interests of a "national Christianity" (Ashe 1973:183–84).

Arthurian romance, from Chrétien de Troyes onward, contained its own allure. Positing a lost Golden Age, a wounded king, and a wasteland whose fertility will be restored through the agency of that archetypal source of nourishment, the Grail, Arthurian romance suggests a magical bond between the king and the land. By the nineteenth century, the Romantic movement had revived Glastonbury's Arthurian mythos. The matter of Britain captured the interest of Blake and Tennyson (who connected the sleeping Arthur's impending return to Glastonbury in his *Idylls of the King*), and later spread within esoteric fraternities such as the Masons and Rosicrucians. This longing for Arthur's return—the hope that a primal superhero might reinstate a golden age in which Britain's glory shines again—has been the archetypal British myth, and the matter of Britain has been taken up in various ways more recently. Anti-Catholic Anglicans in the nineteenth century brought Glastonbury back into an anti-Roman polemic by arguing that the Church of England was heir to an old British church that was distinctive, independent from, and, they claimed, senior to Rome. The so-called British Israelites of the time (and their nationalist followers today) forwarded ideas about the British being the chosen people to whom Jesus will one day return, allowing England to reclaim her rightful spiritual destiny (Ashe 1982:105). In contrast, socialists and New Thought radicals (like Rutland Boughton) have interpreted Arthur's return as an allegory of the birth of the "universal man."

Glastonbury's place in the more recent Arthurian revival has taken various forms. Besides Boughton's Arthurian operatic dramas, John Cowper Powys's vast novel A *Glastonbury Romance* (1933) placed the town in the center of the Grail revival; and T. H. White's *The Once and Future King* helped establish it within the Arthurian mythos. With the publication of Geoffrey Ashe's *King Arthur's Avalon* (1973/1957), the vision of recreating Britain with Glastonbury as its "New Jerusalem" was carried through into the cultural shifts of the 1960s. Ashe sees in Glastonbury a "crucible of cultural fusion" (1982:41) that has legitimate claims to being the birthplace both of the British church and the British state: "This was the first place where Saxons and Britons explicitly renounced conflict and mutual avoidance, and started constructive co-operation" (38). "Within Glastonbury's precinct," he continues, "Englishmen (as Anglo-Saxons were soon, in effect, becoming) mingled with Celts who continued to join the community, including Irish. In their united work and study, it may be claimed, the United Kingdom had its symbolic birth long before its political realization. The descendants of these same Wessex rulers became the first sovereigns of all England. The House of Windsor traces its ancestry to them" (38–39).

But questions and paradoxes abound. As Hutton (1993a) points out, it is all too ironic that the two great villains of the Romantic mystics—the English, and the medieval Catholic Church—are the ones who are largely responsible for Glastonbury's alleged glory: the Anglo-Saxons built the Abbey, while the Church supplied its myths and legends. A second irony is that, for all of Glastonbury's current countercultural trappings, this focus on Britain's former glory and its impending return can only serve a conservative agenda: by defining and defending a traditional image of Britain (though a more Celtic than Anglo-Saxon one) in the face of the country's increasing multicultural and postcolonial realities, it props up the nostalgia for a bygone world which is not only unlikely to return, but may never have existed in the first place.[8] The Arthurian legacy, in Tennyson's words, still "streams over the land like a cloud" (Ashe 1971:50) in the once-Celtic fringes of Britain, where tourists and Arthurian aficionados circulate between Tintagel on the Cornish coast (the castle where Arthur is thought to have been born), Cadbury Castle in Somerset (which presents the most plausible claim to having been Arthur's Camelot), Glastonbury (where he is said to have died), and other sites in England and Wales. And the idea of the rebirth of a parched wasteland, the wasteland, perhaps, of modern industrial Britain, is more appealing now than ever for those who have gathered in Glastonbury in the hope of being witnesses or even midwives to such a rebirth.

Celtic and Occult Glastonbury

Outside of the more immediate political uses of the matter of Britain, Glastonbury's identification as Avalon connects it with a more ancient stratum, that of Celtic myth, and with a more contemporary pursuit—the desire for reconnection with an ancient Earth-centered paganism. As Avalon, Glastonbury becomes a center "between the worlds," bridging the Underworld of Celtic myth with the loftier aspirations of Christianity, humanism, and modernity.

In the folklore of the Celts, Gwyn ap Nudd is said to be the Guardian of the Gates of Annwn (whose colors were red and white), living in a glass spiraling castle in the Otherworld (or Underworld), the Isle of the Dead over which he rules. In the Welsh series of tales called the Mabinogion, Gwyn is locked in a perpetual struggle with his counterpart, Gwythyr ap Greidyawl (the spirit of the light half of the year), for the hand of Crei-ddylad, Shining One, daughter of the solar king Llud Silver Hand (N. Mann 1993:45–48). As King of the Fairies, Gwyn is associated with "fairy hills" in Wales and elsewhere (Ashe 1973:22). In a tale preserved from a sixteenth-century manuscript, Gwyn is said to have appeared to the seventh-century Glastonbury hermit St. Collen, who dispersed Gwyn's fairy kingdom by sprinkling holy water onto the Tor. From this tale, and from the apparently natural concordance of the Tor itself, has grown the idea that the Tor is the Celtic Glass Isle (Ynis-witrin), the Isle of Apples (Avalon), the gateway to the Otherworld. Other lore exists today about entranceways and tunnels below ground, about a vast hollow cavern inside the Tor, and about mysterious disappearances of those who have wandered where they should not have. Glastonbury, Janet Roberts writes, is a "place where two worlds meet—the land of the living and the land of the dead" (in A. Roberts 1992:85). As in Annwn, whose hounds, horses, costumes, and dragons are all of two colors—red and white—so Glastonbury has its Red and White Springs; so, too, Joseph's cruets with the blood and sweat of Jesus were, respectively, red and white. The British monarch Uther Pendragon is said to have flown a banner of red and white dragons, the Welsh flag being a red dragon and the Saxon, white. And in a rare reference to Glastonbury by John Dee, the sixteenth-century occultist, scientist-magus, and physician of Elizabeth I, Dee claimed to have found the alchemical red and white powders of St. Dunstan in Glastonbury Abbey (N. Mann 1993:57ff.).

Other connections are said to exist between the ancient Celts and specific sites in and around Glastonbury. The Ponter's Ball earthwork, found on the east side of the peninsula, is claimed to be dated from the third century B.C., and, according to one tourist guidebook, "most likely to be the enclosure of a great pagan Celtic sanctuary" (McIlwain 1992:7). It is often interpreted as a "ritual boundary" between the outside world and the "sanctuary" within (e.g., N. Mann 1993:47). An avenue of ancient oaks is said to have existed on the east side of the island, and while most of these have apparently disappeared, the two nicknamed Gog and Magog remain. A stump of a yew tree found buried at the Chalice Well site is also claimed to be part of a line of yew trees, possibly indicating some ancient ritual path up the valley (Hardcastle 1990:6). That there was some sort of Druid college of instruction is routinely asserted throughout New Age literature on Glastonbury. A fundraising leaflet for the University of Avalon states, "Tradition tells how Glastonbury had one of the principal Celtic Mystery Colleges, which flourished at the time of the birth of Christ" (Bowman 1993a:149). In a similar vein, Michell calls Glastonbury "the citadel of Celtic esotericism" (1978:167).

Much of this lore about Druids and Celts can be traced to the speculations of British antiquarians in the seventeenth and eighteenth centuries, and to the later Romantic-era Celtic revival. Antiquarians like John Aubrey, the architect John Wood, and clergyman William Stukeley insisted on a connection between the Druids and the megalithic monuments of ancient Britain, most notably Stonehenge. Stukeley's *Stonehenge: A Temple Restor'd to the British Druids*, published in 1740, was an influential source of all manner of speculation about the function of that monument. Stukeley envisioned the Druids arriving in England with the Phoenicians, "during the life of Abraham, or very soon after," with a religion "so extremely like Christianity, that in effect it differ'd from it only in this: they believed in a Messiah who was to come, as we believe in him that is come" (in Grinsell 1978:23; Bowman 1993a:150).[9]

The nineteenth-century revival of interest in Celticism among Britain's artistic and literary circles was at least in part a response to Anglo-Saxon cultural and political hegemony, a way of asserting a modern identity for Scots, Irish, and Welsh that was distinct from English identity. In the present century, this revivalism continues in occult[10] and esoteric spiritual movements (influenced by the Hermetic Order of the Golden Dawn and such early-twentieth-century figures as Anna Kingsford, Rudolf Steiner, founder of Anthroposophy, and Dion Fortune) which posit the idea of a British mystery tradition,[11] part of the longer-standing Western mystery tradition that presumably connects today's occultists with Rosicrucians, Freemasons, Renaissance Hermeticists and Cabalists, and the alchemists and gnostics of previous centuries.[12]

A quaternity of late-nineteenth- and early-twentieth-century figures—John Arthur Goodchild, Wellesley Tudor Pole, Frederick Bligh Bond, and Dion Fortune—connect Glastonbury directly to this tradition.[13] Author of the theosophically influenced *Light of the West*,[14] Goodchild claimed to have been urged by a vision to take a blue glass bowl that was in his father's possession, of supposedly ancient origin, and to bury it beneath a stone in the waters of a well at Bride's Hill (the so-called Women's Quarter) in Glastonbury. Some time afterward, two sisters, Janet and Christine Allen, are supposed to have discovered the bowl and forwarded it to Wellesley Tudor

Pole in Bristol, where it became an object of healings and meetings, and a focus for the idea of Spiritual Womanhood. As Benham notes in his history *The Avalonians*, Goodchild, Tudor Pole, and the others imagined they were inaugurating "the Church of the New Age, a church in which woman was in the ascendant and Bride, the Celtic embodiment of the Universal Feminine, was restored and harmonized with a mystical understanding of the tenets of the Christian faith" (1993:50–51). Tudor Pole, who associated the cup with the Holy Grail, began to interest psychics, academics, and religious leaders (among them an enthusiastic Archdeacon Basil Wilberforce) about the glass vessel.

Tudor Pole himself was an occultist and visionary who, at one point, claimed to have seen a vision of the three spiritual centers of the British Isles—Avalon, Iona, and a mysterious "Western Isle"—and who considered the "energy" of the saint and archangel Michael to be at the center of the forthcoming spiritual era. An influential businessman, he was also the originator of the Silent Minute, a daily moment of united, silent prayer initiated during the British war effort in 1940, and signaled by the BBC-broadcast chiming and striking of "Big Ben" at nine each evening. In 1959, Tudor Pole formed the Chalice Well Trust, which went on to buy and restore the land and buildings at Chalice Well. The mysterious cup itself, after traveling to Palestine, Syria, Egypt, and diverse pilgrimage centers, was eventually put away for safekeeping by the Chalice Well Trustees, and is now rarely seen. (Interest in it subsided after scholarly opinion placed its origins in medieval Europe well after the time of Christ.)

The third of the Avalonian visionaries, Frederick Bligh Bond, was an architect, son of an Anglican minister, and member of the Society for Psychical Research. From the day of his appointment to direct excavations at the Abbey on behalf of the Somerset Archaeological Society, Glastonbury's Abbey ruins became Bond's lifelong obsession. He conducted the most advanced and detailed excavations at the Abbey to date (Rahtz 1993:79), recovering the plan of the great church, and excavating the foundations of the Edgar Chapel. But his approach was notoriously unconventional. He employed psychic methods, including dozens of "automatic writing" sittings (writing under trance or in dissociated mental states) between 1907 and 1912 with the psychics J. A. Bartlett and Everard Fielding, who allegedly entered into "mental sympathy" with an unseen fraternity whom he called the Watchers or the Company of Avalon (Benham 1993:206). Bond also employed dowsing, cabalistic numerology, and other occult methods to locate sites for excavation, and his numerological calculations led to his making extravagant claims about the "sacred geometry" underlying the architecture of the Abbey. In time, some of his religious colleagues split from him, and an anti-Bond lobby developed over the reports of his unconventional methods, as well as the defamatory efforts of his ex-wife. By 1922 the opposition, which included the Anglican bishop and a contender for Bond's position, prevailed, and he was sacked.[15] His work, however, continues to exercise a lasting influence on the later sacred-geometry theorizing of John Michell, Keith Critchlow, and others.

The fourth crucial figure in the cast of Avalonian occultists was Dion Fortune (born Violet Mary Firth). A trained Jungian analyst and a writer of novels and nonfiction on occult themes, Fortune had been prominent in the London-based Theosophical Society and the Order of the Golden Dawn, and later founded her own Fraternity of the Inner Light. Central to Fortune's vision was the reconciliation between pagan nature worship and Christianity. In Glastonbury, her base from 1924 until her death, she found these two forces represented in the "two Avalons, 'the holyest erthe in Englande', down among the water-meadows [the Abbey]; and upon the heights [the Tor] the fiery pagan forces that make the heart leap and burn" (quoted in Benham 1993:262). And though, prior to her death from leukemia in 1946, Fortune saw herself as the "last of the Avalonians," through her teaching and writing she has since become one of the most influential personages (next to Aleister Crowley and Wicca founder Gerald Gardner) in the British neopagan and magical revival.

In the decades since, writers on the so-called British mysteries have forged an alignment with a broader, international neopagan effort to reintroduce and revive "earth-centered" traditions of magical and spiritual practice. In the writings of John and Caitlin Matthews, Gareth Knight, and R. J. Stewart, among others, Glastonbury is portrayed as a place of reconciliation between Christianity and paganism; more specifically, as a site of the Celtic Christianity of Iona and St. Columba, itself a synthesis of Celtic-Druidic paganism and Christianity; and, primarily perhaps, as a site associated with the Holy Grail.[16] An influential addition to this corpus of literature was Marion Zimmer Bradley's *Mists of Avalon* (1984), a novelistic recreation of the Arthurian saga from the point of view of the women involved.[17] In all of this, there is the appeal to an allegedly more enlightened past, one in which the Celts take on the role of Britain's noble savages. As Bowman puts it, "Just as American New Agers are 'rediscovering' Native American wisdom and Australian New Agers are looking to Aboriginal traditions for enlightenment, in Britain the Celts fill that niche" (1993a:154).

Glastonbury's Earth Mysteries

Within the canon of locally influential earth mysteries literature on Glastonbury, the most celebrated ideas are those to do with ley lines, dowsers' energy findings, the sacred geometry of the Abbey, the Tor labyrinth, and the Glastonbury Zodiac (Michell 1969, 1990; Graves 1978, 1986b; Miller and Broadhurst 1989). According to the various accounts, the number of ley lines thought to pass through Glastonbury ranges from four or five to over a hundred. The best known is the so-called St. Michael line (also known as the Michael-and-Mary line). More properly a corridor, since the alignments are inexact, it joins St. Michael's Mount in Cornwall, several churches dedi-

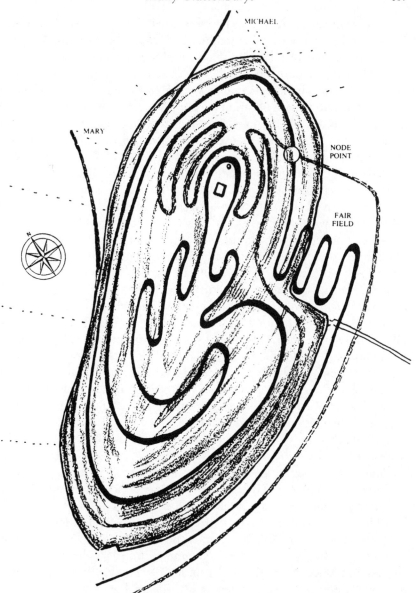

Map 5.1. "Michael and Mary" energy currents, Glastonbury Tor.
Courtesy of Gothic Image Publications

cated to St. Michael (in Brentor, Barrowbridge Mump, Othery, and Glastonbury's remaining tower on the Tor), Stoke St. Michael, and Avebury, the
predominant megalithic site in England. In their cross-country trek dowsing the St. Michael line, Miller and Broadhurst (1989) claim some dramatic findings on Glastonbury Tor: "The Mary energy formed a container

which encompassed the Michael current and its bulbous projection around the Tower. The symbolism was graphic. The female force enclosed the male energy in the form of a double-lipped cup. It was a chalice or Grail." All of this "stunned" the duo and led them to conclude that the Tor was a place "where the male and female energies of the St Michael Line were ritually mating, the actual point of fusion apparently located at the site of the altar of the old church." These were, they realized, "the sexual energies of the Earth" (155). They further traced the St. Michael line through the high altar of the Abbey grounds, King Arthur's tomb site (where the energy apparently divided into two separate streams and flowed around the tomb), and the central axes of the Great Church and of St. Mary's Chapel (the "Mother Church" of Britain, with its Vesica Piscis dimensions, its crypt and well), beyond which the ley finally "flowed out of town."

Combining ley theory with the idea of the human body's chakra system, others have speculated that Glastonbury is the solar plexus of this particular ley, whose root chakra is in Cornwall, its heart in Avebury, and its eye in Norfolk. Frequent mention is also made of ley lines which align Glastonbury with energy centers much farther afield, including the Great Pyramid of Giza, Mecca, Australia's Uluru (Ayers Rock), and Tiahuanaco in Peru. Glastonbury-based Earth alignment theorists see this as evidence for the town's role as a "world energy center." Terry Walsh (1993), for instance, has plotted forty-one widely acknowledged sacred sites on a Gnomonic (spherical-to-linear) Projection of the earth's surface, to obtain forty-eight great circle alignments, five of which pass through Glastonbury (two of these crossing each other at right angles there).[18]

In a related vein, sacred geometry enthusiasts have built on the earlier work of Bligh Bond to argue that Glastonbury Abbey was constructed according to principles of sacred geometry, incorporating ancient knowledge about correspondences between mathematical principles, cosmic harmonies, and natural energies (Critchlow 1982; Pennick 1980; Roberts 1992; N. Mann 1993; Michell 1978, 1990). Mann (1993) and others note that the architecture of the Abbey combines the two Masonic systems of sacred geometry, *Ad Triangulum* and *Ad Quadratum*, into a single pattern which allegedly produces "a twelve-fold geometry symbolically associated with the zodiac, both celestial and terrestrial" (Pennick in Roberts 1992:118). Michell (1990) argues that Glastonbury Abbey and Stonehenge are based on a common octagonal geometry, and that the dimensions of Glastonbury Abbey and St. Mary's Chapel correspond to the "holy city" designs described by Plato in *The Republic* and the New Jerusalem diagram given in the biblical Revelation of John (Michell in Roberts 1992:171–76). At the center of Glastonbury's mysteries, writes Michell, "was a long-sustained priestly ritual which breathed new life into the countryside. It amounted to an invocation of the Holy Grail, and its mythic framework is reflected in the cycle of the Grail romance" (1990:159).

Glastonbury Tor has also been subject to a wide range of speculations, including the idea that it is an artificial mound or that it is hollow inside. The most credible of the various theories appears to be one proposed by Geoffrey Russell in 1969 and later elaborated by Geoffrey Ashe: that the surface of the sides of the Tor had been sculpted in ancient times into a large labyrinth. What is evident is that a series of terraces circle the Tor's summit: archaeologists stand by the idea that these are medieval agricultural linchets—arable terraces, constructed at a time when the surrounding levels were undrained and maximum use of available land for agriculture was desired—though some have suggested that it may have been a Medieval pilgrimage pathway.[19] Mann argues that though there may have been arable linchets on the Tor, the strips were unlikely to be *only* this: "The amount of sheer hard work necessary for the construction of these enormous terraces would have negated the return on all but the lower, broader and sheltered south-facing slopes. And if the need for land was ever that great why were other slopes of a more suitable (less steep) nature not also terraced?" (N. Mann 1993:61). Given what we now know about the population density in neolithic England, it would seem surprising if the Tor did not have *some* special significance in the minds of the ancient Britons; lack of evidence does not equal evidence of lack.[20]

More imaginative has been an idea first proposed in the 1930s by Canadian-born artist and sculptor Katherine Maltwood. When Maltwood was illustrating an edition of *The High History of the Holy Grail*, she noticed what appeared to her to be gigantic effigies of the figures of the zodiac etched into maps of the landscape around Glastonbury. The effigies were inscribed in a circle over thirty miles in circumference and ten miles in diameter, through a combination of river and stream courses, field boundaries and drainage channels, old trackways and turnpike roads. And though some of the signs are represented by figures other than the commonly accepted ones—Aquarius by a phoenix, Libra by a dove, Cancer by a boat, and Capricorn by a unicorn—there are twelve of them, in a circle centered roughly around the village of Butleigh. Maltwood backed up her theory with lavish publications of maps and air photographs, though it was not until the 1960s that her ideas found their natural audience.

The zodiac raises obvious questions, such as: Who designed it, when, how, and why? Maltwood's now discredited theory proposed that Sumerian metal traders constructed the "Temple of the Stars" some five thousand years ago. Others have suggested variations on this theme: for instance, that around 2000 B.C. "a race of astronomer-priests came to Glastonbury and erected various earthworks and standing stones within the precincts of the Zodiac's hallowed ground" (Roberts 1992:29), or that the zodiac goes back ten thousand years to the time of the ancient Atlanteans. A final theory, which Maltwood alluded to herself, is that the effigies are natural—a spontaneous creation of the Earth itself, which could only occur in such a hallowed landscape as this. The tension between these different views—specifically, that the zodiac was formed by an ancient civilization, or that it is

an expression of a power that belongs to the earth itself, a chthonic, formative force related to the ley line networks and mysterious telluric energies—
may constitute part of the idea's continuing appeal, suggesting as it does that
the ancients "felt" the earth energies more acutely than we do. If it is a
natural phenomenon, astrology—or our twentieth-century version of it—
would also seem to be granted the authority of nature itself. Anthony Roberts writes, "The Glastonbury Zodiac is a 'living' manifestation of Gaian
Consciousness . . . a subtle extrusion of telluric currents and earth-mould-
ing movements of a spiritual nature that is naturally geomantic in purpose
and application. . . . The Zodiac is a resolution [sic] of the manifested
Gaian consciousness interacting with the flowing energies of the outer cosmos" (1992:20–21). Like the other Glastonbury mysteries, the zodiac lends
itself to elaboration and multiple associations. The circle and the twelve
signs are obvious stand-ins for the Round Table, the table of the Last Supper with Christ's twelve apostles, the Holy Grail, and the legendary Twelve
Hides of Glastonbury. Arthurian episodes have been assigned to the different constellations. Wearyall Hill, which is in the sign of Pisces, arguably has
a fish-shaped appearance; with Joseph's Holy Thorn near its summit, this
connects it with the idea of Christ as the Piscean fish—both fisher of men
and sacrifice himself. Glastonbury itself is found in the sign of Aquarius,
which is a phoenix rising from the ashes, pouring out wisdom into the New
Age. Leo, the lion, is (naturally) where the kings of Wessex had their power
base. Once one begins to explore the possibilities, there is much fuel for the
imagination here.

   Needless to say, there are a number of problems with the zodiac hypothesis. The grand design would only have been fully apparent at a height of
20,000 feet, so how could it have been constructed by people who could not
have seen it in its entirety? Explanations offered to account for this include
the alleged help of extraterrestrials; the assertion that the ancients actually
could see it, either through "shamanic flight" or with the aid of technologies
whose record has been lost entirely; or the ingenious proposition that megalithic sites and larger earthworks, like the extensive and mysterious Nazca
lines in the Peruvian Andes, were viewed in a mirrorlike "canopy" formation of reflective ice crystals that once hovered some fifty miles above the
earth's surface (Roberts 1992:134ff.). A further difficulty is that part of the
zodiac may well have been covered with water for at least part of the year.
There is, then, the scholars' perpetual complaint that this landscape zodiac,
like ley lines, depends on too many different kinds of topographic features:
hills, streams, woods, ditches, hedges, roads. Some of these, such as rivers
and streams, have been around for quite some time, though not necessarily
for five millennia in their present positions; a few ancient trackways could
also be of quite distant origin. But roads, trees, churches, field boundaries,
and droveways, most of which can only be dated back to within the last few
centuries, beg the question of what their connection is to ancient Atlanteans, Sumerians, or Neolithic farmers. The common answer—that these

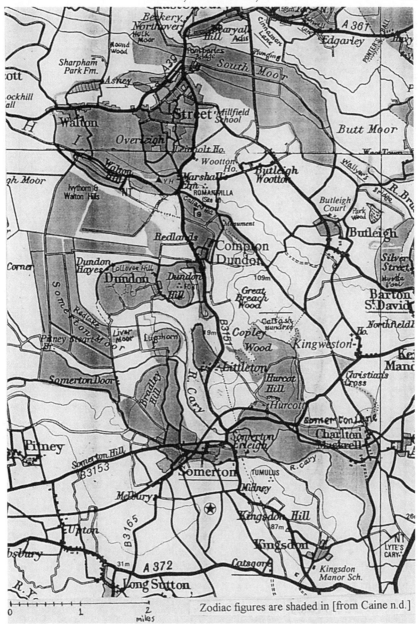

Map 5.2. Glastonbury area, Zodiac shaded

modern features unconsciously perpetuate ancient landscape markings through something called folk memory—does not satisfy most scholars. In the end, it comes down to looking at a map or aerial photograph and judging for oneself: what shapes appear here? (see map 5.2).[21]

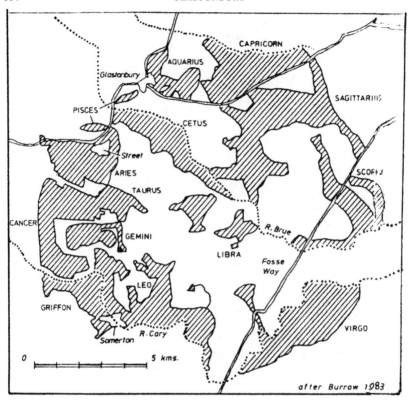

Map 5.3. Glastonbury Zodiac

New Age Glastonbury: Earth's Heart Chakra and New Jerusalem

Although earth mysteries, Celtic and Arthurian themes, and Goddess spirituality are all part of New Age culture in the broadest sense, terms such as "centers of light," "earth chakras," and "etheric networks" are more recognizable as belonging to New Age millennialism proper. The Findhorn community's vision of a network of centers of light (discussed in chapter 2) has spread far and wide, capturing the imagination of spiritual communities across the globe. In Britain, it is often said by New Agers that Findhorn, Iona, and Glastonbury form an "energy triangle." In the writings of New Age visionaries like José Argüelles, Jim Berenholtz, and Martin Gray, Glastonbury is considered a crucial link in the "etheric network" of "power points" whose activation, through visiting, meditation, prayer, and ceremony, is needed to bring about the New Age.

Talk of the "activation" of earth chakras is ubiquitous in the writings of the two most prolific New Age writers associated with Glastonbury, Anthony

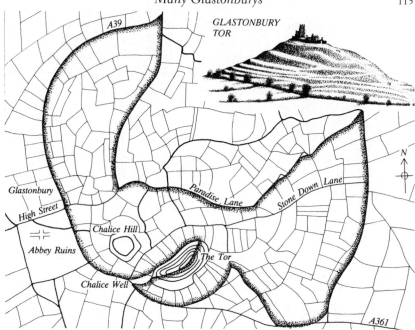

Map 5.4. Phoenix figure, Glastonbury Zodiac. Courtesy of Nicholas R. Mann

Roberts and Robert Coon. Until his death in 1990, Roberts, who founded Zodiac House Publications in 1969 and moved to Glastonbury in 1981, was among the principal figures in Glastonbury's New Age community. He edited the influential collection of writings entitled *Glastonbury: Ancient Avalon, New Jerusalem* (1992 [1978]), which was intended to "show the true, canonical tradition of Glastonbury" (Nicholson, in Roberts 1992:12). Roberts connects Glastonbury to "a divine lineage descending from those ancient priest/magicians the 'Kings of the West'" (in Coon 1986:xiii), to Atlantis, to the Ark of the Covenant. He refers to the "geomantically 'active' sentient landscape of Avalon" (xi), saying that "A 'Great Work' has recently begun in Glastonbury involving the redirection of magical flow of many of the sacred power centres' diverse constituents" (xiii). Glastonbury, in his vision, "protects and guards the Three Great Treasures of Britain in immortal stasis. These are the King Stone, the old Celtic Lia Fail, stone of power and prophecy; the 'electrifying' Spear of Lugh, Sun-God and Sacrificial Warrior, and the Cauldron of Plenty, mystically referred to as 'the hollow filled with Water and Fading Light'" (in Coon 1986:xv). Glastonbury is, accordingly, "a universal Cosmic Beacon. It gathers and fuses magics into its synthesizing strengths, transmuting and blending faiths, philosophies, cultures and . . . most importantly . . . people into awakening transcendence and reunion with God the Father (and through the Shekinah, Mother) of all" (in Coon 1986:xviii). Roberts's language is dense, obtuse, and pontificatory — a style he defends in a foreword to a book by his equally opaque colleague Coon: "The opacity [of this book], facilitated by the jewelled prose, is a necessary initiatory construct that is designed to trigger the psychic synapses (through energy invigoration via the chakras) and so enable the reader to soar into the glittering realms of 'another reality'" (1986:xii).

American-born Coon has inspired and organized gatherings at sacred sites around the world. A self-proclaimed prophet who calls himself "Europe's foremost Immortalist Philosopher," Coon alleges to have received a series of "major Revelations involving Glastonbury and the future of Humanity" in 1967 (Coon 1986). He subsequently settled in the Glastonbury area, convinced that it was the "planetary heart chakra," one of seven chakras which are "Spiritual Initiation areas," to be "activated" in series.[22] Coon portrays the Earth as a living, willful, electrically charged being, and exhorts his readers to "Love the Heart of Planet Gaea with all thy Strength and Passion! Oh where is the physical Heart of our world?" he asks, "The High Altar, within this Global Heart, is Glastonbury Tor." Speaking of the planet's "wiring" and of "blowing fuses in the planetary circuitry," Coon writes that the Great Work of the New Aeon involves "the building of the planetary New Jerusalem and the consequent abolition of all physical death from every life form on earth," a process that requires meditation, magical invocation, visualization, and other spiritual exercises in which he instructs his readers (1986, 1993). For Coon, as for Roberts, Michell (1978, 1990), and their allies, Glastonbury *is* the New Jerusalem, a zodiacal phoenix rising from the ashes, a "cosmo-magical centre, an English Jerusalem" (Roberts 1992:171).

The Goddess in Glastonbury

In a markedly different vein, Glastonbury's core of activist women has interpreted the town's history and landscape from a spiritual feminist perspective, revalorizing chthonic forces, dragon lore, spiral and serpent imagery, mythical underground and Underworld lore, the mysterious processes of women's bodies, and the cycle of birth, death, and regeneration in a manner consistent with the broader Goddess spirituality movement. For them, the medieval Church of St. Michael on the Tor is reinterpreted as the patriarchal Church's attempt to control and subordinate the pagan Tor — an attempt which was never consummated, as the Earth itself destroyed the church in a thirteenth-century earthquake, leaving only its tower standing.[23]

Of the women who have made it their life's work to reenchant the Glastonbury landscape itself, author, theatrical producer, and tour guide Kathy Jones has been the most persistent. Jones's books *The Goddess in Glastonbury* (1990) and *Spinning the Wheel of Ana: A Spiritual Quest to Find the British Primal Ancestors* (1994) weave a spell of connections between land-

Figure 5.2. One of the "Tor burrs" (with votive offerings on tree),
center point of Kathy Jones's maze walks

scape features, Celtic myth, and speculations on ancient goddess religion.
For her, the Glastonbury landscape even looks like the profile of a giant
goddess lying lengthwise across the moors: the Tor is her left breast and
ribcage, Chalice Hill her pregnant belly, and Wearyall Hill her left thigh
and leg. Looking from the banks of the River Brue, the pregnant womb of
Chalice Hill is centered before us and "we stand between her spread legs,"
with the ruins of Glastonbury Abbey situated in the vagina of the birth-
giving Goddess (1990:8). Patriarchal religion, according to Jones, "built
its phallic extravagances in the Vulva of the Goddess, thinking thereby to
crush Her" (10), though the ruined Mary Chapel in the Abbey is interpreted by Jones as situated on one of the most potent spots. To the southwest
of the "island," at the Beckery, a "forgotten, derelict, industrialized area of
Glastonbury, covered in part by the town's sewage works," lies the emerging
head of Her child being born from between the Goddess's spread legs (18).
Known as Bride's Mound, this spot features the buried remains of an early
chapel dedicated to St. Mary Magdalene, at which "tradition holds" that
St. Bridget lived for a time. The names Bridget and Bride (Brigit, Brigid,
Brighde, Brida, etc.) afford a wealth of associations for Jones; Bride/Brighde
is considered by some to have been the name of the "Triple Goddess" of the
Celts, or at least of an important fertility goddess. From this, Jones deter-
mines that Glastonbury is "a place of gestation, where new ideas, feelings
and ways of be-ing [*sic*] are glimpsed and anchored in consciousness and
physical expression" (25). She uses topographical maps to show the Glas-

tonbury landscape in the appearance of a swan, a bird sacred to Brigit, with Wearyall Hill making up the swan's outstretched head and neck; and she sees the Crone Goddess (Cerridwen, Hecate, Morgana or Morrigu), ruler of Annwn, the Celtic Underworld, "rid[ing] on the back" of this swan: "the Tor with its ancient terracing is Her ever-pregnant womb. Chalice Hill is Her soft nourishing breast. The Red waters of Chalice Well are the constant bloodflow from Her womb. The White Spring is Her fertile essence. Her head with its crown and pointed nose is Windmill Hill where many people live and there is a good view in all directions. Her crooked body is formed by the undulations of Stonedown" (34). Glastonbury thereby becomes the "Cauldron of the Crone," a "great melting pot of regeneration and inspiration" (39).

Jones makes much of Glastonbury's "holy waters." Besides the Chalice Well and the White Spring, she refers to a series of other wells, now hidden or forgotten: a well on Old Wells Road (now a fishpond), Paradise Well near the old oak trees Gog and Magog (now covered in brambles), St. Edmund's Well (crumbling in an orchard), Bride's Well (not visible), a well beneath the Tribunal on High Street, and St. Joseph's Well, next to the Mary Chapel (now barred and full of rubbish). Finally, there is the huge volume of water beneath the Tor, whose roar can be heard from beneath a maintenance hole cover partway up the hill.[24] The work of Jones and others to recover these forgotten wells carries practical implications: a group called Friends of Bride's Mound, for instance, has been lobbying for the granting of Scheduled Ancient Monument Protection to the mound which they believe was once a women's sanctuary area.[25]

The writings of other Goddess enthusiasts, including Janet McCrickard (1990) and Nicholas Mann (1985), similarly portray a landscape which is imagined and *felt* to be the body of the Goddess. The Red and White Springs are her life-taking and life-giving aspects (N. Mann 1985); the smoothly rounded Chalice Hill is naturally considered feminine—the breast or stomach of the Goddess; and so on. Obvious connections are made between the Grail, Ceridwen's Cauldron of plenty, and the need to heal the wasteland of "the wounded/piscean/father/Fisherking" (N. Mann 1985:9). Walking Glastonbury's hills and frequenting its wells and other holy sites thus becomes an ongoing pilgrimage within a sacralized landscape, and carries the potential of further discovery: with additional excavations, for instance, the Beckery could turn up more evidence of its role in the distant past. Such sites then attract further interest and speculation, becoming "hot spots" of activity and reshaping the sacred landscape for today's Avalonian believers.

This thread within Glastonbury's contemporary spiritual revival has been vitalized as well by popular books such as Marion Zimmer Bradley's *Mists of Avalon* (1984) and Jean Shinoda Bolen's *Crossing to Avalon* (1994). Bradley's portrayal of the spiritual lives, practices, and struggles of the women of the Arthurian saga, according to Jungian analyst Bolen, struck "a chord in many women," reminding them of "a missing part of our own history" about which "we [women] feel in our bones that it is true" (Bolen 1994:128). Avalon, for Bolen, "is psychologically a motherworld. It is in the shadow of patriarchal consciousness, repressed and thus feared and distorted" (134). Describing and reflecting on her own midlife pilgrimage to Glastonbury, Bolen writes that "to cross to Avalon is to remember the archetypal Mother, the Goddess in her several forms and many names, to rediscover the feminine mysteries and the sacred in embodied experiences. Avalon exists where divinity dwells in nature and quickens it in the pilgrim. . . . But once patriarchal religion and male gods prevailed, Avalon, the Grail, and the Goddess all disappeared into the mists of forgotten time" (136). She repeats the ecofeminist charge that in "Judaeo-Christian cultures . . . the Earth (and goddesses and women) had to be tamed and subjugated," a process symbolically represented by the suppression of dragons, snakes, and serpents, by such saints as Michael, George, and Patrick (90). For spiritual feminists, then, Glastonbury is a site where the hidden heritage of women's spirituality is sought out and found, in the potent imagery of the Grail, the Goddess, and the landscape with its dragon energies, sacred springs, and hills.

The Countercultural Travelers' Glastonbury: Retreat from the Battlefield

In their attempts to live outside the dominant, sedentary, urban or agro-industrial culture and in their questing for nomadic and neotribal identities, the travelers are postmodern refugees. Glastonbury has held an important place in Britain's countercultural geography since the beginnings of the Glastonbury Festival, when one of the festival's organizers wrote:

> Musicians are coming to play, many of them because they feel the magic of Glastonbury and the Vale of Avalon. . . . If the Festival has a specific intention it is to create an increase of awareness in the power of the Universe, a heightening of consciousness and a recognition of our place in the function of this our tired and molested planet.
>
> We have spent too long telling the Universe to shut up, we must search for the humility to listen. The earth is groaning for contact with our ears and eyes, Universal awareness touches gently at our shoulders, we are creators being created and we must prove our worth.
>
> These are the ideals which have inspired the Fayre. (in Elstob and Howes 1987:17)

By the mid-1980s, with the festival having grown substantially, its connections with the Stonehenge People's Free Festival, its travelers and "peace convoy," had waned. Writing from the Rainbow Fields at the Molesworth Cruise Missile Base for the Green Collective, a group which had also organized the first Green Field at the Glastonbury Festival, Bruce Garrard described the disjunction between the two: "From the point of view of people who went to Stonehenge, Glastonbury festival was commercial, middle class, a venue for people who weren't just old hippies but old weekend hippies. . . . From the point of view of people who went to Glastonbury (CND) festival, Stonehenge was a mess, beer cans and bikers, with no direction or purpose, an unhealthy embarrassment" (1994:15). Yet, Garrard mused, "both festivals had their roots in the same spirit, the same culture, even, if you look carefully, many of the same people." They were rooted in the free festival spirit which also gave rise to "the Green Gatherings, the Convoy, the second wave of CND, the peace camps, . . . the squatters' movement" and now Rainbow Fields. Connected by the nomadic routes of the travelers and peace convoy, the Green Collective was interested in making Glastonbury once again "a people's festival, and Stonehenge . . . a peace festival" (15).

So if Glastonbury's New Agers perceived the town to be connected to Findhorn or more distant "power spots," the counterculturalists saw it in relation to the practical battles of their own geography. Glastonbury was a place of retreat and a safe haven, "the lap of the Mother" in contrast to "Stonehenge out on Salisbury Plain in the open, exposed to the wind, exposed to the forces of militarism and repression" (Garrard 1994:15). Stonehenge was "the place to gather together to reclaim our power, for ourselves, for each other, for the tribe, for the Rainbow Tribe that was finding itself and its name up here at Rainbow Fields" (15). Following the Battle of the Beanfield, when younger travelers began appearing in the town or finding temporary refuge at Greenlands Farm, the *Glastonbury Communicator* editorialists wrote: "Before the New Age we have to live through the Police Age. . . . At Stonehenge our annual religious pilgrimage is being attacked by van loads of the new, non-official, National Riot Squad. . . . Is Stonehenge a museum or is it an integral part of the still living tradition, a tradition that recognizes no laws but Spiritual Law. A tradition which we at Glastonbury are, in our own ways, rediscovering and revivifying, a tradition which returns power to *All* the people . . ." (GC 1 [1985]).[26]

Haven of Unreason

To many Britons, it is the Glastonbury Festival which places the town on the map of contemporary England (though the festival takes place in Pilton, five miles outside town). The town itself, when it gets into the national media, is seen more as a source of lifestyle news or even of comic relief, treated with a gently satiric tone as "the de facto headquarters of the New Age movement" and the "town where the national grid of ley-lines criss-crosses like a tartan fabric" (R. White 1994:13; cf. Moir 1993:8). If the center-left broadsheets treat the town with a nod and a wink, the more conservative *Times* and *Daily Telegraph* spare fewer kind words for it. "If you want to see the anti-intellectual side of the English character at its most uninhibited, go to Glastonbury," an article in *Daily Telegraph* exhorts, calling it a "psychic Blackpool" (in *GT* 3:5). A *Telegraph* "Special Report on West Country Living" (September 28, 1994) bemoans the ill effects of mystics and festival-goers on the town's house prices, which, according to the article, are up to one-quarter lower than in nearby Somerton. The rock festival is blamed for "the arrival of a more or less permanent floating population of New Age travellers," with "their uniform of aggression in black with chains, tattoos, cropped hair and bits of metal piercing all their most sensitive body tissues," and their "extra-strong lager" and "morose dogs."

The presence of all those mystics leaves many scholars equally dour about the town. The leading archaeologists and historians to broach the topic of Glastonbury's past portray the threat of the "irrational" as one that looms large over the landscape. Philip Rahtz, for instance, is probably the single most respected scholarly authority on Glastonbury's prehistory, having excavated parts of the Tor and surrounding area since the early 1960s. His English Heritage book on Glastonbury (1993) is undoubtedly the best overview of its topic, and Rahtz writes exceedingly clearly about the issues surrounding Glastonbury's past. His judgments on the various legends and "traditions" associated with Glastonbury is clear: "Most," he writes, "if not all, of the myths associated with Glastonbury are a compendium of invention of medieval and later centuries" (42). When it comes to describing the town today, however, Rahtz brusquely waives any pretense to scholarly objectivity. In his *Invitation to Archaeology* (1991), an introduction to the field, Rahtz includes a case analysis of Glastonbury, in which he writes that all examples of "alternative archaeology" "pale before the Mecca of all irrationality: the sacred Isle of Avalon, Glastonbury," which has "become the magnet for an incredible variety of hippies, weirdos, drop-outs and psychos, of every conceivable belief and in every stage of dress and undress, flowing hair and uncleanliness" (128). Readers expecting an interesting thesis on the causal connection between flowing hair, uncleanliness, and irrationality, unfortunately, would be disappointed.[27] Not mincing words, another scholar, county historian Robert Dunning, has simply called Glastonbury's legends "a load of historical codswallop" (GG 2 [May 1989]: 4).[28]

In fairness to the scholars, the documented history of the area almost completely contradicts the popular mythology. The main archaeological features in the River Brue basin, for instance, are: the timber trackways (at least thirty of them, dated from 4000 B.C. to 500 B.C.), which are the earliest human-made roads known in Britain, and likely in Europe;[29] the Lake Villages—Iron Age settlements from about 700 B.C. to 50 A.D., in the vicinity of Glastonbury and nearby Meare; Romano-British "Pottery Mounds"; and Glastonbury's various medieval remains, which include an early Christian site at the Beckery and a sixth-century habitation on the Tor (which Rahtz, its discoverer, surmises was either a small outpost or stronghold of a local chieftain, or a Celtic Christian religious site). No pre-Saxon remains have been found at the Abbey; no pre-medieval structures or signs of being a sacred place have been found at Chalice Well (though several dozen Paleo- or Mesolithic flints and a shard of Iron Age pottery have been found there, indicating some kind of early use); no pre-1200 A.D. earthwork has been located at Ponter's Ball (it was, apparently, made by monks); and no pre-sixth-century remains have yet been found on the Tor. Rahtz admits that the archaeological potential "has hardly been tapped" (1993:10); but Ronald Hutton (1993a) takes it as "stunning" that Glastonbury is so "mute" compared to the rest of the region—Neolithic henges at Stanton Drew, Priddy, and elsewhere; Celtic and Roman holy sites with votive offerings, goddess figurines, and the like; Celtic Christian sites at Cannington, Congresbury, and Ilchester, with their huge cemeteries; and others. He points out that the Saxons founded totally new administrative and religious centers upon conquering Somerset, and muses that it makes perfect sense that the Saxons would have built a religious center at the *only* numinous, charismatic site in the area that didn't have one already on it—that is, at Glastonbury (Hutton 1993a).

On the topic of ley lines, we would have to turn to Williamson and Bellamy's *Ley Lines in Question* (1983) for the most detailed scholarly repudiation. Examining John Michell's original presentation of the St. Michael line, which they admit is the "most convincing long-distance, or 'primary,' ley that we could find," the debunking twosome write:

> In essence his line connects four churches dedicated to St. Michael, the edge of Avebury Circle, a stone circle in Cornwall and a ruined abbey in Suffolk. This is over a distance of 380 miles, through a country liberally endowed with monuments of the prehistoric past and churches dedicated to St. Michael. However, in its course through Wiltshire, the line passes through none of the 20 churches in that country which are dedicated to St. Michael. Indeed, we cannot help feeling that John Michell has been singularly unfortunate in his choice of line, for random chance could no doubt connect a more convincing series of ancient points than those traversed by his hapless long-distance dragon. (1983:150)

And yet, for all their debunking, even the scholars' viewpoint on Glastonbury owes a significant debt to the religious and popular interest in the area. All the significant research excavations conducted on the Tor, at the Chalice Well, and at the Beckery since the early 1960s have in fact been sponsored and commissioned by the Chalice Well Trust, the organization founded by Wellesley Tudor Pole to preserve and manage the holy well and the mystical chalice which was ostensibly found there (Rahtz 1993:52, 130). The trust established by Katherine Maltwood to further the understanding of her ideas has also been a significant financial supporter of archaeological work in the area (50). Science, after all, can hardly proceed without its benefactors.

CONTESTED SPACES

Smooth and Striated Space: Of Travelers, Traffic, and Trees

Competing ideas about a place inevitably lead to divergent and conflicting land use practices. Glastonbury's history bears evidence of a variety of spatial struggles: between distant kings and local abbots, between competing ecclesiastical estates, between landowners, freeholders and commoners, farmers and fishermen, land drainers and river navigators. As the medieval Abbey's status grew as a pilgrimage center, for instance, it and the town's other religious sites became mark points within the relatively "smooth" space of pilgrims, a broad geography of movement and of spiritual desire which circulated across England and to distant corners of continental Europe. This was facilitated by the dissemination of several place-myths, notably those connecting Glastonbury to Arthurian lore and the myth of the first, "old wattle" church of Britain. At the same time, a "striated" or "gridded" space (in Deleuze and Guattari's terms; see chapter 3), developed to channel and contain that movement, within which pilgrims, innkeepers, and monastic clergy had clearly bounded and complementary roles. The spatial economy of medieval Glastonbury was focused around the status of the Abbey and the political power it represented. For those who lived in the largely agricultural community that grew up around the Abbey, the ultimate governor and landholder of the area was clearly the administration of Glastonbury Abbey (Dunning 1994:27). The Abbey, in turn, was subject to the vacillations of the crown and the machinations of European church and state politics.

The situation was vastly different in the rural southwest England of the late twentieth century, but similar tensions can be seen between different levels of social agency in the production of space. Competing ideas and interpretations of the land have pitted land developers and road builders against ecological activists and conservation groups, while farmers and conservative townsfolk have felt themselves threatened by travelers and assorted itinerants. Roads, hypermarkets (superstores), and real estate developments channel the flow of traffic, money, and people. They open an area up to the smooth space of global capital; but though the flow of capital may appear smooth, to the extent that its free flow is mediated by money, it favors those who have it, and impedes noncommercial uses of and movements across the land. In Britain, the free flow of market forces has been kept in check by state authorities, laws pertaining to the use of common land, public membership organizations like the National Trust, conservation groups, and, more recently, antiroad protesters. Where the state or the National Trust, however, would cordon off land to make it safe from the market while, in the process, preserving the sanctity of capitalist spatial relations, countercultural groups have been more inclined to disrupt those relations. Nomadic travelers, antinuclear and peace activists, and antiroad protesters, by ignoring property rights and capitalist spatial relations in general, have insistently pursued their own smooth spatialities, their own heterotopic counterspaces which cut across the established ones. From within the smoothness of travelers' space, even something as ostensibly alternative as the Glastonbury Festival appears gridded and bounded, and by 1990 the festival's organizers had grown weary of the travelers' disruptive presence. In the broader arena of rural Somerset, such counterculturalists, by cutting against the grain of social expectations, have inevitably set themselves up for social demonization, a process which has in turn contributed a new dimension to the place lore surrounding Glastonbury.[30]

In recent years, very different visions of Glastonbury's future have collided with each other. Should it be a busy, well-trafficked market town, a quiet historical and artistic oasis, an upmarket spiritual haven, or a popular tourist site complete with theme park and motels? The nature of the town has been changing: a high turnover rate in businesses has seen new enterprises coming and going, with traditional High Street shops disappearing and a new breed of shops catering to visitors, tourists, and New Age pilgrims emerging in its place. Varying perceptions of this shift have led to two dominant local interpretations of what is going on. Those accustomed to the "old" Glastonbury see it as slowly withering away, becoming a "dump," "bankrupt" and "dead." In contrast, the alternative community, joined by a growing number of more flexibly positioned entrepreneurs, have been optimistic. "It's as if some great experiment is going on," one observer writes, "which is leading to the establishment of an appropriate, sustainable and new Glastonbury economy" (GT 3 [1990]: 18).

These competing visions have clashed repeatedly in the past several years. The proposed building of a hypermarket on the site of the historical annual Tor Fair (the Fair Field at the bottom of Wearyall Hill) provoked arguments that it will take away business from local traders, and will increase noise and traffic through the town (GC 5:5). But with the support of the Glastonbury Chamber of Commerce, local councillors, and traders, the Safeway Supermarket eventually prevailed. Other controversies have erupted when vacant buildings (such as the Mount Avalon House) have been taken over by homeless squatters. Travelers in the Glastonbury area have rarely been able to settle for very long in one spot. Occasionally their presence leads to the direct actions of landowners or contractors, as when a group of "railway squatters" reportedly had "their mobile homes rocked by forklift trucks, threatened [with] piles of bulldozed rubble, with GBH [clay], with petrol down their chimneys, and suchlike pleasantries" (GC 3:2). In the late 1980s, when a theme park was proposed for the Beckery archaeological site, the local Green Party and other individuals wrote in protest to the Mendip district council and Glastonbury town council. In the end, part of the site was saved by its designation as an "ancient monument," but an "archaeologically sensitive" designation failed to prevent the extension of a car park into the area (GZC 2 [1991]: 25). The theme park idea has not disappeared, however; an Arthurian theme park had been proposed by commercial interests as well as, somewhat surprisingly, by Geoffrey Ashe, presumably as a way of building upon Glastonbury's strengths as a historical and spiritual destination (GT 5 [1991]).

Britain's growing direct-action environmentalism has also made its way into Glastonbury. When the M-11 and other road protests were getting a fair bit of press coverage in the early 1990s, and a relief road protest was building in nearby Wells, the Bove Town Conservation Group was formed to fight plans to fell trees for the building of an estate road in Glastonbury's Bove Town and for a permanent track through Bushy Coombe. The latter is one of the remaining green spaces in the town, a quiet cow pasture shaped like a natural amphitheatre, nestled between Chalice Hill and Bove Town. It is a favorite place for quiet strolls and a green connecting corridor between the town and the Tor. Local press coverage, interestingly, referred to the Glastonbury "green" activists in a way that connected them to a broader English rural green movement (e.g., "Hills under Attack," WG, June 15, 1995:1). Yet, the nature of this movement has remained poorly defined. Many of the antiroad protests around England have enlisted coalitions of local conservationists and concerned residents, together with eco-anarchists, travelers, and counterculturalists. Oddly, though, a *Western Gazette* article (June 15, 1995:1) on such local protests listed among the achievements of "green activists" the successful "fight to get Paradise Quarry New Age travellers' camp, Croscombe, closed down." As this instance suggests, the relationship between travelers and local rural "green" movements can be rather ambiguous; and the place of travelers, "hippies," squatters, and solstice revelers remains a highly contested feature of Glastonbury's local politics.

The county and district councils have frequently found themselves caught between angry residents calling for eviction and removal of traveler sites and the longer-term need to address the issue effectively. When the Glastonbury town council was largely taken over by members of the Glastonbury Residents' Association in 1995, however, voices sympathetic to travelers found themselves once again drowned out. In one case, when the fifteen-family Paradise Quarry camp was being closed down, Conservative councillor Mike Free was quoted as saying, "What we don't want are these dirty vermin in the district" (WG, July 6, 1995:5). A similar attitude was encapsulated in a letter printed in the *Central Somerset Gazette* following the 1995 Glastonbury Festival (July 6, 1995:7). The letter begins, "It is no wonder that Glastonbury is dying on its feet. It is becoming the biggest toilet in the South West." The writer asserts that Glastonbury Festival attracts the worst people—"so-called human beings" who "use the hedgerows, pathways and even behind people's gateways to their homes to empty their bowels and bladders." This new wave of demonization, whatever its basis, transpired in the wake of the largest controversy to hit the town in recent years, a debate over the "pedestrianization" and "enhancement" of the town center.

The Western Relief Road, Pedestrianization, and the Town Center

The idea of building a relief road to cut down the volume of High Street traffic had been discussed since the early 1970s, but had been rejected by most residents on the rationale that it would have cut the town in half. A survey conducted in the late 1980s found that between 6 A.M. and 10 P.M. on a typical weekday some 26,000 vehicles entered Glastonbury (GCSN 56 [July 1990]). The A39, leading from Wells to Street via Glastonbury's High Street, had over the years become increasingly congested and intrusive, to the point where some residents claimed they feared for their lives when crossing High Street. Meanwhile, the A361, leading out to the neighboring town of Shepton Mallet, had been feeding an increasing traffic load along narrow town streets toward parking areas northwest of the town center (and beyond). The solution proposed by the county and district councils was one of the pedestrianization and "enhancement" of Glastonbury's town center, including the closure to traffic of Northload Street and the partial closure or "pedestrian-prioritization" of High Street, along with the building of a relief road on the western outskirts of town.

Pedestrianization elicited a sharply polarized reaction. Pro-pedestrianization forces included conservation groups, parts of the business community, including the town's mayor at the time, and most of the alternative community. Spearheading the anti-pedestrianization forces was the Glastonbury Residents' Association (originally the Glastonbury Ratepayers' Group), which, at the height of the controversy, had a large NO banner strung across the road at the north end of High Street. A reporter for the London-based *Independent* observed at the time:

> The two ends of Glastonbury High Street are worlds apart; deeply divided on the meaning of life—and on pedestrianization of the main thoroughfare. At the top end, traders bemoan the disappearance of household name stores, the emergence of the town as the alternative religious and healing capital of Britain and Somerset County Council's plans to give pedestrians priority. They fear businesses will close and the town centre will become overrun by new age travellers and others attracted by Glastonbury's acclaimed spiritual energies.
>
> Down the road, the growing number of fantasy painters, mystical tour guides, healers, candle makers, incense sellers and gallery owners cannot wait for the barriers to go up, the pavements to be widened and trees planted. They see tourists browsing among the craft boutiques and cafes as representing new life and replacing the gaps left by the multiple stores in their flight to out-of-town shopping centres. (Whitfield 1994:6)

While the "pros" blamed the superstores for Glastonbury's economic downturn, the "antis" feared the closing of High Street would lead to an inunda-

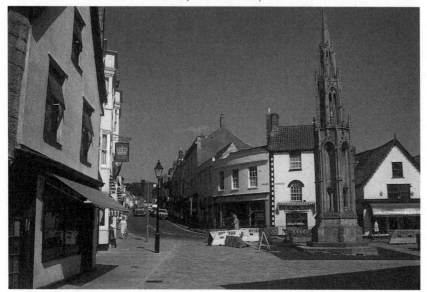

Figure 5.3. Market Cross, High Street

tion by "hippies" and "drongos," New Age travelers and assorted "weirdos," raising crime rates and destroying the town's rural fabric in the process. Town councillor and B and Q Superstore employee Mike Free expressed these fears well: "What is killing [small business] off is the alternative society, the beggars and street musicians. . . . *The High Street will not be safe without passing traffic*" (Whitfield 1994; italics added).[31]

In response to the town council's continued pursuit of pedestrianization, a meeting was called by the Glastonbury Residents' Association (GRA) in the summer of 1994 to put forward a vote of nonconfidence in the council. Attended by about two hundred like-minded residents, the meeting revealed a self-selected community defining itself in opposition to its "others"—those who truly "*live* here" and "belong here" versus those who don't or cannot be trusted (or both):

> "I'm damned if I see this town become a tourist satellite to places like Street." [Huge applause.]

> "You *live* here. . . *You're* not the visitors. You're not the travellers. You're not the tourists." [Huge applause.]

> "The fear here is the fear of pedestrianization making a good home for the '*other* residents' that we have. [Massive applause] . . . Swainbridge, Totnes, Barnstable [towns that have gone ahead with pedestrianization schemes]— have they got the '*other* residents' that we have? . . . Beer bottles, cider bottles. . . . What has happened to our town? . . . going to spend all this money on posh pavement stones. . . . We are frightened of having our roads blocked off. . . . We don't want our town pedestrianized." [Massive applause.]

Throughout the pedestrianization controversy, the press (notably the *Central Somerset Gazette*) gave a broad platform for the GRA, its chairman Mike Free, and town council allies Clive Browning and Andy Andrews. In contrast, their coverage of opposing voices, such as that of Mayor Dennis Allen and County Councillor Susan Openshaw, consistently framed them in a less favorable light. A May 5, 1994, cover story was ominously headlined "New mayor's first words to public: I accuse. . . ." A June 9, 1994, cover story, "Council Faces Town Revolt," was printed only after the GRA had only *booked* the town hall for the meeting at which they planned to stage their own "town revolt." Susan Openshaw later described the meeting as unrepresentative of the town, saying it was attended by "a certain caste and point of view." Councillor Browning, on the other hand, called the meeting's supporters "true Glastonians": it was "the town's heart that came out. We, the people, voted and it was a vote for common sense" (*CSG* July 14, 1994). *Gazette* coverage of the meeting was headlined "'Caste' Jibe Sparks Row," the editors choosing to focus on Openshaw's caste comment rather than on Browning's equally offensive suggestion that only the GRA and its supporters were "*true* Glastonians" and "the town's heart."

The test of how much support the GRA actually had came in the spring of 1995. Advocating a wait-and-see policy to gauge the effect of "enhancement" on High Street, GRA representatives swept into power in town council elections, with its chairman Mike Free leading the way as the new mayor. Dubbed by the *Central Somerset Gazette* "the new broom which swept in to power" around the town enhancement issue (*CSG* May 11, 1995:1), the GRA moved quickly to try to stop the closure of Northload Street to vehicles. The building of the western relief road had meanwhile gone forward. As a project of the district and county councils, and with few local voices strongly objecting to it, the £8 million road was completed in the spring of 1995 (built on the disused Somerset and Dorset railroad line). But efforts to pedestrianize the town center have remained controversial and limited.[32]

The Tor as a Liminal Zone

While Glastonbury's town center has been fought over, and traffic rerouted around its western outskirts, its eastern flank, like the mystical reputation of the town as a whole, has been held up by that heterotopic space par excellence, the Tor. An international meeting place, particularly in the summer, when it attracts visitors from all over the world, the Tor is used by various groups for gatherings and celebrations, and informally for private meditation, music making, and the like. A given summer evening might find anywhere from a dozen to well over a hundred people gathered to watch the sunset, meditate, play drums and didgeridoos, smoke dope, dance or worship in whatever way, or just hang out.[33] A disproportionate number of "neo-

Figure 5.4. National Trust donation box at foot of the Tor

hippies" is generally in evidence in the summer, clothed in the colorful, patchy, and layered "rainbow gypsy" look, and carrying or playing drums and didgeridoos. For travelers in particular, the Tor constitutes a safe haven. As Ann Morgan explains, the Tor acts as "a beacon that draws certain disenfranchised people—a place which says 'Home' in some way or another":

> There's something about [the Tor] that [implies] "public access." And there's something about people walking up that hill from all directions, and actually arriving at the top, and then you're on the top with whoever else has happened to arrive there with you. . . . And there's a sort of a freedom with that— it's like a sense of being able to *freely meet*, by chance, others who have been called to walk up that Tor at the same time. When I walk up the Tor, sometimes when I need a little bit of perspective—when I need to get up on top of my life and actually look down and look around and see what's going on in my own internal landscape—I often go up the Tor to do that. And I think that's what a public hill in a town does—it offers the inhabitants that [possibility]— it's a device [within that kind of process]. . . . (interview; italics added)

Garrard notes that since the early 1970s, "a loose tendency to gather on the Tor on solstice morning has evolved to infuse a large and colourful community, which generally marks the solstices, equinoxes and cross-quarter days with public celebrations" (1994:25). Spiritual groups—among them the Order of Bards, Ovates and Druids, who use the Tor for Celtic calendar festivals (Mathias and Hector 1979), another Druid order which has used the slopes of the Tor for its May Day festivities (Jones 1990:49), and Essenes, Gnostics, and others—conduct ceremonies atop the Tor and on its sides. The idea that the Tor was once a ritual labyrinth has inspired some to walk this maze on the days of the Celtic seasonal "fire-festivals." Kathy Jones, a leader of such ceremonial walks, describes the maze as "like an electric current": "once we were on it there was no stopping. . . . My feet knew where to go" (BBC n.d.). Jones leads walkers through to the center of the maze, where it is suggested they may find themselves—or the unacknowledged "shadow" side of themselves (BBC n.d.; Jones, int.). The prepatriarchal Goddess-centered stratum of the Tor's imagined history has allowed it to develop as a symbol of resistance to the "establishment," whether that be the patriarchal Christian church, as it was portrayed in *The Mists of Avalon*, or rationalist modernity.

The use of the Tor by travelers, however, and especially its use for loud celebrations and drumming in the summer months, is frequently lamented by local residents. Chilkwell Street residents have repeatedly threatened to sue the National Trust for not upholding its own bylaws, which prohibit music or camping on Trust land (CSG, August 10, 1995:1). At the same time, Catholics, with their annual pilgrimage up the Tor, local farmers and residents, and other groups, continue to use the Tor for their own purposes. The National Trust, meanwhile, continues to play a low-key role in managing the Tor for its multiple users: maintaining the stonework, repairing fences, managing wildlife, cleaning up litter, and so on, while continuing its policy of unrestricted access to the Tor (against the wishes of a minority of local residents).[34]

"SACRED GLASTONBURY" AND ITS FUTURES

> The sanctity of Glastonbury . . . was decreed directly by nature. That conclusion is made obvious to anyone who visits Glastonbury, especially at dawn or evening when the mystical quality of the light over its landscape is particularly intense. As one enters the Glastonbury landscape, over the hills which surround its lowlands, one's perception of natural light and color subtly changes. Around the towering cone of Glastonbury Tor is a countryside which gives the impression of being somehow different from any other. It can seem wistful, nostalgic, other-worldly, even intimidating, but it is never quite ordinary.
>
> Those who recognize the spirit of the Celtic culture can find it there, in the limpid greenery of its hills and meadows and secluded among its moorland tracks and waterways, edged with willows and summer garlands of honeysuckle and wild roses. Seeing this, one ceases to wonder why the place has been compared to paradise, why so many mystics and holy men throughout history have been drawn to it and why its medieval abbey was able to boast the finest collection of saintly bones and relics in England.
>
> —JOHN MICHELL, *New Light on the Ancient Mystery of Glastonbury*

For nearly three decades, John Michell has been a controversial and highly visible public figure on the intellectual margins of British society. Michell is the author of numerous books, and his *New Light on the Ancient Mystery of Glastonbury* (1990) is frequently touted as the best overview of the Glastonbury mysteries by believers in them. The two paragraphs quoted above typify his style of argumentation. Glastonbury's sanctity is ascribed to nature itself. He makes much of the "mystical quality of the light," a quality one can find in many other places in England, but which one is more likely to find in Glastonbury—if one is instructed to look for it there. Michell writes, "Those who recognize the spirit of the Celtic culture can find it there." The key words here are *recognize* and *find*: if you know what you are looking for, you may well recognize it. *Re*-cognition implies that what you are looking for has an earlier or objective correlate, a prototype, the reality of which is pregiven, for instance, by nature. Michell has little interest in the many question marks and unknowns in our knowledge of the ancient

Celts. For him, the Celtic spirit is felt "in the limpid greenery of [Glas-
tonbury's] hills and meadows and secluded among its moorland tracks and
waterways, edged with willows and summer garlands of honeysuckle and
wild roses." This indeed sounds like a description of paradise, a pastoral,
very much white-English, countryside version of paradise. There is no question for him but that "so many mystics and holy men throughout history"
have held this same vision; nor are there any politics involved in the Abbey's
"boast[ing] the finest collection of saintly bones and relics in England."
But there *is* a politics in Michell's evocation of the past, a mystical paleo-
conservatism and romantic British (Anglo-Celtic) nationalism, which has
been paradoxically refigured into a late modern countercultural call for a
global spiritual ecology. In the next section I will attempt to show how it is
that this mixture of sentiments flows in to fill the channels which are opened
in and through the encounter of ecospiritual pilgrims' desires and the landscape of Glastonbury.

A Pilgrim Phenomenology

Glastonbury's pilgrims and visitors fall into two main types: the traditional,
and the alternative or New Age. The first includes those interested in England's heritage, many of whom arrive on coach tours and whose primary
focus is the Abbey ruins. This category also includes Christian visitors interested in the religious history of the town, who may come for a spiritual retreat at the Abbey Retreat House, for the Christian pilgrimage weekend in
June, or for some other occasion. It is the second type, however, which concerns us here. Glastonbury's many alternative and New Age guesthouses
and healing centers receive visitors from various parts of the world throughout the year. Group tours, such as those conducted by Gothic Image Tours
or by the Isle of Avalon Foundation, bring in additional numbers, and their
promotional literature is distributed far and wide.

Gothic Image, the bookstore-cum-publishing-house, organizes two broad-
ranging tours which feature Glastonbury as a prominent focus: "Magical
Britain" and "The Quest for King Arthur's Avalon." These boast such hosts
and guides as Geoffrey Ashe, Paul Devereux, John Michell, R. J. Stewart,
John and Caitlin Matthews, Moyra Caldecott, Hamish Miller, and Paul
Broadhurst—in other words, the crème de la crème of Britain's alternative
spirituality scene. Isle of Avalon Tours focus more on Glastonbury itself and
its immediate environs; they offer "weekend breaks" as well as week-long
excursions ("The Magical Journey" and "Esoteric Avalon"). In their promotional literature, Glastonbury is billed as a "World Sacred Site," playing "a
fundamental role in the spiritual transformation of the British Isles." Pilgrims are told about Arthur, Joseph and Jesus, Morgan le Fay and Brigit the
Swan Maiden, the Neolithic "ceremonial labyrinth to the ancient Goddess," and the "Druidic college" of two thousand years ago; and promised
that "the island acts as a spiritual magnifying glass, amplifying the strength

of both positive and negative energies, giving the individual a unique oppor-tunity to accelerate the process of their own growth and awareness" (Isle of Avalon Tours 1995).

A phenomenology of the Glastonbury pilgrim's experience of the land-scape must be, in part, a phenomenology of the symbols and images which organize and inform this experience. In the case of New Age, ecospiritual, countercultural, or alternative pilgrims and visitors, the most prominent symbols and images are the Grail and Arthur's Round Table; the landscape as a network of energy ley lines; the earth as teeming with underground and emergent energies focused at specific places, including the wells, springs, and Tor; the Tor in particular as an entry to the Underworld and place "be-tween the worlds"; the landscape zodiac; and the Goddess. I have eluci-dated some of the meanings and histories of these images; now I will try to present a coherent picture of their role in one's encounter with the land-scape.

In the process of traveling to and arriving in Glastonbury, an array of evocative hints at an ancient importance charges up the pilgrim's imagina-tion. Most visitors to the town have at least a vague idea of some of its many legends and myths, and most have heard either of its medieval status as a significant Christian pilgrimage site or of its imagined status as an ancient holy place. The many legends and tales—most of which can neither be proven nor definitively disproven—offer up a rich matrix of interpretive possibilities for pilgrims. Interpretation is a free-spirited activity, a promis-cuous building up and drawing together of associations, coincidences, per-sonal meanings, and occurrences; and when one is particularly inclined to look for these connections, whether because of a personal predilection or because one may be undergoing a personal crisis and is looking for indica-tions or "signs" of some sort, little effort is needed for this to begin to occur.

> *After more than a week here I find myself increasingly thinking of Glastonbury, and of the Tor in particular, as* subjects, *active agents exercising a mysterious influence over me. For instance, after getting ill following my first climb of the Tor (on this particular visit to the town), I wondered if it was the Tor "getting its revenge on me" for deigning to climb it so soon, instead of respecting my instinct to wait and approach it more gradually, allowing it time to accept me and my work here. But why should the Tor want to "get back at me," and why should it care about me at all? What would put such an idea into my head?* (personal notes, summer, 1994)

Looking out over the town, achieving a visual overview of it, Glastonbury appears as an island of three or so connected hills, with the Tor dominating from behind the smaller and softer curve of Chalice Hill, and Wearyall Hill jutting out to form a limb extended to the southwest. The landscape is soft; it humps out of the surrounding lowland like an outstretched lump of green jelly made up of several rounded clumps. Spending time in Glastonbury, walking its streets, climbing its hills, visiting and drinking from its springs, meditating atop the Tor, one begins to experience and feel it from the inside, as it were, to get to know its intimate particulars. The phenomenology of wells and of underground water sources plays an important role in this. Wells connect this world with the world below the earth; they literally gush out from the Underworld. Their sources are invisible and frequently (as in Glastonbury) unknown, which adds to their mystery. Wells and springs are considered "primary water"—water that is more pure than other kinds, with a higher mineral content, and frequently a constant temperature and flow. Wells have traditionally, in the British Isles, been venerated for their sanctity, or at least for their ability (or that of their resident spirits) to heal and grant wishes. The more popular wishing wells in southwest England and Ireland have accumulated hundreds of votive objects of cloth, stone, metal, or clay, left behind by visitors and pilgrims. (Glastonbury's White Spring has now become such a place.) Connected to this mysticism of water and of subterranean sources of strength, healing, and power, is the Grail mythos. Grails, cups, bowls, like wells and springs, are objects whose form suggests containment and nourishment, a "feminine" symbolism of womb, cave, and tomb, a surface hiding unknown depths. The Grail has an earlier analogue in Celtic myth—the Cauldron of wisdom, inspiration, poetry, and rebirth, connected with the goddess Cerridwen. Its function is to nourish and revivify a wasteland; and for a late-twentieth-century pilgrim, that wasteland may be internal, a perceived spiritual hunger, or it may be that of industrial-capitalist modernity, or it may be both. This mystique is woven into the continuing myth of an ancient yet ever-present isle of Avalon, an enchanted and mysterious place, with its green hills and healing waters, surrounded by swamps and moors.

The Tor expresses this same sense of mystery and subterranean depths, at the same time as it is a hill, a beacon, a "cosmic mountain" overlooking the world and serving as its "world axis"; it reveals a tension between an upward and a downward directed movement. Seen from a distance, the Tor presents itself as an uncanny landmark on the Somerset horizon; taking on different forms depending on the viewer's placement in relationship to it, its uncanniness hardly decreases once it has been reached and climbed. A climber feels herself rising above the surrounding landscape, able to view it more panoptically as its panoramic spread opens up all around. Wind or mist below the summit can increase this sense of separation from the mundane world below. Centered around the Tor's summit, with its crowning tower, the windswept body of the Tor lays itself out toward the sky. In the landscape surrounding it, the terrestrial zodiac is imagined to lay itself out similarly toward the sky: a balanced and harmonious energy field spontaneously ordered like the spokes of a wheel, the twelve apostles, constellations, knights of the Round Table, or the legendary Twelve Hides of Glastonbury.

At the same time, the presence of springs emerging from beneath the Tor, the legends of the Underworld, tales of tunnels and underwater streams, of the Tor being hollow, of earthquakes, such as the one which destroyed the medieval church, and the associations with a reclining Goddess figure—all these draw the attention *down* into the earth beneath the Tor. Nick Mann writes: "Under the Tor is a vortex of elemental energy created by the force-field of water in motion. Several inexhaustible springs rise under it. But the Tor was not sacred only to the Yin, water, earth-goddess, rainbow serpent-energy, for many straight lines of Yang, fire, air, rainbow dragon-power converge on its top" (1985:7). The water beneath the Tor is supposed to be of enormous volume. Though its only overt evidence is a metal door covering a Water Board maintenance hole, the flow beneath which is quite loud, the water is known to cut tunnels into the soft limestone, contributing to insta-bility in the overlying sandstone and fissures in the bedrock. Furthermore, as Mann notes, "Water diviners report a connection between this 'upshoot' of primary water below the Tor, and the terraces which spiral around it. The moving water appears to create a vortex of 'elemental' energy which the terraces synthesize with and elaborate" (1985:16). The Tor's terraces sug-gest a spiraling labyrinth, the inside of a horn or a shell, and a journey in as well as up. Their appearance from above suggests the female labia, entry place to the womb of the earth, place of birth and of spiritual rebirth. They also conjure up dragon associations which evoke another binary pair: that of St. Michael, the Christian dragonslayer (his tower the sole remaining frag-ment of his medieval church) and the pagan earth dragon. Michael's Celtic analogue is said to be Belin, the sun god; so this opposition readily becomes the universal opposition of light and dark, interpreted by mystics not as a struggle but as a complementary duality.

Glastonbury, for the mystically and esoterically inclined, thus becomes a place of rebalancing—between the red and the white, between life and death, light and dark, God and Goddess, Michael and Mary, male and fe-male, fire and water, sky and earth, Christian and pagan. This complemen-tary duality is captured by the emblematic Vesica Piscis, now etched into the wooden door capping the Chalice Well. This balancing motif recurs everywhere—once the habit is gained of seeing it. The Michael and Mary line, invisible to the untrained eye or psyche, is a schematic representation of two interlocking energy currents, which—like the Hermetic and Hippo-cratic caduceus that has been taken as an emblem of healing by the modern medical community—run up and down the body of England: one of them (Michael) more linear, traveling along higher places and church towers; the other (Mary) sinuous and flowing, connecting lower-situated sites and holy wells.[35]

This transformative rebalancing—of the psyche and of the world—oc-curs as an initiatory experience, a rite de passage. The pilgrim travels to the sacred site, undergoes difficult experiences—loss, sacrifice (of whatever needs to be "released"), an initiatory, symbolic death—in order to be reborn and remade, healed and made whole. If Glastonbury is thought of as the Celtic Isle of the Dead, it is a kind of "no-go zone," at least for those un-willing to confront their inner demons or dragons. On the Tor one travels through a labyrinth inward—to the still voice of the Spirit within—and then back out to the world.[36] The physical landscape around the Tor contributes to the aura of mystery such an initiatory place requires.

Bringing these elements together, Glastonbury's particular pilgrim phenomenology can be seen to depend on a combination of factors. First is the wealth of already existing lore: evocative stories and legends, symbols and images, all available for "processing" and interpretive appropriation to suit contemporary needs, such as the desire for a spiritual connection to the Earth, for feminine personifications of divinity, or for healing and regeneration of the wasteland of modern life. Second, and equally crucial, is the creative imagination and intentionality of Glastonbury's pilgrims. In recent years the town's new spiritual pilgrims and visitors have brought with them certain expectations based on what Glastonbury represents to them, along with a readiness to encounter and receive signs, visions, or answers to life-probing questions. These reflect a broader cultural desire for a sense of reconnection with the Earth, with nature, and with extramodern sources of authority. Finally, there is the fact of the landscape itself, already carved by many centuries of forest clearance, drainage, flood control, and land enclosure. It is a landscape which offers up a richness of interpretive possibilities, and which does not foreclose these possibilities through clear historical evidence, but rather makes them available for further expansion, suggestion, projection, and interpretation. Chief among these landscape features are those which particularly correspond to the new pilgrims' desires: the weirdly shaped Tor evokes a sense of mystery and magic, rising like a once-slumbering but now reawakening dragon, with its beaconlike tower signaling to the urban centers of England from the misty, dreamy southwest; wells and springs evoke the imagery of healing, purification, and regeneration of a parched and despiritualized wasteland; and the experience of climbing the Tor and "getting to know" Glastonbury from the inside, in its many contrasting polarities (Tor-Abbey, high-low, etc.), evokes and in turn responds to a desire for the reconciliation of opposites. The lay of the land, its shapes and contours, accommodates itself to the perception of the Earth as a living and energized being: if the Earth is perceived as a Goddess, then springs of clear, primary waters, arising from the mysterious, moist, and dark inner sanctuaries of her body, are her gifts to us; and if she is energetically alive, then her hills are the beacons, protuberances, or energy gathering points on that body's surface.

Glastonbury today contains these three factors in abundance. The particular symbols associated with its lore have ready physical analogues as well as historical precedents (such as the earlier claims around Arthur and the "first church" of Britain/Europe). The rest is imagined into existence on the spot. Today's Glastonbury, then, is a place where landscape and history have conspired with cultural desire to produce a space for imagining an alternative relationship with the Earth, a geography that contrasts with and, it is hoped, might replace the dominant one of industrial modernity. Whether this imaginative and interpretive drift will lead toward any tangible changes is the question around which my remaining musings will focus, and the answer in part depends on the changing role of the alternative community within the town.

A Changing "Alternative"

Evidence for most of the earth-mysteries claims about Glastonbury rests in the realm of the unprovable and, as a consequence, opinions remain sharply divided between the faithful and the skeptical. A situation has arisen in Glastonbury where, as Benham puts it, "strange and wild specimens of humanity" are "drawn to the place by strange and wild rumours of lines of power and forthcoming cosmic revelations"; later "more and more strange and wild people arrive just to be near the others, the purpose of the pilgrimage forgotten" (Benham 1993: xvii). Meanwhile, Glastonbury's association, through its rock festival, with the musical counterculture of the sixties is periodically refreshed with waves of the disaffiliated and unemployed (punks, ravers, etc.) trailing along with the convoy after the dispersals of the Stonehenge gatherings, peace demonstrations, or more recent road protests.

Like Stonehenge, Glastonbury has become a symbol of youthful, and increasingly societal, disaffiliation from contemporary English modernity and from urban industrial civilization as a whole. As a town of only eight thousand, Glastonbury has amplified its extremes, pitting small-town conservatives against colorful dropouts, self-styled messiahs, and New Age visionaries. The former perceive the latter as deviant weirdos, while the latter define themselves by their differences from the "straights" or "locals": as Glastafarians and not Glastonians, and as "alternatives" opposed to some vaguely defined mainstream, "system," or "establishment." The alternative community distinguishes itself especially through its understanding of Glastonbury. Ruth Prince observes, "Every such informant I encountered in Glastonbury considered the area to be 'spiritually significant' in some way; it was common to attribute a concentration of spiritual energy, described as an animating and manipulative power, to the area. The main focal points for such a power are the Tor and the Chalice Well. Over the winter and summer solstice it is common for people to gather on these two points as well as being common places for regular and individual meditations. . . . in conversation an assumed reverence surrounds discussion of these places as sacred" (1991:45). The travelers generally share this positive, "spiritual" assessment of Glastonbury, though it is usually more implicit or vaguely worded. As the alternative residents have endeavored to be accepted or tolerated within Glastonbury, however, the boundary between them and the travelers has been a malleable and, at times, emotionally charged one. Many among the alternative community, especially those who have themselves been travelers in the past, feel a natural affinity for and protectiveness toward them.

When travelers cause problems in town, however, "this backfires upon the alternative community as a whole and people's attitudes become mixed" (58). Reflecting on their differences, members of the alternative community often acknowledge a difference both in lifestyle and in beliefs (59). Conversations I have had with "alternatives" lead me to believe that their patience with the "drongos" and "crusties" can potentially wear thin. Travelers, in turn, feel an ambivalence and sometimes a resentment to the sanitized comforts of Glastonbury's "established" alternative community.

In recent years, the relations between the alternative community and other locals have been evolving as well. Many mainstream residents have come to accept the presence of the alternative community, primarily, it seems, because it has established itself as an economic contributor to the town (Garrard, int.). The rise of the alternative community in the early 1980s was in part a response to local economic conditions. As Bowman (1993:53) explains, the largest local employer, the Morlands sheepskin manufacturer, had made a large percentage of its workforce redundant in the 1970s, with the result that a lot of property was for sale in the town at affordable prices. Small alternative businesses have been started up since then with funds from the Margaret Thatcher–initiated Enterprise Allowance scheme. In the eyes of a growing minority of Glastonbury's more entrepreneurial residents concerned about Britain's integration into the global economy, the alternative community has even become a positive asset for the town's potential as a tourist destination. A long-time activist told me, "We've been here for so long now, and people can see that, actually, we are the color of the town, and we are the new business life of the town. And there are a lot of people, say, in the Chamber of Commerce or Town Council, who would see that if the alternative community suddenly disappeared there'd be very little left, and Glastonbury would end up looking like a clone of Somerton or Dorchester—it would just be another kind of tidy town on the tourist trail" (Morgan, int.).

This process of revaluation of the town's alternative community can be usefully compared with the model of rural social and economic restructuring derived by rural sociologists Paul Cloke, Mike Goodwin, and their colleagues from research on other nonmetropolitan centers in Britain (Cloke and Goodwin 1992; Cloke and Thrift 1987; Cloke and Little 1997). In many places affected by counterurbanization and the commodification of the "rural idyll," Cloke and Goodwin write, one finds the "occurrence of 'two nations' in the same rural place and intra-class conflict therein, with existing residents often feeling marginalized and being least well able to cope with reductions in local services and facilities" (1992:331). This leads, in their analysis, to a "contesting of local political power," with the "historic and hegemonic bloc" of propertied and paternalistic local agrarian elites "first attempting to hold onto their local elite status, then maybe attempting to forge alliances with in-coming class fractions and finally in some cases relinquishing their hegemonic position" (331). Though the "rural idyll" represented by Glastonbury has been a somewhat unusual one, this has prevented neither the initial stage of conflict between the local elite (and long-time residents) and newcomers, nor the emergence of new alliances between originally divergent class fractions. All of this has been accompanied, as Clark and Goodwin suggest it should, by a "contesting of local cultural images" with starkly different place-myths and images shaped by the divergent interpretive communities (331).

Ann Morgan's comments about Glastonbury being *more* than just another "tidy town on the tourist trail" implies a recognition such tidy towns compete against each other, and that Glastonbury's "extras," rather than being liabilities, as the GRA insist, could be seen as assets in this competitive economy of rural differences. The alternative community faces some challenging questions in considering its role in the town's future. Its countercultural origins and inherent suspicion of capitalist values have over the years played ambivalently against the community's growing recognition that an economic base is essential for its existence. In her ethnography, Prince (1991:120–21) notes an unwillingness within the alternative community to discuss people's sources of income, and concludes that this reticence is both a part of the alternative ideology itself, and a result of the paradoxical reliance, for some, on government welfare checks or Enterprise Allowance grants at the same time that they espouse an alternative doctrine. This is reflective of a larger set of ambivalences. On the one hand, the alternative community "criticizes the capitalist, materialist and Thatcherite ethos," considering it contrary to its values of community cohesion and spiritual and ecological interconnectedness. On the other hand it, ironically, mirrors neoliberalism in its strong individualism, its valuation of personal freedom and self-development achievable through material enterprise.

A wide range of views can be found among members of the alternative community on matters of economics and livelihood (cf. Prince 1991:79–97). These include a strong antimarket orientation and a preference for the informal economy of barter, exchange, and low-cost recycling of materials; an "occupational pluralism" within which people take on multiple part-time forms of employment, self-employment, crafts work, or dependence on state subsidies; and frequent reference to ideas of "right livelihood," influenced by E. F. Schumacher's writings on Buddhist economics, and of "prosperity consciousness," a New Age idea developed in the United States and often criticized as a legitimizing philosophy for a yuppie "spiritual materialism." With the growth in New Age tourism, prosperity-conscious entrepreneurs increasingly diverge from the dedicated alternative society advocates—still found among those attempting to live cooperatively off the land, utilizing permaculture farming methods, envisioning an alternative and green economy, and so on. Glastonbury's traveler-turned-shopkeeper Bruce Garrard (1994:28) has written about the possibilities of developing an "alternative sector," "controlled by the people," which would contrast with the "private sector, controlled by big business interests" and the "public sector, controlled by the government."

Meanwhile, popular resistance to state and corporate power, particularly in their collusion with a neoliberal economic agenda, continues to manifest in Britain's DIY culture of antiroad protesters, squatters, travelers, and land rights advocates. Within the imaginative geography of their alternative Britain—in which activists struggle for the designation of traveler sites, conservation of green spaces and public lands, and allowing for cooperative and alternative land uses—places like Glastonbury maintain an important symbolic role, one which would be eliminated (in Glastonbury's case) if the impulse to capitalize on tourism was given free rein.[37] This attraction Glastonbury has held for society's unwanted—travelers and dropouts of different generations—has acted as a form of social insulation, or self-protection, as Ann Morgan calls it: "If Glastonbury hadn't been full of 'dirty hippies' it might have become an upmarket tourist trap. But the 'dirty hippies' sitting around made sure that that didn't happen. So there is a sense in which the town of Glastonbury itself . . . has been continuously protected. . . . Nothing's been spoiled yet" (Morgan, int.). Whether this "self-protection" can be put to good use may depend on whether the region's strengths, which include its religious history and its environmental distinctiveness (e.g., the wetland ecology of the Somerset Levels and Moors), are protected and cultivated. This could best occur through a more constructive dialogue between the different communities that stand to benefit from it—that is, not only the alternative community, but small business owners and other residents, among them the Christian communities in the town.

Christians and New Agers

While the alternative community has been establishing itself as a permanent presence in the town, a recognition has grown among a minority of local Christians that Glastonbury can become an important center of religious renewal. This is especially the case among a growing contingent of Charismatic worshippers, followers of the Pentecostal-style Charismatic prayer movement which appeared fairly suddenly in the Anglican Church in the mid-1990s. An important element of Charismatic worship is its prophetic component, which is exemplified by Reverend David Saunders's Glastonbury prophecy, read to worshippers during a series of meetings in the summer of 1995.[38] In the text of this "prophecy," Saunders describes a vision he had of a cauldron filled with gently bubbling gold, against the backdrop of a detailed map of Glastonbury. "The gold started to rise up and slowly overflow down the sides of the cauldron and form a pool of pure gold beneath it, over the whole town of Glastonbury." It then began "to flow down the lay [sic] lines" to the neighboring towns of Wells, Bath, and Butleigh; and "the Lord told him" that Glastonbury would be "the centre of this outpouring," but that "we must be very wise, to be subject to authority at all times, and to be careful in all we do in His name." As is evident, this prophecy makes use of imagery more commonly found in New Age writings but frames these within a cautious and thoroughly institutional Christian context.[39]

I referred earlier to Marjorie Milne and Rev. James Turnbull, whose willingness to work with hippies and New Agers lies at one end of a continuum of Christian attitudes. A one-time trustee of the Assembly Rooms, Turnbull had conducted prayer meetings at Greenlands Farm in the 1980s, and once spoke of the "hippy invasions" as a form of Jesus' second coming, saying, "I think that Jesus came both in the seventies and in 1985" (Turnbull 1988:17).[40] The majority of Glastonbury's Christian churches, however, have been less than sanguine about the New Age presence in the town. The more reactionary conservatives have been openly hostile, and their periodic accusations of "devil worship" and "black magic" still find their way into the local press.[41] Beyond such overt hostility, however, an increased tolerance has crept in on both sides of the spiritual divide over the years. Though the Christian and New Age communities may not see eye to eye, the creeping parallelism within their ranks around their respective beliefs about Glastonbury and its spiritual role may harbor potential for future convergence (e.g., Spink 1991). As New Age and ecospiritual ideas have become more popular in the broader culture, the alternative community's identity as an *alternative* has lost some of its distinctive focus. This is exacerbated by the apparent difficulties of any organizational efforts within the community, and by its inherent fluidity and high level of transience. The alternative community has weathered many storms in its history—debates over gender equality, the virtues and pitfalls of competing New Age ideas and practices, and soul-searching reflections on its relationship with Britain's traveling and homeless population. The blurring of the community's boundaries and its impending integration with the surrounding culture may mean that these lessons will be lost as the town develops its spiritual-tourist potential—a prospect which is capturing the interest of a growing quiet majority of more sympathetic and open-minded residents. On the other hand, the diverse spiritually and environmentally concerned members of the town (Christians and New Agers, among others), to the extent that their commonalities overshadow their differences, could play a more active role in preserving an appropriate ambience in the town and thereby avoiding the more crass forms of tourist development.

Something Buried, Something Lost, Something Forgotten?

Toward the end of his *New Light on the Ancient Mystery of Glastonbury*, John Michell draws attention to the persistent legend "that some powerful and precious relic lies buried at Glastonbury—at the site of the Abbey, on Chalice Hill or somewhere else nearby" (1990:164). This seems a recurrent dream. Somewhere, something has been buried, lost, or forgotten, and those who feel its loss gravitate to places like Glastonbury as if they might find it there. The search did not end with the "discoveries" of Arthur's tomb or Goodchild's glass vessel, nor with Bond's incessant, obsessive digging. The legends of a golden age restored, a lost object recovered, a New Jerusalem of spiritual enlightenment—are these mere fantasies that haunt the disenchanted mind? Are they a displacement of consumer capitalism's incessant desire for novelty? Are there no mysteries, no secrets to be found? Or is the secret the search itself, the liminal space of the utopian imagination—the realm of imaginative desire which opens liberatory possibilities (but becomes dangerous when congealed into totalizing programs or manifest destinies)? Lady Morgaine's words in *The Mists of Avalon* fittingly describe this Glastonbury of the imagination:

> For this is the great secret, which was known to all educated men in our day: that by what men think, we create the world around us, daily new. . . .
>
> For this is the thing the priests do not know, with their One God and One Truth: that there is no such thing as a true tale. Truth has many faces and the truth is like to the old road to Avalon; it depends on your own will and your own thoughts, whither the road will take you. . . . (Bradley 1984:ix–x)

PART THREE

SEDONA

The very forest-fringed earth seemed to have opened into a deep abyss, ribbed by red rock walls and choked by steep mats of green timber. The chasm was a V-shaped split and so deep that looking downward sent at once a chill and a shudder over Carley. At that point it appeared narrow and ended in a box. In the other direction, it widened and deepened, and stretched farther on between tremendous walls of red, and split its winding floor of green with glimpses of a gleaming creek, boulder-strewn and ridged with white rapids. A low mellow roar of rushing waters floated up to Carley's ears. What a wild, lonely, terrible place! . . . And on the moment the sun burst through the clouds and sent a golden blaze down into the depths, transforming them incalculably. The great cliffs turned gold, the creek changed to glancing silver, the green of trees vividly freshened, and in the clefts rays of sunlight burned into the blue shadows. Carley had never gazed upon a scene like this. Hostile and prejudiced, she yet felt wrung from her an acknowledgment of beauty and grandeur. But wild, violent, savage! Not livable! This insulated rift in the crust of the earth was a gigantic burrow for beasts, perhaps for outlawed men—not for a civilized person—not for Glenn Kilbourne.

—Carley Burch encountering Oak Creek Canyon
in ZANE GREY's *Call of the Canyon* (1924)

Ultimately we read [Zane Grey's] books not because he tells us about life, but because he does not.

—ANN RONALD, specialist in Western American literature

Even middle-aged cynicism doesn't save me from gape-mouthed stupefaction as I drive down from Flagstaff into the Verde Valley one not so fine March day thirty years later to see what, if anything, has happened in my absence. . . . I wind down through a Christmas forest of Ponderosa pine, Douglas and white fir. Visibility zero. The weather is no better twenty-five hundred feet below the rim, and I find myself in . . . *Switzerland?* Well, no, that Matterhorn there is a motel. Which is right next to another motel. Which is across the road from another motel. In front of which there seem to be a dozen tour buses, all of them idling on an apron of asphalt as their cargo mills about, spilling out onto the highway, crowding around a little cluster of outdoor trinket vendors who seem oblivious to the snow. Where am I? I creep along for about a mile, past a continuous strip of gift shops, real estate offices, motels, restaurants, cocktail lounges, craft centers, art galleries, boutiques, Indian pottery, baskets, jewelry, kachinas, sand paintings, pawn, handcrafted this, authentic that, unusual, exclusive, unique. It suddenly occurs to me that I am here. Sedona. *My town trip.*

—WALLACE STEGNER, "The New Riders of
the Purple Sage" (italics in original)

Sedona is not really a town. It is a series of brilliantly colored picture postcards, laid end to end, that have somehow come to life. First, there is all that brilliant, towering red rock. There are those blues and yellows and tints of orange. Then, there is the awesome, somnolent, still very private, Oak Creek Canyon. These two things . . . and these two things alone . . . give Sedona its unique credentials.

—TOM FITZPATRICK, "Picture Postcard"

And the abrupt mountains, the echoing, rock walled cañons, the sunburnt mesas, the streams bankrupt by their own shylock sands, the gaunt, brown, treeless plains, the ardent sky, all harmonize with unearthly unanimity.

—CHARLES F. LUMMIS, *The Land of Poco Tiempo*

Figure 6.1. Passing Bell Rock

SIX

Red Rocks to Real Estate

In an erudite essay on the many definitions of the U.S. Southwest, James Byrkit describes the characteristic physiographic features of this area, the boundaries of which are notoriously difficult to pin down: "Rugged mountains and large rocks; sharp, steep canyons; irregular basins and valleys; wide deserts; high plateaus; small but high-elevation meadows and parks; and hydrologic playas dominate the physiographic Southwest" (1992:289). The Southwest is notable for its overall aridity, a "cleanliness and crispness of the air"(290), wide temperature ranges and long hours of sunlight. "You know," says Erna Fergusson, "When you get that first clear breath of high, dry air. That's the Southwest" (in Byrkit 1992:262). It is a "land of challenge—a harsh country of drastically changing moods which has constantly tested the mettle of man." (Charles DiPeso, in Byrkit 1992:268). "Barren and beautiful," the Southwest is "both a place and a state of mind" (258).

In the cultural production of this enchanted Southwest, images of forbidding nature, vastness, and mystical grandeur have been interbred with a series of cultural stereotypes—Mission/Hacienda Hispanics, dignified and mystical "noble savage" Indians, and rugged individualist cowboys (352). The watershed year for the birth of this particular Southwest, writes Byrkit, was 1884, the year in which both the Southern Pacific and the Atlantic and Pacific railroads were completed, and the same year in which Helen Hunt Jackson's classic "Southwest" novel *Ramona* was published. Until nearly the mid-nineteenth century, in fact, most of New Mexico and Arizona were left virtually untouched by Europeans, except for a few Spanish gold-seeking conquistadores and some scattered enclaves of Hispanic settlers. Few of the Anglos to visit the area wrote anything positive about its inhabitants *or* its landscape (344). But by the turn of the century, the two states were virtually transformed by Anglo-American colonizers—and, correspondingly, the new Southwest genre of fiction, anthropology, adventure, and discovery writing was firmly established in the canons of American identity (345ff.). The railway companies, tourist entrepreneurs, and corporate image makers of the late nineteenth century transformed the region into a "mythological holy land of grand natural wonders, inspirational primitive arts, and domesticated, artistic 'natives'" (Weigle 1989:133). [1]

The selective portrayal of the Southwest as a Land of Enchantment continues to this day, as affluent white Americans from California, Chicago, and New York flock to Santa Fe, Taos, Scottsdale, and Sedona to buy art, play golf, take photographs, have their fortunes told, build homes, and retire; and as, in Byrkit's words, "Louis L'Amour novels, Marlboro Man cigarette advertising, the Cowboy Artists of America, 'Santa Fe' architecture and furniture, cowboy boots and Stetson hats" continue to "generate millions of dollars in sales each year" (Byrkit 1992:358). [2] The spell of the Southwest and the commodification of its "otherness" has exacted a high historical cost—most obviously, the Native American populations decimated during the Indian Wars or forcibly removed from their ancestral lands and herded onto reservations. And contrary to the popular fantasies of writers like Charles Fletcher Lummis, Charles King, Henry Brinkerhoff, Mary Austin, and Zane Grey, the state of Arizona was effectively industrial before it was agricultural. Its economy, Byrkit argues, "developed out of the investment of big eastern capital, the application of advanced technology, and the extraction of great mineral wealth together with a highly industrialized and commercialized agriculture" (320) and featured "highly industrialized mines and smelters, labor-management warfare, powerful energy-generating turbines, corporate-irrigated agriculture and big-business stock-raising" (356–57). Up until the second World War, the limited riparian areas and mineral belts accounted for most of the Southwest's population. After the war, air conditioning and the increased affluence of American society brought tourists, "snow birds," retirees, and high-tech industries to Arizona, together with an increased vulnerability to the by-products of affluence— made riskier by the pollution-entrapping physiography of basins and valleys and their natural inversion layers. The era of the tourist and the retiree has also been the era of atomic energy, uranium tailings, and pollution.

Within this matrix, north-central Arizona carves out a specific niche. Most of the northernmost part of the state consists of Indian reservations, dominated by the huge Navajo and smaller Hopi homelands of the Four Corners area, and of national parks and forests, which encompass much of the Grand Canyon and Colorado River basin. Arizona's southern half is a hotter and drier territory, consisting largely of deserts and mountain ranges, some of them found within the San Carlos, Fort Apache, and Papago Indian reservations or U.S. army and air force ranges, and the sprawling air-conditioned metropolis of Phoenix and its satellites. North of the state's central area, between the Colorado Plateau and the Sonoran desert lies the Basin and Range area, with the Mogollon Rim, running from northwest to southeast, as its northern boundary. The area known as Red Rock Country and its growing resort capital, Sedona, lie in the middle of this area, some twenty-five miles south of Flagstaff and two hours' drive north of Phoenix.

Sedona is an "oasis" community (Foust, Byrkit, and Avery 1991:71) of some 16,000 people, nestled at the mouth of the scenic box canyon Oak Creek has carved out of the Mogollon Rim as it plunges down a 3,000-foot gorge to the sloping mesa of the Verde Valley. The area is set in the spectacular red rock country of the valley's north end, and is marked by its contrast to the arid semidesert of central and southern Arizona (3,200 ft. lower around Phoenix) and the mountains, pine forests, and dry plateaus to the north (2,600 ft. higher around Flagstaff). In and around Sedona, pink, reddish brown, orange, and copper-colored sandstones and shales have been sculpted by wind and water over millions of years into spectacular mesas, buttes, spires, columns, domes, and arches. Sedona's landscape has, in fact, for decades been anonymously familiar: it has been a backdrop for over sixty Hollywood Westerns and countless television commercials and photographic advertisements.

The twentieth century has seen Sedona evolve from an isolated hamlet and cattle ranchers' supply stop to a prime location for Hollywood Westerns, a retirees' haven and artists' colony, and finally a New Age mecca and major tourist attraction. With 4 to 5 million visitors annually, Sedona rivals the Grand Canyon as Arizona's most popular tourist attraction, luring visitors for its combination of spectacular scenery, moderate climate, and increasing reputation as a spiritual "power spot."[3] This mix of tourism, natural grandeur, and a peculiarly postmodern spiritual magnetism has led to its being called a "cross between Lourdes and the Grand Canyon" (LeFevre 1992:5G). Rather than being set aside as a national park long ago, however,

Figure 6.2. Looking up to Schnebly Hill

much of the area's red rock country was designated national forest land, and subject to multiple uses, land exchanges, and incremental development.[4] In order to have greater control over this development, residents voted to incorporate the city of Sedona in 1988 (the neighboring village of Oak Creek remains unincorporated). The city now has jurisdiction over eighteen square miles, half of which is Coconino National Forest land; but erosion of soils and vegetation, pollution of the creek, and traffic jams during the summer influx of tourists have only gotten worse. The question in many Sedonans' minds today is how to contain the growth and attention the area receives from tourists, while still benefiting from the money they bring in. In this sense, Sedona can stand in for any community that is struggling to balance a new imperative for environmental sustainability with the well-established and economically dominant imperative of development, an imperative that has turned nature itself into a multimillion dollar business. The present chapter will trace the history of desire and imagination that has made Sedona the contested terrain it is today; the chapter that follows will focus on the New Age community, its role in the town, and its ideas and practices of place.

SHAPING SEDONA: A NATURAL HISTORY OF DESIRE AND IMAGINATION

Encountering Sedona at the turn of the millennium means seeing it through a filter redolent with historical (mis)representations, tourist desires and environmentalist dreams, the real estate longings of urban refugees, and the agricultural, corporate-industrial, and high-tech histories sketched out by Byrkit. Beneath these lie deeper layers: the frontier imaginary of Anglo-American settlers, pioneering "Mountain Men," and gold-seeking Spanish explorers before them; and histories of uneasy accommodation between Navajo and Apache, Hopi and Pueblo peoples in a landscape dense with the remnants of earlier, more mysterious antecedents (now known as the Anasazi, Hohokam, and Sinagua). To the extent that there is an "original" landscape here, however, its most obvious shapers have been geological and climatological: the eons-slow movement of layered rock, the repeated advances and retreats of oceans and seas, the vast depositions of sediment they left behind, and the slow sculpture of the resultant landforms by wind and water.

The Sedona region lies at the southern edge of the Colorado Plateau, a vast upland area, most of it over 5,000 feet above sea level, which extends across much of northern Arizona and New Mexico and large parts of Utah and Colorado. The Colorado Plateau consists of extensive areas of relatively horizontal strata of sedimentary rocks, deposited over the course of hundreds of millions years and worked over by ancient oceans, seas, and deserts, uplifting and faulting, and volcanic activity. The alternation of wet and dry periods, punctuated by a major species extinction some 225 million years ago, has left behind a series of seven to ten major layers: among them, Red-wall Limestone, the oldest exposed layer, whose reddish coating of iron oxides gets washed down from red sandstones overlaying this formation; five hundred feet or so of alternating beds of siltstone and sandstone known as the Supai Group; some two hundred feet of purplish red limy sandstone and siltstone called Hermit Shale; and the roughly 800 feet of wind-deposited, grayish orange to reddish brown sand that became the Schnebly Hill Formation, which now forms the famous buttes and spires of Red Rock Country. More recently, lava flows and cinder deposits from the over six hundred volcanoes making up the 3,000-square-mile volcanic field that stretches north from the Mogollon Rim, have left behind basalt outcroppings (visible near the head of Oak Creek Canyon, and around House Mountain and Mingus Mountain to the south) and layers of lava in the Verde Valley. A geologist's narrative history of the area would show a quickening telescopic timeline of eons-slow events: tectonic uplifting to create the Mogollon Highlands (65 million years ago) and the Mogollon Rim (35 million years), followed by extensive faulting and volcanic activity, the excavation of Oak Creek Canyon, the sculpting of the land by landslides, glacial advances and retreats, and weathering, and the postglacial thaw and aridification of the last 10,000 years.[5]

The most geologically significant feature in Arizona is the Mogollon Rim, the 300-mile-long escarpment running in a northwest-to-southeast line some 50 to 150 miles south of the Grand Canyon. Shaped over 30 million years by the faulting occurring at the meeting of the Pacific and the North American Continental Plates, this erosional scar of land stands over 1,000 feet high in places. It has been a central actor shaping the climate of the Colorado Plateau and the drainage and hydrology, soil conditions, and cultural history of Arizona. Part of the intimidating *tierra incógnita y despoblado* that Spanish explorers like Francisco Vásquez de Coronado penetrated with difficulty, the rim now divides the forests to the north from the floodplains and agricultural land in the south, providing cool summer retreats for refugees from the torrid southern Arizona summers. With its alluvial deposits brought by the Salt River, the sprawling megalopolis of Phoenix owes its existence to the rim. So, too, does Arizona's hydroelectricity, aquatic recreation, biotic qualities, floods, and irrigation—and the city of Sedona, lying nestled at its foot amid the most dramatically eroded sedimentary rock formations in the world (Foust, Byrkit, and Avery 1991:25–26).

Acting as a barrier to the warm and moist air masses from the Pacific (in winter) and the Gulf of Mexico (in summer), the Mogollon Rim provides for heavy runoff in February and March and a sometimes spectacular, stormy "monsoon" season between June and September. As a result, the Verde Valley has a comparably lush climate that contrasts sharply with the deserts to the south and the pine forests to the north, supplying the Sedona area with four seasons, moderate average daily temperatures, and an average of thirteen inches of rain per year. With its rugged topography (the altitude descends from 6,400 feet at its head to 4,400 feet at its mouth, just north of Sedona), varied microclimates and permanent water, Oak Creek Canyon has a remarkable assortment of diverse habitats: a ponderosa pine and mixed conifer forest on the canyon's upper slopes (where the U.S. Forest Service's overly protective fire management regime of much of the past century has resulted in extreme wildfire danger most summers); desert grasslands and chaparral covering the southern and western portions of Red Rock Country; and a lush riparian habitat extending along the creek's banks, where periodic flooding and a perennial water supply have given rise to a productive and resilient deciduous forest of walnut, sycamore, and Arizona cypress. Most characteristic, especially toward the southern end of Oak Creek Canyon, is the piñon-juniper woodland—short evergreen "pygmy forests" interspersed with shrubs and patches of bare ground or rock. Though the red rock soils (on the elevated plains, escarpments, and hills) and darker basalt-derived soils (on elevated plains and hill slopes) once supported denser stands of grass, erosion from heavy livestock grazing since the latter decades of the nineteenth century have left fewer grasses, but more trees and shrubs. In the last hundred years as well, animal species such as the grizzly bear, Merriam's elk, desert bighorn sheep, and Gila trout, and probably the Mogollon wolf have been eliminated from the area; but the coyote and rarely seen mountain lion remain.

Haunted Land: Natives, Spaniards,
Mountain Men, and the March of Tears

Passing through the area in 1895, archaeologist Jesse Walter Fewkes noted that the "well-wooded valley of Oak Creek" contained "evidence of aboriginal occupancy on all sides—ruins of buildings, fortified hilltops, pictographs and irrigating ditches," and that there was "scarcely a single canyon into these red cliffs in which evidence of former human habitations are not found in the form of ruins" (in N. Mann 1991:5). The area contains remains of hunting-gathering Paleo-Indians going back at least 10,000 years. As in most of the Southwest, the limiting factors of water, fertile soil, and temperatures had required that social groups develop some measure of stability, permanence, organization, and year-round planning as they grew in size. Farming and irrigation was practiced by the sedentary Hohokam and, later, by the Southern Sinagua. The latter group expanded rapidly in numbers between 700 and 1000 A.D., their pit house villages, with dwellings found in recesses along canyon walls and on the summits of mesas, developing into larger pueblos which utilized sophisticated irrigation and dry farming techniques. The remains of terraces, rock-cleared areas, and rock-outlined field borders that resembled checkerboards testify to their presence still, as do ball courts (for purposes unknown) and stylized platform mounds (presumably for ceremonial purposes). The Sinaguans grew corn, beans, squash, and cotton; and the area provided abundant nuts, seeds, berries, fruit, game, stone for crafting, and trade opportunities with cultures to the north. By the early fourteenth century, the Verde Valley Sinagua had consolidated into about forty major pueblos—multistoried and averaging thirty-five rooms each, though some, such as the Tuzigoot pueblo, had nearly a hundred rooms. Each was surrounded by small satellite pueblos and dependent on extensive farming areas (Foust, Byrkit, and Avery 1991:33). But by about 1425 the Sinaguan pueblos were abandoned, for reasons that remain unknown to us; theories proposed include drought, plague, war, over-specialization, and overdependence on canal systems. It is thought that they merged with the Hopis, who claim the Anasazi as their ancestors.[6] In any case, the Sinagua left behind an estimated 60,000 rock-art sites, ruins of cliff dwellings, and other remains between the Verde River and Flagstaff (Ruland-Thorne 1990:3).

By the time the first Spaniards arrived in 1583, the Verde Valley area was inhabited by two seminomadic groups: the Yavapais, thought to have come from the west, and the Tonto Apaches, arriving from the east (Foust, Byrkit, and Avery 1991:35). The Wipukpayas (Cruzados), or "people at the foot of the mountains," one of four subgroups of the Yavapais, regarded the red rock country as their ancestral and spiritual home. Primarily hunters and gatherers who also planted selected crops, Yavapai bands "moved through the landscape in rhythm with the sequence of ripening plants: spring greens for boiling, summer cactus fruits and mesquite beans, the abundant resources of autumn—acorns, piñons, walnuts, and seeds and berries" alongside corn and agave (mescal or century plant) as year-round food sources (Trimble 1993:231–32; cf. also Gifford 1933; Pilles 1981:6; Graff 1990:6). The Spaniards, on the other hand, came looking for El Dorado and the Seven Cities of Gold. More stumbling around, misfortune, and bizarre adventure than success seemed to meet such explorers as Alvar Nuñez Cabeza de Vaca, Marcos de Niza, and Francisco Coronado, and when Antonio de Espejo wandered into Hopi territory in 1582–83 and was led by them to the mineral-rich mountains in the area of present-day Jerome, he was disappointed to find only copper, not gold. Other expeditions followed, notably those of Farfán and Juan de Oñate, but failing in their quest for precious metals and finding hostile natives instead, the Spanish left this unappealing (for them) environment.[7]

For the next two hundred years, Arizona remained Indian country. The region's remoteness, its scorching sun, and predominantly barren, waterless landscape offered little incentive for European settlers—until the discovery of gold in California in 1848. The same year, the signing of the Treaty of Guadalupe Hidalgo ended the war with Mexico, ceding much of the Southwest into American hands and opening up the search for a transcontinental railroad system. Recognizing its potentials for irrigated agriculture and minerals (gold, silver, and copper ores in the eroded surface of the Mogollon Rim and its environs), a few whites had begun to arrive in north-central Arizona as early as the 1820s; and from 1826 onward, trappers and so-called

Mountain Men led the attack that resulted in the gradual confiscation of Indian lands and removal of Indians by the "right of discovery," a policy spelled out in an 1823 Supreme Court decision. By the 1860s, gold had been discovered near Prescott, and a growing number of white settlers were taking over cornfields and killing game animals and Indians (Foust, Byrkit, and Avery 1991:36), their skirmishes leading to the establishment of a military post at Fort Verde. In 1872, General George F. Crook launched his bloody military offensive against natives, which broke the Yavapais, whose renegade leaders Cha-lipun and Delshay surrendered in 1873. Some 1,400 Yavapai-Apaches were forcefully relocated from the Camp Verde Reservation to the San Carlos Reservation in 1875, an event that has come to be known in Yavapai history as the March of Tears. This was a trek over 180 miles of bad terrain in the middle of winter, during which over 100 Indians died from freezing and other causes.

Cattle and Copper Booms

Prior to 1865 the Verde Valley had a semitropical climate: with its high humidity and a regional greenhouse effect created by the encircling escarpment and mountains and an inversion layer over the valley, the area was a "stockman's and hunter's paradise," as the daughter of a pioneer describes it (Foust, Byrkin, and Avery 1991:41). Early settlers aimed to provide food for a growing regional and national market: garden produce, grain and horse feed for the markets in Prescott, Jerome, Fort Verde, and Flagstaff, and beef cattle—raised on the lush valley grasses that grew "up to a horse's belly"— for the nation. With open ranges and growing herds, it only took a few years for pioneer-brought horses, cattle, and sheep to eat most of the grass and trample the spongy land down to solid ground, increasing runoff and flooding in the process. By 1890 the beef market had collapsed and ranchers were forced to turn to orchards and truck gardens. A serious drought hit the valley in the 1880s: the bare ground was hit by heavy rains, causing floods in 1888, 1903, and 1909 (and later in 1938) which washed away much of exposed topsoil and deepened new gullies in the Oak Creek and Verde River watersheds (42). As Foust describes it, "The impact of the cattle boom had been irrevocably destructive. Overgrazing as well as wood harvesting and the creation of hundreds of well-worn cattle and horse trails had left the riparian alluvial topsoil and the foothill areas stripped of the soil-protective vegetation. Flash floods and normal drainage runoffs created sharp arroyos and gulleys everywhere" (Foust, Byrkit, and Avery 1991:43). The river flowed more rapidly, cutting stream beds deeper. At the same time, coyotes, bears, and mountain lions were trapped and killed without restriction, resulting in soaring populations of jackrabbits (which ate the roots of grasses, ruining ranges), quail, and other grass-eating species. By 1905 the federal government recognized a need to manage the use of lands in the West, and it formed the U.S. Forest Service as part of the Department of Agriculture. The Forest Service reflected the Roosevelt administration's conservation philosophy: its mandate included managing state lands, conducting scientific analyses of soil, range cover, and agricultural conditions, and passing regulatory laws controlling land uses. But ranchers and farmers in the western states were resentful of government intervention, new laws and restrictions, and of young, college-educated city-bred "experts" coming to tell them how to do things. (This is a resentment that persists today—despite the state's unusually heavy reliance on federal support; cf. Sheridan 1995a).

On the industrial front, copper mining began in Jerome (some twenty miles southwest of Sedona) in 1876, and by 1903 the *New York Sun* observed that "[a] gray cloud of sulphurous fumes from the enormous smelter always hangs over there" (cited in Foust, Byrkit, and Avery 1991:49). The smelters brought prosperity and markets, but also crop-ruining sulfuric acid, cyanide, other noxious gases, and smoke; and conflicts inevitably developed between farmers, ranchers, and the mining companies. The towns of Jerome and Clarkdale lived and died with their companies' fortunes. Controlled by large mining companies like the United Verde Copper Company and Phelps Dodge Corporation, Jerome was a colony of the industrial-capitalist East; every facet of it was tied to national and international technologies and marketplaces, so that by the early 1950s, when the copper ore became too expensive to extract, the town "gave a barely audible death rattle and expired" (49). The remains of open-pit copper mines, old railroads, acres of huge piles of black smelter slag, waste ore, and toxic mill tailings litter the north end of the valley today, long after the mining boom had busted. With their satellite "suburb" Cottonwood, these old mining towns have drawn working-class retirees, emerging as trade centers with retail and service economies, and now serve as Sedona's laborshed (Gober, McHugh, and Leclerc 1993:14). Byrkit sums up the corporate and industrial transformation of Arizona: "the Industrial Revolution made the unpromising and vast land productive by creating a demand for copper to make electrical wiring for refrigerated railroad cars in which to ship Arizona agribusiness produce. . . . Heavy investment capital from outside the Southwest has made possible hydroelectric generating stations, huge copper mines and state-of-the-art smelters, real estate capital, corporate agriculture, building construction, and 'clean' manufacturing plants. The out-of-state investors have been well repaid in profits" (Byrkit 1992:342).

"A Grand Place for an Outing"

Until the opening of Schnebly Hill Road in 1902, the same year the town was officially founded (and named after T. C. Schnebly's wife), Sedona itself had remained relatively inaccessible. The handful of pioneer families who arrived in the 1870s and 1880s found it tough going: with no road, everything had to be brought in by packhorses, and Flagstaff was a six-day trek. After the road was built, the tiny town served as a stopover between

Jerome and Flagstaff, the regional service center. It took an outsider, Jesse Walter Fewkes, to accurately forecast the area's future: exploring the area between the Palatki (Red House) and Honanki (Bear House) ruins in 1895, he wrote, "The colors of the rocks are variegated, so that the gorgeous cliffs appear to be banded, rising from 800 to 1,000 feet sheer on all sides. These rocks had weathered into fantastic shapes suggestive of cathedrals, Greek Temples, and sharp steeples of churches extending like giant needles into the sky. The scenery compares very favorably with that of the Garden of the Gods, and is much more extended. This place, I have no doubt, will sooner or later become popular with the sightseer. . . ." (in Rigby 1979). By 1902, Oak Creek was recognized as an "ideal trout stream," "the most famous of all trout streams in Arizona," and pleasure seekers were already flocking to the "grand" scenery in the canyon (in Foust, Byrkit, and Avery 1991:56). From around the turn of the century, thousands of fish were being "planted" in the Verde River and Oak Creek by the United Verde Copper Company to provide recreational opportunities for workers. With a canyon road completed to Flagstaff in 1914 (to be paved, twenty-five years later, and extended to Cottonwood), lodges and hotels began appearing, and T. C. Schnebly would sometimes take visitors to see the cliff dwellings and other sites of cultural interest. In 1917 the *Jerome Sun* called Oak Creek one of the beauty spots of Arizona, "an alluring summer resort, where trout abound and [which is] a grand place for an outing" (quoted in Foust, Byrkit, and Avery 1991:57). A 1925 editorial in the *Verde Copper News* recognized two possible futures for the area: one was as a "scenic belt unexcelled anywhere in the world," with streams at the head of each of which "is a varied and fantastic maze of red and white sandstone and malapai wrought into a thousand forms and surrounded by a forest of mixed growths and shades of green." The editors continued: "That region immediately under the rim and embracing Oak Creek should be thrown into a national reserve and national game preserve for deer, elk, antelope, quail, grouse, and any game the section may be able to support. The section mentioned has innumerable prehistoric Indian ruins, varied flora and fauna, a magnificent study of geology, and in winter when the snows are melting in the mountains, contains innumerable waterfalls" (quoted in Foust, Byrkit, and Avery 1991:57). Yet, the newspaper recognized that the area was in danger from woodchoppers and ranchers, and that it needed protection. "This section of country is an orphan," they wrote, "being claimed neither by Coconino County nor by anyone else" (58)—a diagnosis that was to remain accurate for several more decades.

"Water Flows Uphill . . . toward Money"

The dryness that characterizes much of Arizona has meant that water, an ecological limiting factor, has played a key role in the political geography of the area.[8] In the late nineteenth century, Arizonans developed a unique water law according to which water rights could belong to people far away from their sources. This "doctrine of prior appropriation" was based in Spanish water law, which "happened to suit the particular interests of Arizona's nineteenth-century commercial agriculture and the state's mining companies" (Byrkit 1992:378), rather than in the Northern European legal tradition of riparian rights. It has particularly benefited large corporation water users, irrigated farming, and mining operations, being well suited to the diversion of water through flumes, ditches, canals, and dams. Water rights, accordingly, are established by usage, and are subject to legal appropriation for others' "nonusage." In 1900, for instance, the Santa Fe Railroad Company appropriated 1,000 inches of Oak Creek water to be diverted and pumped to the railroad's main line at Flagstaff (Foust, Byrkit, and Avery 1991: 46).

The Verde is a tributary to the Salt River, and is one of the major perennial streams in Arizona. It supports extensive riparian habitat and wetlands, drains some 6,000 square miles of land (Foust, Byrkit, and Avery 1991:73), and is one of the last free-flowing rivers in the Southwest. As one of its tributaries, the Oak Creek begins in the Mogollon highlands and follows the Oak Creek fault into Sedona, where it crosses the Sedona fault and continues further south through Page Springs and Cornville to the Verde. Early in the century, Verde Valley farmers had banded together to fight what they saw as powerful lobbyists and politicians and agricultural special interests in Phoenix and Maricopa County who, they felt, controlled Arizona water law and who wanted the Salt River Project to divert the Salt River basin for their own use. A major court decision in 1910 favored the Verde Valley farmers and ranchers. In the 1940s, the Central Arizona Project—"Arizona's political Holy Grail," as Thomas Sheridan (1995b:49) calls it—proposed to make the desert bloom by bringing Colorado River water to south-central Arizona by using the Verde as a channel to supply the Salt River Valley through extensive dams. The project was eventually abandoned, after decades of trial and error; but the runaway growth of Arizona's sunbelt cities has continued to demand water from the Verde. The Salt River Project Water Users' Association has water rights on the Verde that date back to 1869, and according to the doctrine of prior appropriation, "first in time—first in right." As Marc Reisner puts it in his brilliant dissection of the region's water politics, "In the West, it is said, water flows uphill toward money" (1986:13); a continuing history of court cases serves to prove that point.

Ninety percent of the water consumed in Arizona goes to agricultural irrigation (Reisner 1986:9; Sheridan 1995b:53). The Arizona Department of Water Resources (ADWR) has been studying methods of "augmentation" to increase its water supply further. Proposed methods have included removing trees and shrubs from public lands that drain into the river, to limit the amount "lost" through evapotranspiration, and seeding clouds during winter storms to increase the amount of snowfall. As one proponent of such a scheme put it, "California has been successfully seeding clouds for years"

(Dagget 1989c). None of this bodes well for Sedonans and other Verde Valley dwellers. Water has been a crucial limiting factor in the past; a well discovered (525 feet below Grasshopper Flat) in the 1940s is often credited with starting Sedona's population boom. The well pumped 600 gallons an hour, and the water stood at 170 feet below the surface. Local users formed a private nonprofit cooperative, the Oak Creek Water Company, which has had the lowest cost per gallon of any independent water utility in Arizona. The town's groundwater supply still comes entirely from this underground aquifer, but the pressure from Salt River water users and the lack of adequate water management in Sedona (where the number of golf courses is steadily rising) mean difficulties to come (cf. Forney 1998). The unpredictability of Oak Creek, meanwhile, has been exacerbated by soil erosion from grazing; and the town has seen extensive flooding several times through the last century. Flooding over two days alone in February 1993 damaged or destroyed 291 dwellings in Coconino and Yavapai counties and washed away a low-water bridge at Indian Gardens north of Sedona (Dixon 1993:1).

Hollywood's West

Like the recognition of the Red Rock Country's recreational potentials, Hollywood movie moguls had noticed its cinematic possibilities as early as 1914. Actual movie shoots began here in 1923 with Jesse Lasky's production of Zane Grey's *Call of the Canyon*; Grey's novel had been written while he was staying at the Lolomi Lodge near West Fork. Early movie making led to an economic boost and a growing reputation for the town, and by the late 1930s wealthy people were being attracted to the climate and scenery (though by 1945 there were still no more than 400 permanent residents in Sedona). After World War II, Hollywood's movie makers returned with color film and proceeded to etch Sedona's landscape firmly in the viewing public's visual imagination, most notably as the red, gray, and sandy-colored cliff and hilly backdrops of blockbuster Westerns. More than sixty features have been filmed in Sedona since the 1940s by Paramount, Twentieth Century Fox, Columbia, Warner Brothers, Allied Artists, Universal, RKO, and MGM; notable titles include *Broken Arrow, The Rounders, Johnny Guitar, The Gunfighters, Angel and the Badman, Riders of the Purple Sage, 3:10 to Yuma, The Half Breed, Billy the Kid,* and *Harry and Tonto*. For such blockbusters as *Broken Arrow* production teams visited the region's Indian reservations (Delmer Daves got hundreds of White River Apaches to participate in *Broken Arrow*), built horse mangers at places like Bell Rock, and hauled in gigantic plaster of paris saguaros to make areas of Sedona look like the desert near Tucson (Nasta 1981:42).

By the 1970s, after the era of the classical Western had passed, the Sedona area found increasing use as a backdrop for television commercials and magazine ads. Through all this, it remains ironic that Hollywood's movie industry—an industry which by its nature takes place *out of* place, by deny-

Figure 6.3. "Stage Stop," uptown Sedona

ing any place to the real places in which Hollywood *space* is created—has helped to construct the heterotopic place/space of Sedona. In using Sedona and other such places as backdrops for its Westerns, Hollywood has created a mythic West while erasing both the actual West and the specific places where the shooting has occurred. Like a predator's stalking of its prey, the "hunt" for locations culminates in the "shooting" of movie scenes, the gathering up of their dead carcasses and their preparation (editing and post-production) for the celebratory feasts (blockbuster movies) that are then fed to the larger community of movie-watching consumers. The whole enterprise constitutes a ritual transformation of landscape into myth. And yet, in a kind of reverse movement, one of the main arguments used today by environmentalists and local activists for the preservation of Red Rock Crossing—threatened by a multimillion-dollar road extension bridge (described in the next chapter)—is that it is one of the most photographed and filmed locations in North America. Its role in the creation of the mythic American West has now become part of its own defense against intrusion by further development.

Cowboys of the Art World

Hollywood's exposure of the red rock landscape led to another kind of exposure—by visual artists, especially those contributing to the burgeoning Southwest and "cowboy art" genres. Among the first to discover Sedona's inspirational qualities was German born Dadaist-surrealist Max Ernst, who took up residence with his Californian wife Dorothea Tanning in 1946. More significant for Sedona's development as an art colony was Egyptian sculptor Nassan Gobran, who had been teaching in Boston when he was invited by Hamilton Warren, founder of the Verde Valley School, to come to Sedona. Gobran was reportedly uninterested until he saw *Broken Arrow* and recognized the background from photographs Warren had showed him. Arriving in 1950, he met Ernst and other local artists and soon began organizing the art community, starting a summer graduate arts school in 1956 and purchasing a barn for the Sedona Arts Center. Opened with the fanfare of a fifty-piece orchestra in 1961, "the Barn" became a social and cultural hub of the community.

But Sedona's claim to fame lies less with international stars like Ernst and Gobran than with the founding, in 1965, of the Cowboy Artists of America. Formed out of a milieu that included Joe Beeler, James Reynolds, Frank McCarthy, John Hampton, Charlie Dye, writer Bob McLeod, and George Phippen, the Cowboy Artists set themselves the following goals: "To perpetuate the memory and culture of the Old West as typified by the late Frederic Remington, Charles Russell, and others; to insure authentic representation of the life of the West, as it was and is; to maintain standards of quality in contemporary Western painting, drawing and sculpture; to help guide collectors of Western art; to give mutual assistance in the protection of artists' rights; to conduct a trail ride and camp out in some locality of special interest each year; and to hold a joint exhibition of the work of active members, once a year" (Ruland-Thorne 1990:72). Though the group had moved their show to the Phoenix Art Museum by 1973, the Cowboy Artists' success brought attention and glamour to Sedona's reputation as a regional art center (75). "Cowboy art" functions as a tributary to the broader genre of Southwest Art, a thematic thread that has been milked by the vast majority of the area's galleries, placing Sedona alongside Santa Fe and Scottsdale in its turnover of liquid assets. Several dozen local galleries and boutiques sell oil paintings featuring rock cliff faces or landscapes populated only by wild animals, cowboys, or Indians decked out in traditional regalia, alongside the usual "Southwestern Native American" curios: Navajo rugs, Hopi kachina dolls, pottery, baskets, and jewelry, all thoroughly decontextualized from the reality of Native American life. Meanwhile, the huge boutique and gallery complex Tlaquepaque, built in a Spanish Colonial Revival style, carefully masks the fact that there was never any significant Hispanic presence in Sedona (save for the manual labor in today's hotels and businesses). And to attract buyers from Phoenix (and satisfy its local sophisticates), prestigious festivals like Jazz on the Rocks, the Sedona Arts Festival, Sedona Sculpture Walk, Fiesta del Tlaquepaque, a Chamber Music Festival, and an annual International Film Festival, pepper Sedona's year-round arts calendar.[9]

To Develop or Conserve

As ranching, vegetable growing and horticulture declined in their importance to Sedona's economy through the 1960s and 1970s, the growing image industry, supplemented by word of mouth, established it as a scenic and
cultural center. The climate and scenery, once seen as providing good agricultural possibilities, now became a draw for retirees, artists, tourists, hikers
and recreationists, and a growing community of metaphysically inclined
spiritualists. (Sedona's population had grown from some 400 in 1948 to
5,000 by 1980.) Conservation, environmental quality, and the town's visual
appearance have consequently become primary concerns for residents. After the Coconino County Planning and Zoning Commission, in 1969 (and
over residents' protests), authorized large areas to be zoned for hotel and
motel units, extended commercial areas, mobile home parks and multiple
family dwellings, a group of local citizens formed Keep Sedona Beautiful —
an organization which has since served as a moral guardian and clearing-
house for sign control, litter collection squads, the drawing up of guidelines
for zoning and appropriate landscaping and architecture, and the register-
ing of complaints against "ugliness" and noise pollution (including that
emanating from Luke and Williams Air Force Bases, whose low-level military jets continue to fly over Sedona to this day). The list of other concerns
which have grown over the years includes: pollution and litter in Oak Creek
Canyon (cf. West 1975); bacterial pollution in the popular Slide Rock State
Park, which reached unsafe levels by 1975; water rights and uses; landfills;
unpopular Forest Service land exchanges; zoning regulations; air quality
and the Forest Service's controversial controlled forest burns (the valley's
inversion layer, resulting from rapid ground cooling on clear nights, causes
smoke from these controlled burns in October and November to linger);
open-range grazing (one local rancher has a permit to have his cows grazing
without fences for as long as he is alive); and an inadequate sewage disposal
system.

A series of Sedona Community Plans has reflected the popular desire to
maintain the area's scenic and natural beauty, but citizens had little power
to implement their visions while the town was split between two county
jurisdictions, with the boundary between Yavapai and Coconino counties
running right through the town. The area's overuse by campers, hikers, and
tourists; the impact of off-road vehicles (jeeps, SUVs, and ATVs) on the
fragile soils, vegetation, and wildlife; aircraft and helicopter scenic over-
flights of the area; the appearance of several major developments (with
names like Mystic Hills and Indian Cliffs); and the general question of how
much population the area can sustain—all these issues had, by the mid-
1980s, become woven into the debate over whether or not to incorporate
Sedona. The matter was settled in a 1988 referendum, when both pro- and

Figure 6.4. Capitol Butte (Thunder Mountain) looming over West Sedona

antigrowth factions came to see incorporation as the way to control and manage Sedona's growth.

CONTESTED SEDONA

> "KEEP SEDONA BEAUTIFUL, TAKE SOMEONE WITH YOU
> WHEN YOU LEAVE"
>
> —seen on a car with Colorado plates

Sedona today is a town of affluent retirees and "second-homers," artists, art dealers and gallery owners, real estate agents, developers and entrepreneurs, and New Age spiritualists and healers. Nearly 40 percent of the City of Sedona's 7,720 people in the 1990 census were over the age of sixty (Hall and Pijawka 1992:46), and the town boasts one of the highest per capita incomes in the nation (Valverde 1989:14). Its land prices have skyrocketed in recent years, the median price of a home reaching $157,900 in 1992 (Hall and Pijawka 1992:8). Not surprisingly, this has given rise to socioeconomic stratification and a dearth of affordable housing, with the result that a majority of Sedona's service workers live outside the city's boundaries (Gober, McHugh, and Leclerc 1993:12; Knowles 1995:1A). Sedona's two base industries are tourism and retirement. Services and retail trade accounted for over 70 percent of employment (Hall and Pijawka 1992:11), with real estate and construction providing much of the remainder. Tourism also supports the city's tax base: sales tax is the primary source of Sedona's funding, while Sedona's bed tax is the highest in the state at 10.5 percent (J. Smith 1990:1). Sedona's is a visitor- and commuter-based "petroleum economy," and is becoming more so; destination resorts, golf courses, a cultural park complex, a college, new health care facilities, and a western theme park are among recently launched projects.

Selling the Town: Sedona as Disneyland

A real estate boom in the 1980s left behind a series of financially distressed, swanky resorts—multimillion-dollar edifices intended to raise Sedona's tourist stature to that of Palm Springs, Santa Fe, and Carmel. Resorts like Poco Diablo, Enchantment, L'Auberge, and Los Abrigados, all of which underwent financial turmoil in the late 1980s, were started in the era of short-term, high-profit speculation financed by front-end investment loans from savings and loan institutions. When "business at the resorts failed to produce the kind of working revenue needed to make payments on the enormous loans," the general partners abandoned ship, leaving the lending institutions (and ultimately taxpayers, subsidizing their bailouts) holding the bag (Judy Smith 1990:5). Skyrocketing land prices, high bed taxes, and financial fiascoes have meant that the city's business interests have felt it imperative to bring in even more tourists. The city has consequently been divided between prodevelopment and conservation-minded factions. On the side of growth have been an array of wealthy families, developers, and media moguls—among them the owners of Sedona's sole long-running weekly (now twice-weekly) newspaper, the *Sedona Red Rock News*, and of the town's only AM radio station.[10] In 1990 the pro-growthers formed the Sedona Business Association to fight the anti-growth and environmentalist bias of the 1990 city council—a council which, according to SBA President Ben Miller, "made economic survival extremely difficult" (Miller 1993:34). In 1992, they succeeded, with the election of a pro-growth city council.

Perhaps the most effective medium for the selling of Sedona has been the slick and glossy full-color publication *Sedona Magazine*. Since its launch in 1986, this quarterly has been the chief marketing tool of Sedona's real estate and resort industry. Filled to the brim with full-page picture-postcard photographs of red rock scenery, resorts and subdevelopments, golf courses, and advertisements for art galleries (with their characteristic Native American and Southwest kitsch), it is now available on newsstands across the United States. A typical advertisement produced by the Sedona Oak Creek Canyon Chamber of Commerce extols the virtues of "Arizona's most pristine natural playground": "Swim or fish in the crystalline pools of Oak Creek Canyon, explore the ancient Indian civilizations which once flourished here. . . . Escape to Sedona, a place of sandstone cathedrals, cool pine forests, stunning sunsets and skies of Navajo blue where our warm, friendly people will inspire you to remain long enough to experience it all" (n.d.). Other slick ads, their text usually draped across a backdrop of red rock landscape, sell art, jewelry, properties, condominiums and luxury homes, stays in one or another of Sedona's luxury resorts, tours of the red rock area, "Therapy on the Rocks," "Golf on the rocks!" and the like. An article by the magazine's publisher, Hoyt Johnson, characteristically portrays the town as divided between a virtuous business community and a civic sphere that fails to carry its weight: "It is not appropriate," he complains, "to expect the people who own Sedona businesses to provide the principal support for activities (such as those conducted by the chamber of commerce) that legitimately can be labeled civic responsibilities; especially, considering the sales and bed tax generated by these owners" (1992:51). The activities cited by Johnson, one of the chamber's board of directors, include office space for the chamber, parking, and "marketing and visitor services" (51). The chamber's strategy has been to sell Sedona as a "destination resort" rather than merely a quick stop en route elsewhere. In the past few years, developments and subdivisions have continued to be built, with names like Harmony Hills, Road Runner Rancho, Juniper Knolls, Sedona Meadows, Mystic Hills, Shadow Estates, and the Sedona Golf Resort.

The success of the developers' vision of Sedona depends on bringing in ever greater numbers of tourists, and the result of their efforts has been the virtual transformation of the town into a Disneyland of wonders. The Official Greater Sedona Souvenir Map presents a cartoon panorama of stock characters: cowboy posing for a movie camera, dopey-faced and camera-toting tourist, hot-air balloon rising over Fay Canyon, American flag waving atop Capital [sic] Butte, coffee dripping and steam rising from Coffee Pot Rock, bees humming alongside Sugar Loaf Mountain, judge's hammer preparing to strike Courthouse Rock, musical notes emanating from a Bell Rock struck into motion by a thunderbolt, and scores of jeeps and helicopters buzzing happily around and over everything. Even the street names — among them Road Runner, T-Bird, Sunset Drive, and Panorama Boulevard — seem chosen to resonate with pop-cultural sensibilities. The opposite side of this souvenir map helpfully includes a road map of the town, marked with numbers denoting "some of the fine businesses that help make Sedona such a great place to shop and live"; of these (presumably the map's sponsors), over one-third are realtors.

Defending and Managing Sedona

With powerful forces driving the area's development, the question of Sedona's status as public or private land has surfaced repeatedly. Nearly half of Sedona's land is held by the Forest Service for open space and conservation, while only 28 percent is privately held and developable. Attempts by some citizens to make Oak Creek Canyon a National Monument managed by the Park Service (in the late 1970s), or a National Scenic Area managed by the Forest Service (in 1987), were successfully fought off by owners of land along the creek (cf. MacDonald 1979, Powell 1979, Shaffer 1990), but citizens' groups like Keep Sedona Beautiful, the Responsible Residents of the Red Rocks (4Rs), and the local Sierra Club chapter, continue to argue that the area's public lands need a special designation and a comprehensive land use plan.[11]

A key role in the tug-of-war between conservationists and developers is played by the U.S. Forest Service, which holds 50 percent of lands within Sedona city limits and 90 percent of lands in the Greater Red Rock Area (4RN 1:2 (1994):3). The Sedona–Red Rock area is part of the Coconino National Forest, administered out of Flagstaff, which until recently employed six law enforcement officers, six archaeologists, and several rangers.[12] The role of the Forest Service has changed much over the years: no longer lonely land custodians traveling on horseback, forest rangers have become specialists responsible for outdoor recreation, watershed protection and wildlife care, or office managers and public relations experts trained in settling disputes between different use groups, among them tourists, picnickers, hikers, fishermen, campers, and ranchers (some 800 cows continue to graze in the area). Given that much of the land available for development lies in Forest Service jurisdiction, the only way it can be added to developed areas is through land exchanges, the main purpose of which has ostensibly been to consolidate land ownership patterns, solve administrative problems of land occupancy, and provide for community expansion (Iverson 1989:7). But these exchanges have always been controversial and highly unpopular.[13] Typically, a land trade might involve an outside investment firm (such as Scottsdale-based Incor in the controversial Jack's Canyon land trade) buying up hundreds of acres of prime red rock land at what appears to be unreasonably low prices from the Forest Service. One particular controversy pitted an alliance of developers, the State Land Department, and a Phoenix law firm against the Arizona Game and Fish Department, Keep Sedona Beautiful, the Northern Arizona Audubon Society, two taxpayers associations, and various individuals (Iverson 1989:7). In the debate over Jack's Canyon, the Greater Sedona Conservation Group was formed to fight the land trade, and gathered 3,800 signatures against the deal. Another proposed Forest Service trade centered on Carrol Canyon was opposed by a coalition of conservationist forces, with the city council ultimately rejecting the trade. More recently, however, the Forest Service has made a serious effort to generate greater public participation in their land use decisions.

Participatory politics has had a place in much of Sedona's recent history. The Sedona Academy, formed as a local think tank in 1984, and the annual Sedona Forum, a several-day forum for citizen input into the planning of the city's future, have both allowed a broad cross-section of Sedona's community to become involved in planning and consensus building. The academy's annual reports, featuring the input of invited academics (and sometimes a strong "environmental sustainability" perspective), have raised the level of intellectual discussion in the city. Extensive annual reports have focused on the challenges of growth and development, land use planning, environmental quality in the Sedona/Verde Valley area, sewage and sanitation, community building and cultural values, economic sustainability, and citizen "partnerships" with the Forest Service. There has always been a large gap between recommendation and implementation, but the evidence of recent years suggests this gap may be narrowing.

Another key to an informed and participatory citizenry, arguably instrumental in some of the environmental successes of the late 1980s and early 1990s, has been the existence, for a time, of alternative newsweeklies. Their struggles to survive against the monopolistic tendencies of the more conservative and pro-growth *Sedona Red Rock News* provides an interesting window on the town's politics. Beginning in 1983, the *Sedona Times* served as an informative liberal weekly, more professional in its appearance than the establishmentarian *Red Rock News*. In its own (seemingly accurate) self-assessment, the *Times* was first to piece together issues such as "Incor's massive land purchases in Sedona, spiralling crime rates in the Valley of Oak Creek, the appearance of AIDS at Marcus J. Lawrence Hospital, the raging battle between homeowners and developers at Coffee Pot Rock, the disappearance of Sedona Corporation, and [to] report the profound impact the alleged Sedona vortices (or energy points) was placing on the community" (July 2–7 1986:4). From the *Times's* first few years one gets the impression that Sedona is a culturally sophisticated town dealing with the growing pains associated with tourism and development. By 1988, however, the paper had been bizarrely hijacked by a less than competent management, and was sold to Western Newspapers, Inc., publishers of a regional competitor. Within months, the "new" *Times* was transformed from a handsome and readable weekly into a shabbily designed, ad-saturated paper, full of careless typos and seeming editorial disarray. In summer 1989 a new editor improved the paper marginally, but was soon sacked for, among other things, focusing too strongly on the New Age movement.[14] By November 1989 the *Times* was a free-circulation paper, and in less than two months had stopped publishing altogether.

In January 1989 a new Sedona-based but more regionally focused paper called the *Tab* appeared on the scene. Covering the northern central region of Arizona from Flagstaff to Jerome and the Verde Valley, the *Tab* soon proved to be an incisive and sophisticated, professionally designed weekly with a strong commitment to critical coverage of political and environmental issues. Advertising dollars in the Sedona area, unfortunately, were limited, and when the *Tab* starting cutting into the revenues of the *Red Rock News* (the *News* is controlled by a local real-estate owning family), that paper seemingly declared war on its competitor, increasing its publication to twice a week and persuading its advertisers to pull out of the *Tab*. The *Tab* publisher's problems with the IRS made things worse, and the paper folded less than two years after its inception, restoring what one former Washington journalist described as the *Red Rock News*'s "old-fashioned Hearstian lock" on the town (Bishop, int.).[15]

Conflicts over growth and environmental sustainability continue to color Sedona's politics. A 1998 *Red Rock News* survey (May 22) left little doubt that the number one issue facing the city was its runaway growth. Builders and planners, meanwhile, have arrived at a population figure of 32,000 as the "build-out" density for the Sedona area. As more developments and subdivisions are built and refugees from Phoenix, Los Angeles, Chicago, and elsewhere (R. Brown 1993:68) discover the delights of living in a place like Sedona, infrastructure and roads need to be built and existing ones expanded. In the 1990s the most pressing environmental concerns dominating local discourse remained the degradation of the community's most valued resources—scenery, open space, climate, water availability, native vegetation, and the rural atmosphere—and the waste disposal problems associated with automobiles, sewage, garbage, and landfills.[16]

The city's water system has been under particular strain (water, remember, is precious in Arizona). Its wastewater treatment plant has been operating since 1993, but the Arizona Department of Environmental Quality is forcing Sedona, under National Environmental Policy Act (NEPA) requirements, to find new ways of disposing of its treated effluent. While a new (and much-maligned) sewage system is being built, the city has had to look for buyers of its effluent for reuse; and, naturally, the leading candidates have been yet newer proposed golf courses, most of which would be built on as yet undeveloped land (Aune 1998). As more and more people move to Sedona, the reasons they come in the first place begin to trickle away. A caustic, if somewhat incongruous, reminder of the divergent views on Sedona's future occurred in the winter of 1989–90, when Sedona's so-called Great Wall—a gray cement wall bordering Foothills South, a development owned and constructed by the high-profile Miller brothers—was vandalized three times and sprayed with huge, black block-lettered graffiti, reading, "SMASH IT UP. TEAR IT DOWN. EAT THE RICH." (*SRRN*, January 4, 1989:6A). In the decade since, little has been torn down (with the exception of trees), much more has gone up, and the rich are eating better than ever.

Flows and Counterflows in Sedona's Political Economy

Regionally, Sedona stands out from its surroundings not only in its red rock topography, but also in the social classes it has attracted to itself. Some degree of class polarization has developed within the Verde Valley, with regional stereotypes running roughly north to south as follows: "Flagstaff is inhabited by either transients from I-40 or ivory tower intellectuals from the university; Sedona residents are all either retired or wealthy elitists; the Cottonwood area populace is often seen to be straight out of John Steinbeck's Grapes of Wrath; and Jerome is viewed as a haven for nothing but ex-hippies and radical deviants" (Valverde 1989:7). People from the "other side of the valley" (Cornville, Cottonwood, Camp Verde), I was told, see Sedonaites as conceited and wealthy snobs, while Sedonans view the former as uneducated, uncultured, blue-collar rednecks (Fried, int.). Sedona's analogues, however, are found in such towns as Taos in New Mexico, and Aspen and Telluride in Colorado—magnets of wealth and targets of an aggressive tourist and real estate industry. The process, described by Scott Norris, normally features "the often abrupt and unplanned development of service industries and of a low-wage economy based on these industries; seasonal or permanent increases in the population that exceed the carrying capacity of community infrastructure, resulting in environmental damage and social displacement; overuse and degradation of even 'protected' natural areas and scenic resources; the commodification and commercialization of local history, culture, and ethnicity; and the rapid growth, inflation, and gentrification brought about not just by the flow of visitors but also by . . . 'amenity migrants'—former tourists who move to, or buy second homes in, their favorite vacation site" (1994:viii) Almost all of these factors are evident in Sedona. Such places can be seen as victims of an American "nouveau-frontier" propensity to "destroy what we love," a theme that has surfaced repeatedly in the literature of Wallace Stegner, Bud Guthrie, D. H. Lawrence, Mary Austin, and others (Bishop, int.). At the same time, they present the irony of a region much dependent on federal subsidies, yet whose recipients all too willingly extol the mythic virtues of frontier capitalism and rugged individualism.

The growth of such places, in turn, can hardly be understood without reference to those places which act as a source for their incoming human populations—both the wealthy immigrants and visitors, and the less visible support staff. The move to the Southwest is a by-product of a culture whose better-off members are increasingly eager to escape metropolitan living, and who are encouraged by floods and earthquakes in California, riots in Los Angeles, and so on. As Shirley MacLaine, who moved to New Mexico from Washington state about ten years ago, put it, "There are too many Californians now in Washington"—so California/Hollywood is, in effect, coming to the desert Southwest by way of other abandoned or overcrowded "elsewheres." Meanwhile, the flow of money into the upper strata brings with it a counterflow of those who hope to benefit from its downward trickle: Mexican and Hispanic-American laborers living with their extended families in trailer parks and working at resorts and in restaurants, and others in the service class who cannot afford Sedona's rents (nor its lack of a Laundromat) and choose instead to commute from neighboring towns. In Sedona, visible minorities have been rendered invisible, and real Native Americans have been replaced by the gentle warriors of Southwest kitsch.[17]

Seeing and Feeling Sedona

Much of the selling of Sedona portrays its red rock landscape as scenery, a dramatic backdrop to those activities wealthy visitors or residents would be expected to do (such as shop, play golf, and attend conferences). But a part of the local economy has opted to facilitate a closer and more direct contact with that landscape. Commercial jeep tours take clients out to see, feel, and "reach out and touch" the famous red rocks. Jeep tours have been available since at least 1959 (*ST*, August 2, 1989:1), and, in Darwinian fashion, tour companies have proliferated to fill distinctive and specialized niches within a diversified market. Red Rock Jeep Tours, which calls itself "Sedona's cowboy tour company," provides a "Broken Arrow" tour, named for Jimmy Stewart's movie and the part of Sedona in which it was filmed; Time Expeditions (now part of Pink Jeep Tours) focuses on the history and archaeology of the area (unlike most, it has a Forest Service license to run daily tours to sites like the Honanki ruins); Earth Wisdom Jeep Tours provides a "Native American" focus; Sedona Photo Tours provides ample opportunities for shooting the red rocks, while Pink Jeep Tours at least offers an appropriately colored vehicle from which to view them. Others offer nature excursions, horse adventures, trolley tours, couple's tours, and "brew tours," while hot-air balloons and helicopter and airplane tours offer a grander view of the landscape. Red Rock Jeep Tours was the first to promote "vortex tours" in the early 1980s, but now several companies and independent operators compete to present the area's metaphysical values to visitors.

Meanwhile, Sedona's New Age, or "metaphysical," community has become a growing presence in the city. Its celebrated "energy vortexes" (described in the next chapter) have become an established feature of the city's tourist industry, with vortex maps now given out to visitors at the chamber of commerce.[18] But beyond the commercial potentials of New Age mysticism, there is always also the looming, even overwhelming, presence of the red rock country itself—nature, as it presents itself to be tamed, captured, represented, managed, celebrated, or feared. Between the representations and the reality there is always a necessary gap, one which the New Age community tries to capture in its imagery of energy vortexes, mysterious underground reservoirs of energy, "interdimensional portals," and spiritual presences of various kinds. But nature makes its presence felt in more prosaic, if sometimes dramatic, ways: ravens, hawks, and eagles spotted overhead, coyotes heard howling at night, mountain lions, and even (reportedly) black bears encountered while hiking in the Red Rock–Secret Mountain wilderness area, as well as rattlesnakes and other animal presences; the periodic flooding of Oak Creek's banks; wildfires in Coconino National Forest (a lightning-sparked fire atop Wilson Mountain, four miles north of Sedona, burned over seventy acres of ponderosa pine and oak forest in August 2000); and the near-total reliance of Sedona's economy on its environmental assets. It is a rare postcard or photograph from Sedona that fails to feature the red rock landscape or the riparian beauty of Oak Creek. It is the natural landscape, finally, that is both the setting for, the potential reward, and an inevitable loser, among the different contestants in the struggles over what Sedona is to be. In the following chapter I will look in depth at a couple of these struggles over nature, its definition, representation, and appropriation into everyday practices of living.

Table 6.1. Sedona place-images and -myths

Place-myth/ representation	Representatives	Narratives & claims	Spatial practices, socio-economic activities	Group constructs, "others"
(1) Pioneers' and homesteaders' "West"	local historians	history of Euro-American settlement, homesteaders & squatters, etc.	survival (by any means necessary)	Nature as "other"
	patriotic Americans		ranching, farming	Indians (and Spaniards) as "other" & as enemy
	long-time residents (few)	"man vs. nature"		
(2) Hollywood's West (Sedona as prime location for filmmaking & as representative of the "Southwest" mythos)	Hollywood, movie producers	"wild west," rugged deserts & chaparral, etc.	arrive w/film crews, jeeps, etc., "extract" scenery ("shoot" the landscape) & leave	
	locals (job-seekers, service industry)	"Hollywood!"		
(3) Artists' Southwest	local galleries & boutiques, Tlaquepaque et al.	beautiful landscapes, colors, nature scenery, seasonal chnages, etc.	paint, sculpt & sell art	
	Cowboy Artists of America	"Cowboys and Indians" (and Hispanics)		
(4) Arts/cultural hub	tourist/service industry	arts festivals, galleries, etc.	host, service & attend festivals	
	arts festivals, galleries, boutiques		market & sell art (Southwest art, "cowboy art")	

Place-myth/ representation	Representatives	Narratives & claims	Spatial practices, socio-economic activities	Group constructs, "others"
(5) Retirement haven	retirees real estate industry	climate (dry air, mild yr.-round temps.), amenities, "quality of life"	live	
(6) Recreational and wilderness mecca	recreationalists & nature lovers tourist/service industry	"Red Rock country," scenery, rugged wilderness qualities, amenities	wilderness hiking, cliff climbing, etc. visit & leave	other visitors (require low numbers for maximum enjoyment)
(7) Place of natural beauty	conservationists real estate/tourist/service industry all	landscape, climate, etc.	hike, photograph, etc.	
(8) Prime tourist resort	tourist/service industry tourists	resorts, amenities, climate, etc.	stay at hotels, buy souvenirs, go on jeep & helicopter tours, etc.	
(9) Second-home and "post-urban" amenity community	"second-homers" post-urban "amenity migrants"	scenery, amenities, "quality of life," condo communities	fly in & out cottage industries, business	
(10) Multiple-use management problem	U.S. Forest Service	regulations	range, manage, enforce regulations, guide	townsfolk, New Agers, "land abusers"

(11) Place for employment	low-wage laborers (commuters from nearby towns, Mexicans)	tourist, service & construction industries	work, commute (or live in low-income mobile homes)	
(12) Home, "origin place"	Yavapai-Apache Hopi	documented and oral history " "	ceremonies at Boynton Canyon private use of sacred sites (herb gathering, etc.)	desecrators of sacred sites New Age "cultural appropriators"
(13) *Sacred landscape/ power place:*				
(a) center of "earth energy," "vortexes"	New Age/metaphysical community (healers, psychics) tourist industry (prim. New Age)	experiences at vortexes channeled "messages"	meditation, channeling, etc. group celebrations (Harmonic Convergence, "12:12," etc.)	land developers conservative Christians
(b) Native American sacred landscape	" " (and some Native Americans)	archaeological evidence, speculation, etc.	building medicine wheels, ceremonial work	
(c) ancient (Lemurian?) landscape temple	" "	landscape features, psychic "information"	dowsing, healing work	

Place-myth/ representation	Representatives	Narratives & claims	Spatial practices, socio-economic activities	Group constructs, "others"
(d) High-energy hot spot, spiritual "pressure cooker"	" "	instability in personal & community life; high turnover rate within N.A. community; difficulty of organizing stable institutional structures (e.g. the Center in Sedona)	" "	
(e) UFO hot spot, "interdimensional portals," "secret government" military activity zone	" "	UFO/psychic experiences, channelled "information," military activities?		"secret government," ET "greys"
(14) Battleground between good and evil	evangelical & fundamentalist Christians	proliferation of New Age activities in town	prayer & "spiritual warfare"	New Age as evil, "Satanic conspiracy"
(15) "Weirdo" haven	media (national and state)	New Age activities, strange goings-on	media reports	"irrational, gullible" New Agers

SEVEN

Vortexes and Crossed Currents: Sedona's Multichannel Wilderness

Sedona's New Age, or metaphysical, community—the terms are used interchangeably, though the latter has been in use for a longer time[1]—constitutes a tolerated and not particularly powerful minority of the city's population. However, much of Sedona's reputation in the world at large has resulted from its celebration by the New Age and alternative spirituality movements. Probably more people outside Arizona have come to hear about the town because of this association with New Age activities and famous "vortexes" than for any other single reason; the *Los Angeles Times* has even called Sedona "the Vatican City of the New Age movement" (Rivenburg 1994).

This chapter will examine Sedona's New Age community—its history, spatial practices, and the place-myths and images by which New Agers and metaphysical spiritualists have tried to establish the sacredness of the red rock landscape. The New Age community has evolved in an ambivalent and sometimes antagonistic relationship with several other communities or groups, including the town's evangelical Christians, the local forest service, and Native American communities which have their own claims on the landscape. I will examine the relationships between these and the controversies and debates that have emerged around two spatial conflicts: the issue of New Age medicine wheels constructed on U.S. Forest Service lands, and the struggle over the future of Red Rock Crossing. Always in the background and frequently in the foreground will be the red rock landscape itself, a landscape which swirls with electromagnetic energies and cosmic messages for some, but stands silent beneath the desirous and consuming gaze of others.

GROWTH OF THE NEW AGE COMMUNITY

Sedona's New Age community has its roots in the activities of a handful of metaphysical spiritualists, primarily women, beginning in the late 1950s. At the time, Mary Lou Keller—still alive and known today as Sedona's "matri-arch of metaphysics"—with a circle of friends, held regular meditations in their homes. By the mid-1960s Keller had become a teacher of Hatha Yoga and a real estate saleswoman (a combination that strikes many Sedonans as natural), and was offering space for lectures, seminars, and workshops in her Keller Building on Hwy. 179—a building that was to serve as a commu-nity focus for over twenty-five years. Keller helped a number of metaphysi-cal groups establish themselves in the area, including the psychic organiza-tion ECKankar, the Rainbow Ray Focus group, the Unity Church, and her own Sedona Church of Light (founded in 1973). Among her cohorts was Helen Varner Frye, a woman who "fell in love" with Sedona while flying over it in 1941 with her then-husband Jack Frye, president at the time of Trans World Airlines (TWA): "When I saw this place," she recounts, "I knew it was home" (*SRRN*, June 6, 1974). Later a confidant of Nassan Gobran's, Frye became an active proponent of ECKankar and helped them establish their headquarters near Cathedral Rock. Other groups to establish them-selves in the area in the early years included the Sri Aurobindo Center and Torkom Saraydarian's Aquarian Educational Center.[2]

Sedona's reputation grew through the 1970s. California-based psychic and self-help guru Dick Sutphen lauded its "mysterious power spots" as early as 1976, and popularized the town as a psychic's mecca through his publication *Self-Help Update*, which together with his lectures ostensibly reached up to 100,000 readers (cf. Sutphen 1988). At around the same time, psychic Page Bryant, an apprentice of the Native American teacher Sun Bear, identified seven specific "vortexes" in the area, based on information she allegedly channeled from her "otherworldly guide" Albion.[3] By the early 1980s, jeep tour companies were offering "vortex tours"; and after Sutphen's book *Sedona: Psychic Energy Vortexes* came out in 1986, stories about the miraculous and extraordinary phenomena attributed to the vortex sites be-gan to multiply. By 1987 a large medicine wheel had been constructed by New Agers on Schnebly Hill (more on this below). The wheel soon be-came a focus for New Age ceremonial activities, as well as the first in a series of ongoing controversies over whether the building of such stone circles should be allowed on Forest Service land.

With the celebration of the Harmonic Convergence in 1987, Sedona's New Age community established its irrevocable presence in the town. Some five to ten thousand people converged for the event, some from as far away as Peru, Brazil, and Australia. Events included a Peace Concert, Sunset Services at Posse Grounds, sunrise services held by the Sedona Friends for Peace at the apex of Airport Road, and a celebration on Bell Rock attended by about 1,800 people.[4] And despite some residents' fears of inundation by "hippies" or "devil worshippers," police and Forest Service crews reported no problems, with one ranger remarking on the "very pleasant" and "very cooperative" crowd (*ST*, August 26, 1987:A3). Local business boomed for the weekend, as did rumors, such as the now famous tale of a California man who was arrested for selling $250 tickets for a spaceship that would lift off from Bell Rock; as the story goes, hundreds had gathered there to ascend with it.[5]

By the following year, a New Age information center–bookstore called The Center in Sedona had opened with the mission of providing a hub for the fragmented metaphysical community and acting as an "alternative chamber of commerce" for it. By 1989 the center had some 350 members (*Ariz. Rep.*, August 5, 1989:C1,3), and in the years since—along with at least three name changes (Community Church for the New Age, Center for the New Age, Hub of the New Age Community) and four changes of loca-tion[6]—it has been joined by an array of other healing centers, churches, and spiritual organizations, including the Healing Center of Arizona, the Crystal Sanctuary, and the Center for Advanced Energy Healing. Of the more low-key groups to locate in Sedona in recent years, the Aquarian Con-cepts Community, a semisecretive community whose teachings are based on the early-twentieth-century channeled metaphysical bible, the *Urantia Book*, are fairly typical in their belief that Sedona's "Cathedral Rock is the focal point for the energies of planetary transformation, and that various types of Angelic and extraterrestrial entities can be found around Cathedral Rock at all times" (Dannelley 1993:54).

Spiritual Melting Pot

As a proportion of the city's population, Sedona's alternative spirituality community is perhaps the largest of any comparable town or city in North America, numbering up to a couple of thousand out of a total population of some 16,000 in the greater Sedona area.[7] Many of these are active in the alternative health fields, as bodyworkers and therapists, psychics and spiri-tual counselors, though only a minority make a living from these activities alone.[8] Some work as tour leaders for one of the many jeep tour companies, or in the retail and service industry. Many of Sedona's spiritually oriented immigrants arrived as idealistic, twenty-to-forty-five-year-old seekers, leav-ing behind jobs and sometimes families (and even names) elsewhere, and seeing their arrival in Sedona as part of a spiritual path. Many began by working at odd jobs and taking whatever employment was available. As a result of economic uncertainties, Sedona's New Age community has had a high turnover rate. In recent years, though, another large category of Sedona immigrants—more affluent professionals who have become disenchanted with city or suburban living and have resettled here to what they consider a more "natural" life, to build their dream homes, or to retire—have increas-ingly overlapped with the city's "spiritual immigrants." Wealth, thus, does not seem to be a criterion for inclusion in or exclusion from the commu-nity, and "prosperity consciousness" is a prominent concern even for the less wealthy.

A typical week in Sedona might feature some twenty-five or thirty classes and workshops on such topics as shamanism, dream interpretation, rune reading, "Building Natural Immunity," the "Neglected Child Within," and yoga and meditation, as well as psychic fairs and "energy clinics," Sunday night channeling salons, and a variety of religious services. Periodic festivals bring parts of the community together. For instance, the Women's Spiral Village of Sedona, which celebrates "the Divine Feminine energy of creation," draws on local talent to produce musical-theatrical "celebrations" marking the solstices and equinoxes;[9] while other events, such as the "11:11" (November 11, 1993) and "12:12" (December 12, 1994), mark out "stargate openings" and infusions of new energy into the earth from the heavens, energy which needs to be consciously "anchored" into the planet.[10] An expensive three-day conference accompanying the 12:12 event featured a roster of New Age celebrities including Shakti Gawain, Chris Griscom, Gabrielle Roth, Deena Metzger, Dan Millman, and John Gray. (Interestingly, of the ten highly billed speakers, eight were women; this is a statistic that recurs on other levels of Sedona's New Age community, involvement in which falls into a nearly two-to-one ratio of women to men.)

Like New Age communities in Glastonbury or Findhorn, Sedona seems to have become a place for eclectic spiritual experimentation and theological hybridization. Partly because of its sense of being different from Sedona's mainstream residents and its self-identity as a sacred center for the New Age, and partly because more traditional metaphysical groups have had to open their doors to newer ideas in order to survive, the Sedona metaphysical community has nourished a mixing of traditions and terms of reference. In the resulting melting pot, references to a Father God, the Christ, the Seven Rays, Love and Light, Angelic and Extraterrestrial beings, and Ascension, are found side by side with more pagan, Native-based, or neoshamanic practices such as the use of medicine wheels, sage smudging, drumming, dancing, and Native-styled singing.[11] The two predominant strains, however, are focused, respectively, on beliefs in extraterrestrial contact and beliefs about Native American spiritual traditions.

ETs, Interdimensional Channels, and Conspiracy Cultures

Religious and spiritual groups based on alleged contacts with extraterrestrials (ETs) have emerged in many places since the earliest American UFO sightings in the late 1940s. For the most part, these groups have constituted an interesting, but not prominent, sideshow on the New Age scene. In Sedona, however, they are much more at the forefront. This can be seen in the frequent references to ETs and UFOs in New Age guidebooks to Sedona,[12] the significance ascribed to them by prominent members within the community,[13] and especially by their centrality in the magazine *Sedona: Journal of Emergence*.

In many ways *Journal of Emergence* can be seen as a New Age parallel to

Sedona Magazine (see chapter 6). The latter peddles Sedona's real estate product—the physical, material world; its glossy full-page landscape shots qualify as what some have called eco-porn, selling natural beauty by the acre while obscuring the real vulnerability of the red rock ecology to development and overuse. *Journal of Emergence,* on the other hand, promotes Sedona's channelers and metaphysical seers; indeed, it is (arguably) the flagship of the American ET channelers' community. By 1995 both magazines had attained nationwide, and in the case of *Journal of Emergence,* continentwide, distribution, though their target audiences have little obvious overlap.[14] A large part of *Journal of Emergence* consists of channeled writings, predictions, and spiritual advice, by such regular contributors as Zoosh, Lazaris, Vywamus, Metatron, YHWH, Joopah, and the Beings of Light. The magazine sets itself the following objectives: "1. To provide a forum for those who wish to speak to us from other dimensions and other realities. 2. To celebrate our emergence into multidimensionality and reconnection to the rest of creation. 3. To bring information on the truth of our eternal nature—that we are unlimited beings of Light and Love. 4. To remind us that our Light and our sense of humor will carry us through the next few interesting years" (1994–95 issue: p.2). Within the broader culture of New Age spirituality, *Journal of Emergence* represents a neo-Gnostic, millenarian, otherworldly or Ascensionist current, concerned with shedding self-imposed limitations and "ascending" into the "higher dimensions" of our "light bodies" and intergalactic destinies. A prominent trend within this movement, which may be quite disconcerting to observers, is the large number of references to a shadowy "secret government," sinister extraterrestrial "Greys," "abductions" and "implants," underground alien military bases, "black helicopters" and assorted skirmishes between forces of Light (including Pleiadians and Sirians) and those of Darkness (or "negative ETs"). For some channelers, there is a state of "war in the heavens." Others describe in detailed, quasi-scientific language the technical workings of the "lightbody," the changes which the human genetic code is allegedly undergoing as we ascend through planetary and galactic "energy shifts," and the technical details about the earth's geomagnetic grid and its power points.

In all of this, one sees a heady mixture of millennial angst, the speculative theories of fringe science, popular fascination with *Star Trek* and *X Files*–like scenarios (whose characters range from the benevolent alien messiahs made popular by earlier ET contactee groups to the more paranoid narratives of abductees), and the antigovernment conspiracy thinking that has stewed both in the far right and far left of American politics since the 1960s (cf. Dean 1998). This is a peculiarly American terrain of disaffection with "the system," a disaffection which has in the past fueled leftist sectarianism, more recently (and perturbingly) the right-wing patriotic militia movement, but also the more overtly benign—and more in evidence in Sedona—appeals to sources of "higher authority" such as a UN-styled world federalism, the Ascended Masters, ETs, Jesus and the Virgin Mary.[15] In Sedona, the conspiracy theorist fringe can be found in books and videos distributed by the Secret Information Network, and in sources such as Light Technology Publishing's compilation *Shining the Light,* which bills itself as providing "The truth about ETs, secret government, alien bases . . . the battle begins!" Most New Age thinking differs from the neofascist right in emphasizing the spiritual unity and common destiny of humankind: the "dark" forces, those thought to be preventing humanity's destined evolution toward membership within intergalactic civilization, are commonly portrayed as the inertial remnants of outmoded ways of thinking, and, when identified with particular people, are commonly extraterrestrial races. Equating darkness with evil, of course, has its risks (as postcolonial and antiracist thinkers have persuasively argued).[16] Images of racial otherness in the New Age milieu, however, tend to be more intertwined with the idea that other races, and especially indigenous peoples, have been spiritually advanced and, thus, have knowledge that might bring salvation to humanity today.[17]

Neo-Native Spirituality

Some of that "knowledge" is much in evidence in Sedona, albeit in a highly modified and romanticized form. Several of Sedona's more prominent metaphysical personalities have in fact, at one time or other, been involved in the kind of neo-Native spirituality popularized by such teachers as Sun Bear and Ed McGaa.[18] Medicine wheel ceremonies,[19] popularized by these teachers of "Native spirituality," have been an important part of the community's activities since at least the early 1980s. Since 1992 large Native-styled "encampments"—gatherings involving drumming circles, medicine wheel ceremonies, sweat lodges, and the sharing of teachings—have been held twice a year in the Sedona area, with numbers of participants growing to over three hundred.[20] Among the leaders of this activity are a few actual Natives, such as "Grandfather" Hollis Littlecreek, an Anishnabe elder and master craftsman who moved to Arizona in the late 1980s and who leads "talking circles" in the area. Hollis's presence confers a certain kind of legitimacy to the non-Natives who have taken up the "Red Road," at least in their own eyes. Those who are serious about their Native-styled practice (perhaps several dozen, in my rough estimation) attend sweat lodges regularly, conduct sunrise-to-sunset dancing on important days such as the solstice, and see their spirituality not as a hobby but as a lifetime commitment.

Outside of these circles of more committed neoshamans, suppositions, both real and imagined, about the Native history of the area pervade the marketing of "spiritual Sedona." "To the Native Americans, the red-rock area surrounding Sedona is sacred ground; the home of the Great Spirit." So begins a tour brochure for "Spirits of the Earth—Adventures for the Soul," a program of tours to sacred sites in the Southwest and Peru (VJ En-

Figure 7.1. Celebrating the 12:12 at Cathedral Rock

terprises 1996). Little is said about which Native Americans are being referred to; and, in any case, the same could be said about the entire Southwest. The brochure continues, "A journey to Sedona is an opportunity to open your psychic gifts . . . a land where awareness emerges in your soul and time has no meaning. Past, present and future become one. Our hearts open to the powerful energy here through direct contact with Spirits, visions, healings and unlimited manifestations. A journey to Sedona enables us to experience the power and beauty of the Great Spirit in this magical land." In its itinerary for the first day in Sedona, the text provides the following details: "We travel today to Sedona, the home of the Great Spirit, according to the Native Americans. Zhenya will conduct a Sacred Self-Empowerment Workshop for the group. Immediately following the Workshop, we will begin preparing ourselves for the Lakota Rite of Self Purification, also known as Stone People's Lodge or Sweatlodge Ceremony." Plains Indian (Lakota) rituals are thus being offered by a tour leader with a Slavic name at a place—far from the Plains—that "the Native Americans" consider sacred ground; all for those willing to pay the price. Such vague references to Native Americans abound, and are facilitated by two facts: that there are thousands of burial and other traditional cultural sites in the Sedona area, and that few Native Americans actually live in area—thus making it easier for the mystique to be appropriated into other agendas. I will discuss both of these factors in greater detail below.[21]

THE RED ROCK LANDSCAPE AND ITS
"INTERDIMENSIONAL" CORRELATES

Sedona's Landscape Phenomenology

For most visitors to Sedona, the entry into Red Rock Country is by one of three routes. From Flagstaff in the north, the scenic 89A negotiates several dramatic switchbacks in its 780-foot drop over two miles. Page and Wallace Stegner write: "The road from the top corkscrews through pine and Douglas fir, lower and lower, until it bottoms out in the pygmy forest of juniper-piñon that flows around the weather-battled architectonics of Coconino and Yavapai counties, the buttes, spires, columns, domes, arches of the redrock country" (Porter, Stegner, and Stegner 1981:161). The contrast between the upper part of the canyon—tree-covered and, in winter, frequently snow-covered—and the final opening before one reaches Sedona is dramatic. Negotiating the twists and turns of the road as it winds its way down can be tense, exhilarating, and ultimately cathartic upon entry into Sedona, particularly in winter, when the road may be slippery. The second route, from the south via route 179 leading from the interstate (I-17), provides its first glimpse of red rocks at some distance past Camp Verde. Red soil begins showing through the greenery on hills, and suddenly there is an opening—a view on a huge red rock mesa (Horse Mesa and Lee Mountain). A few more hills and turns later and more red appears, until one sees the looming shape of the aptly named Bell Rock. Passing Bell Rock and its companions (Courthouse Rock on its right and Castle Rock across the highway to the left), there is no question that one has entered a distinctly different place—red rock country. Finally, the third entry route to Sedona, from the southwest, is more straight and the approach more gradual than the others: the road from Cottonville slowly, patiently works its way toward that explosion of red rock in the distance.

Within Sedona one feels cradled, and at times dwarfed, by the red rock landscape. This is especially the case close to the Y formed by the meeting of 179 and 89A, and to its south, where 179 snakes around in the sloping folds of the landscape. There is a monumentality to the landscape, as if it contains a web of powerful ciphers or hieroglyphics, giant rock sentinels beaming out signals to some extraterrestrial observer. Maneuvering one's way through the folds of the earth's surface here, what becomes clear is that the landscape is not so much a unity, with any particular center, as it is a mosaic of shifting forms—a multiplicity of overlapping landscapes, canyons, ridges, rock formations, and distinct sites unified only by their identification as Sedona or Red Rock Country. The texture of the landscape suggests thickness and heaviness, a rough strength and solidity with the seeming authority of having endured across many aeons. There is a persistence and an assertiveness in the way these distinct formations stand out from their surroundings, with their color—invigorating and energizing reds, brownish reds, pinks, coppers—adding to this apparent strength. Compared to its surroundings, in fact, the Sedona landscape seems a unique irruption of reddish brown sculptured rock giants, easily anthropomorphized into distinctive landscape "guardians." Contemporary geomancer Nick Mann, in his speculative interpretation of the Sedona landscape, describes their towering rock shapes as "elemental presences" (1991:36):[22]

> Many of the buttes of the Red Rock Country evoke the qualities of guardianship, of wise and eternal presences watching over the land. There are the examples of the seated figures in the Twin Buttes by the Chapel of the Holy Cross. They are known variously as the Madonna or the Two Nuns, the Apostles or St. Peter and St. Paul. Perhaps all are present if the two adjacent rocks are included. There are the Sentinel Rocks at the head of Soldier Pass where the two buttes display magnificent giants' heads. And there is of course, the bird-being in Coffee Pot or Horus Rock [a.k.a. Eagle Rock]. Yet, for sheer majesty the tall figures enshrined in the central towers of Cathedral Rock stand out above all. . . . The man and the woman standing back to back in Cathedral Rock embody eternal values of humanity: the balancing of male and female, the harmonizing of relationships upon the earth and the essential interdependence of all peoples. These gigantic figures in their sanctified setting form one of the key geomantic signatures of Sedona. . . . (34)

Red is a color associated with heat, fire, blood, high energy; and here, this "vibrating energy" is held in place by these strange rock formations which frame, envelop, and cradle the town. Yet they show no clear logic in their spatial distribution: the framing panoramic backdrop to West Sedona provided by the wall of rock from Capitol Butte to Coffee Pot Rock; the drop down into the Y and Oak Creek; the scattered and fractured multiple formations east of the city—from Schnebly Hill and Mund's Mountain down to Courthouse Rock's horizontal, rectangular slablike presence (with its "Indian chief's head" seemingly carved into its top surface, staring out at the sky), Bell Rock's triangular "beacon," and Castle Rock. As one winds around one formation, others come into view. And there is always the promise of further twists and folds of the land beyond, waiting to be discovered, steep canyons and evocatively shaped rock formations in the outlying areas of the Red Rock–Secret Canyon and Munds Wilderness areas.

Within this broad expanse, the areas that have been singled out as vortexes each have their own distinctiveness. I can hardly present an exhaustive description of even the four or five main vortexes here; so the following description is merely intended to provide the flavor of one possible interpretive encounter with the landscape. In my attempts to understand and apply the process by which New Agers and others interpret the Sedona landscape, over the course of two months in the winter of 1994–95, I arrived at the tentative conclusion that the Y created by the intersecting roads (89A and 179) together with Oak Creek, flowing down from the Mogollon uplands to the valley below, have played a central role in shaping both the growth of

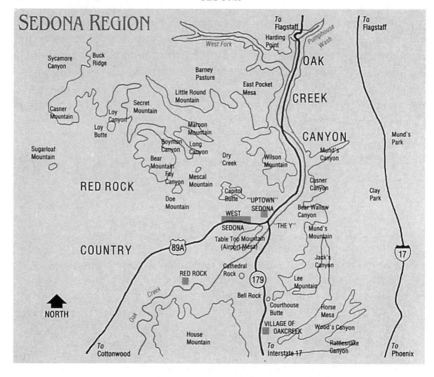

Map 7.1. Sedona area. Note Y formed by routes 89A and 179

the town and its inhabitants' and visitors' perception of the landscape. On their descent down from the Colorado Plateau, 89A and Oak Creek wind their way around each other and within the valley formed by the creek, in a way that is reminiscent of the snake coiled around the modern medic's Hippocratic staff, the Hermetic caduceus, or the kundalini, which, in Indian tradition, is said to travel up the spine[23] — until they finally spill out into the open red rock oasis of the town. The creek continues to flow out between the legs formed by the two roads beyond the Y, and in this area is found Airport Mesa and, farther down, Cathedral Rock and Red Rock Crossing. It is along these arteries of road and creek that traffic and water flows — water being the natural lifeblood of this relatively dry area, and traffic being the town's cultural lifeblood throughout its century-old history and all the more so today. Sedona has developed around the Y and in the areas opened up by the roads (such as West Sedona). Cradling the whole, to the northwest of · 89A and to the east of 179, are located the larger rock formations, mountains, and wilderness areas.

If there is any geographically central formation within this bodylike structure — central in relation to the town itself and in its being located between the legs formed by the roads spreading out from the Y — it is arguably Airport Mesa, also known as Table Top Mountain. Continuing with the body anal-

Figure 7.2. Medicine wheel at the Airport vortex

ogy, this mesa is located at what would be the pubic area of Sedona. Allowing for a bit of imaginative freedom here (if only to illustrate the process of
reading meanings into a landscape), Airport Mesa, given its shape, could be
read either as a phallus or a womb, or, more convincingly perhaps, as the
child emerging from the womb formed by the Y (see map 7.1). It seems not
surprising, given such a reading, that a small outlying area found toward the
north end of the mesa (to call it the clitoris would be stretching the analogy
too far) has been singled out as one of Sedona's major vortexes.[24] This vortex
is said to be located roughly on (or in the air above) a small hill between two
larger hills at Airport Mesa's north end. The middle hill is flat on top, allowing for small groups of people to sit, meditate, or conduct rituals, and is set
between two dips in a saddle flanked by the larger hills, which seem to offer
protection on either side of the vortex.

The top of the hill provides one of the best views on the surrounding
landscape, facing two broad vistas, to the southeast and to the northwest,
framed by the surrounding hills. To the southeast is a broad valley through
which runs Oak Creek, flanked by a dense patch of riverine vegetation; and
a few roads snake their way through the valley. Across it, in the distance, are
the fractured walls of the red rock monuments of Munds Mountain, Courthouse Rock, Bell Rock, Castle Rock, and others. To stand at the Airport
vortex and look out ahead in this direction is to look over a vast expanse of
valley, framed and cradled within looming walls and distinctive formations
of creamy reddish rock. A dialectic seems to occur here between sky and

earth, with the earth opening up to the sky above, and the mesas, buttes, and mountains in the distance both looking up and looking over the outstretched valley, winding creek, and the smattering of homes which appear like dots on the landscape. As one stands looking over this valley, the rock formations in the distance seem to "respond" to one's thoughts or mirror one's projected mental state. Meanwhile, the more immediate vicinity of this vortex presents an abundance of underdefined and underinscribed textural features ready to be filled in with meaning and significance: cracks and fissures within the rock, an interplay of smooth and rough textures, of shadow and light, black streaks and cracks, parts jutting out and others receding into concealedness, and all around, the outstretched bony surface of the earth "pushing itself up" here and there, and the fleshy, green vegetation-covered valleys "laying themselves open" to the sky. The visual qualities are further suffused with smells, vibrant and "electric" air, and other sensory stimuli. Writer Wallace Stegner, decades after leaving the much smaller Sedona of his youth, reminisces:

> I like to remember it by the way it smells when a sudden afternoon shower sweeps by and leaves just enough of itself to clean the dust off the chaparral and darkly stain the rocks. And the way the sky looks as that little storm approaches, one low, isolated cloud framed on the horizon by two silhouetted mesas, rain shot, its underside tattered like the fringe of an old lady's shawl. I like to remember it by the way the light changes from moment to moment on the face of its redwall cliffs as evening comes down and plunges the canyons in cold shadow while the ramparts above still blaze in the setting sun. (Porter, Stegner, and Stegner 1981:162)

Energy Vortexes and the Sacred Landscape

Sedona's identification as a sacred landscape presents certain problems for scholars of religion. Landscapes are considered sacred if they have a history of being sacred for someone; in North America, this often means for indigenous groups. Euro-American ideas of sacredness have traditionally focused on built (religious) structures and on places associated with historical events or significant personae. Natives have frequently argued that Western concepts cannot be applied to understanding indigenous cultures, for many of whom whole landscapes are considered sacred. In *God Is Red*, an influential and sustained argument for such an expanded understanding of sacred land, Vine Deloria Jr. (1994) argues that lands can be sacred not only for historical reasons, but also because "the sacred" at a given site "takes the initiative" to reveal itself in new ways to humans. Emphasizing the historical dimension of sacred place, however, he adds that "No revelation can be regarded as universal because times and conditions change," and therefore, "People must always be ready to experience new revelations at new locations" (277).

In the red rock landscape around Sedona, a sizable community of people has come to believe that the sacred has revealed itself, to them and to others, and that the identification of energy vortexes is a part of this revelation. Definitions of vortexes, however, present a blurred picture. Bryant (n.d.) identifies vortexes as constituting "Earth's emotional body" and as "caused by the Earth's emotional response to its own evolutionary experience." In her view, Earth grids and ley lines are the nervous system of the planet, its "life energy and currents," while vortexes are those points at which the currents meet or "become coagulated into funnels of energy" (Bryant et al. 1991:4). Sutphen (1988:167) defines a vortex as an "energy enhancing field," and he claims to have trained hundreds of individuals in enhancing their "psychic energy" at these fields. Like Bryant, he draws on the common analogy that explains vortexes as power spots akin to acupressure points on the Earth's body (7–8). Similarly, Sedona author and psychic Pete Sanders Jr. calls vortexes areas of "enhanced spiritual energy flow" that "turboboost" meditative, creative and reflective abilities (quoted in Winton 1990b). Tom Dongo (1988:29ff.) calls vortexes "energy springs," but adds that the word is misleading, because Sedona's vortexes don't necessarily spin or rotate; some are "just there, stationary, radiant, vibrant, glowing, powerful" (32).

Vortexes are customarily classified into "electric" ones, said to be stimulating, energizing, and uplifting (yang), and "magnetic" ones, which are thought to make one more focused, receptive, and psychically aware (yin). Other terms used to make this distinction include *uplift* and *inflow*, or *masculine* and *feminine* (e.g., Sanders 1992). The Airport Mesa vortex, Apache Leap, Coffee Pot (or Eagle) Rock, and Bell Rock are all considered electric vortexes; Bryant calls Bell Rock a "beacon vortex" which "shoots out" and "receives" energy from outside the Earth's aura and body. Magnetic vortexes include Cathedral Rock, Red Rock Crossing, and West Fork; balanced electromagnetic "combination vortexes" include Boynton Canyon, which Dongo calls "a clairvoyant's Horn of Plenty" (1988:27); and Oak Creek Canyon as a whole is considered an "electromagnetic grid" (Bryant et al. 1991:91). Certain sites have also been identified as "negative vortexes" because their effect is thought to be unhealthy (e.g., Indian Gardens, and the Sedona Post Office site, which, according to local lore, accounts for the office's unsatisfying delivery record). According to most of Sedona's New Age authors and psychics, the concentration and variety of vortexes in the area makes Sedona unique in the Southwest and one of only a few such places in the world (e.g., Sutphen 1988; Bryant et al. 1991:39). The term *vortex*, however, begins to reveal its elusiveness when it is said that there are "up to 100" vortexes in the area, or that Sedona is itself "one big vortex" (Dongo 1988). Vortexes are also said to change over time, their energy dissipating while new vortexes emerge.

The literature on Sedona's vortexes makes frequent, if vague, reference to their "scientific" basis. For instance, vortexes are said to be anomalous electromagnetic phenomena, caused by the presence of magnetic basalt intrusions (veins of iron-bearing basalt), faulting, or some other force. There are three faults in the Sedona area, the Bear Wallow Canyon, Oak Creek, and Sedona (or Cathedral Rock) faults, intersecting east of the city, which could account for electromagnetically induced phenomena.[25] Some have related Sedona's energy to its "abundant underground water streams." Local "bioelectromagnetic field" and "earth grid" researcher and one-time laser technician Dirk Van Dijk argues, "The friction of water flowing in rock produces electrical currents with circular polarization. The 4% iron oxide content in the red rocks would tend to focus the energy in a tight area. The effect this has on the human biofield depends on the strength and frequency of the field(s) involved" (in Dongo 1993:42). Others, more cautiously, attribute Sedona's "energizing" qualities to the psychological effect of the landscape's predominantly reddish hues, and to negative ion discharges known to be more common in dry, open, and rocky areas.

Contemporary geomancers also commonly draw on ideas taken from traditional Chinese geomancy to read the lay of the land (though, as a rule, this "Chinese geomancy" is taken from often fanciful New Age popularizations rather than from primary sources). As in acupuncture, the Earth's surface is considered to conduct the flow of an invisible life energy, called *ch'i* or *qi*, which ideally is balanced between active *yang* and receptive *yin* forces. Geomancers refer to the White Tiger (yin) and Blue Dragon (yang) energies, which flow in currents following so-called dragon veins in and through the landscape. Where the land is flat, uninterrupted by landforms, high buildings or trees, or flowing water, yin energy is said to accumulate and lead to stagnation, with the land unable to breathe properly. Where it is too dynamic, as in mountainous terrain, yang energy flows rapidly and becomes dispersed. Chinese geomancy further relies on a five-element system, according to which all things are seen as consisting of different combinations of earth, fire, water, metal, and wood. Each different landform is seen as corresponding with one of these elements. Sedona's landscape in its variety is thought to include all these shapes: rounded peaks corresponding to metal (e.g., Capitol Butte); flattened peaks, wood (Table Top Mountain); plateaus, earth (the top of Mogollon Rim); sharp peaks, fire (Bell Rock); and wavy ridges, water (Scheurman Mountain). Flowing underground water also plays a significant role in geomancy. As Nick Mann (1991:21) points out, Sedona sits below the edge of a vast rainwater collector, the Colorado Plateau, whose geological strata consist of permeable Redwall Limestone fragmented by faults (such as Oak Creek Canyon) and fissures, indicated by the fact that basaltic volcanic lava has filled up some faults. There are visible caverns, powerful springs (Oak Creek is an artesian spring creek) and sinkholes, formed by the movement of underground water eroding soft rock in such a way that a circular cavern is formed; in the Sedona area, the Devil's Kitchen sinkhole is 60 feet deep and over 100 feet across, Devil's Dining Room is 75 feet deep and 25 feet across, and a third sinkhole is located south of Boynton Pass. These indicate the existence of large aquifers, suggesting many miles of underground water activity.

Red Rock Country is thus thought to be an energetically active and dynamic landscape, with few places for the flow of life energy to become blocked and stagnant. With its sharp mountainous points and spires, towering red buttes, high incidence of lightning strikes in the summer, and frequent sun, the "electrical" or yang energies are even quite volatile. But these are balanced and grounded by the presence of underground water (yin), which, to the degree it is found here, is comparatively rare in the dry Southwest.[26] Both these factors—the diversity and "intensity" of landscape features, and the presence and flow of water, both underground and overground, in an otherwise generally dry area—are attributable to the conditions created by Sedona's location at the southwest edge of the Mogollon Rim, and are, arguably, what make this area unique.

Inscribing the Land: Place-Stories and Space Claims

The Sedona area's physiographic diversity and distinctiveness provide a wealth of affordances for the imaginative place-making impulse. Rock formations in themselves hold a special allure for many New Agers, at least since the explosion of interest in crystals and their uses for healing—a phenomenon that itself encapsulates many of the back-to-nature, holistic health, and native-romanticist strains of New Age culture.[27] In this sense, Sedona has come to represent a place of *literal* power, a landscape that is charged with an energy that, for some, represents health, healing, and vigor; for others, psychic and spiritual power; and for still others, the power captured in the *image* of the red rock landscape, a power to be transformed into riches through the labor of real estate sales and development—with all these variants located somewhere on a continuum of desire.

Another factor that has facilitated the Sedona area's growth in popularity is the fact that it has neither been set aside as national parkland nor as Indian reservation. It is therefore open for settlement and for spatialization as real estate, as sacred place, or as anything else its Rorschach inkblot–like landscape allows. The relative lack of an obvious Native connection is important, as it has made it easier for New Agers to appropriate the landscape into their own narratives. Though the signs of indigenous habitation are present all around, no contemporary Native community with claims on the landscape actually resides in the Sedona area (though the Camp Verde Yavapai-Apaches have been making their presence felt increasingly in recent years). New Agers have therefore been able to inscribe it with their own meanings with relative ease. These include suppositions about Native American history (i.e. frequent claims that the area has long been holy ground for Hopis, Navajos, Apaches, Anasazi, and other groups), ancient civilizations such as the "Lemurian" (a Pacific analogue to Atlantis), ley lines and earth grids (e.g., that energy lines link Sedona with Glastonbury, the Great Pyramid of Giza, Mount Ararat, and other power spots), beliefs about crystal caverns and underground tunnels, extraterrestrials, and shad-owy government or military activities. The notion that Sedona was once a central city and temple complex of Lemuria, for instance, allows New Agers to upstage any existing Native land claims by invoking for themselves a higher and more ancient authority presumed by them to be equally or more deeply rooted in the land.[28]

Sedona's spatialization also involves the elaboration of many more indi-vidual and site-specific *place-stories*, which serve to spread its reputation within the broader New Age and ecospiritual culture. Anecdotal tales about how people first arrived in Sedona, or how they ended up there, constitute a rich element in Sedona's ethnographic texture, and a central pivot for the self-conscious myth the New Age community propagates about itself. Many of Sedona's New Agers report feeling "irresistibly 'drawn' here" or obsessing over Sedona after they first heard about it or saw pictures of it (Dongo 1988:1). Some, like "biomedical scientist" and parapsychologist Ara Avedissian, claim to have been urged to come by an "inner voice" (Java 1989a:1–2), while others report being profoundly affected by their first en-counter, or feeling an overpowering sense of "homecoming" or of déjà vu, as if recognizing this landscape from a dream or a previous life (e.g., Sut-phen 1988:21,22).[29] The experience of driving into Sedona is sometimes described as "entering another world" (Sutphen 1988:15): "I couldn't be-lieve my eyes or my senses. I stopped, frozen in my tracks, and spun around. Everywhere I looked was red-rock beauty, rock formations that made me feel as though I'd landed on another planet. This was truly like nothing I'd ever seen or even dreamed of, in my life" (Ron Babin, in Dongo 1993:51).

Like Glastonbury and other such places, Sedona is frequently spoken of in anthropomorphic terms, as if it was a sentient being with its own will and agenda. Dongo writes, "either Sedona treats people wonderfully—or it chews them up and spits them out" (Dongo 1988:2). Sedona is a "town situated in a vast zone of powerful, shifting, mysterious and sometimes vola-tile energies" (4). It is a "pressure cooker" (Jelm, int.), amplifying emotions and bringing out the best and worst in people. Sedona is often said to "hold a mirror" to its pilgrims and to "bring you in touch with your real self"; the external landscape becomes a reflection of the internal one, so that "if some-thing's wrong out there, it means there's something wrong in here" (Arm-bruster, int.). This can lead to "red rock fever": "the energy's so intense," says a New Age bookstore owner, "that after a while you have to get out of here" (*ST*, June 4–10, 1986:8). It is frequently asserted that "the Indians didn't live here"; rather, they considered the whole red rock area sacred and only visited it for ceremonial purposes (a Pink Jeep Tours guide quoted in *ST*, July 26, 1989:2). In all this Sedona is thought to contrast sharply with its surroundings: "I began to feel Sedona was one big vortex. . . . and, in gen-eral, when I left Sedona I felt different; and when I was here, I felt a strong vibration" (Jelm, int.). Another interviewee reported:

It seems to be, when people come in from the south, as they approach the Village [of Oak Creek], it's like there's a [specific] place where the energy turns on. . . . I've questioned so many people, and it seems to click in before [Bell Rock], and, uh, as if there is a definite shift, you know. People may start crying, or just feeling tingly, or elated, or, you know, many different kinds of expression of that energy. But they definitely feel that energy when they hit it. So, what I'm saying is you are under the influence of this cosmic battery anywhere on it, which means anywhere on the red rocks and maybe a bit beyond, you know, going up to Schnebly, up to Merry-Go-Round, the top red rock point, up to Cockscomb that way [points north], Isis that way [points west], and Bell Rock, that way [east]. (Lamb, int.)

Tour guides and therapeutic practitioners within the New Age community ascribe specific properties to different sites. According to a local dowser and tour guide, people "have really intense, frenetic experiences" at Bell Rock, so to counterbalance that effect, "we take them over to Rachel's View after they've been here a few days, and they settle down" (Armbruster, int.). Sutphen (1988) claims to have collected "hundreds and hundreds of pages of reports of the experiences people have had in the vortexes," most of them enlisted from participants in his Psychic Seminars: these experiences include "intense spiritual visions," "impressions of what took place in these canyons long ago," "direct contact with spirit entities who remain here," physical healings, past life regressions, auras or "hazes" over Bell and Cathedral Rocks, unexplained sounds, and "a physical change that virtually eliminates the need for sleep."[30] Tales of unusual encounters, mysterious disappearances, unknown rumblings, and UFO sightings or extraterrestrial encounters are said to be particularly common in the Dry Creek and Secret Canyon areas.[31]

Portals into Other Spaces

Much of the New Age activity in the area involves the attempt to communicate with nonphysical entities, and a great deal of this "communication" concerns the "interdimensional landscape," an "etheric" or psychically perceivable, but otherwise invisible, parallel landscape filled with spiritual or extraterrestrial presences, "energy portals" and "interdimensional doorways," "stargates," "third-, fourth-, and fifth-density realities," and the like. The *Sedona Vortex Guide Book* (Bryant et al. 1991), a compilation of accounts by several of the area's better-known channelers, features the same chorus of voices that fill the pages of *Sedona: Journal of Emergence*. We are informed that Sedona is "an affirmation of the linking with the Galactic Core through the specific energy-linkage system provided by the angelic hosts. . . . The space beings flood into the area, . . . coming in on specific energy grids identified through an energy resonance" (44–45). About vortexes we are told that they are "swirling masses of pure energy, rotating about an imaginary axis that extends through the Earth"; "*dissemination points* for the re-

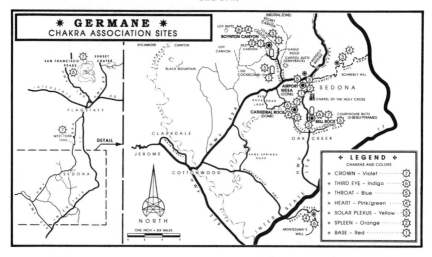

Map 7.2. Sedona chakra association sites. Courtesy of Light Technology Publishing

lease as well as *freeing points* that accept the incoming flow from the solar system"; "renewal centers for consciousness"; "intersection points of varying time-space continuums"; "spiraling streams of energy that contain within them the Light patterns (codes) which define creation"; "a *supermicrobiological interaction* with organisms that function beyond the level of physical biology"; and "the life-support system of creation" which provides the "basic energy units" for the planet's survival. They are said to affect neurons and brain chemicals, expand "auric density," draw out and dissipate people's "inner seismic energy," and "release" the Earth's built up "energy pressure" (various pages; all italics in original).

Sedona, for one channeler, is said to be both "a point of stability" and "a point of dynamic transference or dynamic movement." "In a cosmic sense," the author continues, "Sedona is located in the area of the spleen. . . . Thus it cleanses and then blends. . . ." For another, Sedona "represents a doorway for extraterrestrial consciousness to *enter* your [*sic*] Earth plane," but is *not* "one of the *major*" earth chakras nor of the twelve "*major* vortexes" (italics in original). And a third reveals that "Sedona is laid out, you might say, as a graduate school. There are certain places where one goes when one is beginning to 'do' Sedona." This author warns against starting with Boynton Canyon, Secret Canyon, or Fay Canyon, and suggests instead a more "gentle" area, such as Schnebly Hill. Different authors offer varying recommendations and conceptualizations of the different vortexes and energy sites. Two examples are presented in maps 7.2 and 7.3, which portray the "chakra association sites" and "interdimensional access points" proposed by "Germane" and "Zoosh," two entities channeled, respectively, by local psychics Lyssa Royal and Robert Shapiro. These and other such mappings sug-

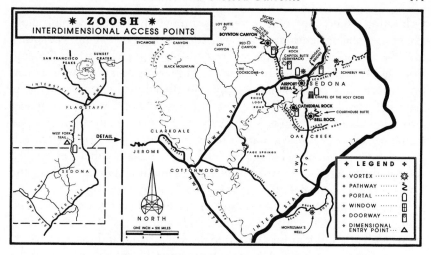

Map 7.3. Sedona interdimensional access points.
Courtesy of Light Technology Publishing

gest two primary concentrations of sites: one extending from Airport Mesa and Oak Creek (including Cathedral Rock) to the area around Courthouse Butte and Bell Rock, and perhaps to the Chapel of the Holy Cross; the other including the Dry Creek and Boynton Canyon areas and beyond, and possibly extending east to Soldier's Pass. Other than the fact that these tend to be away from residential areas (yet within easy reach), few clear patterns emerge from comparing the different authors' suggestions. In this dense polyphony of writings, the red rock landscape becomes a thickly inscribed latticework of crisscrossing electromagnetic fields and pulsating energy streams, rock formations abuzz with cosmic voices, and invisible portals opening onto other times and places. Sedona's psychics log onto this cosmic computer, where particular sites on the landscape correspond to mental states and spiritual lessons, chakras and bodily functions, and planetary constellations with their respective extraterrestrial civilizations. Since no authoritative account exists of them, the landscape is always there to be explored and discovered further, then woven into the millennial stream of cosmically authorized predictions, warnings, practical teachings, grand historical narratives, and up-to-the-minute accounts of UFO crashes, secret government realignments, astrological developments, and the like.

Spatial Practices

Sedona's New Agers and earth spiritualists engage in a variety of individual and collective activities which serve to reinforce their claims about the landscape's sacrality and distinctiveness. These activities include hiking or walking the land and visiting specific sites repeatedly with spiritual intent;

cultivating a state of psychic receptivity through meditation, visualization, chanting, "chakra activation," invocation or channeling of guides or spirits; and the arrangement of stones or rocks in medicine wheels and the conducting of ceremonies within them. Most New Age and ecospiritual ceremonial ritual is founded on the supposition that thought forms and images have real effects on the world, and that focused "work" with such images can bring about real results, such as the effective resacralization of a particular place or the reinvigoration of its earth energies. Medicine wheels are, for that reason, often left in place after their use, rather than being taken apart as the Forest Service would prefer; and sometimes tobacco, coins, pine cones, or other personal offerings are left behind as well.

By celebrating specific events associated with a New Age calendar, such as the Harmonic Convergence or the 11:11s and 12:12s, at particular sites, New Agers attempt to bring them into the sacred time and space by which they are striving to live.[32] A more intensive use of the land occurs at the biennial encampments. One of the leaders of these gatherings explained to me that the nature of the ceremonies performed at them has to do with "working with the energy of the Earth." The encampments are a way of generating a sense of community, and when they include powerfully felt ceremonies, they precipitate a "shift" not only in the participants, but (so I was told) in the Earth itself. "There's a certain vibration that the Earth has, literally, and when we all get attuned to that vibration, we're all on the same wavelength. [The ceremony] doesn't derive its validity from any tradition or from any elder guidance. It derives its validity from the energy of the Earth itself. When the ceremonies work, the energy increases; when they don't, it doesn't." The nature of this form of ceremonial work is reflected in the same person's account of the controversial medicine wheel ceremonies held at Schnebly Hill in the late 1980s.

> We built that thing . . . to heal a huge ley line up there. . . . A lot of people resented that because we were outsiders. And I don't blame them. But that was what we were guided to [do]. . . . It was a big ley line coming from one fault going over to another. [Note: there are two fault lines in the Schnebly Hill area.—AI] And it was just flat broken.
>
> AI: And you could dowse that?
>
> Yeah. And there was one tree that held the ley line. . . . The reason the wheel was so big was not because somebody . . . wanted it to be big—but the ley line was so big 'cause it needed to be big enough to encompass how wide the ley line was, and that was how big we built it. So it was determined by the energy. . . . And the pattern [had been] a vision. . . . Well, later I read that there was supposed to be a man-made vortex made in Schnebly Hill. And thousands of people had come to that place. They still do.
>
> AI: Where'd you read that?
>
> That was Page Bryant [who] had channeled that. And I didn't know that—we

built the thing, and then I read about that. And it literally became another vortex. And so that prophecy was fulfilled.

AI: *There were ceremonies going on up there . . . ?*

Oh, constantly. There has been for years—ever since it was built, and even now when it's been totally destroyed, people still go up there and rebuild it . . . and they still do ceremonies there. Which is true for all the vortexes.

The Schnebly Hill ceremonies unfolded over a cycle of "wheels" (four each for banishing or purification, balance, blessing, and beauty) performed in the morning, noon, evening, and night on a series of thirteen days which culminated on the day of the Harmonic Convergence. With their number of participants growing from a handful to seventy-five or eighty at the final ceremony, the process, according to this informant, was so "powerful" that "after a while, that's all we lived for—just to do those ceremonies. . . . It was transformative."

Through the regular use of specific sites for meditation, ceremony, and other practices, then, the red rock landscape is sacralized by Sedona's New Age and metaphysical community. Their attempts to do so, however, occur in the context of interpretive disputes with other groups, and broader sets of socioeconomic relations. In the remainder of this chapter I will focus on the most important of these, and on a few specific sites where these disputes have become most acute.

INTERPRETIVE CONTEXTS AND CONTESTS

Native Americans, Cultural Appropriation, and the Red Rocks

Relative to other states, Arizona has a very prominent Native presence. Since about the 1960s, the Navajos, Hopis, Apaches, and other tribes, who own 28 percent of Arizona's land (Ruland-Thorne 1990:13), have been re-asserting their traditions and rights with growing success. Native groups have expressed a desire for greater access to sacred places and food collection areas, for exclusive use of religious sites at certain times of the year, and for greater recognition and consultation around heritage and cultural site management issues. Some want inspection rights of certain sites and repossession of religious objects that have been taken from them over the years (Aitchison 1994:12). Though the looting of Native graves and outright desecration of cultural sites has subsided in recent decades, desecration continues, largely out of ignorance and in the cause of development. When a Sedona developer bought a major Sinagua ruin site on Sugarloaf Hill outside Cornville—a fifty-four-room stone complex and major cultural and trading center from around 1300 A.D.—he planned to clear the ruins off the hilltop to build a home. Members of the Hopi, Apache, and Yavapai tribes along with Cornville residents protested and blocked the excavation site, and, in the end, their efforts resulted in the passage of a new state law protecting burial grounds. Eventually, the site was bought and protected by a nonprofit preservation group, the Archaeological Conservancy (Shaffer 1991b).

Yavapai, Tonto Apache, Hopi, and Navajo people all have oral traditions related to this part of Arizona. For the first two groups (which have intermixed during the past 150 years), the Sedona area plays a central role in their cultural histories. Yavapai-Apache elders recount:

> We come out at Sedona, the middle of the world. This is our home. . . .
>
> We call Sedona *Wipuk*. We call it after the rocks in the mountains there. Some of my people, they call themselves *Wipukpa*. That's the ones who live up there around Sedona. All Yavapai come from Sedona. But in time they spread out.
>
> North of Camp Verde there is Montezuma Well. We call it *Ahagaskiaywa*. This lake has no bottom and underneath the water spreads out wide. That's where the people come out first. (told by Mike Harrison [born 1886] and John Williams [born 1904], in *The Yavapai of Fort McDowell*, ed. S. Khera, 1979; cited in Trimble 1993:229)

In one elder's account, tradition holds that the Yavapais climbed into this world from the previous one through the limestone sink now known as Montezuma Well. In the Sedona country the Yavapais locate the sacred caves where Kamalapukwia (Komwidapokuwia), Old Lady White Stone, survived the flood that destroyed the third world of existence, and the cave where her grandson, Skark'a mca (Skata-kaamcha, Sakarakaamche), Lofty Wanderer, taught all beings the proper way to live before he left this world (Trimble 1993:231).[33] "There is a cave in Sedona with lots of marks on the wall. Sakarakaamche made those marks. He took the people in there and gave them the right songs. Teach them dances. . . . Sakarakaamche teach us everything. He teach us how to pray, how to sing right, how to dance." According to tradition, Sakarakaamche gave the Yavapais four sacred things: the black root, a medicine; the yellow powder, cattail pollen, which "stands for the light" and "helps you think and talk right"; the blue stone (turquoise, for men); and the white stone (quartz, for women)—which protect from bad things (cited in N. Mann 1991:12). His footprints, it is said, are still visible as rocks in the Red Rock Country. To date, the Yavapais consider Boynton Canyon, the place where First Woman (Kamalapukwia) resided, particularly sacred. Prayers, offerings, and ceremonial practices are still carried out here and in other locations in the middle Verde Valley and Red Rock area; and the Yavapai-Apaches gather every February at Boynton Canyon to mark Exodus Day, a day of remembrance of the forced exodus and the March of Tears in 1875.[34]

The Hopi and Navajo tribes also acknowledge that supernatural events have occurred in the red rock country, and both continue to gather medicinal herbs and plants in Oak Creek Canyon. Hopis consider that this land was occupied by their ancestors, the Sinagua, and, as a consequence, con-

Figure 7.3. Outside Enchantment Resort, Boynton Canyon

sider all traditional cultural properties to be part of their patrimony (Davenport, int.). Though the Hopis are largely invisible in the Sedona area, their
spirit is sometimes acknowledged or appropriated for New Age purposes.
The famous "Hopi prophecy," for instance, was frequently invoked by non-
Natives around the time of the Harmonic Convergence, despite the Hopi
tribal council's official denial of any Hopi connection to José Argüelles's
pronouncements.[35]

Only a handful of Natives live in or near Sedona itself, and an occasional
event such as a Long Dance or an elders' meeting can bring them into the
town.[36] "Grandfather" Hollis Littlecreek, mentioned above, first came to
Sedona in 1989 to participate in the third annual Native Long Dance, a
four-day celebration organized by locals with invited Native American elders (Java 1989b:1). There are "shamans" and New Age teachers who profess to Native ancestry, though their identification as such could be questioned. Among the more evident traces of Native presence are the ruins of
Sinaguan dwellings, and occasional signs, such as the one at the U.S. Forest
Service trailhead in Boynton Canyon, which reads: "This area is sacred to
many Indian people. Please act as though you were in your own church."
(Sprawled across most of the canyon's mouth, however, is Enchantment
Resort, a gated luxury complex of pink adobe casitas, tennis courts, swim-
ming pools, and restaurants, complete with its very own traditionally attired
Indian concierge and "cultural performer," a Havasupai from the Grand
Canyon area (H. Johnson 1992b:44).)

The issue of the Native connection to the Sedona area is thus an ambiguous one. Existing Native groups are small or some distance away, through
historical circumstance; yet they have succeeded in making many archaeologists and Forest Service workers sensitive to their concerns. The phenomenal growth of New Age interest in Native spirituality has elicited a strongly
ambivalent reaction among Native communities. Some Natives recognize
the need of Euro-Americans to reestablish some sort of spiritual connection
with the earth, and are open to sharing some of their traditions with them;
but others have followed the lead of the activist American Indian Movement (AIM) and a Traditional Elders Circle, which, in the early 1980s, issued forcefully worded resolutions condemning non-Indian use of Indian
spirituality.[37] A common line of critique is that New Age "whiteshamans"
and "wannabes" are said to be actively complicit in processes of cultural
imperialism, denying Natives their dignity, "prostituting" their heritage, and
even contributing to a "final phase of genocide" (Churchill 1994:281). As
Deloria explains, "the realities of Indian belief and existence" become distorted and misunderstood through this commodification of Native spirituality, so that "when a real Indian stands up and speaks the truth at any given
moment, he or she is not only unlikely to be believed, but will probably be
publicly contradicted and 'corrected' by the citation of some non-Indian
and totally inaccurate 'expert'" (cited in Churchill 1992:190). Finally, Native critics resent the marketplace mentality through which everything is

made available, for a price, and where the consumer can not only expect but even demand the right of access to such traditional knowledge. Spirituality, in this way, becomes a matter of personal choice, available to the consumer in a privatized market. Genuine Native traditions, on the other hand, involve a way of life embedded within long-standing communities; but this is hardly possible for white North Americans today.[38]

Holy War: Evangelical Christians Take on the New Age

Despite Sedona's reputation as a capital of the New Age, the city of 16,000 has no fewer than twenty-seven Christian churches. Sedona's Christian communities have tended to divide between liberals and conservatives, the latter forming its own Sedona Association of Evangelicals in 1987, partly in response to liberal Christians' increasing acceptance of the New Age community. In the perception of many evangelical and fundamentalist Christians, fueled by the sensationalist writings of Constance Cumbey (1983), Texe Marrs (1987, 1988), and others, the New Age movement constitutes a threat to Christian America; in some accounts, it is even considered to be satanic in its inspiration.[39] The differences between Sedona's New Agers and its evangelical Christians have simmered uneasily for years. While the former build medicine wheels in the forest, fundamentalists have been known to scrawl graffiti like "Jesus saves" and "Satan deceives" and to conduct their own vigils at places like Bell Rock.[40] The information war between the two camps is even visible at the local Safeway, where supermarket shelves prominently display titles like *The Believer's Guide to Spiritual Warfare, A Woman's Guide to Spiritual Warfare, The Seduction of Our Children: Protecting Kids from Satanism, New Age and the Occult,* and *Mystery Mark of the New Age: Satan's Design for World Domination.* Meanwhile, the bulletin board outside the entrance to Safeway is full of messages advertising Ascension Workshops, "scientific vortex information," the Sedona Spiritual Singles Society, crystal healing, psychic counseling, and other New Age services. So while Safeway's management, in its choice of books for sale, clearly favors the Christian conservatives, the New Agers outside the door go on with their activities in blissful ignorance of the war being waged against them.[41]

Perhaps the strangest and most crude attempt on the part of evangelicals to gain the upper hand in the religious discourse war is a novel called *Sedona Storm* (Scott and Younce 1994). The book is a sophomoric, sword-and-sorcery religious thriller, in which angels fight with demons over the fate of Sedonans' souls, after a ritually murdered body is discovered hanging upside down on a cross on Cathedral Rock. The demons are portrayed as lizards, "scaly," "bat-like," and taloned lords of darkness and "drinkers of blood," with names like Rosh-Rot, the Chief of Decay, Quench-Bersha, Zethar-Zebah (the master of abortion), and Darkon the Scatterer. Their fictional New Age devotees and allied villainous dupes—the authors refer

to them as "winkies" and "crystal gazers"—include Goddess worshipping
"ecofeminist" women who run an abortion clinic in Sedona, where they
perform "sacrifices," channel demons, and praise Gaia. Comparing the work
of these "baby killers" to Hitler, Vietnam, and "the killing fields of Cambo-
dia," the novel serves as a frightening example of fundamentalist "spiritual
warfare" pushed to its furthest degree of hysteria.[42] Though it would be un-
fair to the many more reasonable Christians in Sedona to dwell too much
on it, I will quote a few passages in order to illuminate how the Sedona
landscape has been interpreted by a rather differently possessed religious
mind than I have been detailing so far.

> A slimy, seething black ooze flowed down Cathedral Rock, its stench clinging
> to everything it touched. On closer inspection, it was actually a demon mass
> so thick it appeared to be one putrefying body. The fissure in the rock wid-
> ened with each moment, belching forth even more demons, like an unending
> lava flow. (49) . . .

> The skies over Sedona were dark with the demons spewing like molasses from
> the opening at Cathedral Rock. (66)

Some time after reading this book, on one particular observational encounter with the landscape, I found myself interpreting it in ways that paralleled
this demonically charged imagination:

> It's nearly two months since I arrived here, and only now do I see the poten-
> tial *ugliness* of the red rocks (but a beautiful kind of ugliness): strange, gro-
> tesque forms pushing out from the earth, twisting its body and exposing its
> inner flesh—reddish brown, like an aborted foetus washed in menstrual flu-
> ids; ominous slabs with growths of body hair (vegetation) covering its exposed
> surfaces; tenticular organs; bony, raw, hunched forms vulgarly exposing them-
> selves, defiantly, horns and all, to the heavens. I suppose this is what the au-
> thors of *Sedona Storm* might be seeing here: the Devil himself. (personal jour-
> nal, January 24, 1995)

What is most curious to the outside observer, however, are the parallels,
rather than the differences, between the novel's evangelicals and its New
Agers. Both sides draw on spiritual resources for direction (the novel's Christian characters open up the Bible at random for insight as if it were a pack of
tarot cards). Both appeal to higher-than-human authorities for their actions,
whose directives they "obey and trust" rather than rationally understand,
and who demand sacrifices of them: blood sacrifices in the case of the book's
demon-possessed New Agers, while the Christians must prepare to sacrifice
their lives in the spiritual battle, in emulation of the original flesh-and-blood
sacrifice of Jesus. Interestingly, however, the authors completely overlook
another potential commonality, evident to outsiders observing the two communities in real-life Sedona: this is that both fundamentalists and some
New Agers, at least those of an Ascensionist millenarian persuasion, position themselves on the side of the "forces of Light" in the spiritual battle
that is allegedly being waged in the world. Though the details in their re-

Figure 7.4. Satan's knuckles?

spective belief systems clearly differ, a cynic might be forgiven for asking, With such enemies, who needs friends?[43]

SEDONA'S CONTESTED LANDSCAPES

With such divergent ideas about the significance of the red rock landscape, it is inevitable that conflicts would develop over its use. I will focus on two of these: the conflict over New Agers' construction of medicine wheels on Forest Service land, and that over the future of Red Rock Crossing. In the first of these, the New Agers have been opposed not only by the Forest Service and by their more customary critics (conservatives and fundamentalist Christians), but also by some other citizens, including members of Sedona's arts community, concerned about the potentially damaging effects on the forest environment and about the implications of allowing such a precedent on national forest lands. Disallowing the medicine wheels raises the question of what, if any, are the appropriate *cultural* uses of nature within national forests, and what should be the relationship between New Age practices and the Native traditions which they ostensibly take as their model. In the second case, the conflict over Red Rock Crossing, the battle lines are not so neatly drawn. Examination of this case will, I hope, allow a picture to emerge of how different interpretive constructions of Sedona's landscape play themselves out in practice, and what the possibilities may be for bridging differences and for developing broader alliances around nontraditional environmental solutions.

New Age Medicine Wheels and
Native Cultural Sites on Forest Service Land

The construction of the Schnebly Hill medicine wheel in the late 1980s proved to be the first of a series of conflicts between New Age believers and Forest Service rangers. The circular stone formation was reportedly dismantled several times in succession by the Forest Service, but, as Dannelley (1993:51) recounts, "the rocks always managed to 'find their way' back into place rather quickly" (cf. Sidener 1991:B1). New Agers allege that on at least one occasion the rocks were thrown off the side of the rock formation on which the wheel was laid out; this broke them into fragments and smashed small trees and bushes at the base (Dannelley 1993:51; David, int.). Some New Agers have lamented the Forest Service's apparent vendetta against them; but others see the hand of developers or overzealous fundamentalists behind the action. Another view, however, expressed by a local anthropologist-turned-tour guide, is that, in the process of constructing their medicine wheel, New Agers' ignorance of local geology led them to destroy the "fingerprint" of an extraordinary geological event (Cremer, int.). Similar controversies have surrounded other prominent medicine wheels in the area, including one in Boynton Canyon and another at the Airport Mesa vortex.[44] Smaller "personal use" medicine wheels also appear regularly at various sites, especially in Boynton Canyon and at Bell Rock.

The Forest Service's line of argument against the medicine wheels has been that building any structures—and even rearranging rocks into a circle or piling them into cairns constitutes a "man-made structure"—is illegal on national forest land. Allowing a religiously motivated group to build them, no matter how small or simple such structures are, could be perceived as favoritism, unless other religious groups are allowed to do the same. Such structures and shrines become focal points for practitioners and the curious, leading to heavier use of the area, with the result that vegetation is trampled and erosion occurs. The construction of the wheels disturbs the habitats of smaller animals and insects—all part of a fragile food chain, the ecological integrity of which it is forest rangers' responsibility to protect. Finally, organized "vortex tours" amplify all these effects. In 1990 the Forest Service, citing a forty- to fiftyfold increase in the number of visitors to some sites since the Harmonic Convergence, decided to restrict group access to selected sites. New Agers were displeased, seeing in this a threat to constitutional guarantees of the free exercise of religion and of free expression (Winton 1990a; Dannelley 1991:6).

Forest Service archaeologists have also voiced concerns over New Age use of Native cultural sites. The politics of Native sites on public lands have for long been a tangled issue, and it is only in the last couple of decades that the Forest Service has begun approaching it with the respect Native communities have demanded. In the Sedona area, Forest Service archaeologists have been restoring and "stabilizing" petroglyphs, rock art, and other archaeological sites. Two of these, Honanki and Palatki, are among the largest and best preserved of the many extensive Verde Valley settlements from the Southern Sinagua phase of the region's occupation (from approximately 1150 to 1300 A.D.) (Rigby 1979:8). Archaeologists Peter Pilles and Marietta Davenport have claimed to routinely pick up crystals, tobacco, prayer sticks, jewelry, coins, and other items left buried or exposed at sites such as the popular Honanki ruins. Speaking at the twenty-first annual International Rock Art Congress in Flagstaff, Davenport pointed out that tourists who simply touch the thousand-year-old paintings degrade them with the oil left by their fingers, and that "New Age adherents who use the sites for their own spiritual observances leave campfire and candle soot, and render the images undatable. And they bury offerings ranging from crystals to the corners of $20 bills that ruin efforts to excavate below the art to learn more of its creators" (*Ariz. Rep.*, June 3, 1994:B1). Davenport sees New Agers as responsible for inappropriate "additions" to Native rock art, such as painted occult symbols and graffiti, and accuses them of gradually dismantling kivas by chipping off pieces of rock to keep for themselves (as is the custom at the Christian pilgrimage site of Santuario de Chimayó in New Mexico). Such activities have forced rangers to close off parts of Honanki and Palatki from public access. Medicine wheels, furthermore, are considered to be a Plains Indian tradition, not a Southwestern one, and their promotion by tour guides and New Age entrepreneurs is criticized as misrepresenting the Native heritage of the area.[45]

These concerns call to mind similar questions over the use and ownership of sites such as Stonehenge (see chapter 5). To whom do the rock paintings belong, and what is their proper use? Are they to be used by archaeologists for dating and study of prehistoric cultures, or by people who feel they are perpetuating the spiritual uses such places may have had centuries ago? Is their sacredness, in other words, a part of the past, to be preserved and set aside as in a museum, or can it be a matter of active practice in the present? Finally, are New Age practices analogous to traditional Native uses of such sites, or are they a cheap and inappropriate imitation of them? If all cultural practices are barred from such national forest areas—save for those which "leave no trace"—then what *is* to be the place of culture in these reserves of nature? The ideal of "no-trace" land uses assumes that camping and hiking, jeep and helicopter tours, even the taking and dissemination of photographs (the effects of which are less obvious but, indirectly, potentially more damaging) do in fact leave no traces; and it ignores the other officially sanctioned and more obviously intensive uses, such as military ones. In the case of traditional sites claimed by existing Native groups, such questions have thankfully become more legitimate, and cultural sites are becoming seen as more than just the province of prehistory. But in the case of other sites which have been identified by metaphysical believers as particularly sacred or energetically significant, the answers are more ambiguous.

In an effort to deal with these issues constructively, some members of Sedona's New Age community organized a New Age Sacred Sites Coalition, whose activities have included promoting, with Forest Service input, a sacred site etiquette guide that has been distributed to tourists who ask about the vortexes, and reprinted in New Age magazines. As well, over the past six years, a pilot project has been developed on a piece of privately owned land in Long Canyon known as Rachel's Point or Rachel's Knoll, named after its elderly out-of-town owner. The project consists of several medicine wheels up to about twenty-five feet in diameter, a few stone circles and spirals, and several stone-marked paths criss-crossing each other. Administered by Rachel's Foundation Trust, the site is well maintained (thanks to an annual work party) and much used. Some, like Pete Sanders, have pressed the Forest Service to allow similar work to take place on sites which are under their jurisdiction; the Airport Mesa vortex has been singled out for particular attention. Of greater symbolic significance, perhaps, has been the Forest Service's formal recognition in recent years of the "inspirational" and "spiritual" values in the landscape (Licher, int.). Cooperation between the Forest Service and area residents has been on the rise, for instance, through the Friends of the Forest volunteer program. However, the apportioning of blame for misuse of the land continues on both sides; and this is perhaps better understood in the context of the longer-term struggle over development and land trades, a struggle that through much of the 1990s focused itself around the site known as Red Rock Crossing.

Red Rock Crossing

> There is something in our automated American soul that cannot abide the dead-end drive; we demand that our scenic roads curve across the landscape in great winding loops, freeing us from the detestable necessity of motoring through the same scene twice.
>
> —EDWARD ABBEY, cited in *Red Rock Guardian*

> To me, there is no earthly reason why any attempt should be made to put a bridge at Red Rock Crossing near Sedona. There isn't even a good road anywhere near where they want to put that bridge, and it's one of the most spectacular bits of scenery in the whole state. I join practically every Arizonan in resisting this attempt to desecrate this gorgeous part of our scenery.
>
> —BARRY GOLDWATER, cited in an editorial in the *Arizona Republic*

A low-river point in Oak Creek that directly faces Cathedral Rock, Red Rock Crossing is, according to Forest Service records, the most photographed

Figure 7.5. No bridges here: Cathedral Rock at Red Rock Crossing

place in Arizona (Honan 1994:6), and some claim, in North America. Its visual familiarity stems in part from the films and television ads that have been filmed against its shapely, copper orange (with smatterings of green) form.

The problem with Red Rock Crossing, however, as Edward Abbey's words suggest, is that it is in the middle of nowhere—but a nowhere that has now become not only a destination in itself, but a point en route between two other somewheres. The idea of building a bridge at Red Rock Crossing is not a new one; there had been a low-water crossing, a concrete apron that allowed the passage of horses and wagons, since the 1930s, but this bridge had been washed away (and been replaced) three times between 1958 and its most recent collapse during a 1978 flood. For the purpose of getting cars across dependably today—and the bridge is proposed as an alternate route to the overburdened 89A—nothing less than a large suspended "monster bridge," at an estimated cost of nearly $30 million, would do.[46]

The recent controversy over Red Rock Crossing began in 1983 when the U.S. Forest Service granted Yavapai County an easement for a bridge. Despite environmentalists' allegations that the easement was granted without proper review, the county supervisor applied in 1991 for federal funds to build a highway and bridge at the site. In addition to the bridge proposal, the Forest Service proposed to build a campground at Crescent Moon Ranch (next to the crossing) with facilities for 650 people and their vehicles. Red Rock Crossing has since become an ideological symbol that has polarized the entire community. Those in favor of the bridge include a citizens' group called Citizens for an Alternate Route (C-FAR), who argue that residents of the Village of Oak Creek need an alternate route to the Y to get to the closest hospital, in nearby Cottonwood, both in case of emergencies and for simple convenience. Between 16,000 and 20,000 cars cross the two-lane downtown bridge known as the Y each day (Schill 1994:B1), and traffic on weekends in the tourist season builds to be bumper to bumper. The business community together with the city's old guard have therefore been strong supporters of the bridge.

For environmentalists, on the other hand, Red Rock Crossing is emblematic of the entire surrounding area. As Sierra Club and 4Rs activist Bennie Blake puts it, "if it goes, the whole Sedona area's gonna go" by way of land trades and development. The struggle, as she sees it, is "not about how to get across Oak Creek; it's about how to develop the whole area. It's the biggest expanse of undeveloped land in the whole Sedona area" (int.). In the environmental politics of Sedona's possible future, bridge opponents argue, the bridge would open up a large part of Sedona's as yet relatively undeveloped area to road building and further development. The Sierra Club's Grand Canyon chapter (and its Sedona–Verde Valley group) has taken up the issue as one of their prime causes, focusing an effective campaign around it, for which they obtained legal assistance from the Land and Water Fund of the Rockies. The "antis" argue that the scenic quality of the site is unrivaled and would be destroyed by a large highway bridge. They also point to the potential deterioration of water quality in Oak Creek, which had been designated a "unique and exceptional" waterway by the state;[47] inevitable threats to the stands of cottonwood and willow trees along the creek; and the possible disturbance of ancient Indian sites. Support for the environmentalists has come from far and wide, including from former Republican Senator Barry Goldwater, millionaire grocer Eddie Basha, a former Arizona governor, a one-time Phoenix mayor, and a handful of Democratic congresspersons (*Ariz. Rep.*, May 1, 1994:A28). Both of the state's major dailies, the *Phoenix Gazette* and the *Arizona Republic*, have editorialized strongly against the bridge.

The New Age community's view of the proposed bridge has, not surprisingly, been largely negative. A grassroots group called Concerned Citizens for Sedona was formed to defend Red Rock Crossing from development. A spokeswoman for the group, Ramona Coyote, was quoted in the *Arizona Republic* as saying she considers Cathedral Rock a "sacred site" and important as one of the "four main vortexes." At an event organized by the group at the site itself, "Grandfather" Hollis Littlecreek played flute and others "chanted for serenity, not development, to embrace Oak Creek" (Shaffer 1990:B1). Richard Dannelley wrote: "This area is highly sacred and we must do everything we can to make sure that this bridge is never built. We must hold the line. Cathedral Rock is sacred and a highway through this area can not be allowed. *Cathedral Rock is an ascension point.* We cannot let the vibrations of a highway into this area. Placing a metal bridge over

Oak Creek at this place would also interfere with the spiritual energy that flows along the creek" (1993:62; italics in original). He has also argued that "many people, myself included, have encountered Angelic entities in this area" (1993:54). Page Bryant similarly informs her readers that, according to her teacher "Albion," "two magnificent Archangels stand guard over the 'entrance to the inner sanctum'" at Red Rock Crossing. Bryant claims Red Rock Crossing is the only magnetic vortex in the area, and thus vital to the energetic balance of the landscape (Bryant et al. 1991:13).

The New Age community, however, remains somewhat marginal to local decision making. A few individuals have attempted to bridge the gap between this community and more mainstream citizens. Former Center for the New Age president Pete Sanders, for instance, has represented New Age ideas about vortexes at the annual Sedona Forum, gaining some modicum of recognition for New Age values. Another activist, geologist and one-time mayoral candidate John Armbruster, has attempted to spread ideas about geomancy among city planners. Some local tour guides have succeeded in introducing newcomers to Sedona to the "sacred" dimensions of the surrounding landscape. More recently, a group of environmentally and spiritually oriented residents associated with the Sedona-based World Survival Foundation have launched an ambitious plan to "Save Long Canyon" from a planned development by raising $18 million to set the canyon aside as a wilderness area and ecological architecture demonstration site; they remain well short of their goal, but have built a wide coalition of backers, including the Responsible Residents of the Red Rocks, Keep Sedona Beautiful, the recently formed Sedona Area Coalition, the Grand Canyon Trust, and the Yavapai-Apache Nation and Hopi tribal councils (World Survival Foundation n.d.). The extent of active effort the New Age community on the whole has been willing to put into the fight against the Red Rock Crossing bridge, however, has varied considerably. Bennie Blake, whose role in the issue has been central, explains that though many New Agers "are very involved in Red Rock Crossing. . . . Some of them don't want to do any work toward it, but they'll send good thoughts or prayers."[48] This noninvolvement in part reflects many New Agers' unwillingness to enter into situations of conflict. Given the strength and visibility of prodevelopment and archconservative voices in local political discourse, coupled with the New Age community's lack of political clout, it is not surprising that "there's people who think this is all going to get ruined anyway" (Blake, int.). Many of the more millenarian New Agers consider it more important to prepare themselves spiritually for a kind of earthly purification than to fight losing battles for the preservation of their temporary earthly homes. Despite its environmental attractiveness, then, Sedona, with its otherworldly, hauntingly evocative landscape, may have attracted a disproportionate number of those who are more interested in contacting otherworldly authorities, and even in "ascending" from the planet themselves, than in saving what is left of it.[49]

The Red Rock Crossing issue had taken a positive turn for the antibridge proponents during recent years, with the Yavapai county supervisor recommending another crossing route at West Airport Mesa (some distance upstream from Red Rock Crossing) as the less invasive and more cost-effective alternative, and the county board of supervisors restarting the environmental assessment process for the alternate routes—a process C-FAR has consistently opposed. In response, C-FAR has launched appeals and lawsuits intended to force Yavapai County to "rebuild" the bridge at Red Rock Crossing, but, as of this writing, their lawsuits have not succeeded. Whatever the outcome of the Red Rock Crossing conflict, the red rock landscape around Sedona will continue to face pressures from its increasing population as well as its powerful development lobby.[50]

Of interest in the present analysis is the fact that one of the arguments used to "save" red Rock Crossing—perhaps the most successful argument— has been the recognition the site has achieved through its film exposure. This paradox cuts to the heart of the late-twentieth-century American West: film, photography and television create imagined geographies; they appropriate elements from the real world to create decontextualized images and stars. The defense of places like Red Rock Crossing all too frequently relies on turning these places into media images—landscapes remodeled as stars in their own right. The New Age contention that these sites are vortexes plays into this mediated environmentalism; while the less sensational but more ecological notion that the entire landscape—complete with a clear and healthy Oak Creek and its floodplain—needs to be respected as sacred, is much more elusive. The final irony may be, as Bennie Blake puts it, that "in this peaceful spot"—which attracts so many people precisely for its peacefulness and serenity (bubbling stream, blue skies, riparian vegetation, and picture-postcard scenery)—that here "we're in a constant state of turmoil and of battle" (int.). Nature, the idealized Edenic retreat from urban-industrial modernity, has become a battleground. And the red rock landscape of Sedona has, in this sense, attracted to it the very forces that are waging a battle throughout late-modern Euro-American society.

Crossed Currents, Unanswered Questions

As Richard Foust puts it, "Sedona is a microcosm of the problem the world faces with the common desire to 'put it somewhere else,' as there is no 'somewhere else' here. . . . People come here to get away from the 'somewhere elses'" (Foust, Byrkit, and Avery 1991:166). Most of Sedona's more recent settlers—New Age spiritualists, environmentalists, retirees, and wealthy urban refugees—have come for the beauty of the red rock landscape more than for anything else. But what does that "beauty" consist of? For some, it is in the scenic view, the object of fascination rendered fully accessible to the freely roving eye of the camera or the jeep; or in the penetrative thrill of a helicopter ride veering between buttes, domes, and arches. For a certain, and too powerful, stratum of residents, it is the beauty-once-removed of profit, to be squeezed from the "gape-mouthed stupefaction" of tourists (Porter, Stegner, and Stegner 1981:162). For others, it is the serene beauty still to be found—but ever farther—in the wilderness away from the roads, in unplanned meetings with strangers of the nonhuman (but earthly) kind, or in the afterglow of a triumphant conquering of a cliff.

Sedona's New Agers show little interest in the monumental visuality splayed across the pages of *Sedona Magazine*. The few photographs to be found in their own *Journal of Emergence* are more likely to be grainy, black-and-white images of inscrutable lights in the sky, interpreted as "flying disk photographed while passing through a portal," "negative Sirians pursuing an entity that is consuming gold light," "a hole in time and space," or "the Face of God through the veils" (*SJE* January 1995:24–27; *SJE* April 1995:41). The channeler's entry into the landscape is not that of the colonizer, stretching westward across the continent to possess and dominate it; rather, it is more akin to that of the rock climber or the adventure hiker, pursuing experiential connections in a landscape recognized to be far too vast for possession. But the channeler's entry is into a stranger, and more thoroughly inhabited (so already possessed), landscape, one in which the desires and paranoias festering in the skin of millennial capitalist modernity scramble and multiply into a kaleidoscope of voices and messages. Dreams of ancient wisdom mix with the multiply refracted and contorted languages of science (of a sort), swirling into an electrostatic hum where it becomes possible to hear anything. New Agers' appropriation of the red rock landscape is, in this sense, an escape route, a line of flight outward—away from the rotting corpse (as they would see it) of a civilization in decline, with its single vision and human, all too human, lordship over the earth—and toward a galactic community of the future.

As golf courses, time share resorts, and luxury homes continue to be built, bringing various amenities and associated environmental stresses in their wake, Sedona's actual landscape is being eroded. Unless New Age discourses about energy vortexes can be translated into effective action against the ongoing commodification and development of land (and perhaps the current Save Long Canyon campaign provides a model to be emulated), New Agers may have to look farther afield for places to commune with their angels, ascended masters, and extraterrestrials.

A series of questions remain, which have been implicit in much of my discussion in these last four chapters. Whose land is "public land" and what is its proper use? When the rights to buy and sell, develop, pollute, and pray on a piece of land come into conflict with each other, on what basis should these conflicts be resolved? How can the right to pray and conduct ceremonies be established as a serious right, when those doing the praying are perceived to be members of an eccentric religious minority? And what are the points of tension and connection between contemporary alternative cultural practices (such as New Age and earth spirituality) and indigenous traditions and practices? More to the point, how can New Agers ensure that their

Figure 7.6. Mexican man with son selling rocks in the parking lot of Boynton Canyon

"religious freedoms" do not conflict with the rights and sovereignties demanded by Native groups? In the following, concluding chapter, I will address these questions by arguing for an alternative geopolitics within which the concept of sacred sites could be used to incorporate multiple interpretations of nature and landscape—that is, not merely those according to which land is seen as resource and as property, but also those which perceive land as spirit, as living organism, as elusive and polymorphous trickster, and as home.

PART FOUR

ARRIVALS

After all is said and done, however, the question of why Glastonbury? takes over. Why all this myth-making in one particular place? Why is this wealth of myths and legends not scattered around more evenly?

—FRANCES HOWARD-GORDON, *Glastonbury: Maker of Myths*

The nation is looking to Sedona as the focal point of the new spiritual awakening that has been predicted.

—RICHARD DANNELLEY, *Sedona UFO Connection and Planetary Ascension Guide*

I just want to get out of this metastasized tourist trap and into the desert where I can watch the snow drift into the chaparral.

—WALLACE STEGNER, "The New Riders of the Purple Sage"

. . . there is then not much point in counterposing or restating the great abstractions of Man and Nature. We have mixed our labour with the earth, our forces with its forces too deeply to be able to draw back and separate either out. Except that if we mentally draw back, if we go on with the singular abstractions, we are spared the effort of looking, in any active way, at the whole complex of social and natural relationships which is at once our product and our activity.

—RAYMOND WILLIAMS, "Ideas of Nature"

Wilderness reservations are best viewed as holes and cracks, as "free spaces" or "liberated zones," in the fabric of domination and self-deception that fuels and shapes our mainstream contemporary culture.

—THOMAS BIRCH, "The Incarceration of Wildness"

We *are all* in chiasmatic borderlands, liminal areas where new shapes, new kinds of action and responsibility, are gestating in the world.

—DONNA HARAWAY, "The Promises of Monsters" (italics in original)

EIGHT

Practices of Place: Nature, Heterotopia, and the Postmodern Sacred

In the process of interpreting the sacralization of Sedona and Glastonbury, I have made reference to three distinct approaches or hypotheses. The first, a fairly conventional social-scientific view, typically interprets the construction of the sacred with the aid of social, psychological or political-economic explanations. The second, the explicitly religious perspective of the believer, assumes the real existence of spiritual or transpersonal forces and relies on the effective power of thought, imagination, ritual, or other means of supposed interaction with such forces. The third, a hermeneutic-phenomenological perspective, bases itself on the bodily experience of landscapes, as individuals and social groups encounter particular environments over time, interact with them and make cultural and interpretive sense of their interactions. For the sake of methodological clarity, these three hypotheses can be distinguished and applied to the landscapes of Sedona and Glastonbury as follows.

- *The socio-psychological/social-constructionist hypothesis:* At numinous landscapes, New Agers and ecospiritualists look for, and find, what they believe to be sacred. This can be explained by a set of social and economic factors: the social psychology of the New Age movement, a movement which seeks simple, magical answers to difficult dilemmas in a time characterized by millennial fears and by a crisis of confidence in science and in mainstream social institutions; the suggestibility of New Age believers, a product, in part, of the mass media–precipitated decline in quality scientific education and critical thinking; the individualism and consumerism of the postmodern spiritual marketplace; the culturally produced nostalgia for rural or natural places, fueled by environmentalist discourse and imagery and by the real estate market; and the geographic imperatives of the global tourist economy. The role of particular places or landscapes in this process is a passive one: to the extent that they fit into prevailing and culturally shaped notions of the beautiful, awesome, or sublime, they serve as a backdrop for the playing out of these social forces.

- *The magico-religious hypothesis:*[1] Particular landscapes are in fact sacred; they harbor a numinosity and power which subsists on its own accord. The energies experienced at such places are *real*, either as measurable forces (such as electromagnetism) or as psychic and interdimensional realities knowable through intuitive means (such as dowsing or trance channeling). So, for instance, Sedona's Lemurian history, its extraterrestrial portals and energy gates, and so on, are either literally real or refer to *some* kind of reality, perhaps in another dimension as yet unknown to conventional science.

- *The hermeneutic-phenomenological hypothesis:* Scenic images and cultural lore about a place help to shape the expectations of visitors to a given landscape; but it is the actual embodied experience of encountering the landscape which allows the sense of awe, mystery, magic, or sacredness to *unfold* for a person, and which, when shared with others over time, anchors alternative interpretations of the land within the landscape. This embodied encounter of a landscape may include the movements and physical exertion needed to maneuver one's way through its particular topography; the changing visual, auditory, olfactory, and kinesthetic qualities at different stages of a pilgrimage route; the colors, shapes, textures, and other physical qualities of the landscape; the temporal or durational factor, as one prepares to visit a sacred site and undergoes the process of journeying, expectation and desire, encountering the site, conducting a ritual performance, meditation or "attunement" of some sort, and returning home; and all these factors and qualities as they change over daily, seasonal, and annual cycles. Over time, this experiential and interpretive data collects and is sedimented within the interpretive communities for whom the place is held to be sacred. As such a community becomes more firmly anchored within the landscape, its interpretations take on an increasing matter-of-factness.

Each of these hypotheses provides some insights into the "sanctity" of such landscapes. Many of the socio-psychological factors recounted in the first hypothesis are undeniable. Environmentalist, tourist, and real estate images play a central role in constructing the allure of such landscapes, and New Agers and ecospiritualists can easily be characterized as postmodern consumers in whom a desire for enchantment, and especially a desire to "reconnect with the earth," serves a psychologically or socially compensatory function, providing a sense of personal empowerment they have not found through other channels. This hypothesis, however, fails to elucidate why ecospiritual communities persist at such places, rather than dissembling under the pressures of changing fashions and the economic difficulties faced by many New Agers and ecospiritualists; nor does it provide extensive insight into the values and motivations underlying the more committed forms of New Age and ecospiritual practice.[2] The second hypothesis takes the actual claims of believers more seriously, allowing the analyst deeper insight into believers' motives and experiences. But by remaining at the

level of religious symbols and narratives, many of which appear contradictory or internally inconsistent, we are provided with little means of adjudicating their relative veracity. In any case, the religious (essentialist) hypothesis leaves out any social analysis of why *particular* things become sacred for
particular people in specific settings. Arguably, it also mystifies rather than
clarifies the nature of that which is experienced as sacred (such as the "earth
energies" associated with these places).

In my focus on the relationship between New Age and ecospiritual believers' interpretations of their experience and the actual places which serve
to center and orient that experience, I have found the third hypothesis to be
most fruitful. My attempts, in my fieldwork, to trace the interpretive processes involved in the construction and spatialization of the landscape as
sacred involved paying careful attention to various phenomenological variables while walking, driving, climbing, and otherwise engaging with the
landscape. Subtracting the variables which played a lesser role from those
which were more focal, over repeated efforts, I found certain crucial factors
in each of my place-studies. In Sedona, the qualities of the rockscapes—
their textures (smoothness alternating with rough and jagged shapes and
forms), colors, and shapes—combine to create an ambiguously evocative
landscape that seems to *call for* some sort of interpretation or meaningful
image creation, rather like a Rorschach inkblot. The solidity, monumentality, and jagged surface of the rocks evoke qualities associated with ancient-
ness (e.g., ancient temples, "ancient Indian" faces). Secondly, the vistas,
particularly upon the ascent to a ledge, overlook, or top of a prominent rock
formation such as Cathedral Rock, Schnebly Hill, or the Airport vortex, also
afford an excess of this "ambiguous evocativeness," which, combined with
the heightened suggestivity common among New Age or ecospiritual pilgrims, elicits an unusually rich interpretive flow. As well, the overall combination of diverse microenvironments and other interpretive affordances—
awe-inspiring views, the sense of *presence* of the red rock "giants," relatively
lush riverine valleys, the plenitude of opportunities for personal and group
hikes and excursions into the landscape, and the existence of Native American sites and rock paintings—all contribute to the social and interpretive
construction of Sedona as a *sacred* place. In Glastonbury, on the other hand,
the landscape presents itself as green, wet, and smoothly rounded; harbor-
ing energies which flow through the landscape like water, it conceals a history of secret knowledge whose mysteries require an effort of the heart to be
unlocked for their Arthur-like initiates.

ECOSPIRITUAL HETEROTOPIAS AS INTERPRETIVE
SOCIO-NATURAL CONSTRUCTIONS

I have suggested that the process by which such places become sacred for a
community of people depends on three primary factors: (1) existing discourse, language, narratives, place-images, and lore; (2) a cultural desire for

particular kinds of landscapes and relations, expressed in the intentions and motivations of Gaian pilgrim-migrants; and (3) the landscape itself and its material features. Both Sedona's and Glastonbury's "alternative" communities define themselves largely through their recognition of the sacred and active/agential status of these places, and by their differences from other, more mainstream residents. These communities, in turn, serve a catalytic and exemplary function within the broader New Age and ecospiritual milieu. Individuals attracted to New Age or ecospiritual ideas may hear about the existence of such places and, sooner or later, visit them. Others, coming upon them by chance, may undergo experiences which mark or even trigger some change in their lives. In both cases, visits may lead to the eventual decision to relocate to the new elective center and become part of its spiritual, New Age, or alternative community. The community's resultant growth contributes to the reputation and magnetism of the place itself, while evoking an ambivalent response among the area's other inhabitants. The place becomes a contested zone, a heterotopia incorporating divergent and incommensurable ideologies, values, and practices.

Three crucial processes in the construction of such ecospiritual heterotopias require further elucidation: (1) the reciprocal, or *co-intentional*, relationship that develops between social groups and the landscape; (2) the process by which the pilgrim-immigrants shift into an ecospiritual mode of understanding themselves and the given place, a process which, following Luhrmann (1989), we can call *interpretive drift*; and (3) the growth and congealment of the interpretive community of pilgrim-immigrants, with its fluctuating collective identity and its distinctive place-meanings and narratives.

Spiritual Magnetism and Co-Intentionality

Preston (1992) defines spiritual magnetism as "the power of a pilgrimage shrine to attract devotees." In a relational, interactive, and co-constructive view, the features of a sacred landscape are understood to interact with the images, ideas, and desires of those for whom it is sacred and who take up its affordances in ways specific to this reverent stance. This bipolarity of experience—the fact that an object of experience is always an object *for* an experiencer (and vice versa, the experiencer is always an experiencer *of* something in particular)—is termed by phenomenologists "intentionality." Thus there is a relationship between ecospiritual pilgrims' desire to "reconnect with the Earth" and the fact that places like Sedona and Glastonbury "afford" the possibility of such a connection. Within this interaction, agency (that is, the power to act) is not the exclusive property of people or of transpersonal or environmental forces; rather, it is distributed throughout the network of circulation, a network which encompasses several nodes: pilgrims' perceptions of an ecological crisis, as well as the (contested) reality of that crisis, perceived in the humanization, rationalization, resourcification, and destruction of existing ecosystems; pilgrims' desires to reconnect with that which has eluded these processes; the existence of distinct and readily identifiable places which seem to embody that resistance; and the accumulation of a growing community of such pilgrims around these numinous centers.

Among the features that render a landscape particularly suitable for such an interaction, three are most significant: (1) extraordinary or unusual geographic features, such as the Tor or Sedona's red rock formations, which make these places distinct from others and which facilitate their mediated (photographed, etc.) representation as these landscapes are mythicized, marketed, or popularized; other factors, such as an evocative place-name, contribute as well, helping to conjure up a particular image and shape a readily identifiable and coherent identity; (2) a high degree of hermeneutic and semiotic ambiguity or underdetermination, allowing for multiple interpretive possibilities, partly because their meanings have not been domesticated into a single dominant narrative within the broader culture: the Tor's prehistory, for instance, is unknown, the origin of its terraces is mysterious, just as the historical whereabouts of Arthur, of Jesus and Joseph, and of the Holy Grail are unknown, while the history of Sedona's red rock formations and how they may have been perceived by pre-Columbian Native Americans is also mysterious; (3) discursive links to perceived "power" vested in real or imagined extramodern natural-cultural orders: Glastonbury's lore connects it with pre-Christian British civilization (the Celts, the builders of Stonehenge and other megalithic monuments, the ancient Goddess worshippers, etc.), though not in any specific or prescribed way, while Sedona's connects it unspecifically to Native American prehistory.

Interpretive Drift

During an elaborate program of visits to the Avebury complex at various times of year and in a variety of atmospheric conditions, Paul Devereux observed that

> something subtle began to happen during these visits: I developed the distinct sense that Silbury Hill was communicating in some way. I slowly began to think of it as a teacher—a living, sentient, teacher. Such an animistic idea would of course make any archaeologist, any Western rationalist, wail in despair. I felt uneasy about it myself to begin with, but soon learned to adopt the attitude with ease. Whether or not the idea is taken literally, is it a good mental model to have regarding the site? I found it was. It opened me up to the complex; it put me in receptive mode. I was Silbury's pupil, in the classroom formed by the sacred landscape of the Avebury complex. (1992a:76–77)

Devereux ultimately discovered that the sun on Beltane (the Celtic May Day festival) and Lammas (the August harvest festival) appeared, from the top of Silbury Hill, to rise *twice* over the eastern horizon. Devereux's point in recounting his attitudinal shift is that the act of suspending one's judgment in the *nonagency* of a place or landscape can open one up to experiences or interpretations which might otherwise have been inaccessible.

Interpretations of the world are many layered: new interpretations are built on previously sedimented layers, and new phenomena are made sense of in light of what is already known. An objectivist view of the world presumes that landscapes, places, and the Earth as a whole, are *nonagents* (though the physical "forces" or "laws" which underlie the natural world may be ascribed with the power of agency). But if this assumption is put into question, other related interpretive assumptions may also begin to dislodge themselves from their accustomed places within a person's interpretive and cognitive tool kit. Should such a process of reinterpretation be followed through and reinforced on repeated occasions, the result would be what Luhrmann calls "interpretive drift," the gradual shift into a new "manner of interpreting events, making sense of experiences, and responding to the world" (1989:12).[3]

One Glastonbury immigrant describes her arrival in the town in this way:

> I came here partly because I felt guided here, partly because of a personal situation which could only bring on change, and partly because the Earth Mysteries Camp really affected me deeply. . . . I really felt that a lot was happening here — interesting and spiritual things — and that a lot more would happen in the future. I came here out of love for several people, and since I have returned I have fallen in love with several other people. . . . I also came here to separate myself from a personal situation which was pretty unbearable. And "finally" I came here because so many pointers, signs and omenlike events just said "Be there!" (Vee, GC 5 [1985]: 9)

Vee's story is a typical one, and this fact suggests that she has, over time, drifted into the particular *style* of interpretation that is characteristic of ecospiritual pilgrim-immigrants, for whom a place either *is* or *includes* an active agency of its own which draws people to itself, teaches them things, and so on. Glastonbury's and Sedona's readily identifiable, evocative and enigmatic landscape features easily "absorb" the interpretations imposed onto them. Among the interpretive affordances which their natural and cultural histories make available is the existence of discursive connections to *extramodern sources of perceived power or authority*. These perceived or imagined "authority links" include King Arthur, Jesus and Joseph, Celtic Druids, Culdees (early Celtic Christian monks), and Neolithic Goddess-worshippers, ancient astronomers and geomants, and the energetic body of Gaia herself. In Sedona, extraterrestrials, angels and archangels, Lemurians, and deceased Native American sages are thrown into the mix. As these become privileged figures within the interpretive frameworks of spiritual seekers, events are interpreted in ways that support their presumed authority, and the alleged sanctity of the landscape becomes "authorized" by the narratives they bring together. What these figures have in common is that they are experienced as *numinous Others* (or as connected to a numinous Other), whose Otherness lies, in part, in their opposition to the anthropocentric, rationalist, scientific-industrial modernity—the culture which is being implicitly, and often explicitly, critiqued in the flight of New Agers and eco-spiritualists to such sacred landscapes.

In the process of documenting this flight, I have attempted to sympathetically reimagine these sacred places myself by engaging in similar practices as the pilgrim-subjects of my study. I have followed their steps, but stopped short of literally believing in the figures that guide those steps, or at least of abandoning my skepticism entirely. My own experiences at the vortexes and other sacred sites can be taken as self-reflexive instances of interpretive drift in action, as it were. On some of my visits to sites recognized as sacred, I have been able to become relatively "centered" and focused, and either excited and energized, or reflective and relaxed, depending on the place itself and on my motives and expectations. On a few occasions—most commonly at physically spectacular sites such as Sedona's vortexes—I have been able to feel a kind of pulsating or vibrating "energy" in my body, which could have been interpreted as coming from the ground or from the site itself; and I have been able to work with this energy to heighten a meditative or visualized imaginal experience.[4] On several occasions, either by making a concentrated attempt to meditate or visualize certain things, or spontaneously, I have carried on internal conversations with voices which I could imagine as belonging to beings outside of myself.

To speak about these things adequately, however, I feel a need to splice together words like *felt* and *imagined*, or *heard* and *imagined*. I use the word *imagine* not in the customary sense of something which takes place exclusively in one's head, but, rather, in the depth-psychological sense related to the imaginal faculty—the capacity to form images, inclusive of sounds, movements, bodily sensations, and so on, within one's field of awareness. The images I could see (in my mind's eye), voices I could hear, presences I could feel, and so on, were just as real to me as the images in a dream—and I, like many people, do on occasion have dreams that are more vivid, colorful, three-dimensional, and emotionally involving than much of everyday waking experience. Dreams, of course, are not equivalent to the waking experience of "consensus reality" (Tart 1975b); but they are, phenomenologically speaking, real experiences, whose reality is simply of a different order and consistency than the other kind(s).[5] As subjectively real experiences, they are capable of being woven into the fabric of interpreted reality, a reality which is also always *intersubjective*. The voices and presences seen, heard, felt or imagined in this way at particular places do not necessarily *belong* to those places per se; nor, however, do they emerge purely within the skin-encapsulated reality of one's head. Rather, they arise in and through the interaction between physical body, memory and expectation, the spatial and temporal features of a place or landscape, and the social lore, narratives, and discourses which circulate between all of the above.[6]

Congealment of a Pilgrim-Immigrant Community

Once a landscape has begun to attract ecospiritual pilgrims, the development of an actual residential community of pilgrim-immigrants depends on the capacity of the landscape to accommodate such a community, allowing itself to be orchestrated within their spatial activities, identity claims, place-meanings, and narratives. Here, it would be helpful if the landscape included a mixture of private/residential and public land, making possible both sedentary or residential uses, such that a community might grow there, and nomadic uses, allowing for people to visit and move through it.

Over time, the given spiritual community grows and anchors itself within the landscape through (1) the production of place lore, such as stories about vortexes, personal stories of initial arrival in Glastonbury or Sedona, apocryphal tales about particular events, and so on; (2) a continual influx of spiritually inspired visitor-pilgrims and migrants, often with a high turnover rate and much fluctuation in the community, but with some continuity and regeneration in its sense of collective identity; and (3) the development of ritual and communal spatial practices, including community events and celebrations performed at particular sites on a regular basis (full moons, solstices and equinoxes, etc.), group and private rituals and meditations, and the like.

The nature of such communities, however, makes any sort of stability unlikely for several reasons. Most obvious is the transience of many contemporary spiritual seekers. As one member of Sedona's metaphysical community told me, places like this attract "weirdos": people who have somehow "failed" in other parts of the world might come to "dump their frustrations," while others arrive believing they are Jesus, Nostradamus, or Merlin. "It's like the place attracts people who are searching, people who've been abused, people who've been lost in trying to solve the world's problems. . . . But maybe that's all part of it. . . . They come in to Sedona, *for* this area, and they go through a wide range of experiences with a bunch of people who are searching for the same thing" (David, int.). Many of these individuals have left behind relative stability (though often also pain, abuse, or sheer dissatisfaction) and opened themselves up to change, experiential novelty, and a "psychokinetic" lifestyle dedicated to personal transformation (Bennett 1966:68). These immigrants remain "seekers" and may well wish to leave after a time, either to return to their previous lives or to continue their seeking and self-development elsewhere. As Bowman puts it, "For Avalonians, . . . the quest is not static. There are always more lessons to be learned, more lost knowledge to be recovered, more esoteric teachings to be understood, new phenomena to explore and be experienced" (1993a:59).

How, then, do these communities persist over ten or twenty years in the wake of such instability? One answer to this question is that these communities are in fact very loosely structured, and the discursive lore which accompanies their identity construction *as* communities is not tied to any specific individuals or organizations, but is more free floating. To the extent that this lore persists despite changes in the makeup of the community, it is connected only to the landscape itself (though its actual material forms include books and printed matter, media imagery, and stories and verbal accounts).

A second answer, one suggested by a focus on the interpretive construction of these places and communities, is that such a tension can itself be thematized and interpretively accommodated within the community. Specifically, for both Sedona's and Glastonbury's alternative-spirituality communities, there has developed an accompanying place-myth: the notion that both of these places are "high energy" centers, whose intensity is *intended—* by the places themselves, or by the spiritual forces responsible for them—*to make things difficult,* for the specific purpose of facilitating personal growth and transformation. Almost all those whom I talked to about this agreed that things can be "too intense" for those who live there. These places are thought to be pressure cookers or bubbling cauldrons where things are never quite settled, where everything is always in motion and, more often than not, in crisis. But they are also acknowledged to be places where people do in fact undergo transformative life experiences, individually and collectively. Glastonbury is said to be a place which precipitates a process of self-examination, a place where "the shit hits the fan": "If you're open you can resolve a lot of stuff. If you're not open, you can become aware of a lot of issues; and if you block against that, you manifest a new level of trouble, basically. And it happens from the day you hit Glastonbury. . . . If you stay here for any length of time you find your growth is heightened. The issues are accelerated, and whatever crap you've got going on in your shadow inside comes out whether you like it or not. And people either get repelled rapidly out of Glastonbury, or they get sucked in, and the doors open wildly" (Jenkins, int.). In the latter scenario, Glastonbury plays the role of a "teacher" and "mirror." "And the net result of this is that a person is closer to their life purpose, and they develop commitment in the sense of a responsibility in a new way by the 'instant karma' factor that comes up here. You think something, and *bam!*—it hits you, you know, or you get consequences faster here than you get in other places" (Jenkins, int.). This is said to make it difficult for many individuals to stay long at these places, or for the community to establish permanent organizations or institutions there. Several informants related to me the various disagreements and perpetual difficulties in "getting things done" in Glastonbury; and the experience of the Assembly Rooms, the Glastonbury Experience, and the Isle of Avalon Foundation seem to bear this out (e.g., Mitchell, int.; Prince 1991:176). And yet, this state of perpetual irresolution has been incorporated into the respective mythologies of both places and is taken by some to be one of their strengths and, in fact, continuities. This is understood by one informant as inevitable, given Glastonbury's creative freedom: "But in Glastonbury, not only does ideology (ideas, values, etc.) play such a consciously prominent role in the alternative community, but it is not predetermined or inherited, nor is it given out by one individual such as Bhagwan Shree Rajneesh or Reverend Sun Myung Moon; rather it is in the process of constant formation through discussions, publications, and the popular notion of 'networking' or the 'sharing' of ideas, by all those who wish to be involved" (cited in Prince 1991:175).

Additionally, the economic realities of living in such small communities often exhaust or burn out the very people attracted to them in the first place. In Sedona, this sense of dissatisfaction has been exacerbated by the scale of development and commodification that has engulfed the town in recent years. One frequently hears complaints about pollution, local politics, the raging schism between the metaphysical and fundamentalist communities, the apparently chronic failure of alternative institutions or newspapers like the *Tab* to sustain themselves, and the difficulty of making a living. One informant, a prominent local activist, quite plausibly theorized that conflict in Sedona is exacerbated by an unconscious sense of guilt shared by those who come to live there—guilt for being part of a society that "eats up" and destroys the natural world, and yet for being personally able to enjoy what little beauty remains of it. "All sorts of things are already shook up in the psyche when you move here. . . . You're already in a place where you're dealing with major life change just by making the choice to be here: so it sets itself up for that [heightening of emotions leading to conflict]. And the reason . . . is because of the drama of the landscape. [The landscape is] the impetus that gets [people] to go through something that otherwise might be a scary change. Because they feel so strongly about it, there's something compelling them to do it, instead of just making a choice to move from a big city to a small town in Iowa or something like that" (Licher, int.). Ecospiritual heterotopias tend to amplify tensions between different interpretive regimes, that is, between those for which such places are sacred and those which explicitly deny such a possibility. The presence of New Age "weirdos" or "hippies" who seem to represent a threat to long established ideas and practices often leads to a growing resentment among other local residents, exacerbating tensions. As a result the place takes on an even more conflictual nature: its apparent role, for New Agers and ecospiritualists, as a mirror and amplifier of what is present in a person's (or community's) "unconscious," thereby becomes a self-fulfilling prophecy.

Differences between Sedona and Glastonbury

Much of my focus thus far has been on the similarities between these two communities. Both are geographically marginal in relation to dominant political and economic centers; and both are located in regions that are thought to be more magical, more natural—whether rural (the English southwest) or wild (the U.S. Southwest)—and less industrialized, and to be tied to a deeper historical lore (Arthurian/British or Native/Hispanic) than much of the rest of their respective countries. There are obvious geographical differences—for instance, Sedona is relatively arid, Glastonbury comparatively wet—which undoubtedly play a role in the psychogeography of their respective populations, and result in a different perception of the two places within the international New Age movement. The idea that Glastonbury is the wet, fertile "heart chakra" of the Earth, for instance, could be read as an ethnocentric reference to Arthur's, and therefore Britain's, heartland status within the English-speaking world. Britain is (for good reason) thought of as a wet, rainy, and gray place; and Glastonbury's image as a wet, green, mist-enshrouded landscape resonates well within this perception. New Age perceptions of the Sedona landscape, on the other hand, draw on its aridity to represent it as energized, powerful, and somehow ancient, very much a part of the mythical West Americans have desired and colonized but, perhaps, never tamed.

Sedona's location in the spacious and expansive U.S. Southwest has also made it more vulnerable to the commodification and development of land —there being so much more land available. The fact that much of it is in the jurisdiction of the U.S. Forest Service has slowed this process but not prevented it. The marketing of Sedona as a place of relocation and for resort vacations has been pursued with great vigor by its prodevelopment forces, and its location en route between Phoenix and the Grand Canyon has added to its vulnerability. In the United States as well (especially on the West Coast), New Age spirituality has been more commercially successful and has retained less of its countercultural origins than in Britain. Sedona's New Age community has, in a sense, become a victim of this success.

In Glastonbury, besides the geographical fact that there is not very much land to be bought and turned into real estate subdivisions, million-dollar homes, or shopping malls, there have been at least two additional *social* factors which have mitigated against the town's commodification. On the one hand, much of the local population has been suspicious or, at best, ambivalent, and not particularly welcoming of its outsiders, partly because of its experience with the countercultural travelers and the Glastonbury Festival. On the other hand, the presence of the travelers themselves, with their unusual and, to many, threatening appearance, has served to detract the interest of potential developers. Sedona's New Agers for the most part share the middle-class and largely white appearance of the other locals; Glastonbury's travelers and, to a degree, members of its alternative community, have not blended in quite as readily.

In both cases, however, the presence and appearance of the alternative-spirituality communities has become a factor in the ongoing creation of these towns, and will be significant in the ways they juggle conservation ideals, tourist potentials, and other possibilities for development in the future. New Age and ecospiritual discourses of nature might play an important role in facilitating or constraining development and land use practices; to this I turn next.

CONTESTING THE LAND:
ARTICULATING DIFFERENT NATURES

Over the last 150 years, industrial capitalism has transformed the perception of land into that of a resource for human use, and judged its value according to how productively it is used; the romantic anti-industrial reaction of environmental preservationists has allowed the setting aside of selected marginal areas to be preserved in their idealized "natural" forms; and the conservationist ethos developed by Gifford Pinchot and others has applied a managerial approach to the use of other designated lands, allowing for multiple uses, but subjecting them to bottom-line political-economic considerations. Consumer postmodernity is now transforming the last remaining places of "natural beauty" into outdoor recreation meccas, spiritual tourist havens, second homes for the rich, and escapes for urban refugees. At this point we can ask: Can the identification of a place as sacred save it from such a fate? What does the sacredness of a place or landscape consist of? And what are the implications of different ways of representing this sacredness?

The mystique of natural wonders and of holy places is found practically everywhere. Even today Niagara Falls is thought of by many as a place of wonder, a place where the power of nature expresses itself with an awe-inspiring vivacity—even though the "nature" here has been nearly squeezed out by the multiple turbines of hydroelectric engineering, the gory over-marketing, the billboards, wax museums, souvenir shops, and side shows. Other places have been dealt with by a somewhat gentler hand. Wilderness parks like Yellowstone suffer greatly under the weight of their visitors, but mountains like Fuji, Shasta, and others, despite their ski resorts, still seem to hold some distinctive and vaguely transcendent meanings for various groups of people. From within a society that has transformed most of the earth into property, commodity, and resource, these are places which remind at least some people—those who sense the loss of a connection with other-than-human nature—that there is a *beyond* to the human-controlled world (rather as do tornadoes, earthquakes, volcanoes and other "natural disasters").

In my examination (in chapter 2) of popular ideas about nature, I identified four primary representational discourses: nature as Object, as Resource, as Home, and as Spirit or Numinous Other. Examining Glastonbury and Sedona, my focus necessarily shifted from general discourses of nature to the more specific ones of land (or landscape) and place. The main such conceptions found in Glastonbury and Sedona could be mapped as falling into three categories: (1) *Land(scape) as resource, real estate, property or commodity*, for use by humans according to our needs or desires, without reference to collective values or social conditions. In this perspective, land is seen as basically *there* for our consumption, as a standing reserve, with few or no limitations on what we can do with it. (2) *Land(scape) as home*, coproduced through a specific human (local or regional) history, or available to be shaped into a *new* history. This is both a humanized (anthropocentric) and a relational conception of land, according to which a particular landscape might be seen as "our" land, the epitome of Englishness, the "new world" of immigrant settlers, and so on, but also understood as having its own needs which must be properly tended and stewarded. (3) *Land-(scape) as numinous Other*, characterized by life, sentience, and agency or will, an Other which interacts with humans, teaches us and places demands on us, and with which we can come into closer sympathy or harmony (or from which we can distance ourselves). This latter view is the one most commonly found in New Age and earth spirituality.

These three perspectives can be charted along an axis, at one end of which land(scape) or place is perceived as an *object* of human desires or actions, while at the other it is understood to be an active *subject* and agent in its own right. It is important to note that none of these positions necessarily involves any more "projection" of values, ideas, or ideologies than the others. Land perceived as commodity can be as much a projection of capitalist values and an abstract-mechanistic ontology as land perceived as numinous Other can be a projection of romantic and animist ideals and antimodern sentiments. And although land-as-home would be found somewhere in the middle of the spectrum, this need not indicate that it is a more balanced, middle-ground position; frequently, in fact, it is saturated with exclusionary, ethnic, or nationalist sentiments.

New Age and ecospiritual discourses of nature suggest that modernity has eclipsed certain meanings, certain interpretations, ways of seeing or of "unconcealing" (Heidegger 1977a:117–41) the world. In their attempt to reconnect with the Earth, earth spiritualists feel a need to seek solace and guidance in such places, to reclaim them for purposes unprofaned by commerce, to acknowledge their difference from other spaces, through solitary vision quests or group ceremonies. To articulate this difference, they appropriate whatever language is available for the purpose—Mother Earth or Goddess Gaia, earth energies, sacred grids and ley lines, appeals to extraordinary and divine sources of authority, and so on. Each of these represents a discursive choice, one which may either open up or foreclose possibilities for building discursive alliances; and it is their potential for articulating common images across such broader alliances that can make them fruitful for larger social and environmental struggles.

As the preceding chapters have shown, *Gaia* has become a discourse and a trope, a literary and rhetorical device, which now relays itself across several discursive communities. It is used by scientists as a provocative short-hand image for a holistic theory of the biosphere, and by pagans and New Agers to refer to the divine person or spirit of the Earth. Proponents of planetary resource management and "sustainable development" have been quick to link the image of Gaia with a kind of technocratic managerialism that continues to treat nature, in typically resourcist and mechanistic fashion, as a storehouse of resources for human use.[7] Yet, some feminist critics have pointed out that sex-typing the planet as woman and as mother reinforces stereotypes because it "occurs within the parameters of a patriarchal culture" (P. Murphy 1995:61; cf. Seager 1993:219–21): the "feminine" is idealized yet remains passive, and humanity is still perceived as a masculine agent, "central nervous system" (Lovelock and Epton 1975:306), or "global brain" (Russell 1984) to the unconscious, feminine body of the Earth. If Earth is a woman, then the implicit suggestion seems to follow that women should be more like the Earth, and in a Western, androcentric society, this means passive, irrational, and nurturing like a good mother. And though for some Earth-as-Gaia discourse may suggest a need to care for our mother, loving and honoring her for her selfless nurturance of her many children, androcentric attitudes have historically tended to promote a schizoid love-hate response on the part of the collective male-identified ego toward his mother. It is that mother, after all, whose overbearing presence constrains the growing adolescent and is rejected in the process of becoming a "man." As monolithic as the proverbial mother-in-law, then, the planet reconfigured as Gaia harbors a somewhat restrictive array of potentialities for re-envisioning socio-ecological relations.

In any case, Gaia is meant to describe the Earth as a whole, so when it comes to describing the living quality of specific landscapes, images on a smaller, more local scale are called for. The most common New Age trope which articulates the recognition of a local numinous Other is that of earth energies. Energy metaphorics have their own history, having worked their way into New Age discourse in part from the spiritualist and metaphysical movements of the nineteenth and early twentieth centuries. Energy also sounds vaguely scientific, and the common reference to subtle or astral energies, multiple dimensions of reality, superstrings, holographic paradigm shifts, and other quasi-scientific jargon, is in part intended to grant New Age discourse a sense of ambiguous authority. Energy is an ambiguous word, its meaning more suggestive than precise, so it evokes a hint of an understanding, though a hazy one, even when used in a casual way. For instance, one of Sedona's geomants defines a sacred site as simply a place where the energy is more concentrated than elsewhere: "the ley lines that are normally very far apart and not so dense suddenly become very dense and very concentrated" (Armbruster, int.). The dowsing work of Miller and Broadhurst, Graves, and other earth mysteries researchers sometimes seems obsessive on this point of heightened energy. "Do you feel the energy?" one might be

asked at an "energy vortex," and the effort alone of trying to feel it is generally enough to sensitize a person to *some* sort of energy.

In much of the earth mysteries literature, and in the language used by
New Agers and ecospiritualists in Sedona and Glastonbury, the Gaia and
energy discourses frequently accompany each other. This can in part be
explained by the ubiquity of alternative medical traditions (as well as various kinds of systems theory) within New Age and ecospiritual discourse.
Chinese acupuncture, martial arts like t'ai chi and aikido, unorthodox Western systems such as polarity therapy and Reichian bodywork, and more recently popularized systems such as reiki, all conceive of the body in energetic terms: a healthy body is one in which the flow of life energy is unimpeded.
If the Earth is identified as Gaia, then it is reasonable to suppose that life
energy flows through her body, and that there will be places—chakras or
energy centers—where this flow is more intense and the energy more concentrated than elsewhere.

In its plurality, its suggestiveness and ultimate elusiveness, and to the degree that it doesn't call for proof by measurement, *energies* seems a useful
term for an ecospiritual reimagination of nature, but it is one that channels
the geographic imagination in particular ways. Indefinable and subtle, it
still suggests a physicalistic universe that is in principle subjectifiable to
management by a technocracy of geomancer-engineers. On the one hand,
envisioning the Earth as an energy grid follows on the path of technological
modernity critiqued so pointedly by philosopher Martin Heidegger (1977b):
once the world is "enframed" as image and picture and revealed as standing
reserve, it becomes possible to "set upon" it in a way that "challenges forth
the energies of nature," unlocking and unleashing them, and "driving" nature on to the "maximum yield at the minimum expense" (15).[8] On the
other hand, New Age energy metaphors resist the teleology of this technological maximization, and instead scramble the energy field into so many
possible narratives and imaginings. At a time when rural areas, no less than
urban ones, are being literally converted into "landscapes of speed, light
and power" (Thrift 1994), New Age energy theory spins them further into a
delirious whirlwind of connectivity, an "ecstasy of communication" (Baudrillard 1983) in which modernist time and space have collapsed, and in
which the ghostly images of imagined pasts and desired futures flicker on a
screen of incoherent, multichanneled euphoria. Within this holographic
blur, it becomes hardly possible to reinvent places except as abstract constellations of power, to be experienced as a rush of spiritual intensity.

In contrast, an explicitly *animist* metaphorics more readily allows for specific, place-relevant meanings to emerge. When members of Glastonbury's
alternative community speak of the "angel of Glastonbury" they are suggesting that there is a kind of guardian being or spirit which is identifiable with
or somehow "responsible" for Glastonbury. Sometimes the place-names
themselves are used in this way: "Sedona called me to her," one might fre-

quently hear (with the place or landscape typically being gendered female). More pluralistically conceived, animism becomes the metaphoric basis for an animated world, in which even genes and automobiles can be perceived as more than mere mechanisms. Yet, more frequently, New Agers call upon other agencies to explain the inexplicable goings-on at a place: extraterrestrials, archangels Michael and Gabriel, cosmic messengers, saints and Ascended Masters. These, like Goddess Earth, are not place based or "loric" (Brenneman 1985), but are cosmic in their references. Those which are obviously from off planet provide a sci-fi compensation for the recognition that the earth has indeed been divested of its spirits.

The notion of nature as a *trickster-teacher* resembles the various coyote and trickster figures found in indigenous mythologies, figures which seem to represent an elusive agency beyond the realm of human imperiousness. Tricksters and energies, devas and nature spirits, represent a more pluralistic and open-ended conception of the anima within the other-than-human world: one that defies systematization, deconstructing itself at the same time as it asserts a difference from the merely (and thoroughly) human. When Findhorn's gardeners or the characters of *The Celestine Prophecy* attempt to "attune" themselves to nature devas and invisible energy fields, they seemingly open up to the guidance provided by "nature itself." Science, too, refers to a nature which is in many ways elusive yet active, knowable not in a primary and direct way (as a being one might communicate with, for instance), but indirectly from its effects. As I suggested in chapter 2, Donna Haraway's (1992) notion of nature as a "coding trickster" and "coyote" might serve a balancing role within the ecology of nature metaphors, one which mediates between ecospiritual and more scientific conceptions. It suggests an animacy and elusive agency present in the extrahuman world, appearing now in one guise, now in another: one moment as matter, the next, as mind; now particle, now wave; now datum of knowledge, now of imagination. This latter image is arguably more consonant with a culture of nonlinear systems, polymorphous and transgendered natural-cultural hybrids, and indeterminate but codetermined (by humans and nonhumans), shared futures.

Each of these images or metaphors of nature, in various ways, both enables and constrains our imagination of socio-ecological relations. Rather than seeking a stable identity for the natural world, however, it is more productive for us to understand these images as active *articulations*, spawned within the material and discursive practices of interpretive communities. Recognizing the plurality of such representations allows for greater fluidity in their use. If I have implicitly favored any of them, it is that of a fluid, creative, imaginal co-constitutive "tangled web" of relations, in which neither the human nor the other-than-human retains a fixed and circumscribed identity. Protean,[9] and coyotean, agency and desire circulate through the production of subjectivities, identities, and differences, in ongoing relations worked out temporally, spatially, and at a range of scales—among them that of landscapes, places, and embodied relations between selves and others.

DESIRE, POWER, AND MEANING IN NEW AGE
AND ECOSPIRITUAL CULTURE

> In the beginning was the Golden Age, when
> men of their own accord, without threat of
> punishment, without laws, maintained good faith
> and did what was right. . . . The peoples of the
> world, untroubled by any fears, enjoyed a leisurely
> and peaceful existence, and had no use for
> soldiers. . . . In time the earth, untilled, produced
> corn . . . , and fields that never lay fallow whit-
> ened with heavy ears of grain. Then flowed rivers
> of milk and rivers of nectar, and golden honey
> dripped from the holm oak.
>
> —OVID, *Metamorphoses*

Like Ovid's myth, many New Agers and ecospiritualists posit a time long ago when humans lived in closer relationship with the earth, when we felt the ebb and flow of its subtle energies and channeled them through the landscape in our modest architectural and technical constructions and practices. In time, for whatever reason, humanity has fallen from that exalted state into the world of linear time and toil, into social divisiveness, materialism, spiritual forgetfulness, and the many travails of modern civilization. Surrounded by a popular culture that encourages short-sightedness, greedy indulgence, and an amnesiac ignorance of history, New Agers have responded by identifying the whole of it—science and Western traditions of reasoning along with everything else—as the problem, and have sought a solution outside of it all.

Modern science has its origin myths as well, but with the sequence reversed, so that humanity is seen to progress from the darkness and ignorance of the past to the gradually dawning enlightenment of scientific rationality, with its technological, economic, and intellectual fruits. New Agers and ecospiritualists prefer their own myth of lost origins, but they live within a modern, scientific society; and, in practice, many recognize with ambivalence the gifts of science and modernity. They use scientific language to support their own unorthodox ideas, at the same time as they invoke seemingly premodern, or perhaps postmodern, sources of authority to support their critiques of scientific-industrial modernity and to legitimate their resistance to it.

In a world that is frequently experienced as chaotic and confusing, New Age and ecospiritual discourse offers, on an individual scale, a sense of empowerment for personal life choices and practices. It urges a lesser dependence on consumer-materialist values and on conformity with mainstream culture, and encourages a greater reliance on intuition, inner guidance,

and finding personal answers to questions through a variety of contemplative and divinatory practices. Though these methods can and do encourage
many believers to merely exchange new sources of authority—gurus, psychic channelers, astrologers, or one of many therapeutic techniques or
"psychotechnologies"—for old ones, the underlying theme of New Age ideology is that these are all intended as means to reawaken one's personal
capacities for creativity, wisdom, and inner guidance. This optimistic message of empowerment is well expressed by British New Age celebrity Sir
George Trevelyan: "If we can wake up to our relationship to the wholeness
of life and the fact that the universe is a vast living organism shot through
and through with creative being, and if we can then channel and co-operate
with the energies and forces from that living universe, there is nothing that
cannot be solved, even to the possibility of molecular change which could
de-pollute the planet" (1986:41). Within this ideology of personal empowerment and desired social transformation, sacred sites are the "energy zones"
in which "inner growth is tangibly accelerated, and life-energy is intensified
in receptive people" (P. Jenkins, n.d.). Pilgrims who visit such sites or relocate to them with this in mind almost invariably undergo deep personal life
changes. If it is true, as the New Age cliché has it, that "you create your own
reality," then ultimate authority resides not outside the self, but within it: in
"what feels right," the "gut feeling" suggested by the "Higher Self" or "voice
of Spirit" with which one ought to seek attunement. Religious and magical thinking sees everyday events as meaningful—orchestrated by an inner
teacher, intuitive guidance system, or true Self—and as therefore offering
unconsciously intentional learning opportunities. It sees life itself as a transformative journey in the direction of wholeness—an exciting prospect, for
those who believe in it.

Interpreting Proteus: Alternative Rationalities

If such an alternative way of making sense of the world—an alternative rationality—provides a sense of individual empowerment, the drift into an
alternative interpretive community can also develop its own forms of conformity and authority. So even if you create your own reality, you may not be
willing to question the authority who tells you this. And, in the face of a
perceived threat, any new interpretive community tends to band together to
resist the threat. Williamson and Bellamy argue, for instance, that the view
among proponents of unconventional ideas that they constitute a "threatened minority" tends "to cause the upholders of all kinds of unorthodox
theories to band together in an uncritical alliance against orthodoxy." In the
spirit of "united we stand, divided we fall" they prefer not to question allied
causes, and this only serves to make them "appear gullible and uncritical,"
attracting further scorn from the establishment (1983:171). Thus, while tens
of thousands of miles of hedgerow in England and Wales are being destroyed in Britain and archaeological sites are plowed over or bulldozed,

Williamson and Bellamy lament, "ley hunters agonise over the movement of mark stones" and Tom Graves is busy "hammering copper topped poles into the earth" to improve the flow of its ley energies (183).

In focusing on the differences between scientific and mystical or religious means of knowledge production—differences that are readily visible when one looks at the things themselves (whether protons and genetic sequences, or apparitions and voices from gods or extraterrestrials)—their commonalities can easily be overlooked. Despite having developed different methods and drawn on very disparate ideas, both approaches are, at root, means of interpreting a reality that remains a protean tangled web, a reality whose nature is not known directly, but which is always mediated by signs and interpretive traditions.[10] Both draw on available interpretive resources, languages and discourses which are ready to hand, with which they develop coherent narrative accounts about the phenomena in question. Science pretends to a certain method, involving the testing, refinement, acceptance, or discarding of hypotheses, and some general premises of inductive and deductive logic. Outside the laboratory and the refereed journal, however—and sometimes there as well, as anthropological studies of science have shown— sense making and meaning production is less overtly rigid and programmatic, more promiscuous and pragmatic in its use of whatever is available. Knowledge gained through religious, magical or intuitive means also generally involves self-correcting mechanisms, but its premises and language are entirely different. Among ritual magicians, metaphysical spiritualists, and New Agers, collective knowledge is constructed through consensus, as it is among scientists, but without the benefit of well-articulated procedures of testing and verification. As sociologist Steve Bruce observes of the New Age movement, "If knowledge comes from learning to listen to an inner voice, the light within, then each person's revelation is as good as any other" (1996:213). He concludes that this results in an "individualism raised to a new plane," "individualism taken to the level of epistemology," which is both "complete relativism" and "the acme of consumerism" (221–22). But this is only part of the picture. Even among New Agers, certain things are tolerated or encouraged and others are not. Bruce acknowledges, "It is hard to imagine (though doubtless such things are there on the fringes) a channelling which supported racism, sexism, hierarchy, authoritarianism, cruelty to animals, or the overt promotion of increased consumption, but pretty well anything else must be accepted as being someone's inner guidance. The limited value consensus of the New Age reflects the value consensus of the culture from which its adherents are drawn. . . ." (215).

What is shared among scientists and scholars, New Agers, religious believers of various kinds, and even postmodern philosophers, is that all of us, as interpretive subjects, spin webs of significance and meaning out of the affordances available to us. These webs of meaning are conditioned by our "effectivities," or action capabilities, which include our technical practices, communications media, and so on, as well as by our desires and intentionalities, conscious and unconscious. Different desires and motives lead to different outcomes. The cultural desire for communication and a sense of connection with a numinous nonhuman Other, and frequently with the Earth as a whole, as we have seen, has led to the growth of the New Age and ecospiritual communities I have studied. In contrast, the cultural desire for effective and useable power over the energy locked in an atom, or military power over national enemies, has led to the development of atomic energy and the nuclear bomb. Whatever one may think of New Age answers to empirical questions, New Age desires—particularly the desire for a meaningful sense of connection with the Earth—and the apparent inability of science to assuage these desires, raise questions that deserve serious attention far beyond their specific cultural constituency. The desire to reestablish a reverent working relationship between humans and the extrahuman world is a desire that unites many New Agers with more secular and pragmatic environmentalists and, arguably, with many scientists as well. By redescribing the differences between these different "rationalities" in terms of the desires which fuel them, rather than the different terminologies on which they rely, it may be possible to refocus discussion in ways that facilitate dialogue between them.

New Age Tourism as Global Homesickness

> Making a place sacred once meant protecting it, to preserve it. For us, making a place sacred assures its profanity. We make it a national park. We write a glowing natural history. We put it on a magazine cover or mention it as a *hot* place in *Outside*. The next thing you know, the state travel council people have moved in and are doing inserts for *The New Yorker*.
>
> Brew pubs and traffic jams are only a yuppie away. . . .
>
> Our very culture—environmentally aware, travel crazy—is on the make for great places. . . .
>
> It isn't really about place. It's about response. The place is just a setting, a trigger that helps begin an inner process.
>
> —Rob White, "Sacred Places"

As this lament suggests, New Age culture, for all its high motives, still remains in most respects a symptom of its civilizational milieu. Some social theorists have commented on the "transcendental homelessness" or "global homesickness" (Lukács 1971) which characterizes modern individuals. In many ways, critics of the New Age movement are right to perceive it as being mired in the same individualistic commodity culture of ultramodernity. New Agers may be seeking to retrieve connections to landscapes and the

Earth as a whole, but they do so as privileged members of a society which remains ecologically adrift; and they, arguably, remain incapable of establishing genuine connections to a landscape or to a cultural tradition. In the process, places get refashioned and appropriated into the postmodern marketplace, in which the wealthy can shop around, drifting touristically from one setting to another, while the less well-off are forced to drift in the less romantic quest for wage labor subsistence.

In this context, the line between tourism and pilgrimage becomes interminably blurred, but so does that between nomadism and pilgrimage, where one's pilgrimage may be directed to a place where survival might be more possible, a place of hope and promise. At its extreme, tourism involves a gaze which objectifies and consumes that which is encountered, generally according to preestablished itineraries and meanings. In contrast, pilgrimage, in its "pure" form, sanctifies and reveres its object, opening up to its numinous presence in a way that renders the pilgrim vulnerable to its effective power. The difference, it is often argued, is largely one of attitude, and there is a continuum of shades in between. And there is a point at which pilgrimage turns into nomadism—a sacred wandering, a bohemian quest for cosmic or unifying meaning.

In practice, however, this distinction between tourism and pilgrimage rarely holds up to scrutiny. While pilgrimage may consist of "immersing oneself in a place, letting it do something for one, and perhaps even contributing to the energy or purity of the place," another form of "sacred" travel—"spiritual tourism"—consists of people "simply 'notching up' spiritual sites without getting involved with the place" (from a sacred place tour guide of England's West Country, cited in Bowman 1993a:42). But what kind of "involvement" is called for? Should this be defined by the host community (one or another of them) or by the visitor? If the Earth is covered by a network of sacred sites whose energy flow is facilitated by traveling from one site to another, as some New Agers believe, then what difference does it make how one gets involved with a place? Pilgrimage can be performed for a variety of motives, including personal change or healing, planetary change, the desire for novelty or escape from the confinement of an unsatisfactory or abusive domestic situation; and it could have a variety of different effects. Bowman reminds us as well that whereas traditional pilgrims return home from their travels renewed, "the Avalonians do not return home; they seek instead to live permanently in that state of liminality usually only briefly experienced by the pilgrim" (1993a:59).

In a book on the effects of tourism in the American West, Scott Norris notes, "As a worldwide enterprise based on the packaging and selling of *place*, tourism will play a major role in shaping, for good or ill, the physical, social, and psychological geographies of the year 2000 and the coming century" (1994:vii; italics in original). This is seen by some as a laudable improvement over unsustainable resource-extractive industries, but by others as a "devil's bargain," a "selling of place, history, and cultural identity

in exchange for seasonal, low-wage employment in an increasingly urban-
ized, economically stratified, and corporate-dominated social environment"
(viii). In the global economy, as Alexander Wilson puts it, "The mass circulation of the middle classes around the globe is a phenomenon of vast proportions—now over 400 million people a year" (1991:51). Rural and small
town communities like Glastonbury and Sedona are attempting to carve out
their own niches within this global tourist economy, by promoting one or
another place-image catering to one or another prospective client group.
The packaging of a place necessarily leads to its transformation, as this package is bought, taken up and acted upon. Spatial and technological practices, involving cars, cameras, jeeps and helicopters (in Sedona's case), and
the building of housing estates and tourist establishments, alter and transform the surface of the landscape itself which has been offered for consumption.

The question for New Agers and earth spiritualists is whether the sacred
nature of a place can be maintained in the midst of these transformations.
What does the sacred consist of in this context, and how can it be recognized and preserved? Rather than answering this question directly—a tactic
that would require stabilizing the meaning of the sacred (or the natural)—
we need to understand the broader cultural meaning of New Age and earth
spirituality, and to develop a perspective within which this meaning can be
better articulated and accommodated. Such a perspective would focus on a
possible politics of place, a hermeneutically and dialogically conceived ecological or bioregional politics, in which space is made for divergent understandings of nature, land, and earth, and for practices which adequately
reflect these divergences.

THE DIALOGICS OF SACRED PLACE

I have been describing the dilemma of recognizing what is different or special about a sacred place in order to better argue for its protection. If we step
back from the desire to definitively nail down this difference, however, and
view such places in the context of everyday life as a whole, it becomes clear
that any place is always much more than, say, a conductor of invisible and
elusive earth energies or a residence for animating spirits. Places are also
sites of economic transactions, reservoirs of traditional cultural meanings,
spaces for work, play, learning, socializing, intimacy, movement and rest,
interspecies interaction, and spiritual experience. And places are historical,
products of particular social and ecological relations unfolding over time.

In the context of struggles for the preservation of sacred sites, it has been
indigenous societies which have best represented such a sociohistorical perspective, in which sacred space is recognized to be intersubjective, a part of
communal tradition, ongoing "revelation," dialogue, and negotiation (e.g.,
Deloria 1994; Irwin et al. 1996). A place is sacred because it has been known
to be sacred, and treated as such, over time. Revelation necessitates a genu-

ine openness to the spiritual Other that makes itself known in a place, but known and recognized within a social and communal framework.

This emphasis on intersubjectivity and tradition in the recognition of sacred sites implies several things. Tradition is not static: it changes and responds to altered circumstances. In today's world the notion of tradition is particularly problematic, and cultural adaptation to late-twentieth-century conditions has generated a great deal of religious creativity. The products of this creativity are taken up, accepted or rejected through social negotiation and dialogue. In order for the *social* recognition of the sacredness of particular places and landscapes to spread, in our day, I would argue that certain key premises would need to be more widely accepted. These are not premises about sacredness, subtle energies, or specific deities or forces; they are not premises, that is, about the *identity* or *essence* of such places. Rather, they are working assumptions about human social practices and the relation between humans and the nonhuman. Specifically, these posit (1) that humans are essentially interpretive, linguistic, and meaning-bearing beings; (2) that human society is dialogic, highly differentiated, and pluralistic, and that the democratic working-through of these differences is an important ethical imperative of our time; (3) that relations between human society and its nonhuman others are also, in crucial respects, *social*; and (4) that these latter relations are presently in a state of crisis.

The first of these, a *hermeneutic ontology*, understands that the stories groups of people tell themselves in making sense of their world are basic to who they are. We are interpretive beings, and our interpretations—of the world, of ourselves, and of the spaces and places we live within and cocreate—are social, temporal, and dialogic creations. Over time, within specific histories of interpretive living-within-a-landscape, human communities develop the sense of being at home within that landscape. Once language, discourse, and interpretation are seen as constitutive components of the meaningful world which we inhabit, however, it becomes more difficult to presume a direct connection between a community of people and a single truth about the world (or about a landscape), which is somehow epistemologically privileged over others.

Since different interpretations about the world and our place in it are always possible, the question of adjudicating between these accounts becomes an issue. The second premise, a *dialogic, democratic, and communicatively ethical view of society*, insists on a basic commitment to dialogue and a respect for pluralism and differentiation. It allows us to see that these stories, myths and meaning systems are created over time and worked out in relationship and dialogue: no story, whether it be that of the Christian Bible, the current scientific consensus, or the political-economic discourse of globalization, ought to hold a monopoly on "the way things are." In the present condition (arguably) of increasing global homogeneity, individual, local, and regional differences can be valorized, while those systems of meaning or of practice which strive to dominate or eliminate alternatives can and should be critiqued. By acknowledging that all human groups work out their own specific histories of living in relation to landscapes, histories in which the sense of home or place is constantly being negotiated with other groups and with extrahuman networks of relations, and that this is always an unfinished product or process, a dialogic view can prevent the development of a sense of exclusive right or ownership over a given place. It opens, rather than closes off, dialogue, even if it also recognizes that some stories and interpretive systems may not ever be entirely commensurable with others. A dialogic view of society recognizes that there will always be a tension between the movement toward communicative consensus and that toward divergence and disagreement, and that this tension can be fruitful for all parties.[11]

Third, if relations between human communities and their broader-than-human environments are recognized to be *social* and relational, then the respect to "others" which is facilitated by a dialogic ethics is extended to nonhumans, and potentially to places, landscapes, or environments. This is not some universal principle that can be applied systematically and abstractly. It is, rather, a recognition that the stories that are told to make ourselves "at home" in the world *already* include nonhuman others, without ever fully encompassing them. In practice, this recognition of sociality in nature, not only in human culture, calls for a greater diversity of land use practices, and in particular, more frequent allowance for land to remain unexploited for economic purposes. It means conceiving of communities and landscapes as always already *mixed* communities, that is, as places where humans are already engaged in relationships with other-than-humans.

The fourth premise, *that relations between the human and nonhuman are presently in crisis*, is a basic assumption with which I have worked throughout this book. As the recognition grows that dominant modernist metanarratives and spatial practices, such as those associated with the instrumental rationality of industrial capitalism, are poorly equipped to resolve the world's growing environmental dilemmas, a space can be opened up for alternative practices. These alternatives can take a variety of forms, ranging from ecological restoration initiatives and the setting aside of wildlife corridors to environmentally sensitive community, housing, and landscape design.[12] A sensitivity to the politics of social dialogue would, additionally, confer respect for minority religious views, including those of "alternative rationalities," such as those of New Agers and ecospiritualists. A variety of alternative stories agree on the fallacy of reducing land to its real estate and development value. More importantly, science—the dominant story, in many respects—does not disagree with this. Instead of emphasizing their differences from the scientific worldview, or simply rejecting or ignoring it (which many New Agers and earth spiritualists tend to do) in favor of their own, these alternative discursive communities may fare better by seeking out allies within the scientific community.

Toward a Nonessentialist Bioregionalism

Bioregionalism is the attempt to found the cultural and economic activities of a human community more directly within the particulars of its immediate natural environment or life-region. In response to the increasing globalization of society, bioregionalists counterpose a vision of locally self-reliant, ecologically sustainable, and politically self-governing communities living harmoniously within the boundaries of distinct ecological regions (Berg 1978; Alexander 1990; Andruss et al. 1990; Aberly 1993; McGinnis 1999). In the broader world of politics and economics, bioregionalism is no more than a radical ideal with a small minority of advocates. Some of its theoretical expressions have been critiqued as unrealistic, naive, and even potentially "ecofascist"—a charge directed at some bioregionalists' notion that *culture* should be more firmly rooted in local histories and ecologies, which suggests that the foreign and exotic is somehow out of place. In this sense, any workable democratic bioregionalist theory must include within itself an ethical and critical appreciation of difference and plurality, and a nonessentialist understanding of place which recognizes the ambiguity and mutability of borders and cross-border movements, territorialities and deterritorializations.

As a pragmatic set of ideas, however, bioregionalism suggests an ecosystem-centered approach to the planning and design of human communities, one that is compatible with a pluralistic and democratic society. Such an approach has been taken up not only by countercultural, environmental, and community activists, but even by some urban and environmental planners and politicians.[13] One thing that is made clear by a bioregional approach to planning and politics is that a given bioregion will have places for various kinds of activity—most obviously for everyday dwelling and for intensive economic use, but also for nonintensive uses, such as green space and parkland, marshes and wetlands, cemeteries and cultural monuments, and so on. The identification of numinous or sacred landscapes fits into this latter, nonintensive use category. Within many indigenous societies, sacred places were (and still are) visited ceremonially, and were considered to be particularly powerful because of the spirits or deities residing there. In many societies, sacred places have been those places which play a crucial role in keeping the link between human cultural history and the landscape alive: they serve as anchors for culture within a landscape. Both in locale-specific indigenous traditions and in the larger "world religions," sacred sites provide a kind of symbolic center for a larger and geographically more dispersed community. Such places as the Vatican, Jerusalem, or Mecca are, in a sense, symbolic stand-ins for whole religious systems, representing the coherence of the whole in a specific hierophany, or a set of monuments which draws together the web of meanings that make up its respective tradition.[14] As such, they materially anchor the particular tradition, together with its interpretive and cultural system, in a particular locality.

The preceding chapters have shown how certain interpretive communities have attempted to establish a particular kind of link between culture and specific landscapes. Ecospiritual sacred sites, however, are variously situated on a multitude of cultural geographies: they play a different role within global tourist culture than they do in the lives of individual pilgrims or of particular cultural groups. By placing them within a bioregional perspective (a perspective that should not be imposed over and against the diverse perspectives of a pluricultural society, but rather added to the mix—I will address this point below), we can see additional potential roles such places could play. Taking a cue from indigenous cultures, sacred places could be those places which are visited ceremonially, but otherwise left alone. They may be places which play a special role in maintaining the relationship between regional culture(s), its stories, and the land. They can also facilitate a coherent understanding of the entire life-region—something that is necessarily tied to the phenomenology of landscape. Sacred sites may provide "access points," vantage points or perspectives on the whole surrounding region, which allow a pilgrim to gain an overview of that landscape and to remind herself what the sense and meaning of the landscape is—how it works, how it all fits together within the cyclical round of life in this particular area. Mountains and high places frequently play such a role in traditional societies: they facilitate the generation of insights, via vision quests and unusual encounters with rarely seen animals or other species, distinctive light phenomena, and so on. Other sorts of sites, such as sacred wells, river canyons, and underground caverns, often facilitate a different kind of encounter—one which is more inward or "depth-directed," more to do with personal and community history, ancestry, and the rootedness of self and society in the earth. A variety of such phenomenologies is possible for very different sorts of potential sacred sites; my chapters on Glastonbury and Sedona have suggested a few of these, but the fuller development of this topic will have to await a future effort.

Within the framework of a coherent land-based ecospatial tradition, sacred sites could help to maintain the balance between intensively and non-intensively used areas. Reserved for the latter (nonintensive use), they could remind local inhabitants of the "spirits" of the area—which, viewed hermeneutically, are none other than the stories which make sense of the world and bring it to life for its inhabitants. All societies (and ecologies) tell such stories, and the actors, agents, deities, or heroes of those stories animate the meanings ascribed by the given social group to the landscape, people's relationship to it, and the cosmos as a whole. The crucial characteristic about the sacred stories told within traditional indigenous societies—and what New Agers and ecospiritualists have been groping toward in their own invented narratives—is that they refer to Others who are always interacting with us, but whose agency always remains elusive and autonomous.

In a cultural-hermeneutic understanding of sacred places, such places can be reconceived as *interpretive heterotopias,* "open spaces" at which the human interpretation of the other-than-human would be recognized as necessarily incomplete and inherently *problematic.* Interpretation, after all, is an act which imposes meaning onto a world that is ultimately elusive. Or rather, it generates meaning from the interactive relationality of self and other, identity and difference. *Sacred* places could be those places at which such meanings are not allowed to ossify, but at which they are always kept in play. An ecospiritual opening up to the Other recognizes that this Other has something to teach us. When approached with an interpretive humility, a weakened or minimized impulse to interpretively encompass that Other, this openness can be kept in fluid play; yet, over time, it could lead to the development of traditions of speaking and making sense of the world which are somewhat more locally attuned, more cognizant of ecological relations. This would require self-consciously seeking a balance between *interpreting* the world and *recognizing the limits* of any such interpretation.[15] Sacred places could become places where this openness is sought, individually or collectively, with humility and with a refusal to impose. In contrast to the ongoing buying and selling of place and space until, as Marshall Berman (1976) puts it, "all that is solid melts into air," such places might, in time, help to establish a sense of continuity in the relationship between people and the larger, other-than-human reality as it expresses itself in the natural-cultural life of a given region.

Yet there is a social and historical context which must be kept in mind in any effort to set aside places as sacred. Such an effort, at the present historical conjuncture, takes place in the midst of far-from-egalitarian cultural relations, and against the background of an ecological crisis, a crisis which is associated with industrial-capitalist society. Places already have histories, and sacred places have histories in which their sacredness has been acknowledged, frequently by historically oppressed minority groups in opposition to the meanings the dominant culture would impose on them. In this sense, the refusal to impose interpretations should begin as a *self*-refusal initiated by the privileged beneficiaries of modern industrial, Euro-American culture. A first step away from the imposition of meanings on such places may be to recognize their indigenous coinhabitants, where there are such. (Obviously, this applies to North and South America or Australia but not to Europe, where there is no useful way of distinguishing "natives" from "nonnatives.") A post-tourist recognition of sacred places in the context of local and regional sacred geographies can only reemerge if such sacred places were, in some sense at least, returned to their native "custodians."[16]

Accompanying such a process, however, would need to be a genuine and broad-based dialogue between locally or regionally based residential groups and stakeholders, as well as intercultural facilitators, scholars, and even mystics (that is, those whose interest in the place, or in the issue of sacred sites per se, is spiritually and experientially based). Such a dialogue would need to be oriented not merely around questions of economic justice or tourism, as they tend to be now, but also around questions of *sacred space* within regional geographies. The idea of sacred space would thereby become open to the dialogic determination of what "sacredness" might mean in a given pluricultural regional context. That is, to existing notions of "sacred space" —both those produced by indigenous, land-based historical traditions and those brought by immigrant communities (two poles of a rather blurred continuum)—we would add the ongoing, collective cultural project of determining what might be appropriate regional sacred/spatial practices. Within such a dialogue, New Age and ecospiritual pilgrims' perspectives represent a useful complement to others: they demonstrate contemporary society's spiritual needs (or weaknesses), but also reflect the inevitable loosening of the boundaries and barriers which, in the past, have kept apart different cultural traditions. A broader alliance can thus be built around this issue of recognizing sacred places; and, in the end, such a recognition would have to proceed within the broader project of developing ecologically more sustainable bioregions and communities.

These are, of course, tentative suggestions, and they require much more thought and discussion. In a deeper sense, they carry with them a profound risk that we cannot afford to ignore: this is the risk of contributing to the further extension of a spatial managerialism, an approach which attempts to parcel out rigidly bounded spaces and to manage and control their uses accordingly. This tendency, I believe, should be resisted, and sacred space should ultimately be seen within a nonessentialist framework of relations, flows, and circulations (of desire, power, identities and differences)—yet without erasing the differences of scale and the relative constancies of landscape and nature which make up these relations. Rather than working to *set aside* special places as sacred or "heterotopic," which can ultimately only be a contradiction in terms, *heterotopia* should be understood as a critical practice, an affirmative engagement with places that effectively deterritorializes them from the managerial grip of property and commodity relations, allowing instead for them to remain *open*, not only for individual "vision quests" or collective sacred rituals, but for the play of radical ecological difference.

The cultural politics within which these issues are taken up will always require careful and critical attention. I offer these suggestions with the hope that they may stimulate debate: they are my own translation of what the New Age and ecospiritual quest for sacred landscapes seems, to me, to represent. If the claims made by some of these questers sometimes appear immodest, unsophisticated, or scientifically dismissable, the intuition that lies behind them is certainly worthy of attention: it is that the effort to make sense (and livelihood) of the world can become too forceful in its grasp, squeezing its component parts to the absolute maximum of resource productivity. The economic and technological system that today has extended itself, with all its benefits, side effects, and waste products, over the living body of the planet, exercises such a forceful grip on ecosystems and cultures. If we are not to be left with a dead carcass of a planet, some of the others who inhabit it—whatever forms they are imagined to take—must be allowed to remain, actively, *other*. Our imagination of these "others" has become constrained and restricted. To free it up means to recognize the tangled web of meanings, identities and differences, recognitions and recip-rocations, within which we humans are enmeshed: a web in which power and desire, both human and *un*human, circulate in an unencompassable circuit of relays and flows. Sacred places are the physical and geographic anchor points for our psychic and cultural imaginings, the stories we tell about ourselves, the world, and the relations between them. That world is densely tangled; but the tangles have knots and nodes.

NOTES

1. My interest in this "third position" arises, in part, out of a commitment to thinking through the environmental crisis. Ecophilosophy and critical environmental theory today constitute a polyvocal arena made up of diverse analytical perspectives, including those of ecocentric deep ecologists (Evernden 1985; McLaughlin 1993; Sessions 1995b; Abram 1996), ecofeminists (Plumwood 1993; Bigwood 1993; Cuomo 1998; Sandilands 1999), social and political ecologists (N. Smith 1990; D. Harvey 1996; Peet and Watts 1996; Light 1998; Luke 1999), poststructuralists (Conley 1997; van Wyck 1997; Escobar 1999), and others (cf. Zimmerman 1994; Oelschlaeger 1995; Cronon 1995; Gottlieb 1997; Braun and Castree 1998; Zimmerman et al. 1998). My own particular take on the ecological (and cultural) problematic has been especially shaped by contemporary Continental philosophy, notably poststructuralism, the broad post-1960s theoretical movement which understands discourse, knowledge, power, identity, and materiality to be thoroughly intertwined and dynamically interrelated; and by recent postconstructivist or "posthumanist" attempts in the social sciences to rework social constructivism by acknowledging and theorizing human interdependence and embeddedness within broader-than-human material and ecological relations. I am interested in the development of a relational, performative, discursive, and co-constructive materialism, a theoretical approach which conceives of agency, power, desire, and so on, not as *inhering* in things (humans, scientific laws, nature) but as circulating within relational networks of actors, objects, ideas, and practices — networks which necessarily encompass (and therefore blur the dichotomy between) the "social" and the "natural." The society-nature dichotomy has fulfilled numerous historical functions, some laudable (e.g., allowing the social sciences to carve out their sphere of authority as genuinely *interpretive* sciences in contradistinction to the more quantitative and positivist natural sciences), others far less so (e.g., providing a philosophical justification for some horrendous ways of treating other species), but its limitations today seem to me rather acute.

Such a critical and reconstructive project places my arguments into dialogue with a much broader range of work stretching from the work of such philosophers as Heidegger (1977a,b), Merleau-Ponty (1962), Bachelard (1987), Foucault (1973, 1980), and Deleuze and Guattari (1987), through to various strands of theory and scholarship across the social sciences: in human and cultural geography (Seamon and Mugerauer 1985; Lefebvre 1991; Shields 1991; Duncan and Ley 1993; Keith and Pile 1993; Gregory 1994; Soja 1996; Pile and Keith 1997), cultural anthropology and archaeology (Ingold 1992, 1993, 1995; Bender 1993; Tilley 1994; Hirsch and O'Hanlon 1995; Descola and Pálsson 1996; Feld and Basso 1996; Gupta and Ferguson 1997), cultural studies (Wilson 1991; Ross 1994; Slack and Berland 1994; Wolfe 1998), science and technology studies (Haraway 1989, 1991, 1992; Hayles 1991, 1995; Latour 1993; Sismondo 1996; Kuletz 1998; Law and Hassard 1999), environmental and rural sociology (Dickens 1996; Cloke and Little 1997), environmental history and historical ecology (Bird 1987;

Worster 1994; Crumley 1994), human ecology (Steiner and Nauser 1993), social and ecological psychology (Gibson 1979, 1982; Barwise and Perry 1983; Michael 1996), and other areas.

2. The term *landscape* is not without its problems, largely due to its historical connection with the tradition of Western pictorial representation, which privileges a particular way of seeing based on the objectification of land or places into static aesthetic objects for contemplation (cf. Cosgrove 1984; Mitchell 1994). My use of the word follows in the recent line of cultural geographers and anthropologists (e.g., Bender 1993; Hirsch and O'Hanlon 1995) who critically assess this tradition while expanding the uses of the word to include a broader representational, perceptual/cognitive (soundscape, smellscape, etc.), temporal, and cultural/political scope. Landscape, in this expanded sense, is image, symbol, and perspective (Cosgrove and Daniels 1988), cultural process (Hirsch and O'Hanlon 1995), the material manifestation of human-environment interactions (Crumley 1994:6), and much else.

3. On the New Age movement see Melton, Clark, and Kelly 1990a, 1991; Lewis and Melton 1992; Hess 1993; York 1995; Heelas 1996; Hanegraaff 1998; issues dedicated to that theme in *Religion* (v. 23 [1993]), *Religion Today* (v. 9, n. 3 [1994]), and *Social Compass* (v. 46, n. 2 [1999]); and relevant chapters in Bednarowski 1989; Barker 1989; Albanese 1990; Jorstad 1990; and Bruce 1996. My use of the term *New Age culture* is intended partly to mitigate the implications of the more frequently used term *subculture*, which implies a position of subordination and of marginality in relation to a "dominant" culture. Though my aim includes studying formations of cultural hegemony and dominance, New Age *culture* at least implies a more level playing field at the epistemological level of analysis.

4. On the international dimensions of the movement see Hackett 1987; Heelas and Amaral 1994; Tauxe 1996; Shimazono 1999; and the chapters by Hackett, Mullins, Oosthuizen, and Poggi, in Lewis and Melton 1992.

5. By *earth spirituality* I specifically mean the contemporary, primarily Western, movement which attempts to rediscover, individually or collectively, this sense of reverence for the earth/Earth. Note that my capitalization of the word *Earth* will be restricted to those usages which clearly suggest the planet as a whole (as opposed to the ground, land, or biosphere); in the case of *earth spirituality* this may be one possible usage among several, so I leave it in lower case. My occasional use of the term *ecospirituality* should be seen as merely a shorthand for *earth spirituality*; technically, the term, one could argue, should be reserved for those beliefs which have been specifically shaped by modern ecological thought.

6. On the similarities and differences between neopaganism and New Age spirituality, see Kelly 1992; York 1995; Hanegraaff 1998 (77–93); and Pearson, Roberts, and Samuel 1998. Joanne Pearson (1998), drawing on the views of Wiccan pagans, rejects the notion of an overlap between paganism and the New Age movement; but a cultural hermeneutic perspective such as mine suggests that precisely such a differentiation of religious identities may occur even in culturally similar groups. Useful sources on contemporary (neo)paganism include Adler's (1986) thorough overview of the movement, Luhrmann's (1989) and Orion's (1995) detailed ethnographies, Hutton's masterful history of British paganism (1999), and collections by Harvey and Hardman (1996) and Lewis (1996b). On women's spirituality, see Starhawk 1979, 1982, 1987; Stone 1976; Spretnak 1982; Christ and Plaskow 1989; Eller 1995. On eco-paganism, pagan ecology/ environmentalism and earth religion, see B. Taylor 1995a, 1995b; G. Harvey 1994; Deudney 1995; Adler 1986 (283–318). And on the Rainbow Family and its international Rainbow Gatherings, see Buenfil 1991.

7. See, for example, Marciniak 1992, 1995; Stubbs 1992; Essene and Nidle 1994; or any issue of *Sedona: Journal of Emergence*. Popularly attributed "sources" of channeled literature include Pleiadians, Sirians, the Ashtar Command, and a variety of Ascended Masters. This millenarian stream of New Age culture corresponds loosely to Hanegraaff's demarcation of "New Age *sensu stricto*" (1998:98), but my term *ascensionism* is intended to give it a more specific meaning emphasizing its otherworldly orientation.

8. An example of the Ascension myth is found toward the end of James Redfield's (1993) bestseller *The Celestine Prophecy*. The story is about the discovery of an ancient manuscript which provides a series of nine insights that transform the lives of those who learn about them, and which brings about the beginning of an era of heightened spiritual awareness. The concluding chapter, "The Emerging Culture," offers up a vision of the future that combines a strong endorsement of high technology ("an automation of the production of goods," "fusion, superconductivity, artificial intelligence"), an unapologetic anthropocentrism ("The Ninth [Insight] reveals our ultimate true destiny . . . that as humans, we are the culmination of the whole of evolution"), and a mass Ascension from the physical realm into a spiritual one, which in its apocalypticism rivals the Rapture foreseen by evangelical Christians. One of the characters explains the Ninth Insight thus: "Our destiny is to continue to increase our energy level. And as our energy level increases, the level of vibration in the atoms of our bodies increases. . . . we are getting lighter, more purely spiritual. . . . Whole groups of people, once they reach a certain level, will suddenly become invisible to those who are still vibrating at a lower level. . . . [This] will signal that we are crossing the barrier between this life and the other world from which we came and to which we go after death. . . . At some point everyone will vibrate highly enough so that we can walk into heaven, in our same form" (250–51). This otherworldly millennialism contrasts with other points in the novel, such as the main characters' learning the ability to converse with plants. Such a paradoxical mixture of ecological sentiment, techno-optimism, anthropocentrism, and an apparent desire to get out of the body and off the planet, is characteristic of much of the Ascensionist literature.

9. *Post-Fordism* refers to the decline, since the mid-1970s, of Fordist production practices and their associated political-economic geography, which was characterized by "large-scale, vertically-integrated, industrial production systems; mass consumerism and sprawling suburbanization; the centralized Keynesian planning of the welfare state; and increasing corporate oligopoly" (Soja 1989:61–62).

10. My account of postmodernization relies on the work of Jameson (1991), D. Harvey (1989), Crook, Pakulski, and Waters (1992), Lash and Urry (1994), Featherstone (1995), and numerous others. Insightful overviews of theories of postmodernity include Bertens 1995 and McGuigan 1999.

11. Foucault's definitions of *heterotopia* show some inconsistency, as Genocchio (1995) points out. My use of the term is a loose and general one intended to evoke the polysemic character of the places I will be examining, without resorting to ready-made explanations of what they in fact are (e.g., whether they are "sacred places" or not).

12. Hess's *Science in the New Age* (1993) is an excellent example of the kind of cultural-constructivist, trans-epistemic ethnographic work that serves as a model for much of my thinking. Hess scrutinizes the "paraculture" shared by scientific skeptics, New Agers, and parapsychologists—the different ways they all reconstruct scientific discourse in a broader social context, the ways they construct their own "self-" or "group-identities" as well as those of their "Others," such as by erecting discursive "boundaries" around and between themselves and controlling the "traffic" across them; and he teases out the similarities which underlie their apparent differences.

13. Actor-network theorists use the term *actant* as a way of suspending the question of whether an entity is a willful and intentional agent (actor) or not. Interested in questioning the assumption that "nature" and "culture" constitute two separate and autonomous realms, they take the accreditation of agency (commonly ascribed to humans and denied from nonhumans) as something to be explained, rather than to be taken for granted. For two slightly different definitions see Latour 1987 (70–74, 84, 90) and Haraway 1992 (313, 331).

2. REIMAGINING EARTH

1. Margulis has been known to utter disdainful comments about the religious appropriation of Gaia, though in a more recent interview she acknowledged that it is "less

harmful than standard religion" and that "at least it is not human-centered" (L. Joseph 1990:71). The primary popular expositions of the Gaia hypothesis are Lovelock's (1979, 1988); useful overviews of its scientific reception are presented in Bunyard and Goldsmith 1988, and Schneider and Boston 1991. L. Joseph chronicles Gaia's movement from science to its becoming "a guiding, galvanizing metaphor for that large, loose association of ecological, holistic, spiritual, and feminist activists described collectively, sometimes derisively, as New Age" (1990:66); while W. I. Thompson (1987, 1991) offers a range of more speculative thinking on the implications of Gaia theory. See also Roszak 1978, 1992; Berry 1988; Sheldrake 1991; Abraham 1994; Spangler 1984; Oates 1989; and Allaby 1989.

2. For instance, Peter Russell's influential *Awakening Earth* (1984) introduced the idea of a planetary consciousness or "Gaiafield," drawing on Teilhard's "noosphere" and Hindu sage Sri Aurobindo's "Supermind" concepts. Marilyn Ferguson's widely read manifesto-cum-progress-report of the New Age movement, *The Aquarian Conspiracy* (1980), listed Teilhard at the very top of a list of most frequently mentioned influences on those surveyed in her sociological questionnaire (420). Teilhard's (1955, 1964) views have been much criticized by radical ecologists for their anthropocentrism; in his view, humanity was the crowning achievement of earthly evolution, which was to culminate in the development of the "noosphere," a kind of collective consciousness enveloping the planet. Theologian Thomas Berry has rectified Teilhard's anthropocentrism and been praised for it by deep ecologists. Ecologically speaking, Berry (1988) is considered to be at the "deep" end of a spectrum, with New Paradigm thinker Fritjof Capra closer to the middle, and anthropocentric humanists like Henryk Skolimowski and Peter Russell at the opposite end (see, for example, Sessions 1995a and other articles in the same volume).

3. The book's publication led to an acrimonious debate in the pages of the British archaeological journal *Antiquity*, with Hawkins supported by Cambridge cosmologist Fred Hoyle but attacked and sloughed off by much of the archaeological establishment. By the end one of Hawkins's principal foes, archaeologist R. J. Atkinson, had become a measured supporter of astro-archaeology; John Michell, with characteristic aplomb, called his a "Saul-like conversion" (1989:80). Hawkins's ideas, however, have not fared well with time, and the present archaeological consensus is that there is not enough evidence to conclusively accept *any* of his astronomical hypotheses, with the exception of the solar orientation of the axis of Stonehenge, which is unmistakeable (Chippindale 1994).

4. In the past two decades, Thom's theories have been extensively tested and found to be based on flawed assumptions and imprecise calculations. Theoretical astronomer Douglas Heggie has extensively modified Thom's conclusions, demonstrating that there is no incontrovertible evidence for the existence of an accurate and standard megalithic unit of measurement; that there is no statistical evidence that the arrangements of megalithic sites were complex geometrical designs based on advanced mathematical knowledge; and that orientations toward astronomical phenomena, including solsticial markers (the most convincing) and lunar standstill orientations, are on the whole approximate and nonsystematic. Few academic scholars accept Thom's conclusions in their full form today (cf. Hutton 1993b:113; Chippindale 1994:230). There is, however, a general recognition that some sorts of alignments with celestial events were important in the design and use of many stone circles. Rather than a vast prehistoric intelligentsia, then, the picture today looks more like an intensely regionalized activity of circle and mound building, fulfilling a variety of social, political, economic, and religious purposes. Megalith builders, thus, were hardly astronomers (in the modern sense of the word) building "observatories," but they *were* interested in coordinating seasonal celebrations with heavenly bodies (e.g., Burl 1976, 1979, 1981). Archaeoastronomy continues to develop on the peripheries of astronomy, archaeology, and other disciplines (cf. Ruggles 1993). Michell (1989) usefully provides the subject's more partisan "countercultural" history; unfortunately, he also blurs the distinction between archaeoastro-

nomy and the much more speculative ley line and earth energies work (see below). See Critchlow 1982 for another account.

5. Useful histories of the earth mysteries movement are found in Hitching 1976; Williamson and Bellamy 1983; Marcus 1987; Michell 1989; Pennick and Devereux 1989; W. Howard 1990; Heselton 1991; and Screeton 1993.

6. Archaeologists today are agreed that megalith building occurred over millennia, not, as Michell says, over a few centuries. Even at single sites like Stonehenge and Avebury, construction took place in several stages over the course of two or three thousand years, with apparently different social and philosophical goals expressed at different times (cf. Hutton 1993b; Chippindale 1994; Ucko et al. 1990).

7. Michell and others have claimed to discover the proportions and principles of sacred geometry at work in the stone circles of the British Isles, the pyramids of Egypt, Greek and Hindu temples, medieval and Renaissance cathedrals and churches (including Glastonbury Abbey), and, it seems, almost everywhere they have looked. Geometry and proportion had, of course, been highly valued and utilized by the ancient Greeks and Egyptians and by the builders of the Gothic cathedrals. Overviews of sacred geometry include Pennick 1980; Lawlor 1982; Critchlow 1982; Michell 1972, 1983; and Charpentier 1972.

8. Dowsing is an intuitive art that makes use of tree branches or metal (usually copper) rods to discover underground water sources and, less frequently, other objects or phenomena. It is also more generally used as a form of divination, whereby a source of knowledge outside the diviner's consciousness is thought to provide answers to questions posed. Having observed dowsers in action and attempted it myself, I tend to agree with the moderate skeptics' view that most (though perhaps not all) dowsing phenomena can be attributed to unconscious muscular activity and other nonparanormal influences (e.g., Hancock 1998). A successful dowser, in this view, unconsciously—mainly through arm and wrist muscles—changes the angle of the rods (using L-rods) so as to move them in the appropriate direction. The slightest change has an obvious, and visually compelling, effect: the rods really seem to move on their own (though a shift too great merely sets them spinning). Other media, such as tree branches or pendulums, act in an analogous fashion. All these instruments can be thought of as props for "tuning into" the unconscious or "body-mind"; but there is little way of knowing whether this "unconscious" is genuinely "receiving" information from an external source (e.g., underground water channels, electromagnetic energy currents) or simply transmitting information that is subjective (i.e., finding things according to the dowser's expectations), intersubjective (i.e., conforming to the actions of one's fellow dowsers), or indicative of other environmental conditions (such as uneven ground). The only way to make dowsing a reliable method of gaining information is through repeated testing, experimentation, and verification, under controlled conditions; and so far, results of such testing have been ambiguous or unconvincing. For contrasting accounts, see Bailey, Cambridge, and Briggs 1988; Betz 1995; Hancock 1998; Jansson 1999; van Leusen 1999; and Enright 1999. Practical introductions to dowsing include Graves 1986a and Lonegren 1986.

9. Graves points to the work of the Findhorn Community—made famous by Paul Hawken (1975) for growing huge cabbages in the soils of northern Scotland with the aid of meditative communication with "nature spirits"—as laying the "groundwork" for a new "psychology" or "sociology of nature," a sociology which includes "nature spirits or 'elementals' . . . concerned with what we might call routine maintenance work," and "devas and landscape angels," which are the "archetypes and essences" of species, places, and things (Graves 1986b:161–62). Similarly, demons are "thought-images" constructed over time, "personifications of our own imbalances—our greed, our ignorance, our self-aggrandisement," "complete archetypes which have been built up over millennia" (166). But the Catholic Church, Graves argues, "in constructing an image of a demonic hierarchy . . . has effectively unified these inchoate forces behind one massive super-archetype, *the* Devil" (166; italics in original), constructed partly out of

the image of the nature-god Pan, but "better described as a sort of 'dustbin' for all the aspects of human nature that the Church preferred to hide" (or demonize) (166).

10. Similarly, Bloom and Pogacnik (1985) propose that ley lines "form the matrix of energy which is the *dynamic physical principle* of the geological body of earth. Ley lines are the essential structure of the etheric body of the Earth Spirit." At places where they meet, "both dense (normal) and etheric matter vibrate at higher, therefore more conscious, frequencies" (in Leviton 1991:249; italics in original). The American dowser Sig Lonegren defines an "energy ley" as "usually a six-to-eight-foot-wide beam of yang energy" whose width varies but whose length is straight. Where such leys cross there is a body of "primary water" underneath (251); and the yin underground water element balances the overground yang energy beams. Richard Leviton writes, "Under great internal pressure in the earth, water at faults was originally forced upwards, condensing into fractures as it neared the surface and forming water domes with numerous exiting veins" and "moving out laterally through the veins or fractures" (1991:252). "A power center or holy site is found 'at any point on the earth's surface where one or more energy leys and primary water converge'" (Lonegren cited in Leviton 1991:252). At such a power center, everyday reality is supposed to interpenetrate with other "paraphysical" realities.

11. Pennick and Devereux's critique of the energy ley concept is strongly worded. They write: "But the energy ley thesis is more serious than an internecine quarrel. It represents a movement into abstraction, away from the land and the archaic whisper that lies upon it. It is all *projection on to* rather than a *learning from* the land and the planet. A jamming signal which blots out reception" (1989:244; italics in original). One could argue that some writers' emphasis on "sacred geometry" involves a similar type of abstraction and "projection on to the land" (though neither Devereux nor Pennick has such reservations about the latter). A reader of Pennick and Devereux might also wonder to what extent *their* shamanic energy line thesis is such a "projection." Skeptical scholar Ronald Hutton (1993b:123), however, lauds their *Lines on the Landscape* (Pennick and Devereux 1989) as "by far the most well researched, intelligently written and beautifully produced work yet published on leys." Devereux's most recent writing (1996, 1997; Devereux and Jahn 1996) further downplays his earlier enthusiasm for leys themselves, while emphasizing the real examples of straight or nearly straight landscape lines and other physical properties of prehistoric sites.

12. Cathie's and others' energy grid theories have found a sizable audience among the readers of such magazines as *Nexus*, a magazine which boasts of its coverage of "suppressed technology, prophecies & the future, big brother conspiracies, health coverups, behind the news, ufos & the unexplained, hidden history, & more" (October–November 1994, back cover). With their dense mathematical calculations and physical, chemical, and geometrical references and formulas, Cathie's attempts to link "UFOs, Earth Grids, Sacred Geometry, Light, Gravity, Matter, and Time," not to mention antigravity, space transmitters, pyramids, harmonics, and government cover-ups of various sorts, "into one unified theory" (Cathie 1994:37), speak volumes about the quasi-scientific predilections of his conspiracy-minded readers. A less freewheeling work on earth grid alignments is Walsh 1993.

13. According to Hindu and Buddhist tradition, the chakras run along the spine from its base to the crown of the head, via centers just below the navel and at the solar plexus, heart, throat, and "third eye." Transposing them to the round surface of the earth seems rather forced; and speculation about the geographical locations of the various chakras generally rests on an intuitive assessment or on subjective preferences. Glastonbury is often called the heart chakra, for instance—which is sometimes explained with reference to the introspective, meeting-one's-own-shadow sort of process that is said to occur for pilgrims to the town. By the same token, however, it seems a revealing oversight when New Agers *fail* to acknowledge that cities like New York, London, Los Angeles, Calcutta, or Mexico City, are *immense* "energy centers."

14. Psychologist and neurophysiologist Michael Persinger, for instance, has demonstrated a connection between seismic phenomena, tectonic stress, and increased report-

ing of UFOs. Persinger hypothesizes that piezoelectric effects and other electromagnetic discharges associated with tectonic plate movements, specifically at geological fault zones, stimulate specific areas of the neocortex, producing hallucinatory images which the brain interprets as apparent UFO encounters, poltergeistlike episodes, and even elements of near-death experiences (NDEs). Persinger has reportedly duplicated such phenomena in subjects through direct electrical stimulation of the temporal lobe (see Persinger 1987; Regush 1995). Wilder Penfield's (1975) work on electrical stimulation of the cortex also showed that such stimulation could reawaken vivid memories and elicit dream states or "psychical seizures." The biogenetic structuralist school (e.g., Laughlin, McManus, and d'Aquili 1990) has especially pursued the relationships between transpersonal experiences and neurological activity. Transpersonal psychologists have surmised that alleged alien abduction experiences (AAEs) and NDEs share a common structure which parallels that of shamanic and initiatory spiritual experiences (e.g. Grosso 1996; Bailey and Yates 1996), and that these are facilitated by geophysical phenomena. Devereux, parapsychologist Serena Roney-Dougal (1993:158), and others speculate that anomalous electromagnetic readings, radioactivity, and ionization levels have been found near Britain's megalithic monuments because many of the British stone circles are built on quartz-bearing granite intrusions, and are themselves built out of quartz-bearing stone.

On the UFO and alien abduction phenomenon, see Keith Thompson 1991 and Jodi Dean 1998. A good source of peer-reviewed scholarly writing is the *Journal of UFO Studies*. Of interest to my own thesis, K. Thompson (1991), Vallee (1969, 1988), and Baisden (1996) have all suggested that UFOs be viewed as part of the centuries-old phenomenon of encounters with some anomalous extrahuman "source" (interpreted, in the past, as fairies, angels, gods, and so on). Thompson argues, convincingly, that the long-standing polarization between believers and skeptics itself serves to maintain the enigmatic and emotionally charged nature of the topic.

15. The term *geomancy* is also used to refer to forms of divination based on the interpretation of figures or patterns drawn on the ground with sand or other granular materials. Such geomancy was common in the ancient Near East, the Arab and Mediterranean worlds, and medieval Europe. My usage, however, will be restricted to the interpretation or divination of the landscape (cf., e.g., Pennick 1979).

16. For instance, Gimbutas's position that male divinities were not prominent before the Indo-European invasions has been disputed; male, androgynous, zoomorphic, and indeterminately gendered figurines and deities are largely ignored by her. Her portrayal of Old Europe as culturally homogeneous, socially egalitarian, and devoid of human or animal sacrifice has also been disputed. Feminist archaeologist Lynn Meskell argues that, in Gimbutas's accounts, "every figure that is not phallic—and some that clearly are—are taken as symbols of the Goddess. This includes parallel lines, lozenges, zigzags, spirals, double axes, butterflies, pigs and pillars. Why this miscellany are self-evidently emblems of a female, much less a deity, is never explained. And indeed even the *male* may be symbolically *female*: 'Although the male element is attached, these figurines remain essentially female' (she writes (1989:232)). Gimbutas denied that phallicism was symbolic of procreation since Neolithic peoples did not understand the nature of biological conception (1974:237)" (Meskell 1995:80). Gimbutas's overarching theory of the patriarchal, steppe-nomadic origins of Indo-European-speaking peoples (known as the Kurgan theory) is one of several alternative theories. Parts of it have gained acceptance in the archaeological community, while others are rejected. One of the most prominent supporters of the theory, James Mallory, has argued against the simplistic portrayal of "the Proto-Indo-Europeans as a single people constrained within their homeland, perfecting their language and then bursting all over the earth waving swords and spreading paradigms" (1989:22). Yet this is precisely the image that gets presented by many popularizers of Gimbutas's work. On the debate surrounding Gimbutas's ideas, see Spretnak 1982; Hayden 1986, 1998; Mallory 1989; Hutton 1993b, 1997; Anthony 1995; Meskell 1995; Conkey and Tringham 1995; Keeley 1996; Goodison and Morris 1999; Marler 1999; and Eller 2000.

17. Similarly, the prevalence of Virgin Mary statues in Catholicism or of Barbie dolls in modern-day North America says little about the position of women in those societies. But for an argument that there *is* a correlation between origin myths and the secular power of women in a society, see Sanday 1981. The women's spirituality movement has also come under the critical scrutiny of feminist and environmental scholars (notably social ecologists); e.g., Biehl 1991; Heller 1999.

18. Hess 1993 is an excellent study of the science-paranormal boundary dispute; while Hansen 1992 provides a thorough and enlightening overview of the "scientific skeptic" movement, documenting some of its less-than-scientific excesses and near-religious fervor.

19. I am focusing here on British writing because this is where the best-known English-language work has occurred. In North America, archaeologists have had analogous rival theories from which to defend themselves, ranging from "ancient astronauts" to transoceanic voyages by Celts, Phoenicians, and other ancient seafarers. Stephen Williams's *Fantastic Archaeology* (1991) provides the most comprehensive (and outrightly hostile) scholarly rebuttal to these alternative prehistories. For an indication that these diffusionist theories warrant more attention than mainstream prehistorians like Williams are willing to grant them, see Stengel 2000.

20. A case in point is Christopher Chippindale, who replaced Glyn Daniel at the helm of *Antiquity* in 1986. After the (in)famous "Battle of the Beanfield," fought between well-armed policemen and unarmed "hippies" near Stonehenge in 1985, Daniel used his editorial page in *Antiquity* to commend the authorities for routing the "pop festival desecrators": "We are grateful to them for their wisdom and resolution in maintaining law and order at Stonehenge which is a sort of prehistoric Westminster Abbey, Westminster Cathedral and St Paul's all rolled into one. No one would dream of allowing hippies to camp around these London Christian temples or permit neo-Druids to perform their rites of worship in them"(1985). Chippindale, in contrast, has claimed to "like" the alternative researchers "for their *irrationality*" (1994:249; italics in original) and has actively engaged in constructive dialogue with earth mysteries researchers, Druids, Welsh nationalists, and others, over such issues as the fate of Stonehenge. Exploring the implications of the Beanfield battle, Chippindale commendably admits that "as long as the methods of archaeological research remain largely destructive, we are ourselves not 100 per cent in the business of preserving the past" (1986:55).

Other instances of dialogue between fringe and orthodox prehistorians was that between John Michell and Aubrey Burl in a series of 1983 issues of *Popular Archaeology*; and a conference later that year, "The Alignment of Ancient Sites," which featured Michell, Devereux, and Pennick facing off against Burl, John Barnatt, and other "establishment" prehistorians. Devereux's work has occasionally been published in scholarly journals (e.g., the December 1996 issue of *Antiquity*); and recent developments in symbolic, cognitive (Renfrew and Zubrow 1994), interpretive and phenomenological (Bender 1993; Tilley 1994; Thomas 1996; R. Bradley 1998), and post-processualist (Hodder 1986; Shanks and Tilley 1994) archaeology have suggested further avenues for potential collaboration. Some of these areas of overlap have been explored in the British publications *At the Edge* and *Third Stone: The Magazine of the New Antiquarian*.

21. They base their assessment on leys given in eight of the most popular ley books: Alfred Watkins's *The Old Straight Track* and *The Ley Hunter's Manual*, Janet and Colin Bord's *Mysterious Britain*, Paul Screeton's *Quicksilver Heritage*, Francis Hitching's *Earth Magic*, Paul Devereux and Ian Thomson's *Ley Hunter's Companion* (which they credit as the best and most convincing of the eight), John Michell's *The View Over Atlantis*, and Guy Phillips's *Briganti*. When they included as mark points only those sites generally thought to be neolithic, not a single line passed the generally accepted test of having at least five points in less than ten miles. When they included Bronze Age, but not Iron Age, mark points, only four passed the test. Yet most ley hunters assume the ley network is a neolithic production, largely established between about 5000 B.C. (or earlier) and the introduction of metallurgy at the beginning of the Bronze Age (around 2600 B.C.).

22. The use of place-names by Watkins and others ignores the fact that most place-names in England are of Anglo-Saxon origin, and that in Wales, where one would expect to find Celtic, and thus more ancient, place-names, there are none of those which ley hunters are fond of (e.g., variations on "end," "ley," "red," etc.). "The names are purely English, and can tell us nothing whatsoever about the neolithic period" (Williamson and Bellamy 1983:130).

23. Williamson and Bellamy acknowledge isolated instances of longer-term continuity, but nothing indicating the sort of "widespread continuity of religious significance, from the neolithic to the medieval period, which ley theory demands" (1983:81). On this, see also Hutton 1993b (128–29). In response to ley enthusiasts' views that the medieval churches were built by people who still understood the prehistoric system of earth energy wisdom, Hutton points out that there is not a single known mention of leys among the thousands of documents left behind by medieval church builders, nor in the writings of either the accusers or the defenders of medieval heresies, of magic and supposed witchcraft, and so on.

24. The Scots pine was particularly favored by Alfred Watkins and is still taken by some of his followers as an indication of a ley line. Yet pollen evidence has indicated that the Scots pine died out in England during the Roman period, and was only reintroduced in the seventeenth century. Even if it had not, it would seem far-fetched to assume that these trees had reseeded themselves and continuously grown in exactly the same place for innumerable generations (Williamson and Bellamy 1983:90–92). In an entertaining passage, Williamson and Bellamy describe the nature of ley hunting fieldwork: "We wanted to find out how difficult it is to discover these 'confirmatory' mark points and so we decided to do a bit of fieldwork ourselves. We prepared a number of alignments, 'pseudo leys', which were made up of various nineteenth- and twentieth-century features, such as schools, hospitals, telephone boxes and large houses, which could not possibly have 'evolved' from prehistoric sites. We then carried out field investigation on five of these alignments, to see if they were 'confirmed' by additional mark points. This was intended to show whether the confirmatory features, Scots pines, ponds and mark stones, occurred more often on ley lines than on pseudo leys, and also to demonstrate how difficult it is to find these things. One of the lines ran for several miles from Saffron Walden to Shudy Camps (Essex), through two schools, a hospital, a telephone box and a water tower, and another connected four nineteenth-century country houses in the five and a half miles between Pampisford and Strethall (Cambs./Essex). Walking along the former we discovered an impressive Scots pine and a respectably large pond; along the latter a mark stone. All these confirmatory features were lying right on the alignments and this suggests to us that the discovery of such things can do nothing to justify an otherwise untenable theory" (146).

25. Ley hunters have not been convinced by the book, and have responded to it with a combination of hurt, anger, holier-than-thou righteousness, or silence. Screeton, for instance, admits "the book makes many telling points—and ley hunters will need to tighten up some procedures if they wish to retain [sic] full credibility." Yet he goes on to make his main point that "it is essentially a pitiful, niggling, jealous, and, in essence, childish work" (1993:57). I read the book quite prepared to find this "niggling jealousy"; but, in the end, found it to be on the whole well argued and relatively fair. Interestingly, Williamson and Bellamy acknowledge, "When preparing this book we wrote to many ley hunters in order to get permission to quote their work, and we were most touched and not a little embarrassed by the incredibly friendly and helpful response that we received. We could not imagine receiving quite such encouraging letters from establishment academics" (1983:133). Consequently, when the book's verdict came out so strongly against them, one can understand the alternative archaeologists' sense of being betrayed by the two scholars. After all, Screeton and other ley hunters have dedicated so much of their lives to exploring the possibilities of the "linear vision."

26. Williamson's and Bellamy's own project can be picked apart somewhat. They acknowledge at the beginning of the book that the study of leys "forms a parallel, although at times a bizarre one, to the orthodox study of the past," and, significantly, that

"[n]o other intellectual discipline has such a convincing and coherent rival" (1983:28). Thus, as they proceed to pick apart the ley theory brick by brick, one can't help but sense their triumph at vanquishing this "convincing and coherent rival." A sophisticated rebuttal to their book, to my knowledge, however, is yet to be written; so one might assume that, on the scholarly front, they have successfully vanquished their rival. Books on ley lines and earth mysteries continue to sell by the truckload, of course, and most of these reiterate the same "facts" as if in blissful ignorance of their vanquishment. (The better earth mysteries researchers, like Devereux, have revised their views in recent years; but others, like Heselton 1991, have remained oblivious to criticism.) *Ley Lines in Question*, on the other hand, might, with luck, be found in a university library. So ley critics are not entirely winning the battle over public opinion.

But, in all fairness, Williamson and Bellamy realize that the "real battle" is a different one. They express sympathy for ley hunters' ecological (and, to a degree, spiritual and political) sentiments, and argue, significantly, that the study of the past is important in encouraging "the view that there is nothing immutable, natural, or divinely ordained about our western industrial capitalism" (1983:184). In the end, they argue that "drawing lines on a map and inventing myths about the past" are little better than a "diversion" for practical solutions to our present crises (183). In this, I agree with them. It is a pity they didn't make more of the commonality between their own aspirations and the *intentions*, however misguided they may be, of ley hunters and earth mysteries researchers. They thus leave the work of alliance building to others.

27. Hutton captures the scientific incredulity to Michell's work well when he writes, "All I can say is that virtually all his work within my own provinces of history and prehistory is unacceptable." This is so "even (for) that most admired by his followers for its apparent objectivity, namely his study of the monuments of West Penwith," which, Hutton asserts, is marred both by a selectivity of evidence, an unjustifiably broad range of *admissible* evidence, and by the "high probability that somebody could draw straight lines through a map of this district and hit a large number of prehistoric sites with each, purely by chance" (1993b:127). On the other hand, he acknowledges that one of Michell's alignments (and one other recognized by another ley hunter) "does look convincing" (130); and he lauds Michell and other ley line researchers for at least producing valuable surveys of the districts they research.

28. I have drawn on the classificatory mappings of Killingsworth and Palmer 1992, and Herndl and Brown 1996 (11). Both works present three categories (resource, object, spirit), to which I have added *nature-as-home* (i.e., as a living context of interrelationships extending out from the human social sphere). Certain traditional and indigenous societies, as well as social ecologists, bioregionalists, and segments of the environmental justice movement, could be seen to hold to this fourth conception. Rather than relying on government structures, for instance, to set aside wilderness preserves in which "nature as spirit" could be encountered by wilderness enthusiasts, social ecologists and environmental justice activists would prefer to empower local communities to rid existing urban environments of toxic chemicals, nuclear power plants, and other sources of "environmental oppression." For comparable typologies of environmental discourses, see Spangle and Knapp 1996, and van Buren 1995.

29. Modern science has historically been dominated by the model of nature as an object or machine, but in recent years this has become increasingly supplemented, if not overtaken, by cybernetic and computer-derived, informational models. Botkin (1990) suggests that cybernetic models of ecosystems are blurring the distinction between life and non-life, "spirit" and "matter." Such models, arguably, blur the human "down" to the level of matter and artificial intelligence, so that perception is understood in terms of informational flows, representations, and cognitive operations. In contrast, Gaia theory would seem to suggest the opposite—a "raising" of planetary biogeochemical processes toward the level of near sentience.

30. Findhorn is best known for its "spiritual gardening" methods, which use on-site meditation techniques as an integrated part of gardening so as to "attune" to the plants,

organisms, and nature spirits, or "devas." In the early days, Dorothy Maclean (1990) and others would directly "communicate" with the nature spirits, and the community became known for the forty-pound cabbages they grew in the supposedly dry soils of northern Scotland (though the journalist who had announced this "wonder" [Hawken 1975] had exaggerated the low quality of the area's soil [Riddell 1990:175]). Carol Riddell's insider's account of the history of the Findhorn community contains a chapter entitled "Nature and the Environment," in which she relates "the great change that took place in the community during David Spangler's stay," when the "main purpose" became "neither advanced communion with nature, nor to find perfect ecological awareness," but "the practice of developing a loving relationship with all things, the environment included" (163–64). She admits that though Findhorn residents' aim is to "live lightly on the earth," their "ecological consciousness has been partial so far," and has included some "extremely energy-wasteful" buildings and motorized trailers (campers) which are "ecological nightmares" (166–67). On the other hand, its gardens are organic, its energy-generating windmills are now operative, and the community has begun building a series of ecologically designed Scandinavian-style homes which they hope will serve as prototypes for other ecocommunities.

31. The distinction between New Age and New Paradigm is a blurred one, but the latter tends to be more intellectually and spiritually discerning, more critical about technological fixes, and less naively idealistic about the future. New Paradigm views are exemplified by the writings of Capra (1982, 1995), Roszak (1977, 1978, 1992), Morris Berman (1984), Harman (1988), W. I. Thompson (1987, 1991), Eisler (1987), Spretnak (1991), Grof (1985), Swimme and Berry (1992), and the later writings of scientists Sheldrake (1991) and Abraham (1994). New Paradigm thought includes or draws on the writings of physicists, mathematicians and chaos theorists (David Bohm, Ralph Abraham, Brian Swimme, Fred Alan Wolf), geologists, biologists, and chemists (Lovelock, Francesco Varela, Ilya Prigogine, Charles Birch, Rupert Sheldrake), theologians, philosophers, and religious leaders (Frederick Ferré, John Cobb, David Ray Griffin, Thomas Berry, Matthew Fox, the Dalai Lama), and transpersonal theorists and parapsychologists (Ken Wilber, Willis Harman, Stanley Krippner). See Dunbar (1994) for an overview of the movement, which he sees as an attempt to "reintegrate an ecological, feminine impulse" into Western culture's dominantly masculine, rational value system; and as continuing a legacy initiated by Emerson, Nietzsche, Jung, Eliade, and Joseph Campbell. Hanegraaff (1998) makes little distinction between New Age and New Paradigm; Zimmerman (1994) presents a good assessment of the relationship between the New Age and New Paradigm movements and radical ecology; while deep ecologist Sessions (1995a) critiques the anthropocentrism, techno-optimism, and resource managerialism in much New Age discourse.

32. The "quantum mystics" include Zukav (1980), Davies (1983), Bentov (1979), Talbot (1986), Wilber (1985b), Herbert (1985), and Wolf (1981, 1986, 1991). For scientific critiques see Grim 1990, Restivo 1985, and M. Gardner 1981; and for critiques of the quantum mystics' representation of Eastern traditions, see Diem and Lewis 1992 and Wilber 1985a. More generally, New Paradigm and New Age thought has been criticized as connecting ideas from widely disparate fields in an ad hoc manner. Marilyn Ferguson (1980), for instance, makes use of Kuhn's notion of paradigm shifts, theoretical physicist David Bohm's implicate and explicate orders, Alfred Korzybski's General Semantics, Stephen Jay Gould's and Niles Eldridge's punctuated equilibrium theory of evolution, Ilya Prigogine's theory of dissipative structures, neuroscientist Karl Pribram's holographic brain theory, Bell's theorem, and General Systems Theory, to argue her case for an imminent societal paradigm shift. Capra, Roszak, W. I. Thompson, and others show the same weakness. In his *The Turning Point: Science, Society and the Rising Culture* (1982), Capra builds his narrative around the clash between the "Newtonian world-machine" and the "new physics." By 1984, with cowriter Charlene Spretnak, an ecofeminist and Goddess theologian, Capra had identified the international Green movement as the protagonist (Capra and Spretnak 1984); and by 1987 he championed

the "deep ecological" worldview promoted by "the ecology movement, the peace movement, the feminist movement, the holistic-health and human-potential movements, various spiritual movements, numerous citizens' movements and initiatives, Third World and ethnic liberation movements, and many other grassroots movements" (Capra 1995:24), the differences between which he does not care to address.

Regarding the environmental implications of Gaia theory, now increasingly influential in the discourse of global management as well as in popular environmentalism, Lovelock's own presentation of the concept blends organismic, mechanistic, cybernetic, and animist or "sentientist" metaphors to explain the functioning of the biosphere. He disclaims his own occasional talk of Gaia "as if she were known to be sentient," saying, "This is meant no more seriously that is the appellation 'she' when given to a ship by those who sail in her, as a recognition that even pieces of wood and metal when specifically designed and assembled may achieve a composite identity with its own characteristic signature, as distinct from being the mere sum of its parts" (1979:ix–x). More recently, though, he has inveighed that Gaia "is stern and tough, always keeping the world warm and comfortable for those who obey the rules, but ruthless in the destruction of those who transgress. Her unconscious goal is a planet fit for life. If humans stand in the way of this, we shall be eliminated with as little pity as would be shown by the microbrain of an intercontinental nuclear missile to its target" (Lovelock 1988:212). See also note 1, this chapter.

33. For some responses to David Ray Griffin, the main proponent of "constructive postmodernism," which he attempts to found on the organicist process philosophy of Alfred North Whitehead, see Tilley and Westman 1995 and Raschke 1992.

34. See Hayward 1984, 1987; Grof 1985; Wilber 1985b, 1990; W. I. Thompson 1987, and 1991; Sheldrake 1988, 1991; Griffin 1985, 1988b; Swimme and Berry 1992; Hayward and Varela 1992; Abraham 1994; and Sheldrake, Abraham, and McKenna 1992.

35. On cognitive science, see Varela, Thompson, and Rosch 1991. On the debate over the scientific status of parapsychology, see McClenon 1984, Kurtz 1985b, Edge et al. 1986, Grim 1990, and Hess 1993. Among the most fruitful scientific outgrowths of the post-1960s interest in spiritual experience and altered states of consciousness have been the field of transpersonal psychology (Tart 1975a, 1975b, 1990; Ring 1976; Grof 1976, 1985; Fischer 1980; Wilber 1977, 1983, 1990, 1995; Wilber, Engler, and Brown 1986; Washburn 1988, 1994) and its more recent analogue in anthropology (Laughlin, McManus, and d'Aquili 1990; Campbell and Staniford 1978; Laughlin, McManus, and Shearer 1983; Laughlin 1989; Young and Goulet 1994). In studying those experiences which extend beyond the personal, or which expand or extend consciousness "beyond the usual ego boundaries and beyond the limitations of time and/or space" (Sundberg and Keutzer 1984:442), transpersonalism implicitly critiques conventional Western notions of selfhood, identity, and the mind-body dichotomy, and thus provides interesting parallels with recent postmodern social theory. The field of alternative health is even more vast.

36. Additional models could be suggested: for instance, nature as a spiritual-cybernetic-informational "living library" (e.g., Marciniak 1995); as a hologram; as Lover (in some pagan interpretations); as Unconscious to humanity's consciousness (i.e., biosphere to "noosphere"); and as a school for spiritual growth.

3. ORCHESTRATING SACRED SPACE

1. Following Durkheim (1964 [1915]), this distinction between the sacred and the profane is often taken to be the hallmark of religious behavior and belief. To suggest that *every* society maintains such a conceptual distinction, however, is ethnocentric and misleading. Nevertheless, the discourse of "sacred sites" has become widely used in the context of land use disagreements involving traditional and indigenous peoples, issues of cultural heritage protection, preservation and management, and struggles for the freedom of religious belief and expression (e.g., Carmichael et al. 1994). Useful schol-

arly accounts of sacrality, sacred sites and pilgrimage include E. Turner 1987; Brereton 1987; Bhardwaj and Rinschede 1988; Eade and Sallnow 1991; Scott and Simpson-Housley 1991; Morinis 1992; Preston 1992; Reader and Walter 1993; Park 1994; Chidester and Linenthal 1995a; Coleman and Elsner 1995; Stoddard and Morinis 1997.

2. *Hierophany* denotes "the act of manifestation of the sacred," in other words, "that something sacred shows itself to us" (Eliade 1959:11). Maureen Korp (1997) argues that Eliade's notion of *kratophany* provides a better means of understanding contemporary sacred landscapes (and earth art, the focus of her book). In his *Patterns in Comparative Religion* (1958), Eliade suggested this term to denote "manifestations of power" (14), but he later dropped it in favor of the more general *hierophany* and the less ambiguous *theophany* (manifestations of divinity or deity). Jonathan Z. Smith's influential reconsideration of Eliade (1972) launched the first in a series of critiques which have made Eliade's name somewhat passé among religious studies scholars. Nevertheless, his thinking continues to inform scholarship in the phenomenology of sacred space and pilgrimage (e.g., Brenneman, Yarian, and Olson 1982; Seamon and Mugerauer 1985; Lane 1988; Walter 1988; Swan 1991; Korp 1997; Prokop 1997; and see Grimes's 1999 critique of J. Z. Smith), and it underlies much popular writing on these topics. On the debate over Eliade, see Idinopulos and Yonan 1994, and Rennie 2000.

3. See, for instance, Soja 1989, 1996; Lefebvre 1991; Shields 1991; Anderson and Gale 1992; Keith and Pile 1993; Gregory 1994; Pile and Keith 1997.

4. The descriptions of Eade and Sallnow (1991) and Chidester and Linenthal (1995a) seem to hedge between the view that sacred spaces are tabulae rasae which can contain an "*endless* multiplication of meaning," "open to *unlimited* claims," and a barely registered admission that this multiplication of meaning is *not* quite "endless": a shrine's power "derives *in large part* from its character *almost* as a religious void," "a sacred space could signify *almost* anything," its meaningful contours being "*almost* infinitely extended," and so on (italics added). Their focus on cultural meanings prevents them from clarifying this tension, which, for my purposes, limits the usefulness of their approach.

5. I take the metaphor of orchestration in the making of pilgrimage sites from Coleman and Elsner (1995), whose approach is broadly similar to my own.

6. A third form of geographical mobility within the New Age and alternative cultural milieu has been purely urban, involving the formation of countercultural enclaves within large cities (e.g., San Francisco's Haight-Ashbury, New York's Greenwich Village, Toronto's Yorkville, Vancouver's Kitsilano) in the 1960s and 1970s, and their economic upscaling and gentrification in the years since. In some of these gentrified neighborhoods, a certain countercultural or New Age flavor has persisted; see, for instance, Mills's (1994) study of Vancouver's Kitsilano. Other visible forms of New Age–style spatial activity include aspects of the "DIY," anarchist, and Rainbow youth cultures in Britain and some European countries (cf. McKay 1998; Buenfil 1991), expressed in the growing phenomenon of "Reclaim the Streets" parties or the large outdoor drumming gatherings that take place in many metropolitan centers.

7. The height of the movement back to the land, according to Zablocki's (1980) authoritative study of communes, was between 1967 and 1971. Zablocki notes an interesting regional differentiation, whereby rural differences "became exaggerated as their stereotypical reputations served as magnets, selectively attracting recruits from different personality stocks. For example, rural communes on the north California coastline could in general be characterized as anarchistic, violent, individualistic, and highly practical. Those in the Rio Grande Valley, by way of contrast, were characterized as spiritual, hierarchical, and matriarchal" (75). Later studies (e.g., Anders 1990) do not necessarily support such characterizations; but what is of interest for my own study is that certain regions became known for distinct qualities and attracted new settlers to them based on their specific kind of "magnetism."

8. On New Age and other spiritually oriented intentional communities, see Popenoe and Popenoe 1984; McLaughlin and Davidson 1986; and the various editions of the

Directory of Intentional Communities (e.g., Fellowship for Intentional Community 1995). *Communities* magazine has chronicled the intentional communities movement since 1972.

9. Examples include the *Spiritual Community Guide*, which by its fifth edition had become *The New Consciousness Sourcebook* (Khalsa 1982), and included introductions by Marilyn Ferguson and peace activist Daniel Ellsberg; and *The Pilgrim's Guide to Planet Earth: A Traveler's Handbook and New Age Directory*. The latter was introduced by Apollo astronaut Edgar Mitchell, founder of the transpersonal think tank the Institute for Noetic Sciences. The book featured "Sites of natural and man-made splendor," "Addresses of thousands of New Age centers, natural foodstores, vegetarian restaurants, hotels, etc. around the world," and "Description of Planetary Power Points" (cited in Khalsa 1982).

10. Argüelles's theories about the Mayas, based on his own idiosyncratic decipherment of the ancient Mayan calendar, are rejected by most Maya scholars. Similarly, the use of Hopi prophecy by New Agers is meticulously critiqued by Geertz (1994).

11. Quotes are taken from Argüelles's "Open Letter to 144,000 Rainbow Humans" (cited in Buenfil 1991:177–78). According to media reports, over 1,500 people gathered in Chaco Canyon, 6,000 on Mount Shasta, 45 at the Great Pyramid in Giza, 1,000 at an ancient mound in East St. Louis, and more than 1,500 at a site in New York's Central Park. The actual number of convergers, however, whose "participation" could have included simply meditating or "linking thoughts" with the global action in the privacy of their backyards, is impossible to know. (My sources here include "No Muggings? It's a New Age," *International Herald Tribune*, August 18; "Humming Chorus Saves the World," *Daily Mail*, August 17; "Believers Celebrate Dawn of 'New Age'," *Albuquerque Journal*, August 17, 1987; "Glastonbury Comes of Age," *Guardian*, August 19; "Unharmonious Start to Bright New Age," *Daily Telegraph*, August 17; "Hippies Miss the Dawn of Aquarius," *Today*, August 17; all 1987.)

12. Besides crediting Coon ("whose esoteric writings on the earth's sacred places provided the initial impetus to put the project together and helped to identify the pilgrimage which, as it turned out, I had already been on for several years"), Milne also thanks sacred site theorist Jim Berenholtz for giving him "specific direction" (1991a:vi). Milne describes his thinking during the project: "Was I at this sacred spot as a pilgrim to meditate or as a photographer to get the job done? As the project progressed, however, I realized that I had been training myself for years to meditate, not by sitting in the lotus position with my legs crossed but by looking through the viewfinder at the exquisite shapes and forms and letting the 20th century evaporate from my consciousness" (42). Curiously, his twentieth-century photographic equipment seems to have "evaporated" from his consciousness as well. (Incidentally, the foreword to *The Sacred Earth* was written by His Holiness the Dalai Lama.) A similar pilgrim's journey—to more than 800 sacred sites around the world—is documented on Martin Gray's extensive text-and-photo web site <www.sacredsites.com>. See also S. Miller 1989; Devereux 1992b; Molyneaux 1995; McLuhan 1996.

13. In their travel guide to "Goddess sites" in Europe, Rufus and Lawson (1991) list well over a hundred shrine, temple, sanctuary, and Marian church sites. As for Atlantis and Lemuria, the lack of physical evidence for their existence does not detract from believers' propensity to ascribe to them a present-day geographical reality. Many metaphysically inclined residents of Sedona believe the area was once part of Lemuria; some even believe there are remains of ancient temple structures beneath the ground. Belief in Lemurian (and Atlantean) remains is also popular in parts of California, particularly around Mount Shasta. One account claims that the ancient Atlantean city of "Tlamco," a temple city of seven hills, once existed at the present-day site of San Francisco, in and around Golden Gate Park (cf. F. Joseph 1992:57–68).

14. I draw on Chidester and Linenthal's (1995b:5) distinction between *substantial* and *functional* or *situational* approaches to studying sacred space. I have changed their first category to "substan*tive*" to underline that their *focus* is on the "substance" or "con-

tents" of religious experience (but that does not necessarily mean they are theoretically more substan*tial*).

15. Several scholars have argued, contra Turner, that pilgrimage serves more to reinforce the social status quo than to threaten or destabilize it (cf. Eade and Sallnow 1991:5). Their studies would seem to support a traditional Durkheimian, structural-functionalist understanding, according to which pilgrimage welds together diverse local communities and social strata into more extensive collectivities, whether regional or tribal, national or civilizational. Recognized pilgrimage places, as Morinis explains, "embody intensified versions of the collective ideals of the culture" (1992:4). New Age pilgrimage sites, in this sense, could be seen as "welding together" this particular subculture.

16. On this kind of Othering, see Torgovnick 1990 and Root 1996. On New Age "neo-orientalism" see Mehta 1991; Bartholomeusz 1998; and King 1999.

17. The following example shows how commodification of land could be seen as compatible with sacred site pilgrimage. In 1994, Suzanne McMillan-McTavish and Glen McTavish, workshop and retreat leaders and founders of Sacred Sight Journeys International, were in the midst of a several-year mission to complete a circuit of "Transceiving Stations" intended "to unite the Americas on the ley lines (earth's energy grid) and assist the earth in her ascension through harmony, balance and stability." By 1994, forty-four of these "stations" had already been created, and forty more were planned by the year 2000. After they were "given the word to move to Sedona," Glen spent three weeks in Phoenix "taking an accelerated course to get an Arizona real estate license in order to sell vacation interval ownerships. Spirit had let us know that Glen's mission had shifted after he had arrived in Sedona. *Glen's mission now is to move large amounts of financial energy and real estate (earth energy) around to create the physical spaces for Suzanne to anchor the Light for Spirit to move into*" ("Holiday Greetings from Suzanne & Glen," flyer, Sedona, December 1994; italics added).

18. Tourism is said by some to be the largest single industry in the world today, in terms of the employment it provides and the trade it generates (Boniface and Fowler 1993:xi; Urry 1992:5; Urry 1995:173). In recent years tourism has diversified to include such categories as heritage tourism, cultural or ethnic tourism, sport tourism, adventure tourism, nature tourism or ecotourism, and spiritual tourism. The evolving nature of global tourism is also related to the development of heritage protection efforts, such as those of UNESCO and its World Heritage List. Established by the 1972 Convention Concerning the Protection of World Culture and Natural Heritage Convention, the World Heritage List in 1994 included 469 properties, of which 350 were "cultural sites," 102 were "natural sites," and 17 were "mixed." Interestingly, in recent years UNESCO has begun including "natural" landscape features within its designation of significant "cultural landscapes" (Carmichael et al. 1994:2).

19. The activities New Agers and ecospiritualists at sacred sites can of course be much more varied than my rather schematic account suggests, especially for those of them affiliated with more specific traditions of practice. My account draws on the more popular guidebooks for sacred site pilgrims, among them Corbett 1988; Devereux 1989b; Heselton 1991; Bryant 1991; F. Joseph 1992; Swan 1990, 1992; Kryder 1994; LaChapelle 1988; Johansen and Barclay 1987; Dannelley 1991; A. Moore 1994; and Gray n.d.

20. An environmental psychologist by training, Swan was one of the co-organizers, with Chippewa-born medicine man Sun Bear, of the first Medicine Wheel Gathering near Mount Rainier in 1980. (Since then, these gatherings have become possibly the most effective instrument in the spread of a New Age "Native spirituality" among non-natives in North America.) He was also centrally involved in a seminal 1985 conference of scientists, environmentalists, and religious figures, sponsored by the Audubon Expedition Institute, called Is the Earth a Living Organism? In 1988 he coordinated a gathering called Gaia Consciousness: The Goddess and the Living Earth, and in 1988 and 1989 he co-organized the Spirit of Place Symposia, which brought together over a hundred presenters including architects and landscape designers, scientists, artists, aero-

space engineers, environmental psychologists, and geographers, along with members of indigenous cultural groups. Swan has been a long-time faculty member at the California Institute of Integral Studies, a leading New Age educational center. Far more probing than many books on the topic, his *Sacred Sites: How the Living Earth Seeks Our Friendship* (1990) includes an extended legal and philosophical argument for the protection of Native American sacred sites. The book's foreword, incidentally, was written by Swan's friend James Lovelock.

21. He particularly recommends *dreaming* as the most practical and effective state-altering method, a means, he claims, that is most appropriate at magnetic stones, at stone circles (or rock outcrops at non-engineered places of power), and at ancient holy wells. According to Devereux, wells have an ancient connection with dreaming and with earthy, feminine deities. He cites Francis Hitching's speculation that over 300 early "medical centres" in ancient Greece, which included dreaming as a healing method, were placed at or near water sources (Devereux 1989b:190). Many of the Virgin Mary apparitions have also taken place at wells, springs, and grottoes. Similarly, according to Devereux, megalithic enclosures, such as dolmens and fogous (underground passages), if made of the appropriate geological components (such as granite), seem to evoke "time-lapse" experiences "in which people, objects or scenes appear momentarily with complete realism."

22. As mentioned earlier (chap. 1), my use of the term *landscape* intends to capture more than the pictorial and aesthetic qualities associated with the Western representational tradition. Landscape, as defined by Cosgrove, denotes the "external world" as it is "mediated through subjective human experience" (1984:13). The suffix *-scape* assumes the presence of some underlying unity to the given area or region of the earth's surface that is being considered. Landscapes have been variously conceived and "read" by geographers, anthropologists, and others; for instance, as compositions, panoramas, symbolic creations, cultural texts, organismic or mechanistic systems, and contested sites. See Cosgrove and Daniels 1988; Duncan 1990; Bender 1993; Greider and Garkovich 1994; Mitchell 1994; Hirsch and O'Hanlon 1995.

23. My account is presented in summary form (I develop its theoretical implications elsewhere; cf. Ivakhiv 2000). On ecological psychology see note 24, this chapter, and on actor-network theory, note 25. For different approaches to the hermeneutic phenomenology of landscape and environment, see Mugerauer 1985; Ingold 1992, 1993, 1995; Casey 1993; and Tilley 1994. Overall, my model bears some resemblance to those developed by cultural geographers and sociologists (e.g., Giddens's structurationist model) to account for the interaction between structure (i.e., the social and institutional constraints shaping social actions) and agency (people's actions and their understandings of the meaning of those actions). But my interest here is more on the role played by the features of particular landscapes as these are appropriated both within people's actions and lifeworlds and within broader geographical and economic relations. In a model that in some ways resembles Gibson's, Maturana and Varela's (1980, 1987) theory of autopoietic systems also sees cognition as an ongoing "enactment" or "bringing forth of a world through the process of living itself" (1987:9), a process which takes place through a history of "structural coupling" between an organism and its environment. Since our process of coming to know the world takes place *within* that world, we are always bringing our world forth *with others*; thus, for Maturana and Varela, knowledge is always a social, and therefore ethical, phenomenon (cf. 1987:239–49). See also Harries-Jones 1995 for a lucid account of Gregory Bateson's recursive systems epistemology.

24. This concept of affordances provides a way of describing an environment that is scaled to a perceiver and that entails meaning (Carello 1993:126–27). See Gibson 1977, 1979, 1982. My usage of Gibson's work is more indebted to others who have developed his ideas, especially Ingold (1992, 1993, 1995), Carello (1993), Reed (1988), Turvey and Carello (1981), Barwise and Perry (1983), and Costall (1995). See also Mugerauer 1985.

25. I draw here, rather loosely, on the language of actor-network theory. See Callon 1986; Latour 1987; Callon and Latour 1992; and Law and Hassard 1999.

26. Shields defines *place-images* as "the various discrete meanings associated with real places or regions regardless of their character in reality" (1991:60); while *place-myths* are collective sets of such place-images which form systems according to which relations between different places and spaces are socially established and demarcated.

4. STAGE, PROPS, AND PLAYERS OF AVALON

1. Touted as a "male counterpart of the Goddess" and "the archetype of our oneness with the Earth" (Anderson and Hicks 1990), the leafy-headed Green Man is a composite of the folkloric Jack in the Green, Pan, the cloven-hoofed Greek god of nature, mythic unicorns and centaurs, and other half-man, half-animal figures. In some neo-pagan traditions the God (of which the Green Man is at least one aspect, if not the entirety) is placed in as high esteem as the Goddess.

2. These figures were provided by the wardens of Chalice Well Gardens. The trust is deliberately low key in managing the Chalice Well and makes no special claims for it; but Prince Charles's visit during a 1990 tour of Glastonbury increased popular interest in it (Bowman 1993a:33).

3. All of this is fairly recent. In the late nineteenth century, the White Spring had been a mossy bank of bushes, pools, and running water (Hennessy 1991:22). Its capping and diversion into a large stone reservoir in the 1870s obliterated the natural spring; the water afterward rose up in a small brick chamber above the reservoir. Since the building of the Well House Cafe (now the White Spring Cafe) in the early 1980s, it has been plagued by controversy, and some of Glastonbury's alternative community avoid it as if it were somehow tainted. The owner of the land on which the cafe and spring are located is former town councillor Ian Tucker. Together with John Morland, in the 1970s, Tucker had been responsible for the so-called Hippie Wrecker—a truck that was to remove hippies from Glastonbury; Tucker convinced other Glastonians to buy £1 shares in the "wrecker." Later, the engineering works connected with the White Spring's conversion into a cafe caused the surrounding land to subside, which some residents criticized. Tucker's idea for a new car park (a perfect money-making venture for him) angered some as well. Ironically, the White Spring today seems to attract precisely the "hippies" Tucker once disdained.

4. From 1536 to 1541 the number of monasteries, nunneries, and friaries in Britain fell from over 800 to zero. Over 10,000 monks and nuns were dispersed; buildings were seized by the Crown, and sold off or leased to new occupiers. The reasons were primarily political and financial.

5. Peat is formed from the accumulation of compressed, partially rotted remains of plants growing in water-logged conditions. Central Somerset's peat deposits were formed in a submerged landscape—its original valleys are estimated to have been up to 90 feet below the present sea level. Commercial peat extraction began in the area in the late nineteenth century, and by the middle of the twentieth century, peat was being extracted by machine and increasingly from below the natural water table. By the early 1990s there were some thirty peat producers in Somerset providing about 250 full-time jobs. But the industry has come under strict control, and extraction is expected to cease in the near future (Somerset County Council Peat Local Plan, Environment Dept., August 1992).

6. With the opening of Clark's Village in 1995, this town of 9,000 was brought sudden prosperity, homes and amenities, guaranteed jobs, and 1.5 million visitors in its first year. Unfortunately, the same global economy that inspired the expansion of Clark's shoemaking empire has made the town vulnerable: imports are cheap, while British labor is expensive, and by 1996 several hundred of its employees were already being made "redundant" as the company struggled against competitors from China, Indonesia, Thailand, Vietnam, and Brazil (Oulton and Garrett 1996:17).

7. Rahtz's *Glastonbury* (1993) is the best scholarly introduction to the history and legends of Glastonbury. Where evidence is meager and Rahtz hesitates to speculate, others, like John Michell (1990), Anthony Roberts (1992), Robert Coon (1986, 1990),

Kathy Jones (1990, 1994), and Nicholas Mann (1993, 1996), allow their imaginations to run free. Somewhere closer to the middle ground between the academics and the mystics is the work of Geoffrey Ashe, whose *King Arthur's Avalon* (1973 [1957]) and *Avalonian Quest* (1982) present arguably the most complete and coherent overviews of the Glastonbury mythos. Ashe is an Arthurian scholar and amateur historian whose devotion to the Arthurian theme has been instrumental in generating much scholarly work on early British history. As cofounder and Secretary of the Camelot Research Committee, he coordinated and coauthored an important interdisciplinary collection of archaeological and historical writings exploring the Arthurian legends (Ashe 1971). His books on Glastonbury, which has been his passion since the late 1950s and his home for nearly as long, present a spirited defense of many, though not all, of its legends. Though Ashe candidly admits that he sees "rebirth" of Glastonbury "as more important than history" (1973:10), he manages to maintain the sort of balanced and critical perspective that generally eludes the earth mystics and New Age visionaries. Other useful historical works on Glastonbury include those by Carley (1988) and Abrams (1996; Abrams and Carley 1991) on the Christian historical period, and Dunning's (1994) social history of the town.

8. This period is covered by sociologist of religion Irving Hexham's unpublished 1971 master's thesis (Hexham 1981), which recently became available over the internet. According to Hexham, the early countercultural community of Glastonbury—which at the time preferred the label *Freaks* to the more commonly used *hippies*—was distinguishable into Settlers, who lived in Glastonbury for at least six months of the year, and Visitors, who stayed for a number of days or weeks and then moved on. Between Christmas 1970 and Easter 1972 Hexham counted "around eighteen Settlers and ten Visitors to be found in Glastonbury at any one time," though the number went up in the summer, climaxing at over a hundred during the weeks preceding the Glastonbury Fayre. The majority of Visitors were between sixteen and twenty years of age (most of them male), while Settlers tended to be older (between 20 and 25, though a minority were as old as 50 or up). In addition, Hexham notes the existence of semi-institutionalized spiritual groups and a small population of independent "spirituals" residing in Glastonbury at the time, who were for the most part "very sympathetic to the Freaks, seeing in them fellow pilgrims seeking religious truth" (though they did not necessarily approve of all the Freaks' activities). Hexham's is an insightful look into the spiritual beliefs of what was to become the alternative community at an embryonic point in its development.

9. The history of Greenlands Farm is documented in Bruce Garrard's passionately argued pamphlet on the subject (1986). Less sanguine is the pseudonymous Ali Baba, who wrote in the *Glastonbury Communicator* (15:3) that Greenlands Farm had become "a haven especially for psychic casualties, disenfranchised hippies, anarchists, Hare Krishnas and Rainbow People"; it became a kind of "ghetto," a "grim scenario" which finally ended with the court eviction order.

10. One polemic pitted feminist Goddess proponents (the editors, at the time) against the Immortalist philosophy of guru Sondra Ray and techniques such as rebirthing. In an editorial that followed the release of an earlier, overtly feminist issue (no. 6), Nick Mann reported, "It appears Glastonbury's dark goddesses are too much for Findhorn's Hierarchy of Light and the dozen copies of *Communicator* #6 sent there last time were returned with excuses about lack of shelf space. This seems a shame given the similarity between the two communities." (GC 7 [1985]).

11. Another sign of the green presence in the area was the second-place finish in the 1989 European elections of Green Party candidate David Taylor, an active member of Glastonbury's alternative community.

12. Some locals have continued to frown on the Festival, but none more so than Mrs. Anne Goode, who has erected a thirty-two-foot cross in her garden overlooking the site to bear "Christian witness" to the event's "corrupting influences" (M. Brown 1993).

13. Seven Faculties of the Isle of Avalon Foundation are being developed, including Faculties of Consciousness, Health and Healing, Human Potential, Planet Earth, Sacred Arts, Sacred Sciences, and Spiritual Revelation. Topics covered in the foundation's

courses, workshops and occasional symposia cover the whole gamut of New Age concerns, from permaculture, deep ecology, herbalism and folk magic, global energy alignments, dowsing, and crop circle mysteries to shamanic healing, ancient Egyptian magic, the Holy Grail, and personal prosperity. According to foundation records, over 1,500 students from several countries had attended courses or workshops during the 1993–94 year.

14. The temple has more recently been renamed the Sanctuary, and sacred geometry author Keith Critchlow appointed as its architect. The entire Avalon Project has been notable for its attempt to convey an ecumenical inclusiveness, expressed in its brochure as follows: "Today's Glastonbury has many active religious groups from traditions diverse as they are many. These include Sufi, Buddhist, Essene, Born-again Christian, New Age, Pagan and many others which are drawn to the spiritual nature of this place. It is clear that a Temple should reflect all of these people since they represent the essential essence [!] that is Glastonbury." Ultimately, the Temple of Avalon is envisioned as containing a "Celebration Space, Chapels, Healing Spaces, a Library, Gardens, Hot Baths, Meeting Rooms, Children's facilities, Underground chambers etc." Like many Glastonbury projects, however, this one has been long on vision, but short on the material energy to bring itself about.

15. Prince spent a year living and interacting with Glastonbury's alternative community in 1989–90. She presents the alternative community as a somewhat utopian attempt to put "New Age" ideas—conceived as an alternative to mainstream Western society—into concrete practice.

16. About this impracticality and inefficiency: the need to feel good about how things are going often means that organizational efforts dissipate, people lose interest, and little gets done. Schisms develop as a matter of course in many projects, with the more spiritually inclined Glastafarians interpreting these in historical, spiritual, or cosmic terms, for instance, as a kind of "test," a "clearing away of the debris of centuries," or karma accumulated since the dissolution of the Abbey. Frustrations with such organizational difficulties were expressed to me on several occasions, and they concur with Keith Mitchell's (unpublished) professional assessment of the organizational and managerial possibilities of the community (Mitchell, int.). My own sense of the alternative community—gleaned from informal participant observation, time spent doing volunteer work for the University of Avalon, and interviews with key participants (among them Bruce Garrard, Ann Morgan, Keith Mitchell, Kathy Jones, Palden Jenkins, Jan Preece, and Taras Kosikowsky)—tends to confirm Prince's and Mitchell's characterizations here. To them could be added Ann Morgan's (int.) observation that both the Assembly Rooms and the Avalon Foundation "have been guilty of becoming obsessed with their own ideas" rather than addressing the wider needs of Glastonbury as a whole, though that may have begun to change in recent years.

17. Living styles, for instance, range from town-based "Glastafarians" living in council and private flats and bedsits (rooms in shared houses), though the more affluent own houses, to country dwellers living in farm cottages, communally rented farmhouses, or in caravans (trailers), tipis, domes or tentlike "benders" on privately owned fields.

18. I heard some version of this local folk wisdom recited to me by several informants.

19. Of the alternative community's more successful enterprises, Gothic Image, the oldest New Age bookstore in town, has become something of an institution, with its own publishing, mail order, and tour-leading branches; and Unique Publications, founded by one-time hippie-traveler Bruce Garrard, continues to serve as the town's printer, publishing materials on such topics as the history of Glastonbury's alternative community, Stonehenge, travelers, and green economic initiatives. Other organizations or centers which survived, at least over the couple of years over which I visited the town, included the Glastonbury Natural Health Clinic, the National Federation of Spiritual Healers' Glastonbury Healing Centre (forced to move out of its Market Cross location in 1994 and, at the time of writing, searching for new premises), and the Tareth Centre (founded in 1992 by spiritual healer Geoff Boltwood and his group, who claim to have been "guided" to Glastonbury "to open a sealed energy centre: the most significant in

England"). On the outskirts of town or near the Tor there are the Shambhala Healing Centre, the Ramala Centre, Berachah House, the Unicorn Light Centre, Waterfall Cottage, EarthSpirit Centre, and several others. Most of these offer some forms of healing or therapy on the premises, run workshops and retreats, and so forth.

20. It is difficult to know the exact number of travelers. Estimates have ranged from 10,000 to 40,000, the latter provided by the London daily *Independent* (June 22 1993, Comment, p. 19), while Stangroome (1993:1) and Hetherington (1993:194–95) suggest lower figures. On the distinction between "traditional" travelers (Gypsies of Romany ancestry, who trace their origins to the Indian subcontinent) and New Age travelers, see Stangroome 1993 and Halfacree 1996. Stangroome points out that the distinction is overused and somewhat misleading, as the majority of Gypsies are now of mixed racial groups; but it is of help to Romanies, as it protects them from the popular scapegoating of "New Age travellers." For a history of New Age travelers in Britain, compiled and written by travelers themselves, see Earle et al. 1994; more scholarly accounts include McKay 1996 and G. Martin 1998.

21. The first Stonehenge People's Free Festival is often taken as a convenient marker for the origins of New Age traveling culture. The details of the festival's origins are shrouded in a foundation myth, a version of which is related by John Michell: "Phil Russel, commonly known as Wally Hope, established the Stonehenge People's Free Festival. His followers, all of whom claimed the name Wally and were collectively called the Wallies, camped in fields near the site which they declared sacred ground. Their festival and those which followed were of a pagan religious character. Babies were baptized and marriages were performed at the stones on the longest day. Wally Hope was arrested and sent to prison, and soon afterwards died in unexplained circumstances. At the Wallies' second festival, in 1976, his ashes were ceremonially scattered among the stones" (1985:6).

22. On the Battle of the Beanfield and the history that led up to it, see Michell 1985 and Earle et al. 1994. Chippindale has written two of the most perceptive accounts of the contested politics of Stonehenge and of the beanfield battle (1986, 1990). Barbara Bender, author of a series of fascinating analyses of the history and prehistory of Stonehenge (1992; 1993:245–79; 1998), was instrumental in creating an excellent traveling exhibition of photographs and texts on the contested politics and perceptions of Stonehenge. (I was fortunate enough to see this exhibition at the 1994 Glastonbury Festival, and am grateful to her for sending me a photocopied version of its twenty-five or so panels.) Goodwin (1995) provides a retrospective summary of the events and their aftermath; his figure of arrested travelers is 420, which may be a misprint (others state 520).

23. Selected material for this section is taken from interviews with Bruce Garrard, Ann Morgan, and Jan Preece.

24. In one twenty-six-week period (August 1985 through January 1986) the two local newspapers, the *Western Gazette* and the *Central Somerset Gazette*, together featured the "hippy problem" as front page headline news no less than twenty-one times (Garrard 1986:4). Their insistence on the use of "hippy" rather than "traveller" (the term preferred by travelers themselves) in such headlines as "Trust's Plea to Authorities: Stop Hippies," "'Hippy Haven' Owner in Court Action," and frequent references to the "hippy problem," underscored their bias. One front page of the CSG (November 7, 1985) featured two headlines—"More Hippies Heading for Glastonbury?" and "New Disease Fear as Vermin Virus Hits Greenlands." The first paragraph of the cover story, in bold type, read: "Rats found at Greenlands Farm are to be wiped out by vermin control experts following the discovery of a suspected new killer disease at the controversial camp site." The vermin virus turned out later to have been nonexistent (Jennifer Cobb, "Our Local Press," GC 8:12), yet this was played down when it was revealed.

25. Constructive solutions to the dilemma were proposed by, among others, alternative community members Ann Morgan and Bruce Garrard in a series of articles in the *Glastonbury Times*. Morgan and Garrard argued that the traveling population could supply seasonal help, crafted goods, and other special skills, and would add color to the

town; the town, in turn, would need to improve its washing facilities and open a casual employment agency. Unfortunately, their proposals were largely lost in the din of public fears and local media scapegoating.

26. The left-wing newsweekly *New Statesman and Society*, for instance, called it "one of the most oppressive laws to have been passed in a modern democracy" (Malyon 1994:iii), and even moderate critics have likened it to an increasingly authoritarian and fascistic temperament in Britain. Unfortunately, much of the mainstream media have tended to disregard the issue of the CJA on the basis that it "only affects a minority." Exceptions have been Duncan Campbell and Simon Fairlie in the *Guardian* and Camilla Berens in the *Independent* (Malyon 1994:vi).

27. For histories of "DIY culture," see McKay 1996, 1998. Among the movement's theorists is the young anthropologist and former Oxford University Fellow, George Monbiot, who has been called "the new Gerrard Winstanley" (*Pod* 6:17) in honor of the seventeenth-century anti-enclosures resistance leader.

28. See Nick Cobbing's photo exhibit of materials on low-impact homes, travelers sites, antiroad campaigners' tree-top houses, and the Tinker's Bubble Land Trust at <www.oneworld.org/media/gallery/cobbing>.

5. MANY GLASTONBURYS

1. Insofar as "business as usual" suggests maintaining the conditions of everyday livability, such groups as the Glastonbury Conservation Society and the Bove Town Conservation Group could be considered a part of this category, though their political stance may rest, at best, uncomfortably next to that of the Glastonbury Residents Association.

2. The number of visitors to Glastonbury is difficult to estimate. Extrapolating from the Abbey's records of individual ticket buyers and visiting groups, it appears to host some 150,000 visitors a year. Glastonbury's Tourist Information Centre reports between 50,000 and 60,000 annually, from countries the world over, in recent years, a figure that is based on numbers of people who come with questions and sign their names in a guestbook (personal correspondence, August 10, 1995).

3. The National Trust plays a key role in managing relations between local residents and the Tor's more "alternative" users. An independent charity whose mandate is to "protect the best of our heritage forever," the trust has worked since 1895 to preserve places of historic interest or natural beauty in England, Wales, and Northern Ireland. In 1907 the trust was granted, by act of Parliament, the unique power to declare its property "inalienable," meaning that it can never be sold or mortgaged (nearly all its properties are now inalienable, though properties can be leased). It is currently the largest private landholder and conservation society in Britain, with over 570,000 acres of land in its possession (National Trust 1992). The trust conducts Archaeological and Historic Landscape Surveys on its properties, and employs a small number of archaeologists and other heritage managers with the goal of balancing out visitor access with conservation goals. Among other sites, the trust manages Avebury and Stonehenge, both UN World Heritage Sites.

4. Geographically, the earlier higher water levels around Glastonbury render Joseph's arrival at least a theoretical possibility, and certain finds discovered this century at the "Celtic lake villages" suggest that such seagoing trade contacts were possible. Whether Jesus or Mary ever set foot on British land remains unproven and, one would think, unlikely. As for the many saints said to have come to Glastonbury, evidence is for the most part lacking, though strategic reasons are easy to see for the monks' desire to forge such connections.

5. The Roman Catholic pilgrimage has been attracting around 3,000 to 4,000 annually since the 1950s, reaching a high point of some 20,000 in 1965 (Mathias and Hector 1979:44). It is primarily a diocesan pilgrimage for the Clifton Diocese, and mainly attracts people from Somerset, Gloucester, and Wiltshire (Bowman 1993a:46). The

1988 millenary of the death of St. Dunstan attracted 14,000 to the Anglican pilgrimage (Bowman 1993:44). According to the secretary of the West of England Pilgrimage Association, most Anglican pilgrims come from a radius of 150 miles around Glastonbury, some of them making the trek on foot. An Orthodox presence has grown in the weekend's proceedings, and now includes a service of prayer and veneration of the Icon of Our Lady of Glastonbury. It is also notable that the Catholic pilgrims make their way up to the summit of the Tor, while the Protestants, perhaps more wary of the hill's traditional pagan overtones, do not.

6. The idea of a distinct, "Druidic" form of "Celtic Christianity" is not supported by most historians of the era; cf. Hughes 1983; Firey 1983; and Hutton 1993b (287–88).

7. During one particular conflict Milne invited Muz Murray, editor of the countercultural journal *Gandalf's Garden*, to pray together to arrive at a resolution. Murray later heralded Milne's work behind the scenes to bring people together on either side; however, "though their ideas gained consent locally, they came to nothing because of wider politics" (Frost 1986:145–46).

8. Occasionally one hears of Glastonbury's (and the Grail's) importance in the psyche of the "White races," an idea that ties into Alice Bailey's and H. P. Blavatsky's theosophical notions of seven root races. (Bailey's and Blavatsky's turn-of-the-century writings reflect the Eurocentrism of their times.) A related myth has been that of Britain's connection to the legendary island of Atlantis: according to the version promulgated by Dion Fortune (and recently taken up by Marion Zimmer Bradley in her *Mists of Avalon*), Britain became the refuge for the ancient wisdom of the priests of the long-vanished Atlantean civilization. Conservatism, it should be mentioned, can take many forms, however: as the connection with William Blake suggests, an anti-industrial, mystical radicalism (such as Blake's) has also served as a predecessor to the countercultural new-leftist critiques of recent decades.

9. On the mythology surrounding Stonehenge, see Chippindale's thorough *Stonehenge Complete* (1994). Chippindale notes that Stukeley "set Stonehenge under a fog-bank of mystification which lasted a century. The modern-day Druids, acting out weakly para-Christian ceremonial in a slacker version of his Druidic garb, are the last vestige of it" (86). When John Wood developed the thesis that Stonehenge was a temple of the moon, dedicated to the goddess Diana, Stukeley was appalled. He wrote in his diary that dragging pagan moon-worship "into this sacred enclosure seems to me like Satan breaking over the hallowed mound of Paradise with no other than a murderous intent" (94).

10. The word *occult* simply means hidden, secret, or beyond the range of ordinary knowledge. The tradition of occult thought is a long-standing one in Western culture: it has included a variety of studies and ideas ranging from those associated with magic, astrology, and various methods of divination, to spiritual practices that have been passed down through esoteric teaching orders, fraternities, and religious institutions (both within the major religions and outside of them). Misunderstandings around the term have persisted, however, especially in North America, fueled by fundamentalist Christians' appropriation of it to refer to all manner of "heretic" practices.

11. At the same time, several Druid orders have been formed (or revived, as it were), including the Druid Order (also known as the British Circle of the Universal Bond), the Order of Bards, Ovates, and Druids (now the largest and most established Druid order), the Glastonbury Druids (a smaller organization), and the Scottish College of Druidism. As Grinsell puts it, "The creed and philosophy of the members of the modern Druid Orders contain little or nothing which a good Christian would wish to repudiate" (cited in Bowman 1993a:152).

12. On the Western esoteric, magical, or mystery tradition, see Faivre and Needleman 1992; Faivre 1994; Godwin 1994; Knight 1979; J. Matthews and C. Matthews 1985–86; Ivakhiv 1996.

13. I leave aside Rutland Boughton, mentioned elsewhere in this chapter, and writer Alice Buckton, who bought the Catholic Seminary at the foot of Chalice Hill and established there the Guild of Glastonbury and Street Festival Players, which produced

her pageant plays such as "The Coming of Bride," modeled on old religious and folk mystery plays and seasonal festivals (Benham 1993).

14. The book combined Goodchild's interests in Irish tradition, Celtic Christianity, and the feminine forms of divinity. Much of my information in this section is gleaned from Benham's (1993) thorough (if not all verifiable on my part) study of Glastonbury's early twentieth-century "Avalonians."

15. All the while Bond believed he was, as Benham puts it, "the high steward of the mysteries enshrined in the ruins of Glastonbury for the age to come" (1993:221). Rejected by Glastonbury, he ultimately ended up a priest of the Old Catholic Church in the United States, and a friend of Father Francis, that church's archbishop and metropolitan. With his "Church on the Mount" in Woodstock, New York, Father Francis was to become known as the Hippie Priest, a radical priest, friend, and confessor of the Woodstock hippies (as well as, reportedly, of Bob Dylan, F. D. Roosevelt, and Frank Lloyd Wright), and a co-organizer of the Woodstock Festival. Francis endearingly referred to Woodstock as the "Hippieopolis of America," and scorned local opposition to the hippie developments. The parallels between Woodstock in the 1960s and Glastonbury in the 1970s, with their seminal rock festivals and countercultural pilgrimage status, are obvious. Intriguingly, the archives of Francis's rustic wooden "cathedral" in Woodstock contained a collection of Bond's "automatic scripts" related to Glastonbury Abbey (Benham 1993:234–35).

16. The Matthewses have been especially prolific, churning out book after book on Arthurian themes, the Holy Grail, the Mabinogion, Welsh bardic poetry, neopaganism, Celtic shamanism, Glastonbury itself, and the Western mystery tradition (J. Matthews 1981, 1987, 1991a, 1991b, 1991c; C. Matthews 1987, 1995; Matthews and Matthews 1985–86, 1994). See the chapter entitled "The Island of Glass" in *Legendary Britain* (Matthews and Stewart 1989) for the authors' take on Glastonbury. The Grail, for these writers and Western mysteries practitioners, is a mystical symbol, to be experienced psychologically and spiritually with the aid of meditation, "pathworking" (visualization techniques), and ceremonial ritual. For an excellent ethnography of the British neopagan and magical subculture, including Western mysteries groups, see Tanya Luhrmann's *Persuasions of the Witch's Craft* (1989).

17. Luhrmann (1989) notes that most British ritual magicians and Wiccans have read the book, and that many have been inspired by it to practice magic (87). *The Mists of Avalon* caused a stir in Glastonbury: it was, of course, very well received among the Goddess-oriented feminists, but scathingly reviewed by Anthony Roberts (in GC 8:32), who claimed that Ms. Bradley has reversed the "sacred ethos" of the Grail legends (the male brotherhood, etc.) and made the saga of Arthur and his knights "into a Goddess obsessed propaganda exercise for militant matriarchy."

18. Walsh's list of sites drew on similar lists prepared for the Harmonic Convergence by Jim Berenholtz and Robert Coon, with some additions of his own. The Gnomonic Projection is a method of mapping great circles (the shortest distances between two points on a spherical surface) to straight lines. Walsh's criterion for accuracy in an alignment was a standard error of 60 km (37.5 mi.), which he takes as a small margin of error compared to the total length of great circles, which is about 40,000 km (25,000 mi.). (A critic might argue, though, that if the earth were to have such geometrical straight-line alignments at all, they should probably be perfectly straight, with no margin of error.) Walsh found the "most aligned site of all" to be Rapa Nui (Easter Island).

19. Rahtz has agreed that it is *possible* the Tor was such a maze-labyrinth, and has dated it as second or third millennium B.C. *if* so; popularizers have capitalized on Rahtz's open-mindedness to the idea. Archaeological opinion, however, seems to have grown more solidly in favor of the lynchets theory (National Trust n.d.:10–11).

20. Other ideas about the Tor have come and gone. It had been thought, for instance, that there may have been stone circles on the Tor; Alexander Thom sought them in the 1970s and found nothing. Legends of lost tunnels leading from the Abbey to the Tor (A. Pennick in Roberts 1992:147), or even across the whole ancient Somerset landscape, have similarly failed to materialize any evidence. A tunnel running from the old water-

works property next door to Chalice Orchard (once Dion Fortune's home, more recently Geoffrey Ashe's) is, it turns out, a brick-lined heading drilled by the Bristol Waterworks Company in 1873 to tap underground springs (Ashe 1982:116).

21. Geoffrey Ashe suggests, "The phenomenon is akin to the Rorschach ink-blot test, or to seeing pictures in a fire" (1982:123). "Zodiac-finders," he writes, "do not themselves agree on these 'obvious' figures." "I have studied these photographs; I know what I am meant to see; I honestly try to see; and I simply do not" (121). To this, New Age patriarch Anthony Roberts (1992:19) retorts, "The foolish contention that the Zodiacal figures are 'not really there' and are in fact a ludicrously overblown Rorschach phenomenon shows a lack of wisdom, not to say psychic acumen, that is truly staggering." The (presumably wiser) Glastonbury Zodiac Companions have for years held monthly pilgrimage outings to different sites on the Zodiac planisphere, which have been attracting perhaps twenty people on average (Bowman 1993a:48). The Companions seek official recognition for the zodiac, which would presumably allow its designation as a site of national importance, along with strict controls on construction or road building within its bounds.

22. The base/root and "initiatory" center is Mount Shasta; the sexual center is Lake Titicaca in South America; the solar plexus is Australia's Uluru; the Glastonbury-Shaftesbury area constitutes the heart and "culminating" center; the Great Pyramid, together with the Mount of Olives is the throat center; the "Immortal Shamballic Focus" is mobile; and the crown is located at Mount Kailas in Tibet. For Coon, "Shasta and Glastonbury are the 'Alpha and Omega' of major planetary chakras" (1986:17).

23. These Goddess-inspired ecofeminists (a term most of them use only on occasion, but which is appropriate) have run into conflicts with more androcentric New Agers, Arthurians, and others with whom they otherwise share the "alternative" end of the Glastonbury spectrum. A long-standing conflict between the "Goddess women" and "patriarchal" male Avalonians like Anthony Roberts and Robert Coon has resulted in harsh words being spilled in both directions. In return for the abrasive Roberts' frequent denunciations of "matriarchal" feminists, his unexpected death on Glastonbury Tor (at age fifty, from cardiac arrest) was greeted by one reviewer with the following ominous epitaph: "The Goddess will not be mocked! Unless they wake up soon to the folly of their ways then Roberts & Co., who are sowing the seeds of such a lot of negative karma will reap a bitter harvest." (Valerie Remy, *Pipes of Pan*, 24; in Screeton 1993:65). Coon, in turn, has fired invectives against "those who have been duped into believing they serve the Goddess, when their real Master is Death. . . . Beware the so-called *Aquarian midwives* of death" (1986:79; italics in original). Quoting (imprecisely) a widespread neopagan chant, he continues, "The mindless drivel of 'We all come from the Goddess—to the Goddess we shall return like drops of rain in the ocean' is a deathist [*sic*], reactionary, and historically brief aberation [*sic*] that shall rapidly fade away as a bad dream in the morning light of Everlasting Life" (80).

24. Below the maintenance hole cover, apparently, is a Water Authority room filled with dials and wheels which control the water flow in the reservoir beneath; it was built in 1949 (N. Mann 1993:53). What this implies for the holy waters I am not sure.

25. Their plan, presented to English Heritage, Mendip district council, and the Archaeological department of the Somerset county council, is to restore the "sacred" character of the site by creating a shrine enclosed within an herb garden and permaculture-based orchard; they also advocate further archaeological work in the area. As evidence for the site's prior status, they cite William of Malmesbury's (ca. 1135) and John of Glastonbury's (ca. 1400) writings mentioning a chapel dedicated to St. Bridget at the location, and legends about the "Women's Quarter" there <www.isleofavalon.co.uk/places/bride-1.html>.

26. A wonderful illustration of the depth of overlap between earth mysteries research, neopagan Goddess spirituality, and the musical and traveler counterculture, is postmodern hippie Julian Cope, former star singer with the Teardrop Explodes and author of an extensively documented popular guide to megalithic Britain, *The Modern Antiquarian* (1998).

27. Though they might prefer it being otherwise, some members of the alternative community have acknowledged to me that Rahtz's book is the best scholarly overview of the topic, even if limited by his fear of risk taking and speculation. And for all his indignation at the "hippies, weirdos, drop-outs and psychos," Rahtz is one of the few archaeologists on record to support dowsing as a supplement to other archaeological research methods. He employed the services of a local dowser to successfully locate a Norman tunnel under the defenses of Old Sarum—and was rebuked for it by the Council of British Archaeology (Rahtz 1988).

28. A friendlier model of a scholar engaging in dialogue with the nonscientific community is provided by Ron Hutton, whose associations with Glastonbury's New Age community I described in chapter 2. The University of Avalon, now the Isle of Avalon Foundation, has made available a tape of one of his lectures, "The History of Glastonbury," in which Hutton skillfully but sympathetically debunks many of the legends associated with the Glastonbury landscape.

29. Another spectacular archaeological find was the recent discovery of the second oldest oak trees to be found, preserved in the peat outside Glastonbury. These were dated by trunk rings to between 4655 and 4135 B.C.—well before Stonehenge and the Egyptian pyramids. This shows that the moorland area was covered with a mix of fen woodland and sedge swamp for 3,000 years, because of rising sea levels and poor drainage; and also that primitive agricultural clearings had taken place in Glastonbury as long ago as the New Stone Age.

30. See Halfacree 1996 for an analysis of the New Age traveler phenomenon in terms of smooth versus striated space, Lefebvre's (1991) analysis of capitalist spatiality, and the Thatcherite construction of travelers as "folk devils."

31. In an intriguing illustration of the convoluted politics of local decision making, a letter of support to the council from local Friends of the Earth spokesperson Keith Dixon appeared in the *Central Somerset Gazette* (June 9, 1994). Dixon mused: "We find it somewhat unusual to be fighting on the side of the decision-making authority against a few mavericks [the GRA] in the town."

32. In May 1995 an 800-name petition was drawn up to stop the closure of Northload Street. A *Gazette* cover story (May 18, 1995) related accusations by protesters of Northload St. pedestrianization that Somerset County Council officials are "tearing the heart out of Glastonbury"—that is, by diverting not only heavy but also light traffic. (The story, typically, was titled "'Town Has Gone Dead'"; in effect, only the quotation marks here serve to differentiate the views of the petitioners from those of the newspaper reporting on them.)

33. Numbers seem to average around a few dozen, though they could be as few as a handful (I have never seen less in the summer) or as many as a few hundred (on special days like the solstice), depending on the weather and the day of the week, with people coming and going at all hours. In summertime, dozens of vehicles can often be found parked overnight at the base of the Tor.

34. A recent National Trust Consultation Process surveyed Tor users and concluded that most support continued unrestricted access to the Tor and an absence of commercial tourist amenities, but also are in favor of more information and signage, and the provision of parking at some distance from the Tor. See <www.isleofavalon.co.uk/local/features/tor-cnsl.html> and <www.isleofavalon.co.uk/local/biz/unique/freestate/archive/tor.html>.

35. The notion of balancing polarities such as dark and light, male and female, heaven and earth, recurs in frequent comparisons of Glastonbury's alternative community with the Findhorn community in northern Scotland, with which a number of "Glastafarians" have been associated at one time or another (among them the respective custodians, through most of the 1980s and 1990s, of Chalice Well Gardens). The two communities have at times seemed to carry on a rivalry over Britain's New Age leadership. Palden Jenkins notes that Glastonbury is "a much more *raunchy* kind of spiritual center," less "into the Light" than Findhorn, and more "into sex and drugs and rock 'n' roll," with people who are clearly "going through very, very human neuroses on the

growth path." Jenkins (among others) sees Glastonbury as closer to the Celtic heritage whose mysteries are accessed "in the dark of night, and when it's rainy and foggy and mysterious" (int.). The connection between Findhorn, Glastonbury, and (sometimes) Iona was a topic of writing in the *Glastonbury Communicator* and is reflected in the travel itineraries of many New Age visitors. But, as Ann Morgan explained to me, the connection between the two communities has weakened as Findhorn members now tend to see Glastonbury as "a messy, disorganized bunch of hippies who sit around smoking dope and don't want to work; and 'Glastonbury' thinks that Findhorn's a bunch of elitists, therapists who don't understand the pro issues of life, who've got money and want to [host] international conferences talking high-falutin' stuff and not really dealing with the real world" (int.).

Glastonbury's identification specifically as a *heart* chakra is also consistent with the notion that it is a place of rebalancing. The heart tends to be valued as the central, as well as the most "human" of the chakras (see chap. 2, n. 13). It is here where the tension between being both a physical body and a spirit or soul is said to work itself out, where some of the deepest lessons of human incarnation are learned, and where love and compassion have their source. The heart is, arguably, also a place where the watery, magnetic, maternal and nurturing impulse is transformed through will to serve the needs of the "Higher Self"—as Glastonbury is a place where watery nature (the primordial Somerset wetlands) rises up (in the shape of the Tor) toward the sky.

36. This interpretation is Roland Pargeter's, presented in a talk at the Glastonbury Experience (August 11, 1994). I am also indebted to various persons for certain other ideas in this section.

37. Another aspect of the alternative community that will inevitably come under stress is its members' reticence to specify what it is that makes Glastonbury special. As Garrard puts it, there is "a common acknowledgement that everybody's here for the same reason, as long as you don't try and define the reason in words" (int.). Others speak in no more tangible terms of an "angel of Glastonbury" to account for the "unidentifiable intelligence and coherence in the way things go on here, giving Glastonbury a particular flavour—the flavour and atmosphere which attracts us all here instead of anywhere else" (Jenkins, GC 3:3). This amorphousness leaves Glastonbury open to respond to people's imaginings, but also allows individuals to assume a responsiveness towards "it." As Jenkins sees it, this results in a balancing dynamic that occurs between a person's expectations, desires, or fears, and their inner psychospiritual needs. The "Glastonbury initiation," as he calls it, teaches its initiates "to loosen up, open our feelings, increase our vulnerability, straighten our dealings, drop unworkable illusions, work on our relationships" and encounter "crunches which are direct expressions of unwanted ghosts in our unconscious" (Jenkins, GC 3:3). Failure to appreciate this "balancing intelligence" that is said to reside in Glastonbury purportedly provokes disappointment or calamity in one's life. "Too many" would-be revivalists or gurus, Ashe writes, "have tried to force some preconceived idea on [Glastonbury], to use it as a base for pre-packaged teachings, to 'lay their own trips on it'—in fact to exploit the mystique. . . . The interesting thing is that there seems to be some quality in the place which defeats or diverts them" (1982:128–29).

38. In 1995 these meetings were attended by well over a hundred people on a given Sunday evening, and included live acoustic music, highly physical forms of worship (including shaking and rolling around on the floor), Pentecostal-style glossolalia (speaking in tongues), and cathartic emotional releases. They were mainly led by lay ministers, whose gentle elocutions stress the themes of "opening up" to the "power" of "the (Holy) Spirit" and a feel-good Christian message conducive to self-acceptance and healing. All quotes are from the text of Rev. Saunders's prophecy, first presented in a service on May 21, 1995.

39. A (New Age) healing group meeting I attended a few days after this charismatic prayer meeting, and which was put on by the local chapter of the National Federation of Spiritual Healers (NFSH), held with a full-capacity attendance of some fifty people

in the Miracles Room of the Glastonbury Experience, was opened by a guided meditation that used almost identical imagery of light pouring out onto Glastonbury and flowing out along ley lines to other centers. One wonders whether the Christians inspired by Saunders's prophecy, many of whom have lived in the Glastonbury area for years and not considered themselves to be part of any New Age, are aware that this imagery and terminology is almost identical to New Age visions that have been circulating for much longer.

40. Others, like Rev. Patrick Riley and the Quest Community's John Sumner, have contributed to an ecumenical dialogue among Glastonbury's diverse religious identities, though some within the alternative community have remained skeptical of these inroads, sensing a preachy condescension on the part of the churchmen. In the fall of 1994, however, a conference entitled "Meeting the Presence" was held at a Christian camp near Avebury. According to reports in London's *Times* and *Telegraph*, it was a gathering of "outward-looking pagans" and Wiccans joining "ecumenically-inclined Christians" in order to open a dialogue between Christians and "pre-Christian nature religions." Christian clergymen John Sumner, the Anglican leader of Glastonbury's ecumenical Quest Community, and Canon Tom Curtis Hayward, a Catholic priest in Stroud (not far from Glastonbury), were to address the gathered pagans. I am not aware of what ultimately transpired from the meeting; but it is encouraging to note that both (conservative) newspapers avoided the distortions commonly found in portrayals of pagans and Wiccans. Both reported that there are some 250,000 British pagans, who, in the words of the *Telegraph*'s religious affairs correspondent Damian Thompson, "follow a nature-based spirituality and worship pre-Christian deities." ("Churchmen to Address Pagan Group," *Telegraph*, September 23, 1994; "Witches Worship at Christian Camp; Avebury, Wiltshire," *Times*, September 24, 1994, 10). Further instances of pagan-Christian bridge building and "borrowing" are described in Marion Bowman's chapter on Glastonbury in Sutcliffe and Bowman 2000 (a book I received as this one was going to print).

41. For instance, in the 1980s hostility to the alternative community's Living Dance and Astrology Camps led to several parish councils asking local landowners to refuse the New Agers use of their land in coming years (GC 6). There have also been attempts in the past to disrupt the business activities of Assembly Rooms tenants through statutory devices (GC 4:15), and to prevent the use of the town hall for events such as Psychic Fairs. Other Christians have remained more quietly disdainful of Glastonbury's alternative religious groups. A typical view is that expressed by an Anglican priest, quoted by Bowman, that "Christian pilgrimage, like Christianity itself, is centred on God; New Age pilgrimage, like New Age, is centred on self" (1993a:57). More pointedly, a Catholic lay activist told me with noticeable anger in his voice that "Glastonbury has been hijacked by the New Age." To an outsider, though, the parallels between religious believers of different persuasions are often more evident than their differences. Perhaps only an outsider like myself could so easily notice the resemblance between a bearded young Orthodox priest in black robes, black hat, and thick cross dangling around his neck, and a long-haired Wiccan priest (I assume that's what he was) in similar black robes, with pentagram and ankh hanging around his neck—both real persons spotted a couple of days apart in Glastonbury.

6. RED ROCKS TO REAL ESTATE

1. Byrkit traces the Southwest genre back to the displaced desires of New England's Mugwump literati, whose sense of being left behind in the march of American industrial progress left them longing for a new American South to romanticize, fetishize, and "orientalize." Looking for an antidote to their New England "Protestant ethic and spirit of capitalism," these culturemakers alchemically combined "land, sky and people" to create "an almost hallucinogenic 'Land of Enchantment'" (1992:355). On the invention of the *idea* of the Southwest by transcontinental railroad corporations (like the

Santa Fe Railroad Company), cultural and tourist entrepreneurs (like the Fred Harvey Company), and others, see Weigle 1989, 1990; Byrkit 1992; Riley 1994; Weigle and Babcock 1996; and some of the essays in Norris 1994.

2. More than 30 million people are supposed to have visited the Colorado Plateau's national parks in 1992 (M. Murphy 1994:A1). Tourism in Arizona generates an estimated $7.2 billion a year, most of it centered around sun and scenery. But the global tourist economy has become increasingly unstable and competitive, dependent on media representations, unpredictable weather and crime patterns, and the like. A 1994 study sponsored by the Arizona Tourism Office warned of increasing competition with Arizona's tourist industry coming from luxury cruise ships, mega–gaming casinos, and amusement and theme parks elsewhere. Acknowledging that Arizona had benefited from the "wave of crime, riots, hurricanes and other woes besetting Florida, southern California and Hawaii in recent years," it warned that those states were "bouncing back," and that new competitors, including Mexico and Central America, and theme parks in San Antonio and Las Vegas, would make it difficult for Arizona's industry to keep up if it failed to take action soon. The study urged the state's tourist industry to become more "customer-driven" by appealing more to "target groups" (families seeking theme parks, "Mexican skiers to Flagstaff," and "German visitors who love the Old West") and by cashing in on its "Southwestern character" and organizing its attractions around such "itinerary themes as the Old West, recreation/adventure, geology/scenery, ecotourism, astronomy, cultural/historical/archaeology, military history and bases, and New Age."

Sedona's position between the mountains around Flagstaff and the desert valleys closer to Phoenix allow it to benefit from the seasonality of Arizona's tourist economy—with tourists migrating northward in the summer months and southward in the winter. But, according to the report, the issue of capacity constraints has to be dealt with. Long lines of traffic snake through the Grand Canyon and Sedona in the summer, resulting in newspaper headlines warning of "mobfests" (Western 1994:H1). The solution, for technocrats oblivious to the arid landscape's low carrying capacity, is to build more roads.

3. The estimates for Sedona range from two to six or seven million visitors annually. The *Arizona Republic* provided the figure of five million (Shaffer 1992); seven million was suggested to me by a local environmentalist (Blake, int.). Most figures in the early 1990s hovered around the three to three-and-a-half million mark, up from 2.5 million in 1988 (R. Brown 1993:114); but the numbers have gone up as the town's reputation (and the U.S. economy) have grown. The Grand Canyon, according to figures provided by the U.S. Bureau of the Census in 1990, has attracted a similar number, four million or so visitors annually.

4. Wayne Iverson, a planner for the National Park Service who chanced upon Oak Creek Canyon in the early 1960s, recalls his disbelief that it was never made a part of the national park system (in Shaffer 1992:B1). In the United States, National Parks are the jurisdiction of the Department of the Interior, and are the most protected land designation; national forests, administered by the Department of Agriculture, are subject to multiple uses, including mining, forestry, grazing, and recreation.

5. For the information here on geology, climate, natural history, and indigenous history, I have relied especially on Aitchison 1992, 1994; and Foust, Byrkit, and Avery 1991. The best recent history of Arizona is Thomas Sheridan's masterful *Arizona: A History* (1995a); while the social history of Sedona is well covered in R. Brown 1993.

6. There is a Hopi story about Palatkwapi—Place of the Red Rocks, which some think may be the Sedona area (though opinion is divided)—which suggests that the Palatkwapi clans had it too easy: plentiful water, food, and a good climate led to their becoming self-indulgent, for which they were punished by a great flood, and they eventually migrated northeast to present-day Hopi lands (Foust, Byrkit, and Avery 1991:34–35).

7. At this point in my narrative the Spaniards disappear, reappearing only as a spectral historical presence connected, however vaguely, with today's small population of

Hispanic or Mexican residents or (more commonly) commuting laborers in Sedona. I should mention, however, that the southwestern states, especially New Mexico and Arizona, have been mythicized by Chicano cultural nationalists, especially in the late 1960s and 1970s, as the Chicano/Mestizo homeland Aztlán, named after the legendary northern homeland of the Aztecs. See Chávez 1984, and Riley 1994 (235–39).

8. In *Rivers of Empire*, Donald Worster (1985:7) resurrects Karl Wittfogel's "hydraulic society" hypothesis to argue that the American West is "a social order based on the intensive, large-scale manipulation of water and its products" through an increasingly "coercive, monolithic, and hierarchical system, ruled by a power elite" of bureaucrats and their wealthy patrons (agribusinessmen, ranchers, mining executives, and utility companies). Arthur Maass and Raymond Anderson (in Pisani 1989:259) reject Worster's view, emphasizing instead the degree to which water users have controlled their own destinies through local forms of control and management; but Sheridan (1995b:48) argues that resource control in Arizona has been more like a "feudal society of competing warlords," among them "copper companies, railroads, ranchers, farmers, loggers, utility companies, real estate developers, municipal governments," all held together by a weak state (the federal government). On the politics of water in the western United States, see also D. Mann 1963; Ingram 1969, 1990; Wiley and Gottlieb 1982; Reisner 1986; and Gottlieb 1988.

9. Sedona is presently home to some three hundred professional artists and performers including painters, sculptors, printmakers, potters, jewelers, weavers, and photographers. About forty-five galleries are found in the city itself, though cultural facilities for artists and affordable studio and living spaces are felt by some to be inadequate (Hall and Mankin 1990:32–33). The hub of the arts community is the Sedona Arts Center, whose membership grew from 700 in 1986 to over 2,000 in the mid-1990s. Sedona is also the site for the construction of the Sedona Cultural Park, a large, ambitious ($9 million), corporate-funded project whose intent is to develop a major, fifty-acre arts center that would serve both the local area and the international market.

10. The vast bulk of the *Red Rock News*'s advertising revenues come from the real estate industry (80%, according to the now-extinct, conservationist *Red Rock Guardian* [1 (1): 7]). The publisher of the *News*, Bob Larson Jr., is a member of the board of directors of the chamber of commerce, where he sits alongside developer Frank Miller, *Sedona Magazine*'s Hoyt Johnson, and other prominent businessmen. To this group one might add the "Sedona Thirty," a fraternity of wealthy, influential local men. Meanwhile, the radio station's outspoken owner, Joe Tabback, frequently shares his right-wing, pro-growth, and anti-environmentalist views over the air.

11. In the mid-1990s, Keep Sedona Beautiful had close to 800 members; while the 4Rs (originally called the Retirees and Residents of the Red Rocks) had over 500, but was growing more rapidly. The latter group has been one of the major players active in the struggle against the building of a bridge at Red Rock Crossing (see chap. 7). The regional Sierra Club chapter has succeeded in making the Red Rock Crossing controversy an issue of regional and even national importance. Among the suggestions made for a better land use plan have been the development of an interconnected trail system, restrictions on national forest land exchanges, obtaining a Class 1 Air Quality designation, and limiting water diversions (e.g., Iverson 1994).

12. The U.S. Forest Service has been undergoing a structural overhaul in recent years, with downsizing and cost cutting affecting employee numbers, and with a greater emphasis being placed on local volunteerism. Coconino is one of eleven national forests in Arizona and New Mexico, together (along with one national grassland) covering nearly one-eighth of the surface area of the two states. They make up the majority of the Southwestern Region (Region 3) of the USFS office.

13. A Keep Sedona Beautiful survey found 92 percent of respondents favored more open space and opposed trading any more public land. Relations between the Forest Service and townsfolk, however, have always been tinged with local resentment against outside experts. As early as 1908 a Coconino National Forest supervisor resigned because of conflicting pressure from superiors and from ranchers and grazers (Byrkit and

Hooper 1994:31). When, in 1935, the USFS erected a 34,000-gallon tank to pump water from an "inexhaustible well" to supply the house and lawn (and flush toilet) of a forest ranger, locals complained that this was an unnecessary luxury at a time when children at the Sedona school used unsanitary outdoor toilets and got drinking water from an irrigation ditch (Foust, Byrkit, and Avery 1991:47).

14. The story of the *Sedona Times*'s downfall (slick, smooth-talking easterner comes from nowhere, steals the owner's wife and the paper, and then tries to set up an authoritarian regime . . .) is told in an article by Jim Robinson (*Tab* 2:18 [May 23, 1990]: 5).

15. This reconstruction is based on my interviews with several sources, including a prominent personality in the town, the *Tab*'s former publisher, and a couple of former *Tab* employees. I did not attempt to confirm it against the "other side's" version.

16. In 1997, Sedonans approved a Sustainable Growth Initiative, which included an ordinance reducing by one-third the number of building permits that could be issued in the town. The measure was lauded by some as the first attempt by an Arizona city to control growth and sprawl. The Sedona Private Property Owners Association, led by real estate broker and businessman John D. Miller, responded (rather typically) by suing the city to block the ordinance; they won the case in Yavapai County Court. Many conservation measures have ended in similar circumstances.

17. Nonwhites constitute only a tiny percentage of the city of Sedona's permanent residents. In the 1990 census, just over 100 were registered of a total population of 7,720 (1990 Census of Population and Housing, U.S. Dept. of Commerce, Bureau of the Census, Data User Services Division, 1991). On labor and wealth differentials more generally, in Sedona and in the Verde Valley, see Gober, McHugh, and Leclerc 1993.

18. There are conflicting reports about the importance to the tourist industry of New Age–related activities. Some have called it Sedona's number one industry. The chamber of commerce office manager estimated in 1989 that less than 5 percent of tourists ask about vortexes or New Age matters (*Ariz. Rep.*, August 5, 1989:C1); however, the chamber's executive director Patti Henry was quoted in 1990 as saying that about 20 percent of Sedona's three million annual visitors are "interested in the so-called sacred sites" (Winton 1990a); and the *Sedona Times* had reported back in 1986 that the vortexes "are probably the primary reason most new residents are moving to the area" ("Children of the Vortex," *ST*, June 4–10, 1986:1). Retired geographer and Sedona resident Robert Brown (1993:105–6) surveyed residents and found that 26 percent, evenly gendered, believed that the vortexes include "forces that affect humans psychologically," while 69 percent denied this, often vehemently, and 5 percent were unsure. A tour company, Pink Jeep Tours, reported in 1989 that some 15 percent of their customers (mostly women, aged 25 to 45) chose the vortex route tours (*Ariz. Rep.*, August 5, 1989:C1). On the other hand, it should be stressed that it is not only the natural attractions which bring visitors to Sedona. Its arts festivals, galleries, boutiques, and various amenities by now play an equally important role.

7. VORTEXES AND CROSSED CURRENTS

1. The use of the term *metaphysics*, when in reference to the New Age movement, generally refers to the tradition of spiritual and religious thought that seeks to know the invisible, spiritual world, which it considers primary (but corresponding) to the manifest, visible one. The term is sometimes used interchangeably with *occultism* or *esotericism*, though, strictly speaking, they are not identical. The metaphysical tradition includes Swedenborgianism, Spiritualism, Christian Science, New Thought, Theosophy, and the many spin-offs and splinter groups within each of these denominational families. Most subscribe to the idea that the physical world is one of several levels of reality; that the others are accessible, either through meditation, dreams, or mediumistic trance (now known as channeling); and (less centrally) that a liberal, tolerant, and rational approach to life is basically sound when it embraces, rather than closes itself off from, spiritual experience. Most also emphasize God's identity or similarity with humans, rather than their difference, often resulting in a monistic worldview according

to which the universe *is* God/divinity; and most consider health and healing to be primary tasks of earthly life. The metaphysical tradition is one of the main strands that has shaped the New Age movement. For a history of metaphysical religion in America, see Judah 1967, as well as Melton's (1993) bibliographic and reference works. In relation to Sedona, my usage will reflect the fact that the term *metaphysical* was more common in earlier days, while *New Age* has become popular more recently. Among other things, the metaphysical tradition shares with New Age spirituality (besides similarities in worldview) a high proportion of women leaders.

2. The Rainbow Ray group and the Aquarian Educational Center are still active today. According to Keller (1991) and Dannelley (1993), Rainbow Ray cofounder Evangeline Van Pollen was "the first person in modern times to identify a Vortex in the Sedona area," and the center they established on Airport Road (allegedly "under the direction" of St. Germaine and "Christ Sananda") was the first major "New Age Center" in the area (Dannelley 1993:44). The Aquarian Educational Center, of a similarly Eastern and theosophical orientation, is perhaps the largest and most active of these groups today, attracting sometimes over a hundred participants to its regular Sunday services. In an interview, Keller (int.) also fondly recollects the "Tibetan connection" to Sedona. Now well-known and respected teacher Tarthang Tulku Rinpoche had come to Sedona some thirty years ago. Keller recounts that the Tibetan lama had said he'd been there in an earlier incarnation some "fifty civilizations ago" and that he "seemed to know where everything was." Another Tibetan lama, she claims, had been sent there by the present Dalai Lama. During my stay in Sedona in 1994, several Tibetan monks came to create a sand mandala, dedicated to world peace, and to publicly meet with Navajo and Hopi elders.

3. Bryant has been involved with Sun Bear's Medicine Wheel Gatherings and his brand of neo-Native millenarianism for years, and her book *Earth Changes Survival Handbook* (1984) has been influential in the neotribal Rainbow movement.

4. The latter number is according to the Forest Service head count at the event (*ST,* August 26, 1987:A3,5). Total attendance figures for the Convergence varied between 2,000 and 10,000, depending on whom one talked to. The FS estimate was 5,000 to 10,000 (*ST,* August 26, 1987; *SRRN,* August 19, 1987:14), with some 4,000 hiking into the Bell Rock area on both Saturday and Sunday, and 1,500 going out each day to Boynton Canyon (*SRRN,* August 19, 1987:14).

5. Despite the lucrative commercial possibilities, a few devoted believers, like Pat Northrup, owner of the Golden Word, Sedona's oldest New Age bookstore, and a former executive director of the Sedona/Oak Creek chamber of commerce, chose "the temple rather than the marketplace" by closing for the weekend (*ST,* August 26, 1987:A5). Ironically, this adds weight to an observation made that same weekend by the chief archaeologist at New Mexico's Chaco Canyon, in reference to the Harmonic Convergers who had gathered there: "These people are not from a bizarre sect. They come from middle-class to upper-middle-class Anglo White America. They're the people who check you out in stores. They own the stores" (cited in "New Agers Flock to Chaco," *High Country News,* November 30, 1992:11). (Chaco Canyon, the vast archaeological complex that apparently played a central ceremonial function for the ancient Anasazi, has been called the Stonehenge of the Southwest and the Camelot of New Agers. Close to a thousand gathered at Chaco for the Convergence. See Bensinger 1988 for one account.)

6. Always struggling to make ends meet (and to iron out its internal politics), the center had, for a time, changed from being a nonprofit membership cooperative to being a church organization under IRS Code 501(C3). During a serious crisis in the mid-1990s, the center's first president and cofounder, Christopher Jelm, put forward a proposal intended to revitalize the center by urging individual members to focus on bringing in one of twelve Divine Virtues—beauty, compassion, courage, curiosity, imagination, joy, justice, love, loyalty, power, purity, and will. The proposal, to my eyes, had little to say about practical matters; and it is a wonder that the center has survived for as long as it has.

7. My conservative estimate of the size of Greater Sedona's metaphysical community, based on the numbers I counted at large events, the percentage of residents who say they believe in vortexes, and other data, is between 1,000 and 2,500, though newspapers have suggested figures as large as 5,000 (e.g., Shaffer 1991a:B1). A 1991 article in the *Arizona Republic* on a National New Age and Alien Agenda Conference held in Phoenix stated that 600 Sedonans were on a mailing list of UFO and New Age enthusiasts; of a total 1990 census population of 7,200 for the city of Sedona, the author reasoned, one in twelve people "is a UFO buff or New Ager" ("Short Takes," September 5, 1991:C3). That particular mailing list was one which would have appealed only to a part, and perhaps not the majority, of those who make up Sedona's "New Age culture."

8. For instance, at a networking meeting for healing practitioners, of about twenty people in attendance, only three made a living from their practice; most others called themselves "part-time" healers (i.e., getting some income from their practice, or, for the rest, even none at all). Presumably, however, the ones attending were those who needed to "network"; more successful ones would have been busy elsewhere.

9. The 1994 winter solstice celebration, which involved some fifty performers and attracted an audience of close to 200, portrayed a Goddess-theological revisioning of Christmas themes: the Divine Mother/Earth Goddess/Sarasvati gives birth to a son/consort/Sun (and to the divine within), having been impregnated by a Solar Regent. Besides the pagan Goddess imagery (founder-director Dove is a "Priestess, Reverend & Minister," who has been facilitating Goddess Circles and Celebrations for most of her ten years in Sedona), there were plenty of angels, the singing of Christmas carols and "Ave Maria." The overall thematic dynamic emphasized the complementarity, rather than opposition, between spirit and flesh, light and darkness (a prominent theme also in the 12:12 conference). The Darkness within, participants sang, is "the Light disguised." One can see here the extent to which the New Age community attempts to come to terms with, while reworking, the Christianity of the surrounding culture (and of individual believers' upbringing).

10. According to a brochure put out by the World Ascension Network, "A stargate is a dimensional doorway. In recent years, global link-ups, sacred site activations and the growing commitment to lightwork in general, go hand in hand with the opening of stargates. *The opening of a stargate creates a consciousness shift, that is its simple definition.*" ("12:12 Gateway to Freedom Part II: Return to Innocence," WAN 11 [Winter 1994]: 1, Santa Fe: Goddess Press; emphasis in original). The way these events occur seems to be that someone somewhere "channels" information about them, and *that* information gets picked up on by others and developed further, until it snowballs into an event.

11. All these were in evidence at a Full Moon ceremony I attended at an "ascension wheel" outside Sedona. The majority of participants were associated with the Rainbow Ray group, with the notable presence of a few "shamanic" individuals whom I recognized from the circles led by transplanted Anishnabe elder Hollis Littlecreek. Twenty-one people were gathered, standing or sitting in chairs around the fire pit at the center of the medicine/ascension wheel, on this cold January day. The ceremony began with sage smudging (purification) and a go-round of prayers and dedications. One of the leaders, a woman I will call K., talked about Jesus Christ visiting this place 2,000 years ago, and then again 1,000 years later. According to her story, things got mixed up about a century ago when Natives and whites got into conflict (by doing "what they knew," which was "survival"). Now, she continued, we are preparing for Christ's return—not only for one Christ but for seven "Christs," representing the seven rays, who are "preparing to go public." (This is an idea familiar from Alice Bailey's teachings.) K. proceeded to sing a song which was supposed to have been sung by a Native shaman woman who had served Christ here in the past. Sung in an earthy, not at all churchy or ethereal style, it blended (according to her) Christ's Hebrew and Aramaic language with "Native American" (and was well balanced in its gender imagery, light-dark metaphorics, etc.). Then the drumming and dancing began, quite restrained compared to pagan celebrations, but enjoyable nonetheless.

Like other events I had participated in, all the participants seemed very friendly and theologically nondogmatic. Except for one of the "shamans," most of the leading figures were women, ranging in age from their thirties to their sixties. Diversity of religious expression ranged from the enthusiastic Christian hymns sung by one man, to the obvious Native-inspired pagan chants and dances—a strange blend of the heterodox Christianity of the Rainbow Ray group (based partly in the Alice Bailey/Theosophical tradition) and the more earthy, shamanic, Native/pagan strain. It seems that even a relatively staid and conservative metaphysical group like this one has opened up to the drumming and song stylistics and medicine wheels of the (New Age) "neo-Natives"—probably as a result of need (to survive as a religious group) and of being thrown together in the bubbling cauldron of Sedona. The differences between these many strands within Sedona's eclectic New Age fabric do not, in fact, seem to trouble most New Agers: they have been integrated into a belief system which respects the validity of (what is thought to be) Native American spiritual wisdom at the same time as it identifies a universal truth behind all the world's religions. In the babbling cacophony of ascended masters, teachers, angelic beings, extraterrestrials, and other intermediaries, one person's path may be a "native" one, another's "more extraterrestrial" (Jelm, int.), or may include personal "guides" channeled from diverse times and places.

12. In the mid-1990s the most popular of these guidebooks were Sutphen 1988; Dannelley 1991, 1993; Dongo 1988, 1993; and Johansen and Barclay 1987. Nicholas Mann's *Sedona—Sacred Earth* (1991) has garnered respect for his application of a variety of geomantic ideas to the Sedona landscape. (This is the same Nick Mann who has lived in Glastonbury and written extensively about its mysteries.) Some of the hiker's guides to the area also mention the "vortexes" (e.g., Magnum and Magnum 1994).

13. For instance, two of the past presidents of the Sedona Center for the New Age (the Center in Sedona), the only two with whom I conducted lengthy interviews, both stressed the centrality of the extraterrestrial influence to their own spiritual lives (Jelm, int.; Danu, int.).

14. For a journal which began as a local directory of metaphysical events and services, the success of *Sedona: Journal of Emergence* has been phenomenal. It is, at the time of writing, the best-selling periodical devoted to channeled teachings in the largest New Age bookstore in Toronto (the Omega Center), and likely many other places. As for my claim that the magazine's target audience is entirely different from that of *Sedona Magazine*, this would be difficult to verify. It is conceivable that there may be overlap—that readers of *Journal of Emergence* become interested in traveling to Sedona and subsequently discover the other magazine, or vice versa. However, the entire tone and tenor of the two magazines is distinctly different. The object being promoted by *Sedona Magazine* and the source of titillation for its readers is Sedona, its landscape, and its opportunities for recreation, tourism, and high-style living. *Journal of Emergence* also makes frequent reference to the red rock landscape, but (arguably) less to titillate or compel readers to move there (though it may have this effect anyway); rather, the subject of titillation, if it can be called that, are the ET sources of its channeled wisdom and the "emergence" into the New Age which they herald. An apt description of the *Journal's* content might be Riordan's analysis of the entire channeling phenomenon: "A bewildering cacophony of cosmic voices babble, gossip, and prophesy on every aspect of human and nonhuman life, offering a myriad of ingenious revisionist (and often mutually contradictory) versions of history, theology, and science, and a profusion of clashing—but equally unorthodox—commentaries on current events" (1992:107). Because of the Sedona-centered nature of the magazine's contributor pool, though, *Journal of Emergence* is more consistent than this would suggest, and also features a frequent concern with the Sedona landscape itself.

15. Magazines like the Australian-based *Nexus*, one of the most popular sources of New Age conspiracy theorizing, and the U.K.-based *Rainbow Ark*, have made the boundary between New Age and far right more permeable in recent years than it had been previously; the amorphousness of both movements seems to virtually guarantee that there might be some boundary traffic between them. Kalman and Murray (1995a,

1995b) have documented some of the intercourse between right-wing, neofascist figures and individual New Agers like one-time U.K. Green Party prominent David Icke. A kind of group multiple-personality disorder seems to result from this in places where New Agers congregate. In Glastonbury, for instance, a talk by David Icke was picketed by antifascists and by the local Green Party candidate. And while *Nexus*, books by Icke, and similar literature was being sold in stalls outside an August 1995 Crop Circle Symposium held at Glastonbury's Assembly Rooms, the town's flagship New Age bookstore and publishing house, Gothic Image, prominently (and provocatively) displayed a copy of Kalman and Murray's accusatory "New Age Nazism" article on its front window across the street.

16. For a strong antiracist critique of the New Age movement (from an ecofeminist and Goddess spirituality perspective), see Sjöö 1992, 1994.

17. By emphasizing the differences between New Age and New (far) Right, I wouldn't want to imply that New Agers tend to be left-wing in their politics; such a generalization wouldn't hold either. Among the most in-depth, extended treatments of world politics from a New Age perspective (one specifically informed by Alice Bailey's Arcane School teachings, which have strongly influenced Ascensionist thought), is McLaughlin's and Davidson's *Spiritual Politics: Changing the World From the Inside Out* (1994). The book includes a foreword by His Holiness the Dalai Lama, and has been lauded by New Age prominents like David Spangler, Willis Harman, economist Hazel Henderson, and World Policy Institute board member Patricia Ellsberg. The authors articulate such ideas as "whole-systems thinking," the mental and psychological causes of world events, the political effects of the laws of karma and reincarnation, "the soul of nations," and the "invisible government" of the "Masters of Wisdom"; and they advocate meditation, "thought-form building," and similar methods for developing a "new planetary order." Like other previous attempts to articulate a New Age politics (e.g., Satin 1979), their view could be called "neither left nor right." At its best, one might say it represents a politics of touchy-feely compassionate action; at its worst, it is open to the criticism that it uses ideas of karma and reincarnation to justify present-day inequities, while focusing on rather abstract and potentially undemocratic solutions (i.e., world order). Nevertheless, even if (as two of their chapter headings spell out) "Form Follows Thought" and "The World Is Our Mirror," these authors are at least addressing large-scale political issues—something which many New Agers tend to avoid altogether.

18. Page Bryant, as mentioned earlier, was one of Sun Bear's closest apprentices. Richard Dannelley claims to have received "the vision and the guidance that has held [his] life together ever since" while at a Medicine Wheel ceremony led by Sun Bear in 1984. Dannelley writes that he understood then Sun Bear's vision that "with ceremony we could heal the Earth and ourselves"; and his turning-point "shamanic initiation" (or conversion) experience occurred on top of a "power spot" mountain sacred to the Modoc Indians at the 1984 Rainbow Gathering in the Modoc National Forest in California (1993:117–20). I will discuss the politics of this "neo-Native" spirituality below.

19. Medicine wheels are formations of rocks laid out in a wheel-like circle, with several spokes going out from a small central circle to the large one on the outside. They have traditionally been made by Native North Americans in the prairies and Great Plains; a few hundred remaining medicine wheels are known to be standing today, many of them on high plateaus or hilltops. Non-Native fascination with medicine wheels stems in part from their use by such Native author-teachers as Sun Bear, Hyemeyohsts Storm, Ed McGaa, and others, for group ceremonies and individual meditation and self-examination. In current usage, a medicine wheel generally has four (or eight) spokes pointing to each of the four (or eight) directions. These, in turn, represent the four seasons, times of day and stages of the human life cycle, and are associated with particular "power animals" and types of energy. Systems of symbolic correspondences vary widely. Medicine wheel ceremonies are thought of as a way of balancing the four directions, animal powers, and so on, within an individual. For an influential account of medicine wheel usage, see Sun Bear and Wabun (1992).

NOTES TO PAGES 178–187

275

20. Estimates from two participants (David, int.; Armbruster, int.).

21. Earth Wisdom Tours kindly took me along on a two-hour tour, which included Boynton Canyon, the popular meditation spot Rachel's Knoll, and the Airport vortex. (Different jeep tour companies have permits for different sites; the oldest companies, Red Rock and Pink Jeep Tours, have the most site permits.) The guide, who identified herself as "third generation German-American," frequently referred to her "many Native relatives," and rather than speaking, as is customary, of "electric" and "magnetic" vortexes, she used the terms "Grandfathers" and "Grandmothers." Commenting on the commercial development around Oak Creek canyon (the "womb of the Mother"), she referred to it as a "violation of the Mother," and suggested that a recent flood and two magnitude 5.0 (moderately strong) earthquakes are a fulfillment of Native prophecies about the Earth's retribution for such violations.

22. In his eagerness to provide a thorough geomantic analysis, Mann imposes various ideas onto Sedona's landscape in a somewhat abstract manner. "Trained," as he puts it, "in the European Geomantic Tradition" (1991:1)—he is, in fact, one of the more useful of Glastonbury's guides (see chap. 5)—Mann follows this tradition's tendency to look for abstract geometrical designs, such as pentagrams, hexagrams, straight-line alignments, and chakra systems, in their quest for a "landscape temple." It seems to me, however, that nature is much more wild and interesting than that. Nevertheless, once patterns have been identified in a landscape (and Mann finds a huge bird and a serpent in Sedona's, just as Katherine Maltwood found an entire zodiac in Glastonbury's), they can become a part of its lore and, subsequently, of the cultural landscape, if not of its "natural" one.

23. This spinal "staff" is among the central images in both Eastern and Western forms of mysticism: the basis for the chakra system of Hindu and Buddhist yoga, and for the Kabbalistic Tree of Life (which itself is central to many Western magical and esoteric traditions). I describe this chakric axis in chapter 5 in relation to the so-called Michael-and-Mary ley line in southern England.

24. Of Sedona's published geomants, to my knowledge only Mann has credited the Airport vortex with this central importance. His reasons are somewhat different than mine. In one reading (and he performs several different ones), Airport Mesa is located at the head (and the vortex is at the throat) of a large bird formed by topographic contour lines; in another it is the "solar plexus chakra" within a "Realised Chakra System" that stretches from Isis Rock (between Long Canyon and Secret Canyon) at the crown, to a point that forms a triangle with Lee Mountain and Courthouse Rock at the base. Perhaps the point here is that many readings are possible, limited only by the reader's imagination and by the technical instruments—contour maps, photographs, automobiles, helicopters, and so forth—at her disposal. My reading, however, stays closer to the real circulation of "energy" (people, cars, and water) in and through the town. Any such readings, in the end, are simply evocative imaging tools for visualizing the landscape.

25. As related in chapter 2, neuropsychologist Michael Persinger has for years been researching, with interesting results, the idea that electromagnetism, such as could be generated piezoelectrically by rock faulting (with rock layers squeezing against each other, as happens more frequently in earthquake zones), can activate the brain's temporal lobe and stimulate stored images, memories, and visual hallucinations. Persinger's account tends to be more reductionist than others. One of my informants in Sedona, tour guide and environmental activist John Armbruster, explained to me his more "holistic" theory, according to which the temporal lobes and electromagnetic stimulation are connected to the "astral energies," which, in his reckoning, are the "missing link," the nonrecognition of which has prevented science from developing a coherent unified field theory.

26. Mann (1991) presents the most comprehensive geomantic reading of the Sedona landscape. I have drawn on it (with additional insights of my own) in my description. Mann points out as well that the action of water is evident in even the most *yang* formations: "The round, smooth, red Supai bedrock has been sculpted (by ancient oceans)

into massive piers at the summit." However, the presence of water hundreds of thousands of years ago is not the same as its presence today, so this argument seems to me a weak one.

27. The topic of New Age crystal worship deserves a book in itself. For a popular New Age view, see Baer and Baer 1984, 1987; but for Randall Baer's later conversion to evangelical Christianity, see Baer 1989. For a highly informative, critical perspective on the crystal craze (by a writer better known for her encyclopedic books on women's spirituality), see B. Walker 1989.

28. Lemurian references abound in Sedona; several of my informants believed they lived in the area during the "Lemurian era." The idea of Lemuria has been passed down from the speculations of nineteenth-century scientists about a lost Pacific continent, and reshaped through the imagination of psychics and spiritualists, including Theosophical Society founder Helena Blavatsky, Edgar Cayce, Ruth Montgomery, Col. James Churchward, John Newbrough, and others. They have little or no basis in any currently recognized scientific theory of prehistory.

29. "When I first drove to Sedona coming up Route 17," one informant told me, "you get off at 179, and you make that . . . turn, and it opens up, and you finally see the red rock: well, I burst into tears. It was one of those 'coming home' things" (Jelm, int.). Another recalls her cross-country drive from Florida to California and her decision, for no apparent reason, to take the alternate route through Sedona. "Driving down the canyon . . . it's like, all of a sudden going—God! [drops jaw, exhales] . . . I'm sure my mouth was hanging open, you know, as I was driving." On a whim, she decided to turn toward the Chapel of the Holy Cross (built into the side of a mountain). When she parked and walked into the chapel, she recalls being "pulled like a magnet" to the Bible at the front of the chapel. "I walked down there, my eyes fell on the right side of the page to Isaiah 43, and it said, 'Fear not. I have called you by your name. You are mine,'" followed by "'You'll walk through the fire and not be burned. You'll go through the waters and you'll not drown.'" Retrospectively, she explains that she had been "seeking" her "spiritual path" in the Human Potential movement and elsewhere, but that the visit to the chapel in Sedona had served as a turning point, "a real—kachung!—I don't know how to say it. . . . Conscious mind doesn't really know what that's about; but it was very important." On her next visit to Sedona, while looking up at Capitol View, "something inside just went 'poof!'—just kind of like an opening in my heart." (G. Lamb, int.).

For other such experiences, see Sutphen 1988. Dongo (1993) collected written testimonies from twenty-two of Sedona's metaphysical immigrants, among them healers, counselors, psychics and channelers, a few artists, authors and workshop leaders, a former scientist and now an "energy consultant," a store manager, a bartender, an "intergalactic communicator," a naturalist, and a wilderness guide. He posed each of them the questions: "What drew you to Sedona? How has Sedona affected you? and Why do you think Sedona is such a mysterious place?" In their responses, nearly all mention Sedona's "energy" or its "vortexes"; eleven make reference to UFOs or extraterrestrials, ten to Native Americans (three of whom describe being Native American in past lives); nine describe feeling drawn or being directed to Sedona by some sort of spiritual guidance; nine describe Sedona as a place of learning, transformation, and great changes; eight mention a feeling of recognition or of "coming home" upon their arrival; eight draw on the discourse of "Light" or "Light and Love."

30. Among many apocryphal stories I heard was that of a film crew which had shot in the "Saddle Rock" area of the "Airport vortex" for twelve straight hours, and when they were finished, their batteries were still entirely charged up (David, int.). Another story told of a man who had had something implanted in his head by extraterrestrials. For ten years he was supposedly in contact with them, after which the device was taken out, leaving him confused and "a mess." At the time he was in contact, he had been "absolutely accurate" in his predictions, being able to say when a group of UFOs would come around, and others confirmed that, sure enough, they did (Keller, int.). A third, and less fantastic, story was that about the old ECKankar house on Wings of Wind point, over-

looking the Oak Creek Canyon west of Sedona. This house had once belonged to Helen Frye, and afterward incurred a history of power struggles; it was thought to be located at an ideal "lift-off point" for astral traveling (which ECKankar is known for). According to a real estate agent, the house was almost sold recently—to an Arabian princess, according to this account—but the buyer died in a plane crash and the deal was never consummated.

31. Many New Agers seem to believe that a secret military base is located underground somewhere in the Secret Canyon area. Dannelley (1993:59–61), however, helpfully points out that an actual army and National Guard base and "Navajo Weapons Depot" are located just a few miles north of Secret Canyon. Dark green helicopters fly there on regular routine training or supply flights, and even occasional practice flights at night using night-vision equipment. They make no effort to avoid being seen, and occasionally detour into the area for sightseeing, or to refuel at Sedona Airport.

32. In practice, to an outsider, such activity can appear haphazard and poorly coordinated. The 12:12 celebration at Cathedral Rock, for instance—the best-advertised and most public of several events occurring at various local sites that day—took shape as about 120 people slowly assembled into concentric circles around a metal pyramid. We were then led in chanting and in visualizing tetrahedrons of light connecting Sedona with other planetary grid points; heard a tape of the event's main organizer, who was supposed to be doing something similar at the Great Pyramid in Giza at the time; and listened to local and visiting speakers talk of Light-beings, Earth spirits, the Goddess, the Lord, Christ consciousness, Ascension, and the opening of other dimensions. After a few more chants of "Love . . . " and "Aloha . . . ," the event ended as breezily as it began, with people drifting into private conversations and small group activities, or wandering on elsewhere.

33. I have relied here primarily on Khera's (1978), Barnett's (1968), Gifford's (1933, 1936), and N. Mann's (1991) accounts of Indian legends.

34. As recounted in the previous chapter, the Yavapai-Apache were pressured out of the Verde Valley by General Crook's offensive in the 1870s, and finally by the March of Tears, a forced mass relocation of 1,400 Yavapai-Apaches to the San Carlos Reservation over 180 miles of bad terrain in the middle of winter, during which over a hundred died from freezing and other causes. By 1900 some Yavapai-Apaches were given permission by the federal government to return to the Verde Valley and the Sedona region (mainly because coal miners and dam builders wanted their land at San Carlos). Many did, but were not given enough land to cultivate. They adapted by working on farms, ranching, constructing roads, mining for copper and smelting in Clarkdale; but the closure of mines in the 1930s and 1940s forced most of them back onto reservations near Camp Verde. Today most Yavapai-Apaches live on or near four small reservations at Camp Verde, Middle Verde, Clarkdale, and Fort McDowell. Of the 1,200 Yavapai-Apaches at Camp Verde, about half live on the reservation. Tourism (their assets include a Best Western hotel) and a gambling casino have, in the last decade, placed them in an increasingly important economic position in the area. Another hundred-plus Yavapais live at the Yavapai-Prescott reservation, which includes an industrial park, a commercial park, a hotel complex, a casino (which opened in 1994), and a state-of-the-art tribal museum-in-the-making (Trimble 1993:242–44).

35. Hopi prophecy is a complex matter whose unraveling reveals some deep divisions among the Hopi. The non-Native counterculture of hippies, radical environmentalists, and New Agers has, in the past, drawn much inspiration from the Hopi prophecies as presented by Traditionalist Hopi leaders like Dan Qötshongva (Katchongva), David Monongye, and, until his death in 1999, Thomas Banyacya (Banyancya). The Hopi tribal council, which represents about half the Hopi villages, has, on the other hand, frequently derided those same leaders and challenged their claims to represent Hopi prophecy. Divisions have emerged on such contentious issues as the Navajo-Hopi land dispute, with Traditionalist Hopis coming out in defense of the several hundred Navajos who were to be resettled from land that the Hopi Tribal Council, in tandem with

Peabody Coal Company, opted to develop. A well-researched account of this dispute is presented in Feher-Elston 1988, though a reader might wish to supplement it with a view more sympathetic to the Navajo side (e.g., Benedek 1992).

Armin Geertz's *The Invention of Prophecy* (1994) provides a masterful analysis of Hopi prophecy and its many uses within the Hopi community, and should be required reading for anyone interested in the topic. Though a non-Hopi, Geertz's years of work alongside the Hopis has earned him respect among Hopis. Some of the implications of his analysis, however, particularly his critical debunking of the Traditionalist movement and his thrashing of their New Age allies and followers, remain, to my mind, unfairly biased. In the end, Geertz's social-constructionist tactics are directed against the critics of industrial society—"hippies and New Age practitioners" with their "voraciously apocalyptic vanities" (294) and "spiritual imperialism" (307)—which leads him to conclude with a trite dismissal of the global ecological crisis (338–39). His scholarship also raises questions about the extent to which a scholar, and by definition an outsider, should take sides within his subject community's internal politics. A different perspective on Hopi prophecy is presented by Clemmer (1995) in *American Indian Quarterly*. Geertz criticizes Clemmer's work as "highly ideological," noting that the latter was an activist for the Traditionalist movement (Geertz 1994).

36. At least one well-known Hopi, Oswald White Bear Fredericks, an artist of the Hopi Bear Clan and Frank Waters's collaborator on his highly influential, but controversial, *Book of the Hopi*, still lived in Sedona in the mid-1990s.

37. Some Hopis, for instance, have sought out white followers, and through their popularization of Hopi prophecy, have brought about the kind of attention more "progressive" Hopis disdain. A meeting of Hopi and Navajo elders with visiting Tibetan lamas, which took place in Sedona in December of 1994, was intended, in part, to generate dialogue between these cultural traditions and their non-Native audience. The Hopi spokesman present, however, lamented the antitraditional views of many of his kin. The Hopi Cultural Preservation Office, meanwhile, has been clear in expressing the problems arising from New Age use of Hopi cultural sites (e.g., Jenkins et al. 1996). Incidentally, the Cultural Preservation Office kindly refused to give me any information about their own claims or interests in the red rock area, leaving me dependent on secondhand information from archaeologists and written sources. A former tribal chairman of the Yavapai-Apache tribe at Camp Verde expressed to me a similarly ambivalent view about New Agers, though acknowledging their apparent sincerity; and was more generously forthcoming about Apache traditions, such as their medicine wheel and creation stories (Smith, int.).

38. Those who have been criticized for cultural appropriation tend to fall into several distinct categories: (1) Natives who teach non-Natives, often for money; these include Sun Bear, Ed "Eagle Man" McGaa, Hyemeyohsts Storm, Brooke Medicine Eagle, Wallace Black Elk, Grace Spotted Elk, Rolling Thunder, Harley Swiftdeer, Dhyani Ywahoo, and Oshinnah Fast Wolf; (2) non-Native teachers who have been given some traditional teachings, and who proceed to "take up the pipe" and "set up shop," or to make their careers out of their supposed authority; these include popular New Age authors like Lynn Andrews, Ruth Beebe Hill, Mary Summer Rain, Marlo Morgan, and "Native authorities" like Jamake Highwater; and (3) less well known Natives who teach non-Natives out of sheer economic, and perhaps cultural, desperation. Vine Deloria writes, "How can there be so *many* medicine people who have been commissioned to hold ceremonies for non-Indians while their own people suffer without religious ministrations?" The answer, he asserts, is that Indians in "the 'New Age' circuit" have devised the "clever" title of "pipe carriers"—"an office that has rather hazy historical and cultural antecedents. No definition is ever given of the exact duties of the pipe carrier except that he or she can perform all the ceremonies that a shaman can perform without being called to account when nothing happens. . . . Now everyone from movie stars to gas station attendants has claimed to be an authorized pipe carrier" (1994:43; italics in original). Other critiques of New Age cultural appropriation include Hobson 1978;

A. Smith 1991; Rose 1992; Churchill 1992, 1994; Donaldson 1999; and articles in *Wassaja* 2 (1974): 7.

In response to such criticisms, McGaa, introducing his book *Rainbow Tribe: Ordinary People Journeying on the Red Road* (1992:ix), defends himself with the argument that "[t]oo many of the red-way people (North American Indians) are standing idly by complaining and not realizing that they can be of tremendous assistance to many across the planet. . . . We all perish together if we lose this earth to overheating, pollution, greed, and overpopulation." Some non-Natives also argue, with poet and deep ecologist Gary Snyder, that "Spiritual knowledge belongs to all humanity equally. Given the state of the world today, we all have not only the right but the obligation to pursue all forms of spiritual insight" (cited in Churchill 1992:192). Some neoshamans, eco-ritualists, and Men's Movement and "wild woman movement" (Estes 1992) activists, have tried to recover shamanic and nativistic practices—such as chanting, vision quests, the use of drums, gourd rattles, feathers, pipes, and talking staffs—that are less culturally specific and, one could argue, therefore more appropriate to white Westerners. See, for example, LaChappelle 1988; C. Matthews 1995; and Glendinning 1995.

In practice, though, such events as the World Unity Festival, a "rainbow festival" held in August 1994 on national forest land near Flagstaff, can easily demonstrate an insensitivity to Native concerns even among those who profess the greatest respect for Native spiritual traditions. The World Unity Festival proved to be an organizational fiasco and embarrassment which angered some Natives when its organizers decided to move the festival's location from national forest land to Hopi-Navajo disputed lands without asking the Hopi tribal council for permission. The festival billed itself as featuring "international food and crafts, [the] world's largest drum circle, sacred sciences . . . healing arts village, tibetan [*sic*] sand painting, laser and light show," and guests including Richie Havens, Jefferson Starship, Big Brother and the Holding Company (flashbacks of the 1960s!), and Babatunde Olatunji. Both the Hopi and Havasupai tribes had protested the event's being held on national forest land in the vicinity of their traditional cultural sites. (Cf. Schill 1994a:B1).

39. Constance Cumbey's 1983 book *The Hidden Dangers of the Rainbow* first alerted evangelical and fundamentalist Christians to the "dangers" of the "New Age Movement." Drawing on Marilyn Ferguson's "Aquarian conspiracy" image, Cumbey developed a full-fledged conspiracy theory, according to which all things New Age, including several trends within Christianity itself, as well as ecological movements and international peace efforts, were part of a grand design, masterminded by Satan himself, to subvert Christianity and take over the world. The Plan, as she called it, was supposedly promulgated by Theosophists, Alice Bailey followers, H. G. Wells and his "Open Conspiracy," Nazis, and an assortment of others. Cumbey's alarmist claims were later rejected by most Christian apologists (e.g., E. Miller 1989); but in the mid-1980s they caused a great stir within evangelical circles (Miller 1989:193). More carefully reasoned, semischolarly critiques were eventually formulated by Groothuis (1986, 1988), Chandler (1988), E. Miller (1989), Martin (1989), and the Berkeley-based Spiritual Counterfeits Project (Hoyt 1987); these authors have tended to expose the wilder claims of popular New Agers and offer a reasoned, if faith-based, critique of New Agers' pantheism, monism, syncretism, and eclecticism.

In some ways, the New Age movement has served as an easy scapegoat for conservative Christians' disappointment with an increasingly pluralistic (and culturally relativist) America. The demonization of the New Age movement (frequently abbreviated NAM in evangelical writings) has had some wider social repercussions. In a report entitled "Attacks on the Freedom to Learn, 1992–1993," the U. S. anticensorship organization People for the American Way listed 347 attempts at censorship reported in forty-four states during a single school year. Fifty-one of these listed "New Age religion" or "New Age techniques" as the reason for the challenge. Among the "New Age" techniques criticized by such groups as Citizens for Excellence in Education (CEE) or Focus on the Family are relaxation, meditation, affirmation, visualization, and journal-

keeping, as well as such "New Age beliefs" as the interconnectedness of life, global-
ism, and a person's ability to make decisions without reference to the Bible (Willeford
1993:78–79; and see Marzano 1993).

40. A public debate was held in 1989 between anti–New Age crusader Constance
Cumbey and a representative of the New Age community, transpersonal psychiatrist
Dr. Stanley Zurawski (though many from the New Age community were unhappy with
being represented by any single person). Another attempt to mediate the antagonism
between the two camps was Pete Sanders's efforts, during his term as president of the
Center for the New Age, to initiate outreach and interaction between religious groups,
including around a food drive for Somalia. For a variety of reasons these efforts seemed
to fail, at least in the short term.

41. The war metaphor is prominent in the evangelical community. D'Antonio quotes
an assistant pastor at Sedona Community Church as saying, "We view people in the
New Age as prisoners of war in Satan's camp" (1992:396). My discussions with staff at
Harvesters' Christian Fellowship bookstore conveyed a sense of paranoia about the New
Age movement that had seemingly overtaken the town.

42. Disturbing parallels could be drawn between characters in the novel and actual
Sedonans. In the novel, for instance, a New Age bookstore owner channels, and is ultimately possessed by, an Aztec goddess who directs her "daughters" "all around the
globe" to "sacrifice" at the "sacred sites," which include the four best known of Sedona's
vortexes. The bookstore owner's name is rather similar to that of an actual bookstore
owner in Sedona, the authors verging perilously close to publishing slander and hate
literature. Understandably, many local booksellers have declined to sell the book. I saw
it prominently displayed only at the centrally located Book Worm in uptown Sedona
(though, as far as I could tell, this was for commercial reasons) and at the Harvesters'
Christian Fellowship Bookstore in West Sedona. The book was one of a few recom-
mended to me by the salesperson at Harvesters' when I asked about books related to
Sedona (after introducing myself as a researcher on perceptions of landscape).

Sedona Storm follows in the tradition begun by Frank Peretti, whose novel *This Present Darkness* (1986) had sold over a million copies within six years and was rumored to
be under consideration for a major motion picture (Hexham 1992:156). The novel,
which Christian religion scholar Irving Hexham describes as "surrealist" and "sanctified
Stephen King," portrays the "spiritual warfare" that ensues in a small American town
when two journalists and a local fundamentalist minister discover a plot by a vast New
Age conspiracy to control the world. Interestingly, a comparative analysis of Christian
and New Age literature conducted by Hexham showed that "while the average New
Age book required a 'grade 14' reading level, Christian books were written at 'grade 9'
level" (1992:161). In the end, various fundamentalist "bogey men," including feminism, secular higher education, skeptical journalists, psychology, Eastern mysticism,
witchcraft, and paganism, are all "exposed" as parts of a global conspiracy of evil. Hexham notes that this type of literature has created "new social boundaries for many evangelical Christians who escaped from a restrictive fundamentalism during the 1970s and
1980s," thereby replacing "older social taboos like the cinema, makeup, and smoking as
the criteria used to identify 'true' from 'false' Christians by many evangelical church
members" (156). See Lewis 1996a for another analysis of Peretti's fiction. Other works
in this genre include Peretti's *Piercing the Darkness* and Roger Elwood's *The Christen-
ing* and *Angelwalk*.

43. A week-long 1987 documentary series, *Supernatural Sedona*, produced by Phoe-
nix-based KTVK focused on the supposed "standoff" between the evangelical Christian
and New Age/metaphysical communities. As with much media coverage of New Age
activities, the series tended to fall into the category of "let's see what the weirdos are up
to." At one point in the filming of the series, Village Bible Church pastor Rev. Gardy
Cronk was asked, "Why do you think people delve into metaphysics?" His response was
long and detailed, yet, in the end, a single remark was used as a hook to end one of the
mid-week broadcasts: "There are also those oppressed and possessed by demons." The
show was later critiqued by the *Sedona Times* as well as by some in the New Age com-

munity for turning Sedona into a "carnival," focusing on unrepresentative people, and the like, in its effort to boost the station's ratings (Dame-Glerum 1987c:A1–2). A 1991 episode of CBS's *Forty-Eight Hours* ("Secrets of Sedona," March 27, 1991) presented a similarly sensationalized portrait of Sedona (G. Joseph 1991:E6).

44. New Age lore holds that an old Indian medicine wheel had been at the Boynton Canyon site for centuries. The one which was there in late 1994, of obviously recent vintage, was about three feet tall and twenty feet across.

45. This is a common critique of New Age use of the land. However, a former Yavapai-Apache tribal chairman (Smith, int.) told me that although the practice of laying out stones in wheel-like formations and using them ceremonially in the way New Agers do is a Plains tradition, medicine wheels (circles with four directions, etc.) *have* in fact been used historically as teaching devices by the Apache.

46. An up-to-date source of information on the controversy (with links to many primary documents) is the Red Rock Crossing web site, hosted by the Responsible Residents of the Red Rocks <www.redrockxing.org/4r.htm>.

47. Water quality is surprisingly poor, given the clean surface appearance of the creek. Septic tanks all along Oak Creek, and particularly human uses of the creek at Slide Rock and at Red Rock Crossing cause pollution levels which the creek's low volume of water cannot adequately clean out.

48. One particular group, a metaphysical community that has for years been based very close to Red Rock Crossing, has been "very passionate about Red Rock Crossing, but they don't get active. And it is hard—it's hard on your spiritual well-being to get involved in these [issues], because you meet so many angry people, and it is very easy to become angry within yourself" (Blake, int). Interestingly, Blake's own spiritual orientation, which she calls "in some ways a very traditional Christian" one, plays an important role in her activism. In contrast to other local Christians, Blake is not threatened by religious differences, but focuses instead on commonalities between her beliefs and those of New Agers. On Red Rock Crossing and its surroundings, she says, "This is so spiritual for me—this spot, and this whole area. Especially the red rock area—there's a powerful spirituality here." She also related to me how she has tried to feel the energy of vortexes, even standing at the specific spot at the Airport Mesa where the vortex is said to be, but was unable to feel any distinct energy. "But really," she added, "I'm just so entranced with this whole place that I don't really need a vortex" (int.).

49. For all its mythologizing of the red rock landscape, it is a rare event when *Sedona: Journal of Emergence* actually urges its readers to do something (in this "third dimension" of material reality) about a social or environmental issue. When it does, though, it is clear about it. For instance, the April 1995 issue featured a four-page insert at the beginning of the issue, in red ink, no less, under the caption "Shadow Government of Planet Earth Planning to Mine Uranium under the Hopi Reservation." Arguing that this mining would be a violation of Mother Earth, two of the magazine's channeled "entities" urged readers to write their congressional representatives and to demonstrate against the mining. Hopis, on the other hand, are themselves sharply divided on the matter. In a similar situation, when the Yavapai-Apaches were attempting to fight off a development in Boynton Canyon (Enchantment Resort), according to former Apache tribal chairman Vincent Randall, "none of those New Age people were there to help us" (D'Antonio 1992:47).

50. A more visionary set of transportation alternatives has been developed by a group of forward-looking but pragmatic idealists who realize the need for some way of reducing traffic flow through downtown Sedona. The so-called Pathways proposal and local architects the Design Group envisioned a transportation system which included bicycle paths, park-and-ride lots, auto-free zones, a public transit shuttle loop, and a low-water bridge at Red Rock Crossing (to be used only by pedestrians, cyclists, the shuttle, and service and emergency vehicles, and therefore requiring only minimum development of new infrastructure at the site). Red Rock Pathways proponents have acted alongside the conservation-minded Responsible Residents of the Red Rocks, the Sedona-Verde Valley chapter of the Sierra Club, Keep Sedona Beautiful, and others (on the

Citizens' Alternate Route Task Force) to influence the decision-making process; but progress is slow, and always uphill.

8. PRACTICES OF PLACE

1. By *magical* I mean, roughly, the view "that mind affects matter, and that in special circumstances, like ritual, the trained imagination can alter the physical world" (Luhrmann 1989:7); and that this effect on the physical world occurs by "supernatural" means or through channels unrecognized by science—for instance, through "action at a distance" or the "sympathy" of a particular object or person with another object separated from it in space or time. A problem with this definition, however, is that it relies on scientific and commonsense notions specifying what would qualify as supernatural, and also on a clearly set out distinction between *mind* and *matter*, though such boundaries are rather elusive in the real world of experience. A subsidiary and less common definition of magic, which draws on the "high magic" or *magia* of the Renaissance and which is held by many ritual magicians today, sees magic as a view of the world which emphasizes *participation* in that world (facilitated by interrelationships and correspondences which are not necessarily recognized by science) rather than linear *causality*. For a few influential discussions of the relationships between science, rationality, and magic, see Tambiah 1990; O'Keefe 1983; and Luhrmann 1989 (345–56).

2. One could, for instance, analyze the social psychology of New Age believers and find (as I have) that a high proportion of them consists of women who have left behind personal or domestic situations that were confining, unsatisfactory, or even abusive in some way. My observations of this remain impressionistic, as they were not a focus of my research, but my suspicion is that such an analysis would complement, rather than contradict, my own theses. On the social psychology of the New Age movement, see especially Heelas 1996.

3. In Luhrmann's account, interpretive drift is characterized by systematic changes in one's structure of interpretation; experiential changes, involving "new phenomenological experiences, a vivid imaginative engagement, a world awash with personally powerful symbolism"; and rationalizations which solidify the new interpretive framework. "Intellectual and experiential changes shift in tandem, a ragged co-evolution of intellectual habits and phenomenological involvement" (1989:312–15).

4. It is equally likely that this sensation of vibration or pulsation arose as a result of the combination of environmental (dryness, altitude), psychological (expectations), and somatic (held bodily positions, fatigue from climbing) factors. It was not too different from a shaking or vibrating sensation which I have felt under numerous other circumstances, and which I have never thought to be more (or less) than natural.

5. My experiences at specific sites have not normally been sufficiently intense to seem to me to be "channeled messages" from "external" sources. In contrast, some of my more vivid and lucid dreams (not to mention psychedelic experiences) *have* felt as if they arose from a source outside of my normal sense of self, and I have no qualms about calling them transpersonal. But I am not sure that there is an obvious threshold between the merely imagined and the genuinely transpersonal. In any case, I have sometimes waived these categories and intentionally blurred the boundaries in order to test the experiential possibilities of a given situation.

6. If this sounds like a hypothesis about reality—an interactive and co-constructive view according to which identities and relations are produced and reproduced in an ongoing and dynamic "tangled web" of self and world, selves and others, or "self-imagination-culture-world intertwining"—then I would have to admit that it is my own hypothesis, which I began with, though in a less developed form, and which I have "confirmed" over the course of my investigation here. It is, of course, one account among others, and I can hardly appeal to "the evidence" to make my case for it (if only because what counts as evidence is rather slippery and elusive here). I can only hope to successfully convey its greater adequacy in accounting for the social spatialization/sacralization of landscapes, when compared to previous scholarly models of sacred space. In

a sense, this entire book is an extended argument for a slippery, muddy, densely entangled, interactive, and hermeneutic view of the world. I use these metaphors (slippery, muddy, entangled) in part as a way of facilitating, or at least rendering more plausible, something like the very process of interpretive drift that I have been describing. At the same time, by emphasizing the interpretive nature of what humans do to make sense of the world—by emphasizing the *process* of interpretation itself rather than arguing for the superiority of any specific interpretations—my hope is to encourage greater interpretive flexibility and reflexivity.

7. For instance, in a systematic, collaborative international research effort published as *Gaia: An Atlas of Planet Management* (Myers 1984), the two conflicting tendencies—of anthropocentric global resourcism and of Gaian organicism—are subsumed into a view that sees humanity as rising to the level of manager and arbiter over the entire earth. (The 1988 Brundtland Commission Report, *Our Common Future*, and the 1991 Rio Summit have provided high-profile forums for this growing international discourse of global resource management, though the application of sustainability ideals has been selective at best.) As if in response to this appropriation of his ideas, James Lovelock has written that imagining that such "good stewardship or planetary management" could alleviate the increasing human impact on the earth is "the greatest of our errors" (1992:14). "We cannot manage the Earth," he concludes, "but we can usefully regulate our own lives and our human institutions," by, for instance, reducing our dependence on what Lovelock calls the "three Cs"—cars, cattle, and chainsaws (15).

8. For a critical perspective on environmental managerialism, or "environmental governmentality," see Luke (1995, 1997, 1999). In Luke's Foucauldian perspective, it is only a short step from the environmental "worldwatching" of Lester Brown's World Watch Institute (or the desires infusing many New Age geomancers, though Luke does not mention their work specifically) to the panoptical surveillance technologies of a corporate-controlled "big brother."

9. Proteus was the shape-shifting Greek god dwelling in the sea, whose mutability he mimicked "in his remarkable capacity to change himself into myriad shapes and forms—a lion, panther, swine, serpent, or, if desperate, the contour of water or fire—in order to avoid those who would press him to demonstrate his prophetic powers." As Keith Thompson puts it in his study of the UFO phenomenon, we are all "participants in the social construction of an essentially protean reality moment by moment" (1991:17–19).

10. Different things "count" as significant or relevant data within different interpretive traditions. For instance, those phenomena which seem inexplicable within the interpretive tradition of science—UFO reports and abduction experiences, Marian apparitions, poltergeists, instances of psychic surgery, stigmatism, and so on—are customarily dismissed as anomalies. I have found my own experience of such a scientifically "anomalous" phenomenon deeply instructive, however. The phenomenon was that of "kundalini awakening" (the spontaneous discharge of currents of psychophysical energy in or coextensive with one's physical body), which began to occur for me at the age of about seventeen or eighteen. At times uncontrollable, overpowering, and accompanied by visions and other sensations, this phenomenon presented me with a troubling hermeneutic dilemma, since I knew nothing about what was going on. In time, I found out that there is in fact a voluminous literature on kundalini and the human body's "subtle energy system" in the Indian and Tibetan yogic traditions (where they are clearly *not* considered anomalous). At the time, however, my own interpretive resources suggested a different reading—that of "possession" (by some entity, whether demonic, divine, or neutral but powerful)—and science offered no satisfying alternative explanation. In other words, the interpretive resources at my disposal were incapable of satisfactorily accounting for the experience, which to me was a distinctly physical event that occurred on its own, without conscious prompting on my part. As these experiences, initially at least, were solitary and quite unexpected, only their later interpretation could in any way be called socially constructed.

11. Jürgen Habermas's (1984) carefully developed model of communicative rational-

ity provides some guidance for such a democratic politics of social dialogue. For Habermas, a society or collective is considered communicatively rational "to the extent that its interactions are egalitarian, uncoerced, competent, and free from delusion, deception, power, and strategy" (paraphrased by Dryzek 1995:106). Habermas's framework is limited in its applicability to the interaction between humans and the nonhuman world; Dryzek (1995), and in some ways van Buren (1995) and S. Vogel (1997), have insightfully attempted to expand it beyond its exclusively anthropocentric focus. Poststructuralists, some feminists, and others have also critiqued Habermas's universalism and his limited ability to grapple with radical cultural difference. Deconstructive ethics (e.g., Cornell 1992; Caputo 1993) and Bakhtinian dialogics (e.g., Todorov 1984; Gardiner 1992) provide crucial insights complementing a Habermasian approach to communicative ethics, though a working through of their differences is beyond the scope of this book.

12. Alexander, Ishikawa, and Silverstein (1977) and Hough (1995) present an array of arguments and proposals for redesigning homes, communities, and cities along more environmentally sensitive lines. The important thing, as Weston (1995) argues, is to incrementally expand the opportunities for interaction and reciprocity between humans and the rest of nature.

13. For instance, the Royal Commission on the Future of the Toronto Waterfront applied a loosely bioregional, ecosystem approach in its series of much lauded (if not so widely applied) reports with recommendations for local and regional revitalization (e.g., Royal Commission, *Regeneration: Toronto's Waterfront and the Sustainable City. Final Report*, 1992).

14. Secular traditions have their sacred sites as well (e.g., Westminster Abbey, Mount Rushmore, the Lenin Mausoleum, Graceland). Sites which provide such "symbolic coherence" can also represent relations *between* traditions, as, for instance, the United Nations (and their various symbols and icons) represent peaceful coexistence or dynamic unity and harmony between nations. Peaceful coexistence between the human and *non*human worlds may be represented in certain sites; in North America, such places as Niagara Falls, Yosemite, or Yellowstone could be understood as symbolically cohering stand-ins (though not this alone) for the power of nonhuman nature.

15. Italian philosopher Gianni Vattimo (1988) advocates the notion of "weak thought" (*il pensiero debole*), a form of hermeneutics which is constantly reminding itself of its limits. Other "deconstructive ethicists," such as Caputo (1987, 1993) and Cornell (1992), both inspired by the philosophy of Jacques Derrida, have argued for a similar approach—a hermeneutics which is responsive to the world, but which undercuts its own system-building and interpretation-imposing tendencies through a self-deconstructive reflexivity.

16. On the struggle for recognition of Native claims to sacred lands, see Michaelson 1986, 1995; Jaimes 1992; Carmichael, Hubert, Reeves, and Schanche 1994; Hornborg 1994; Kelley and Francis 1994.

BIBLIOGRAPHY

GENERAL REFERENCES

Aberly, Doug, ed. 1993. *Boundaries of Home: Mapping for Empowerment*. Philadelphia: New Society.

Abraham, Ralph. 1994. *Chaos, Gaia, Eros: A Chaos Pioneer Uncovers the Three Great Streams of History*. San Francisco: HarperSanFrancisco.

Abram, David. 1996. *The Spell of the Sensuous: Perception and Language in a More-than-Human World*. New York: Pantheon Books.

Abrams, Lesley. 1996. *Anglo-Saxon Glastonbury: Church and Endowment*. Studies in Anglo-Saxon History, 8. Woodbridge: Boydell Press.

Abrams, Lesley, and James P. Carley, eds. 1991. *The Archaeology and History of Glastonbury Abbey: Essays in Honour of the Ninetieth Birthday of C. A. Ralegh Radford*. Woodbridge, Suffolk: Boydell Press.

Adler, Margot. 1986. *Drawing Down the Moon: Witches, Druids, Goddess-Worshippers, and Other Pagans in America Today*. Rev. ed. Boston: Beacon Press.

Aitchison, Stewart. 1992. *Red Rock—Sacred Mountain: The Canyons and Peaks from Sedona to Flagstaff*. Stillwater, Minn.: Voyageur Press.

———. 1994. "Natural History, Archaeology, and the Environment." In Sedona Forum, *Building Partnerships with the Forest Service* (Sedona Forum X Background Report), ed. W. Vannette et al. Flagstaff: Northern Arizona University/Sedona Academy.

Albanese, Catherine L. 1990. *Nature Religion in America: From the Algonkian Indians to the New Age*. Chicago: University of Chicago Press.

———. 1993. "Fisher Kings and Public Places: The Old New Age in the 1990s." *Annals of the American Academy of Political and Social Science* 527 (May): 131–43.

Alexander, Christopher, Sara Ishikawa, and Murray Silverstein. 1977. *A Pattern Language: Towns, Buildings, Construction*. New York: Oxford University Press.

Alexander, Donald. 1990. "Bioregionalism: Science or Sensibility?" *Environmental Ethics* 12.

Allaby, Michael. 1989. *Guide to Gaia*. London: Optima.

Alternative News Digest. 1988a. *Stonehenge '88: News Cuttings*. Supplement. Glastonbury: Unique Publications.

———. 1988b. Stonehenge Special Issue (September). Glastonbury: Unique Publications.

Anders, Jentri. 1990. *Beyond Counterculture: The Community of Mateel*. Pullman: Washington State University Press.

Anderson, Kay, and Fay Gale, eds. 1992. *Inventing Places: Studies in Cultural Geography*. Sydney: Longman Cheshire.

Anderson, Walter T. 1987. *To Govern Evolution: Further Adventures of the Political Animal*. Boston: Harcourt Brace Jovanovich.

Anderson, William, and Clive Hicks. 1990. *Green Man: Archetype of Our Oneness with the Earth*. London: HarperCollins.

Andrus, Van, Christopher Plant, Judith Plant, and Eleanor Wright, eds. 1990. *Home! A Bioregional Reader*. Philadelphia: New Society Publishers.

Anthony, D. 1995. "Nazi and Eco-Feminist Prehistories: Ideology and Empiricism in Indo-European Archaeology." In *The Nationalism, Politics, and Practice of Archaeology*, ed. P. Kohl and C. Fawcett. Cambridge: Cambridge University Press.

Appadurai, Arjun. 1990. "Disjuncture and Difference in the Global Cultural Economy." *Public Culture* 2 (2): 1–24.

Argüelles, José. 1987. *The Mayan Factor: Path beyond Technology*. Santa Fe: Bear.

———. 1988. *Earth Ascending*. Santa Fe: Bear.

Ashe, Geoffrey. 1973 [1957]. *King Arthur's Avalon: The Story of Glastonbury*. London: Collins.

———. 1982. *Avalonian Quest*. London: Fontana.

———. 1990. *Mythology of the British Isles*. London: Methuen.

———. 1997. "Magical Glastonbury." <http://206.66.98.16/history/glaston1.html>. Britannia Internet Magazine <http://www.britannia.com>.

———, ed. 1971. *The Quest for Arthur's Britain*. London: Paladin/Grafton Books.

Ashe, Geoffrey, Michael Eavis, Steve Hillage, et al. 1979. *Glastonbury Fayre 1979*. Booklet. N.p.

Aston, Michael, ed. 1988. *Aspects of the Medieval Landscape of Somerset: Contributions to the Landscape History of the County*. Bridgwater, Somerset: Somerset County Council.

Aune, Michael J. 1998. "Anatomy of the New Land Rush." <www.savelongcanyon.org/new-land-rush.htm>. Accessed August 2000.

Aveni, Anthony F. 1989. *World Archaeoastronomy*. New York: Cambridge University Press.

Bachelard, Gaston. 1987. *On Poetic Imagination and Reverie*. Translated by C. Gaudin. Dallas: Spring.

Baer, Randall N. 1989. *(For the First Time Ever . . . A Former Top New Age Leader Takes You on a Dramatic Journey) Inside the New Age Nightmare*. Lafayette, La.: Huntington House.

Baer, Randall N., and Vicki V. Baer. 1984. *Windows of Light: Quartz Crystals and Self-Transformation*. San Francisco: Harper and Row.

———. 1987. *The Crystal Connection: A Guidebook for Personal and Planetary Ascension*. San Francisco: Harper and Row.

Bailey, Lee W., and Jenny Yates, eds. 1996. *The Near Death Experience: A Reader*. New York: Routledge, 1996.

Bailey, Richard N., Eric Cambridge, and H. Denis Briggs. 1988. *Dowsing and Church Archaeology*. Wimborne, U.K.: Intercept.

Baisden, Gregory. 1996. "Close Encounters of an Imaginal Kind: Are Aliens and Angels Guiding Us into the Third Millennium?" *Magical Blend* 48.

Banks, Leo W. 1991. "U. S. Forest Service in Arizona Is Stuck between a Rock and Religious Freedom; Dispute Is over Sacred Symbols Set Up on Public Land." *Los Angeles Times*, April 20: A24.

Barker, Eileen. 1989. *New Religious Movements: A Practical Introduction*. London: Her Majesty's Stationery Office.

Barnett, Franklin. 1968. *Viola Chimulla: The Indian Chieftess*. Prescott: Yavapai-Prescott Tribe.

Bartholomeusz, Tessa. 1998. "Spiritual Wealth and Neo-Colonialism." *Journal of Ecumenical Studies* 35 (1) (Winter).

Bartholomew, Alick, ed. 1991. *Crop Circles—Harbingers of World Change*. Bath, U.K.: Gateway Books.

Barwise, J., and J. Perry. 1983. *Situations and Attitudes*. Cambridge, Mass.: MIT Press.

Basil, Robert, ed. 1988. *Not Necessarily the New Age: Critical Essays*. Buffalo: Prometheus Books.

Baudrillard, Jean. 1983. *Simulations*. New York: Semiotext(e).

BBC. n.d. "Everyman" television special on Glastonbury. Videocassette; private copy.

Becker, William S., and Bethe Hagens. 1991. "The Rings of Gaia." In *The Power of Place*, ed. J. Swan, 257–79. Wheaton, Ill.: Quest/Theosophical Publishing House.

Bednarowski, Mary F. 1989. *New Religions and the Theological Imagination in America*. Bloomington: Indiana University Press.

Bell, Daniel. 1976. *The Cultural Contradictions of Capitalism*. New York: Basic Books.

Bender, Barbara. 1992. "Theorizing Landscape, and the Prehistoric Landscapes of Stonehenge." *Man* 27: 735–55.

———. 1998. *Stonehenge: Making Space*. Oxford: Berg.

———, ed. 1993. *Landscape: Politics and Perspectives*. Oxford: Berg.

Bender, Barbara, et al. 1994. *Stonehenge*. Traveling exhibition, on view at 1994 Glastonbury Festival, Pilton, Somerset.

Benedek, Emily. 1992. *The Wind Won't Know Me: A History of the Navajo-Hopi Land Dispute*. New York: Knopf.

Benham, Patrick. 1993. *The Avalonians*. Glastonbury: Gothic Image.

Bennett, John G. 1966 [1961]. *The Dramatic Universe*. London: Hodder and Stoughton.

Bensinger, Charles. 1988. *Chaco Journey: Remembrance and Awakening*. Santa Fe: Timewindow.

Benterrak, Krim, Stephen Muecke, and Paddy Roe. 1984. *Reading the Country: Introduction to Nomadology*. Fremantle, Australia: Fremantle Arts Centre Press.

Bentov, Itzhak. 1979. *Stalking the Wild Pendulum*. New York: Bantam Books.

Berg, Peter, ed. 1978. *Reinhabiting a Separate Country: A Bioregional Anthology of Northern California*. San Francisco: Planet Drum Foundation.

Berger, John. 1972. *Ways of Seeing*. Harmondsworth: Penguin.

Berger, Peter, Brigitte Berger, and Hansfried Kellner. 1974. *The Homeless Mind*. Harmondsworth, Middlesex: Penguin.

Berman, Marshall. 1976. *All That Is Solid Melts into Air: The Experience of Modernity*. London: Verso.

Berman, Morris. 1984. *The Reenchantment of the World*. New York: Bantam/Cornell University Press.

———. 1989. *Coming to Our Senses: Mind and Body in the History of Western Culture*. New York: Simon and Schuster.

Berry, Thomas. 1988. *The Dream of the Earth*. San Francisco: Sierra Club Books.

Bertens, Hans. 1995. *The Idea of the Postmodern*. London: Routledge.

Bettey, Joseph. 1988. "From the Norman Conquest to the Reformation." In *Aspects of the Medieval Landscape of Somerset*, ed. M. Aston, 55–66. Bridgwater, Somerset: Somerset County Council.

Betz, Hans-Dieter. 1995. "Unconventional Water Detection: Field Test of the Dowsing Technique in Dry Zones," parts 1 and 2. *Journal of Scientific Exploration* 9 (1) and 9 (2). <http://www.jse.com/betz_toc.html>.

Bhardwaj, S. M., and G. Rinschede, eds. 1988. *Pilgrimage in World Religions*. Geographia Religionum. Berlin: Dietrich Reimer Verlag.

Biehl, Janet. 1991. *Rethinking Ecofeminist Politics*. Boston: South End Press.

Bigwood, Carol. 1993. *Earth Muse: Feminism, Nature, and Art*. Philadelphia: Temple University Press.

Birch, Thomas H. 1995. "The Incarceration of Wildness: Wilderness Areas as Prisons." In *Postmodern Environmental Ethics*, ed. M. Oelschlaeger, 137–61. Albany: State University of New York Press.

Bird, Elizabeth Ann R. 1987. "The Social Construction of Nature: Theoretical Approaches to the History of Environmental Problems." *Environmental Review* 11 (Winter): 255–64.

Bishop, James, Jr. 1987. "Bring Them Back!" *Sedona Times*, August 26.

———. 1991. "The Rise of New Gods and Goddesses on Earth: Across the United States Seminars Are Popping Out Like Wildflowers on the Mogollon Rim." *Arizona Republic*, May 5: C5.

Bloom, William, ed. 1991. *The New Age: An Anthology of Essential Writings*. London: Rider.

————. 1992. *Devas, Fairies, and Angels: A Modern Approach*. Glastonbury: Gothic Image.

Bloom, William, and Marco Pogacnik. 1985. *Ley Lines and Ecology: An Introduction*. Glastonbury: Gothic Image.

Bohm, David, and F. David Peat. 1987. *Science, Order, and Creativity*. Toronto: Bantam.

Bolen, Jean Shinoda. 1994. *Crossing to Avalon: A Woman's Midlife Pilgrimage*. San Francisco: HarperSanFrancisco.

Bond, Frederick Bligh. 1918. *The Gate of Remembrance: The Story of the Psychological Experiment which Resulted in the Discovery of the Edgar Chapel at Glastonbury*. Oxford: Blackwell.

Bonham, Neill. 1986. *This Is Glastonbury*. Glastonbury: Glastonbury Conservation Society.

Boniface, Priscilla, and Peter J. Fowler. 1993. *Heritage and Tourism in "the Global Village."* London: Routledge.

Botkin, Daniel R. 1990. *Discordant Harmonies: A New Ecology for the Twenty-First Century*. New York: Oxford University Press.

Bowman, Marion. 1993a. "Drawn to Glastonbury." In *Pilgrimage in Popular Culture*, ed. I. Reader and T. Walter, 29–62. London: Macmillan.

————. 1993b. "Reinventing the Celts." *Religion* 23: 147–56.

Bradley, Marion Zimmer. 1984. *The Mists of Avalon*. New York: Ballantine/Del Rey.

Bradley, Richard. 1998. *The Significance of Monuments: On the Shaping of Human Experience in Neolithic and Bronze Age Europe*. London: Routledge.

Braun, Bruce, and Noel Castree, eds. 1998. *Remaking Reality: Nature at the Millennium*. New York: Routledge.

Brennan, Martin. 1983. *The Stars and the Stones*. London: Thames and Hudson.

Brenneman, Walter L., Jr. 1985. "The Circle and the Cross: Loric and Sacred Space in the Holy Wells of Ireland." In *Dwelling, Place, and Environment: Towards a Phenomenology of Person and World*, ed. D. Seamon and R. Mugerauer, 137–58. Boston: Martinus Nijhoff.

Brenneman, Walter L., Jr., Stanley O. Yarian, and Alan M. Olson. 1982. *The Seeing Eye: Hermeneutical Phenomenology in the Study of Religion*. University Park: Pennsylvania State University Press.

Brereton, Joel P. 1987. "Sacred Space." In *The Encyclopedia of Religion*, ed.-in-chief M. Eliade, 526–35. New York: Macmillan.

Britannia. 1996a. "Glastonbury Abbey and the Development of the Legends of King Arthur and St. Joseph of Arimathea." <http://206.66.98.16/history/h9.html>: Britannia Internet Magazine, <http://www.britannia.com>.

Brown, Kenneth, Robert Croft, and Russell Lillford. 1988. "Conserving the Historic Landscape." In *Aspects of the Medieval Landscape of Somerset*, ed. M. Aston, 109–27. Taunton, Somerset: Somerset County Council.

Brown, Mick. 1993. "Milking the Pop Scene at £50 a Go." *Daily Telegraph*, June 25.

Brown, Robert H. 1993. *Sedona: Arizona's Red Rock Community*. Phoenix: Bronze Age Publishers.

Bruce, Steve. 1996. *Religion in the Modern World: From Cathedrals to Cults*. New York: Oxford University Press.

Bryant, Page. 1984. *Earth Changes Survival Handbook*. Santa Fe: Sun.

————. 1991. *Terravision: A Travelers' Guide to the Living Planet Earth*. St. Paul, Minn.: Llewellyn.

————. n.d. *The Sedona Vortices*. Cassette tape.

Bryant, Page, Robert Shapiro, et al. 1991. *Sedona Vortex Guide Book*. Sedona: Light Technology Publishing.

Buenfil, Alberto Ruz. 1991. *Rainbow Nation without Borders: Toward an Ecotopian Millennium*. Santa Fe: Bear.

Bunyard, Peter, and Edward Goldsmith, eds. 1988. *Gaia, the Thesis, the Mechanisms, and the Implications: Proceedings of the First Annual Camelford Conference on the Implications of the Gaia Hypothesis.* Camelford, Cornwall: Wadebridge Ecological Centre.

Burl, Aubrey. 1976. *The Stone Circles of the British Isles.* New Haven: Yale University Press.

———. 1979. *Prehistoric Avebury.* New Haven: Yale University Press.

———. 1981. *Rites of the Gods.* London: Dent.

Burrow, I. J. 1983. "Star-Spangled Avalon." *Popular Archaeology* 4 (8): 28–31.

Byrkit, James W. 1988. "The Palatkwapi Trail." *Plateau* 59 (4): 3–31.

———. 1992. "Land, Sky, and People: The Southwest Defined." *Journal of the Southwest* 34 (3) (Autumn 1992; special issue).

Byrkit, James W., and Bruce Hooper. 1994. "History of the Forest Service in the Red Rock Area." In Sedona Forum, *Building Partnerships with the Forest Service (Sedona Forum X Background Report),* ed. W. Vannette et al., 19–56. Flagstaff: Northern Arizona University/Sedona Academy.

Caine, Mary. n.d. *A Map of the Glastonbury Zodiac: Arthur's Original Round Table.* N.p.

Callon, Michel. 1986. "Some Elements of a Sociology of Translation: Domestication of the Scallops and the Fishermen of St Brieux Bay." In *Power, Action, and Belief: A New Sociology of Knowledge?* ed. J. Law, 196–229. London: Routledge and Kegan Paul.

Callon, Michel, and Bruno Latour. 1992. "Don't Throw the Baby Out with the Bath School! A Reply to Collins and Yearley." In *Science as Practice and Culture,* ed. A. Pickering, 343–68. Chicago: University of Chicago Press.

Campbell, Joseph. 1989. Foreword to *The Language of the Goddess,* by M. Gimbutas. San Francisco: Harper and Row.

Campbell, R. L., and P. S. Staniford. 1978. "Transpersonal Anthropology." *Phoenix: The Journal of Transpersonal Anthropology* 2 (1): 28–40.

Capra, Fritjof. 1976. *The Tao of Physics.* Bungay, Suffolk: Fontana/Collins.

———. 1982. *The Turning Point: Science, Society, and the Rising Culture.* New York: Simon and Schuster.

———. 1995. "Deep Ecology: A New Paradigm." In *Deep Ecology for the Twenty-First Century,* ed. G. Sessions, 19–25. Boston: Shambhala.

Capra, Fritjof, and Charlene Spretnak. 1984. *Green Politics: The Global Promise.* New York: E. P. Dutton.

Capt, E. Edmond. 1983. *The Traditions of Glastonbury.* Thousand Oaks, Calif.: Artisan Sales.

Caputo, John D. 1987. *Radical Hermeneutics: Repetition, Deconstruction, and the Hermeneutic Project.* Bloomington: Indiana University Press.

———. 1993. *Against Ethics: Contributions to a Poetics of Obligation with Constant Reference to Deconstruction.* Bloomington: Indiana University Press.

Carello, Claudia. 1993. "Realism and Ecological Units of Analysis." In *Human Ecology: Fragments of Anti-Fragmentary Views of the World,* ed. D. Steiner and M. Nauser, 21–40. New York: Routledge.

Carley, James P. 1988. *Glastonbury Abbey: The Holy House at the Head of the Moors Adventurous.* New York: St. Martin's Press.

Carmichael, David L., Jane Hubert, Brian Reeves, and Audhild Schanche, eds. 1994. *Sacred Sites, Sacred Places.* New York: Routledge.

Casey, Edward. 1993. *Getting Back into Place: Toward a Renewed Understanding of the Place-World.* Bloomington: Indiana University Press.

Cathie, Bruce L. 1977. *The Pulse of the Universe: Harmonic 288.* London: A. H. and A. W. Reed.

———. 1994. "The Harmonic Conquest of Space." *Nexus (New Times)* 2 (22) (October-November): 37–43.

Center in Sedona. n.d. *Statement of Purpose, The Center's Philosophy, etc.* Sedona: Center in Sedona.

Certeau, Michel de. 1984. *The Practice of Everyday Life*. Berkeley: University of California Press.

Champion, A. G., ed. 1989. *Counterurbanisation: The Changing Pace and Nature of Population Deconcentration*. London: Edward Arnold.

Chandler, Russell. 1988. *Understanding the New Age*. Waco, Tex.: Word Books.

———. 1991. "Bad Vibes Rock New Age Mecca." *Los Angeles Times*, August 4: A1, A28–29.

Charpentier, Louis. 1972. *The Mysteries of Chartres Cathedral*. Wellingborough: Thorsons/RILKO.

Chávez, John R. 1984. *The Lost Land: The Chicano Image of the Southwest*. Albuquerque: University of New Mexico Press.

Chicago, Judy. 1979. *The Dinner Party: A Symbol of Our Heritage*. Garden City, N.Y.: Anchor Press.

Chidester, David. and Edward T. Linenthal. 1995a. *American Sacred Space*. Bloomington: Indiana University Press.

———, eds. 1995b. Introduction to *American Sacred Space*, ed. D. Chidester and E. Linenthal. Bloomington: Indiana University Press.

Childress, David Hatcher. 1987. *Anti-Gravity and the World Grid*. Stelle, Ill.: Adventures Unlimited Press.

Chippindale, Christopher. 1986. "Stoned Henge: Events and Issues at the Summer Solstice." *World Archaeology* 18 (1): 38–58.

———. 1994. *Stonehenge Complete*. London: Thames and Hudson.

Chippindale, C., P. Devereux, R. Jones, and T. Sebastian, eds. 1990. *Who Owns Stonehenge?* London: Batsford.

Christ, Carol, and Judith Plaskow, eds. 1989. *Weaving the Visions: New Patterns in Feminist Spirituality*. San Francisco: Harper and Row.

Churchill, Ward. 1992. *Fantasies of the Master Race: Literature, Cinema, and the Colonization of American Indians*. Edited by M. A. Jaimes. Monroe, Maine: Common Courage Press.

———. 1994. *Indians Are Us: Culture and Genocide in Native North America*. Monroe, Maine: Common Courage Press.

Clemmer, Richard. 1995. "'Then Will You Rise and Strike My Head from My Neck Down': Hopi Prophecy and the Discourse of Empowerment." *American Indian Quarterly* 19 (1) (Winter): 31–73.

Clifford, James. 1988. *The Predicament of Culture: Twentieth-Century Ethnography, Literature, and Art*. Cambridge, Mass.: Harvard University Press.

Cloke, Paul, and Mark Goodwin. 1992. "Conceptualizing Countryside Change: From Post-Fordism to Rural Structural Coherence." *Transactions of the Institute of British Geographers* 17: 321–36.

Cloke, Paul, and Jo Little, eds. 1997. *Contested Countryside Cultures: Otherness, Marginalisation, and Rurality*. London: Routledge.

Cloke, Paul, and Nigel Thrift. 1987. "Intra-Class Conflict in Rural Areas." *Journal of Rural Studies* 3: 321–34.

Cohen, Erik. 1992. "Pilgrimage and Tourism: Convergence and Divergence." *Sacred Journeys: The Anthropology of Pilgrimage*, ed. E. A. Morinis, 47–61. London: Greenwood Press.

Coleman, Simon, and John Elsner. 1995. *Pilgrimage: Past and Present*. London: British Museum Press.

Conkey, Margaret W., and Ruth E. Tringham. 1995. "Archaeology and the Goddess: Exploring the Contours of Feminist Archaeology." In *Feminisms in the Academy*, ed. D. C. Stanton and A. J. Stewart. University of Michigan Press.

Conley, Verena A. 1997. *Ecopolitics: The Environment in Poststructuralist Thought*. New York: Routledge.

Coon, Robert. 1986. *Voyage to Avalon: An Immortalist Introduction to the Magick of Glastonbury*. Glastonbury: Griffin Gold Publications.

——. 1990. *Glastonbury and the Planetary New Jerusalem*. Avalon [*sic*]: Excalibur Press.

——. 1993. *Spheres of Destiny: The Shaftesbury Prophecy: A Planetary Vision for the Twenty-First Century*. Glastonbury: Glastonbury Circle.

Cope, Julian. 1998. *The Modern Antiquarian: A Premillennial Odyssey through Megalithic Britain*. London: Thorsons.

Corbett, Cynthia L. 1988. *Power Trips: Journeys to Sacred Sites as a Way of Transformation*. Santa Fe: Timewindow Publications.

Cornell, Drucilla. 1992. *The Philosophy of the Limit*. New York: Routledge.

Cosgrove, Denis. 1984. *Social Formation and Symbolic Landscape*. London: Croom Helm.

Cosgrove, Denis, and Stephen Daniels, eds. 1988. *The Iconography of Landscape: Essays on the Symbolic Representation, Design, and Use of Past Environments*. New York: Cambridge University Press.

Costall, Alan. 1995. "Socializing Affordances." *Theory and Psychology* 5 (4): 467–81.

Crain, Mary M. 1997. "The Remaking of an Andalusian Pilgrimage Tradition: Debates Regarding Visual (Re)Presentation and the Meanings of 'Locality' in a Global Era." In *Culture, Power, Place: Explorations in Critical Anthropology*, ed. A. Gupta and J. Ferguson. Durham, N.C.: Duke University Press.

Crang, Michael. 1994. "On the Heritage Trail: Maps of and Journeys to Olde Englande." *Environment and Planning D: Society and Space* 12: 341–55.

Crick, Julia. 1991. "The Marshalling of Antiquity: Glastonbury's Historical Dossier." In *The Archaeology and History of Glastonbury Abbey*, ed. L. Abrams and J. P. Carley. Woodbridge, Suffolk: Boydell Press.

Critchlow, Keith. 1982. *Time Stands Still: New Light on Megalithic Science*. New York: St. Martin's Press.

Cronon, William, ed. 1995. *Uncommon Ground: Toward Reinventing Nature*. New York: Norton.

Crook, Stephen, Jan Pakulski, and Malcolm Waters. 1992. *Postmodernization: Change in Advanced Society*. London: Sage.

Crumley, Carol, ed. 1994. *Historical Ecology: Cultural Knowledge and Changing Landscapes*. Santa Fe: School of American Research Press.

Cumbey, Constance. 1983. *The Hidden Dangers of the Rainbow: The New Age Movement and the Coming Age of Barbarism*. Shreveport, La.: Huntington House.

Cuomo, Chris J. 1998. *Feminism and Ecological Communities: An Ethic of Flourishing*. New York: Routledge.

Dagget, Dan. 1989a. "Hurry Up and Flush! Phoenix Owns That Water!" *Tab* 1 (8) (March 16): 16.

——. 1989b. "Less Trees, More Snow—Forecast for the Northland?" *Tab* 1 (7) (March 9): 7.

——. 1989c. "The Long Gone Dried Up River Blues: Verde River—Dry Ditch?" Special Report. *Tab* 1 (6) (March 2): 8.

Dahms, Fred, and Janine McComb. 1999. "'Counterurbanization,' Interaction and Functional Change in a Rural Amenity Area—A Canadian Example." *Journal of Rural Studies* 15 (2): 129–46.

Dame-Glerum, Kathie. 1987a. "Did Harmonic Convergence come off as advertised?" *Sedona Times*, August 26: A3–A5.

——. 1987b. "'Sacred Sedona' Buzzing over 'Harmonic Convergence'." *Sedona Times*, July 22: A1–A3.

——. 1987c. "Supernatural Sedona?" *Sedona Times*, May 20–27: A1–2.

Dames, Michael. 1976. *The Silbury Treasure*. London: Thames and Hudson.

——. 1977. *The Avebury Cycle*. London: Thames and Hudson.

Daniel, Glyn. 1985. Editorial. *Antiquity* 59: 161–62.

Dannelley, Richard. 1991. *The Sedona Power Spot, Vortex, and Medicine Wheel Guide*. Sedona: Richard Dannelley/Vortex Society.

——. 1993. *Sedona UFO Connection and Planetary Ascension Guide*. Sedona: Richard Dannelley/Vortex Society.

D'Antonio, Michael. 1992. *Heaven on Earth: Dispatches from America's Spiritual Frontier*. New York: Crown.

Davies, Paul. 1983. *God and the New Physics*. New York: Simon and Schuster.

Dean, Jodi. 1998. *Aliens in America: Conspiracy Cultures from Outerspace to Cyberspace*. Ithaca, N.Y.: Cornell University Press.

Deleuze, Gilles, and Felix Guattari. 1987. *A Thousand Plateaus: Capitalism and Schizophrenia*. Translated by Brian Massumi. Minneapolis: University of Minnesota Press.

Deloria, Vine, Jr. 1994 [1972]. *God Is Red: A Native View of Religion*. Golden, Colo.: Fulcrum.

Derr, J. S., and M. A. Persinger. 1990. "Geophysical Variables and Behavior: 63. Quasi-Experimental Evidence of the Tectonic Strain Theory of Luminous Phenomena: The Derba, Colorado, Earthquakes." *Perceptual and Motor Skills* 1990 (71): 707–14.

Descola, Philippe, and Gísli Pálsson, eds. 1996. *Nature and Society: Anthropological Perspectives*. New York: Routledge.

Deudney, Daniel. 1995. "In Search of Gaian Politics: Earth Religion's Challenge to Modern Western Civilization." In *Ecological Resistance Movements: The Global Emergence of Radical and Popular Environmentalism*, ed. B. R. Taylor, 282–99. Albany: State University of New York Press.

Devereux, Paul. 1989a. *Earth Lights Revelation*. London: Blandford Press.

——. 1989b. *Earthmind: A Modern Adventure in Ancient Wisdom*. With John Steele and David Kubrin. New York: Harper and Row.

——. 1990. *Places of Power: Secret Energies at Ancient Sites: A Guide to Observed or Measured Phenomena*. London: Blandford.

——. 1992a. *Earth Memory: Sacred Sites—Doorways into Earth's Mysteries*. St. Paul, Minn.: Llewellyn.

——. 1992b. *Secrets of Ancient and Sacred Places: The World's Mysterious Heritage*. London: Blandford.

——. 1992c. *Shamanism and the Mystery Lines: Ley Lines, Spirit Paths, Shape-Shifting, and Out-of-Body Travel*. London: Quantum.

——. 1992d. *Symbolic Landscapes: The Dreamtime Earth and Avebury's Open Secrets*. Glastonbury: Gothic Image.

——. 1996. *Re-Visioning the Earth: A Guide to Opening the Healing Channels Between Mind and Nature*. New York: Simon and Schuster/Fireside Original.

——. 1997. "The Archaeology of Consciousness." *Journal of Scientific Exploration* 11 (4): 527–38.

Devereux, Paul, and Robert G. Jahn. 1996. "Preliminary Investigations and Cognitive Considerations of the Acoustical Resonances of Selected Archaeological Sites." *Antiquity* 70 (269).

Devereux, Paul, and Ian Thompson. 1979. *The Ley Hunter's Companion*. London: Thames and Hudson.

Dickens, Peter. 1996. *Reconstructing Nature: Alienation, Emancipation, and the Division of Labour*. London: Routledge.

Diem, Andrea Grace, and James R. Lewis. 1992. "Imagining India: The Influence of Hinduism on the New Age Movement." In *Perspectives on the New Age*, ed. J. Lewis and J. G. Melton, 48–58. Albany: State University of New York Press.

Dixon, Jennifer L. 1993. "Flood: Number of Houses Destroyed Continues to Grow." *Sedona Red Rock News*, March 5: 1.

Donaldson, Laura E. 1999. "On Medicine Women and White Shame-Ans: New Age Native Americanism and Commodity Fetishism as Pop Culture Feminism." *Signs* 24 (3) (Spring).

Dongo, Tom. 1988. *The Mysteries of Sedona: The New Age Frontier*. Sedona: Hummingbird.

———. 1993. *The Mysteries of Sedona.* Book 3: *The Quest.* Sedona: Hummingbird.

Dryzek, John. 1995. "Green Reason: Communicative Ethics for the Biosphere." In *Postmodern Environmental Ethics,* ed. M. Oelschlaeger. Albany: State University of New York Press.

Dunbar, Dirk. 1994. *The Balance of Nature's Polarities in New-Paradigm Theory.* New York: Peter Lang.

Duncan, James S. 1990. *The City as Text: The Politics of Landscape in the Kandyan Kingdom.* New York: Cambridge University Press.

Duncan, James, and David Ley, eds. 1993. *Place/Culture/Representation.* New York: Routledge.

Dunning, Robert. 1994. *Glastonbury: History and Guide.* Stroud, Gloucestershire: Alan Sutton.

———, ed. 1975. *Christianity in Somerset.* Taunton: Somerset County Council.

Durkheim, Emile. 1964 [1915]. *The Elementary Forms of the Religious Life.* London: Allen and Unwin.

Eade, John, and Michael J. Sallnow, eds. 1991. *Contesting the Sacred: The Anthropology of Christian Pilgrimage.* New York: Routledge.

Earle, Fiona, et al. 1994. *A Time to Travel? An Introduction to Britain's Newer Travellers.* Lyme Regis, Dorset: Enabler Publications.

Edge, Hoyt, ed. 1986. *Foundations of Parapsychology: Exploring the Boundaries of Human Capability.* New York: Routledge, Chapman and Hall.

Eisler, Riane. 1987. *The Chalice and the Blade.* San Francisco: Harper and Row.

Eliade, Mircea. 1958. *Patterns in Comparative Religion.* New York: World/Meridian.

———. 1959. *The Sacred and the Profane: The Nature of Religion.* Translated by W. R. Trask. New York: Harcourt, Brace and Jovanovich.

Eller, Cynthia. 1995. *Living in the Lap of the Goddess: The Feminist Spirituality Movement in America.* Boston: Beacon Press.

———. 2000. *The Myth of Matriarchal Prehistory: Why an Invented Past Will Not Give Women a Future.* Boston: Beason Press.

Elstob, Lynne, and Anne Howes. 1987. *The Glastonbury Festivals.* Glastonbury: Gothic Image/CAHLME.

Enright, J. T. 1999. "Testing Dowsing: The Failure of the Munich Experiments." *Skeptical Inquirer* 23 (1) (January-February): 39–46.

Escobar, Arturo. 1999. "After Nature: Steps to an Antiessentialist Political Ecology." *Current Anthropology* 40 (1): 1–20.

Essene, Virginia, and Sheldon Nidle. 1994. *You Are Becoming a Galactic Human.* Santa Clara, Calif.: Spiritual Education Endeavors Publishing.

Estes, Clarissa Pinkola. 1992. *Women Who Run with the Wolves: Myths and Stories of the Wild Woman Archetype.* New York: Ballantine.

Evernden, Neil. 1985. *The Natural Alien: Humankind and Environment.* Toronto: University of Toronto Press.

———. 1992. *The Social Creation of Nature.* Toronto: University of Toronto Press.

Faber, M. D. 1996. *New Age Thinking: A Psychoanalytic Critique.* Religions and Beliefs Series, no. 5. Ottawa: University of Ottawa Press.

Faivre, Antoine. 1994. *Access to Western Esotericism.* Albany: State University of New York Press.

Faivre, Antoine, and Jacob Needleman, ed. 1992. *Modern Esoteric Spirituality.* World Spirituality: An Encyclopedia History of the Religious Quest. New York: Crossroad.

Featherstone, Mike. 1995. *Undoing Culture: Globalization, Postmodernism, and Identity.* London: Sage.

Feher-Elston, Catherine. 1988. *Children of Sacred Ground: America's Last Indian War.* Flagstaff: Northland.

Feld, Steven, and Keith Basso, eds. 1996. *Senses of Place.* Santa Fe: School of American Research Press.

Fellowship for Intentional Community. 1995. *Communities Directory: A Guide to Cooperative Living.* Langley, Wash.: Fellowship for Intentional Community.

Ferguson, Marilyn. 1980. *The Aquarian Conspiracy: Personal and Social Transformation in the 1980s.* Los Angeles: Jeremy Tarcher.

Fewkes, Jesse Walter. 1895. "Preliminary Account of an Expedition to the Cliff Villages of the Red Rock Country and the Tusayan Ruins of Sikyatki and Awatobi, Arizona, in 1895." *Smithsonian Institution Annual Reports* 1985: 557–88.

Findhorn Community. 1975. *The Findhorn Garden.* New York: Harper and Row.

———. 1980. *Faces of Findhorn: Images of a Planetary Family.* New York: Harper and Row.

Firey, A. 1983. "Cross-Examining the Witness: Recent Research in Celtic Monastic History." *Monastic Studies* 14: 31–49.

Firsoff, George. N.d. "Why We Need Stonehenge: A History of Worship and Celebration." N.p.

Fischer, Roland. 1980. "A Cartography of the Ecstatic and Meditative States." In *Understanding Mysticism,* ed. R. Woods. Garden City, N.Y.: Doubleday.

Fitzpatrick, Tom. 1982. "Picture Postcard: Splendid Scenery Makes Sedona Almost a Religion but Growth Threatens to Overwhelm Simple Beauty." *Arizona: The Arizona Republic Magazine,* March 7.

Forney, Ross. 1998. "Water Resources Can Evaporate in More Ways than One." *Responsible Residents of the Red Rocks Newsletter,* June.

Fortune, Dion. 1989 [1934]. *Glastonbury: Avalon of the Heart.* Wellingborough, Northamptonshire: Aquarian Press.

Foucault, Michel. 1973. *The Order of Things.* New York: Vintage Books.

———. 1980a. *Power/Knowledge.* Translated by C. Gordon. New York: Pantheon.

———. 1980b. "Questions on Geography." In *Power/Knowledge: Selected Interviews and Other Writings,* ed. C. Gordon. Brighton: Harvester Press.

———. 1986. "Of Other Spaces." *Diacritics* 16 (1): 22–27.

Foust, Richard D., Jr., James Byrkit, and Charles Avery. 1991. Environmental Quality in the Sedona/Verde Valley Area. Flagstaff: Northern Arizona University/Sedona Academy.

Fox, Steve. 1994. "Sacred Pedestrians: The Many Faces of Southwest Pilgrimage." *Journal of the Southwest* 36 (1) (Spring): 33–53.

Frost, Brian. 1986. *Glastonbury Journey: Marjorie Milne's Search for Reconciliation.* Oxford: Becket.

Gadon, Elinor. 1989. *The Once and Future Goddess.* San Francisco: Harper and Row.

Gardiner, Michael. 1992. *The Dialogics of Critique: M. M. Bakhtin and the Theory of Ideology.* New York: Routledge.

Gardner, Martin. 1981. *Science: Good, Bad, and Bogus.* New York: Avon.

———. 1991. *The New Age: Notes of a Fringe Watcher.* Buffalo: Prometheus Books.

Garrard, Bruce. 1986. *(The Children of the Rainbow Gathered in the Free State of Avalonia at the Christian Community of) Greenlands Farm.* Glastonbury: Unique Publications.

———. 1989. "'Glastonbury Hippies'—A Potted History." In *Travellers in Glastonbury,* ed. A. Morgan and B. Garrard, 4–5. Glastonbury: Glastonbury Gazette/Unique Publications.

———. 1994. *The Alternative Sector: Notes on Green Philosophy, Politics, and Economics.* Glastonbury: Unique Publications.

———, ed. 1987. *Stonehenge '87: A People's Pilgrimage.* Glastonbury: Unique Publications.

Garrard, Bruce, and Steve Hieronymous, eds. 1986. *Stonehenge '86.* Glastonbury: Unique Publications.

Garrard, Bruce, and Lucy Lepchani, eds. 1990. *Glastonbury Earthweek Magazine.* Glastonbury: Unique Publications.

Geertz, Armin W. 1994. *The Invention of Prophecy: Continuity and Meaning in Hopi Indian Religion.* Berkeley: University of California Press.

Genocchio, Benjamin. 1995. "Discourse, Discontinuity, Difference: The Question of

'Other' Spaces." In *Postmodern Cities and Spaces*, ed. S. Watson and K. Gibson, 35–46. Oxford: Blackwell.

Georgoudi, Stella. 1992. "Creating a Myth of Matriarchy." In *A History of Women: From Ancient Goddesses to Christian Saints*, ed. P. S. Pantel. Cambridge, Mass.: Harvard University Press.

Gibson, James J. 1977. "The Theory of Affordances." In *Perceiving, Acting, and Knowing*, ed. R. E. Shaw and J. Bransford. Hillsdale, N.J.: Erlbaum.

———. 1979. *The Ecological Approach to Visual Perception*. Boston: Houghton Mifflin.

———. 1982. *Reasons for Realism: Selected Essays of James J. Gibson*. E. Reed and R. Jones, eds. Hillsdale, N.J.: Lawrence Erlbaum.

Gifford, Edward W. 1932. "Northeastern and Western Yavapai." *University of California Publications in American Archaeology and Ethnology* 29 (3): 177–252.

———. 1933. "Northeastern and Western Yavapai Myths." *Journal of American Folklore* 46.

———. 1936. "Northeastern and Western Yavapai." *University of California Publications in American Archaeology and Ethnology* 34 (4): 247–354.

Gimbutas, Marija. 1982. *The Goddesses and Gods of Old Europe, 6500–3500 BC: Myths and Cult Images*. Berkeley: University of California Press.

———. 1989. *The Language of the Goddess*. San Francisco: Harper and Row.

———. 1991. *The Civilization of the Goddess: The World of Old Europe*. San Francisco: HarperSanFrancisco.

Glacken, Clarence J. 1967. *Traces on the Rhodian Shore*. Berkeley: University of California Press.

Glastonbury Temple Design Group. 1994. *The Avalon Project*. Glastonbury Temple Design Group.

Glendinning, Chellis. 1995. "Yours Truly from Indian Country." *Yoga Journal*, January-February: 79–85.

Gober, Patricia, Kevin E. McHugh, and Denis Leclerc. 1993. "Job-Rich, Housing-Poor: The Dilemma of a Western Amenity Town." *Professional Geographer* 45 (1): 12–20.

Godwin, Joscelyn. 1994. *The Theosophical Enlightenment*. Albany: State University of New York Press.

Gold, Mick. 1984. "A History of Nature." In *Geography Matters!* ed. D. Massey and J. Allen. London: Macmillan.

Goodison, Lucy, and Christine Morris, eds. 1999. *Ancient Goddesses: The Myths and the Evidence*. London: British Museum Press.

Goodwin, Neil. 1995. "Jackboot and the Beanfield." *New Statesman and Society*, June 23: 22–23.

Gottlieb, Robert. 1988. *A Life of Its Own: The Politics and Power of Water*. New York: Harcourt Brace Jovanovich.

Gottlieb, Robert S., ed. 1997. *The Ecological Community: Environmental Challenges for Philosophy, Politics, and Morality*. New York: Routledge.

Graburn, Nelson. 1989. "Tourism: The Sacred Journey." In *Hosts and Guests: The Anthropology of Tourism*, ed. V. Smith. Philadelphia: University of Pennsylvania Press.

Graff, Cynthia E. 1990. The Rancho Del Coronado Land Exchange: Final Report on Data Recovery at Four Sites, Sedona Ranger District, Coconino National Forest. Flagstaff, Arizona: Northern Arizona University.

Graham, Brian, and Michael Murray. 1997. "The Spiritual and the Profane: The Pilgrimage to Santiago de Compostela." *Ecumene* 4 (4): 389–409.

Graves, Tom. 1978. *Needles of Stone*. Wellingborough, Northamptonshire: Turnstone Books.

———. 1986a. *The Diviner's Handbook*. Wellingborough, Northamptonshire: Aquarian Press.

———. 1986b. *Needles of Stone Revisited*. Glastonbury: Gothic Image.

——, ed. 1980. *Dowsing and Archaeology: An Anthology from the Journal of the British Society of Dowsers.* Wellingborough, Northamptonshire: Turnstone Books.

Gregory, Derek. 1994. *Geographical Imaginations.* Cambridge, Mass.: Blackwell.

Greider, Thomas, and Lorraine Garkovich. 1994. "Landscapes: The Social Construction of Nature and the Environment." *Rural Sociology* 59 (1): 1–24.

Gray, Martin. 1991. "Sacred Sites and Power Points: A Pilgrim's Journey for Planetary Healing." *Shaman's Drum* (25) (Fall): 32–44.

——. n.d. "Places of Peace and Power." Electronic manuscript (accessed 1999–2000). <http://www.sacredsites.com/manu/Intro.html>.

Griffin, David Ray. 1985. *Physics and the Ultimate Significance of Time: Bohm, Prigogine, and Process Philosophy.* Albany: State University of New York Press.

——. 1988a. *Spirituality and Society: Postmodern Visions.* Albany: State University of New York Press.

——. 1990. *Sacred Interconnections: Postmodern Spirituality, Political Economy, and Art.* Albany: State University of New York Press.

——. 1993. *Postmodern Politics for a Planet in Crisis: Policy, Process, and Presidential Vision.* Albany: State University of New York Press.

——, ed. 1988b. *The Reenchantment of Science: Postmodern Proposals.* Albany: State University of New York Press.

Griffin, Wendy, ed. 2000. *Daughters of the Goddess: Studies of Healing, Identity, and Empowerment.* Walnut Creek, Calif.: AltaMira.

Griffith, Diana, and Ronald Hutton. 1990. "Mothers, Amazons, and Goddesses." Glastonbury: Library of Avalon Symposium. Audiocassette.

Grim, Patrick, ed. 1990. *Philosophy of Science and the Occult.* Albany: State University of New York Press.

Grimes, Ronald L. 1999. "Jonathan Z. Smith's Theory of Ritual Space." *Religion* 29: 261–73.

Grinevald, Jacques. 1988. "Sketch for a History of the Idea of the Biosphere." In *Gaia, the Thesis, the Mechanisms, and the Implications: Proceedings of the First Annual Camelford Conference on the Implications of the Gaia Hypothesis,* ed. P. Bunyard and E. Goldsmith. Camelford, Cornwall: Wadebridge Ecological Centre.

Grinsell, L. V. 1978. *The Druids and Stonehenge: The Story of a Myth.* St. Peter Port, Guernsey: Toucan Press.

Grof, Stanislav. 1976. *Realms of the Human Unconscious: Observations from LSD Research.* New York: Dutton.

——. 1985. *Beyond the Brain: Birth, Death, and Transcendence in Psychotherapy.* Albany: State University of New York Press.

Groothuis, Douglas R. 1986. *Unmasking the New Age.* Downers Grove, Ill.: InterVarsity Press.

——. 1988. *Confronting the New Age: How to Resist a Growing Religious Movement.* Downers Grove, Ill.: InterVarsity Press.

Grosso, Michael. 1996. "UFOs and the Myth of the New Age." *Mythos Journal* 6 (Fall).

Gupta, Akhil, and James Ferguson, eds. 1997. *Culture, Power, Place: Explorations in Critical Anthropology.* Durham, N.C.: Duke University Press.

Habermas, Jürgen. 1984. *The Theory of Communicative Action I: Reason and the Rationalization of Society.* Boston: Beacon Press.

Hackett, Rosalind, ed. 1987. *New Religious Movements in Nigeria.* Lewiston, N.Y.: Edwin Mellen Press.

Halfacree, Keith H. 1996. "Out of Place in the Country: Travellers and the 'Rural Idyll'." *Antipode* 28 (1): 42–73.

——. 1997. "Contrasting Roles for the Post-Productivist Countryside: A Postmodern Perspective on Counterurbanisation." In *Contested Countryside Cultures,* ed. P. Cloke and J. Little, 70–93. New York: Routledge.

Hall, John S., and Lawrence D. Mankin. 1990. *Our Cultural Values: Past, Present, and Future.* Tempe: Morrison Institute for Public Policy/School of Public Affairs, Arizona State University.

Hall, John S., and K. D. Pijawka. 1988. *Sedona: Assuring a Quality Future.* Tempe: School of Public Affairs, Arizona State University.

———. 1992. *Sustaining Sedona's Economy: Planning toward the Year 2000.* Tempe: School of Public Affairs, Arizona State University.

Hancock, P. A. 1998. "Dowsing the Rollrights." *Skeptical Inquirer* 22 (1) (January-February): 32–37.

Hanegraaff, Wouter J. 1998. *New Age Religion and Western Culture: Esotericism in the Mirror of Secular Thought.* Albany: State University of New York Press.

Hannigan, John. 1998. *Fantasy City: Pleasure and Profit in the Postmodern Metropolis.* New York: Routledge.

Hansen, George P. 1992. "CSICOP and the Skeptics: An Overview." *Journal of the American Society for Psychical Research* 86 (January).

Haraway, Donna. 1989. *Primate Visions: Gender, Race, and Nature in the World of Modern Science.* New York: Routledge.

———. 1991. *Simians, Cyborgs, and Women: The Reinvention of Nature.* New York: Routledge.

———. 1992. "The Promises of Monsters: A Regenerative Politics for Inappropriate/d Others." In *Cultural Studies,* ed. L. Grossberg, C. Nelson, and P. Treichler, 295–337. New York: Routledge.

Hardcastle, F. 1990. *The Chalice Well, Glastonbury, Somerset, England: A Short History.* Rev. ed. Glastonbury: Chalice Well Trust.

Harman, Willis. 1988. *Global Mind Change: The Promise of the Last Years of the Twentieth Century.* Indianapolis: Knowledge Systems.

Harries-Jones, Peter. 1995. *A Recursive Vision: Ecological Understanding and Gregory Bateson.* Toronto: University of Toronto Press.

Harvey, David. 1989. *The Condition of Postmodernity: An Enquiry into the Origins of Cultural Change.* Oxford: Basil Blackwell.

———. 1996. *Justice, Nature, and the Geography of Difference.* Oxford: Blackwell.

Harvey, Graham. 1994. "The Roots of Pagan Ecology." *Religion Today* 9 (3) (Summer): 38–41.

Harvey, Graham, and Charlotte Hardman, eds. 1996. *Paganism Today.* London: Thorsons/HarperCollins.

Hawken, Paul. 1975. *The Magic of Findhorn.* New York: Harper and Row.

Hawkins, Gerald S. 1963. "Stonehenge Decoded." *Nature,* October 26.

———. 1964. "Stonehenge: A Neolithic Computer." *Nature,* June 27.

———. With John B. White. 1965. *Stonehenge Decoded.* Garden City, N.Y.: Doubleday.

Hayden, Brian. 1986. "Old Europe: Sacred Matriarchy or Complementary Opposition?" In *Archaeology and Fertility Cult in the Ancient Mediterranean,* ed. A. Bonanno. Amsterdam: Gruner, 17–30.

———. 1998. "An Archaeological Evaluation of the Gimbutas Paradigm." *Pomegranate* 6: 35–46.

Hayles, N. Katherine. 1991. "Constrained Constructivism: Locating Scientific Inquiry in the Theatre of Representation." *New Orleans Review* 18: 76–85.

———. 1995. "Simulated Nature and Natural Simulations: Rethinking the Relation between the Beholder and the World." In *Uncommon Ground: Toward Reinventing Nature,* ed. W. Cronon. New York: Norton.

Hayward, Jeremy. 1984. *Perceiving Ordinary Magic: Science and Intuitive Wisdom.* Boston: Shambhala/New Science Library.

———. 1987. *Shifting Worlds, Changing Minds: Where the Sciences and Buddhism Meet.* Boston: Shambhala/New Science Library.

Hayward, Jeremy, and Francisco Varela, eds. 1992. *Gentle Bridges: Conversations with the Dalai Lama on the Sciences of Mind.* Boston: Shambhala.

Heelas, Paul. 1993. "The New Age in Cultural Context: The Premodern, the Modern, and the Postmodern." *Religion* 23: 106–16.

———. 1996. *The New Age Movement.* Oxford: Blackwell.

Heelas, Paul, and Leila Amaral. 1994. "Notes on the 'Nova Era': Rio de Janeiro and Environs," *Religion* 24 (2): 173–80.

Heidegger, Martin. 1977a. *Basic Writings*. Edited by David F. Krell. New York: Harper and Row.

———. 1977b. *The Question Concerning Technology and Other Essays*. Translated by W. Lovitt. New York: Harper and Row.

Heller, Chaia. 1999. *Ecology of Everyday Life: Rethinking the Desire for Nature*. Montreal: Black Rose.

Hennessy, Lin. 1991. "The White Spring: A New Place of Pilgrimage in Glastonbury." *Glastonbury Zodiac Companion* 2 (Winter Solstice).

Herbert, Nick. 1985. *Quantum Reality: Beyond the New Physics*. Garden City, N.Y.: Anchor Press/Doubleday.

Herndl, Carl G., and Stuart C. Brown, eds. 1996. *Green Culture: Environmental Rhetoric in Contemporary America*. Madison: University of Wisconsin.

Heselton, Philip. 1991. *The Elements of Earth Mysteries*. Shaftesbury, Dorset: Element.

Hess, David J. 1993. *Science in the New Age: The Paranormal, Its Defenders and Debunkers, and American Culture*. Madison: University of Wisconsin Press.

Hetherington, Kevin. 1992. "Stonehenge and Its Festival: Spaces of Consumption." In *Lifestyle Shopping: The Subject of Consumption*, ed. R. Shields. New York: Routledge.

———. 1993. *"New Age Travellers: An Analysis of a Neo-Tribal Lifestyle."* Unpublished paper.

———. 1994. *"New Age Travellers: Heterotopic Places and Heteroclite Identities."* Paper presented at the Alternative Political Imaginations Conference, University of London, April 1994.

Hewison, Robert. 1987. *The Heritage Industry*. London: Methuen.

Hexham, Irving. 1981. "Glastonbury and the New Age Movement." In "Some Aspects of the Contemporary Search for an Alternative Society (In Glastonbury, England, 1967–1971)." M.A. thesis, University of Bristol, 1981. <www.ucalgary.ca/~nurelweb/glastonbury/glast-1.html>.

———. 1983. "Conversion and Consolidation in an English Town: The Freaks of Glastonbury: 1967–1982." *Update*, March: 3–12.

———. 1992. "The Evangelical Response to the New Age." In *Perspectives on the New Age*, ed. J. R. Lewis and J. G. Melton, 152–63. Albany: State University of New York Press.

Hirsch, Eric, and Michael O'Hanlon, eds. 1995. *The Anthropology of Landscape: Perspectives on Place and Space*. Oxford: Clarendon Press.

Hitching, Francis. 1976. *Earth Magic*. London: Picador/Pan Books.

Hobson, Geary. 1978. "The Rise of the White Shaman as a New Version of Cultural Imperialism." In *The Remembered Earth*, ed. G. Hobson, 100–108. Albuquerque: Red Earth Press.

Hodder, Ian. 1986. *Reading the Past*. Cambridge: Cambridge University Press.

Hoffman, John F. 1987. *Sedona Oak Creek Canyon Visual*. San Diego: Scenic Visuals.

Holden, Dean, and Paul Scott. 1991. "Keys to Hidden Doorways." In *Crop Circles: Harbingers of World Change*, ed. A. Bartholomew. Bath: Gateway Books.

Honan, R. 1994. "Sierra Club Obtains Support to Halt Bridge." *Canyon Echo*, February 6.

Horigan, Stephen. 1988. *Nature and Culture in Western Discourses*. New York: Routledge.

Hornborg, Alf. 1994. "Environmentalism, Ethnicity, and Sacred Places: Reflections on Modernity, Discourse, and Power." *Canadian Review of Sociology and Anthropology* 31 (3): 245–67.

Hough, Michael. 1995. *Cities and Natural Process*. London: Routledge.

Howard, James K. 1976. *Ten Years with the Cowboy Artists of America: A Complete History and Exhibition Record*. Flagstaff: Northland Press.

Howard, Michael. 1990. *Earth Mysteries*. London: Hale.

Howard, William. 1981. *Sedona Reflections: Tales of Then for the Now*. Sedona: Pronto Press.

———. 1992. *Once upon a Time in Sedona*. Sedona: Runamuck Publishers.

Howard-Gordon, Frances. 1982. *Glastonbury: Maker of Myths*. Glastonbury: Gothic Image.

Hoyt, Karen, ed. 1987. *The New Age Rage: A Probing Analysis of the Newest Religious Craze*. Old Tappan, N.J.: Fleming H. Revell.

Hughes, Kathleen. 1983. "The Celtic Church: Is This a Valid Concept?" *Cambridge Medieval Celtic Studies* 1.

Hurd, Michael. 1993. *Rutland Boughton and the Glastonbury Festivals*. Oxford: Oxford University Press.

Hutton, Ronald. 1993a. "The History of Glastonbury." Public lecture, University of Avalon, Glastonbury. Audiocassette.

———. 1993b. *The Pagan Religions of the Ancient British Isles: Their Nature and Legacy*. Oxford: Blackwell.

———. 1997. "The Neolithic Great Goddess: A Study in Modern Tradition." *Antiquity* 71: 91–9.

———. 1999. *The Triumph of the Moon: A History of Modern Pagan Witchcraft*. Oxford: Oxford University Press.

Idinopulos, T. A., and Yonan, E. A., eds. 1994. *Religion and Reductionism: Essays on Eliade, Segal, and the Challenge of the Social Sciences for the Study of Religion*. Leiden: E. J. Brill.

Ingold, Tim. 1992. "Culture and the Perception of the Environment." In *Bush Base: Forest Farm: Culture, Environment, and Development*, ed. E. Croll and D. Parkin, 39–56. New York: Routledge.

———. 1993. "The Temporality of the Landscape." *World Archaeology* 25 (2): 152–74.

———. 1995. "Building, Dwelling, Living: How Animals and People Make Themselves at Home in the World." In *Shifting Contexts: Transformations in Anthropological Knowledge*, ed. M. Strathern, 57–80. London: Routledge.

Ingram, Helen M. 1969. *Patterns of Politics in Water Resource Development*. Tucson: University of Arizona Press.

———. 1990. *Water Politics: Continuity and Change*. Albuquerque: University of New Mexico Press.

Irwin, Lee, et al. 1996. "To Hear the Eagles Cry: Contemporary Themes in Native American Spirituality" (special issue). *American Indian Quarterly* 20 (3–4).

Isle of Avalon Tours. 1995. "The Magical Journey and Esoteric Avalon." Glastonbury. Promotional brochure.

Ivakhiv, Adrian. 1996. "The Resurgence of Magical Religion as a Response to the Crisis of Modernity: A Postmodern Depth-Psychological Perspective." In *Magical Religion and Modern Witchcraft*, ed. J. R. Lewis, 237–65. Albany: State University of New York Press.

———. 1999. "Whose 'Nature'? Reflections on the Transcendental Signified of an Emerging Field." *Pomegranate* 8: 14–20.

———. 2000. "Theorizing Landscapes: A Co-Constructive Model." Unpublished manuscript.

Iverson, Wayne. 1989. "Peddling and Back-Pedaling in the Coconino National Forest." *Tab* 1 (23): 7.

———. 1994. "The Oak Creek Canyon/Red Rock Country: What Can We and the U.S. Forest Service Do to Save Its Beauty and Spirit?" 4R Special Report. *4Rs Newsletter* 3 (July).

Jaimes, M. Annette, ed. 1992. *The State of Native America: Genocide, Colonization, and Resistance*. Boston: South End Press.

Jameson, Fredric. 1991. *Postmodernism, Or the Cultural Logic of Late Capitalism*. Durham: Duke University Press.

Jansson, Rasmus. 1999. "Dowsing: Science or Humbug?" Rev. January 27. <http://www.lysator.liu.se/~/rasmus/skepticism/dowsing.html>.

Java, Judy. 1989a. "'Inner Voice' Brings Science to Sedona." *Sedona Times*, July 26: 1–2.

——. 1989b. "Sedonans Gear for Third Long Dance." *Sedona Times*, August 2: 1–2.

Jenkins, Leigh, et al. 1996. "Managing Hopi Sacred Sites to Protect Religious Freedom." *Cultural Survival Quarterly* 19 (4) (Winter): 36–39.

Jenkins, Palden. 1994. "Coming Home: A Tale of the Glastonbury Camps and the Oak Dragon Project." Glastonbury. Mimeo.

——. n.d. *Energy Centres, Ancient Remains, Leylines, Coast and Islands: A Map of the Ancient Landscape around Glastonbury*. Glastonbury: Planetary Paths.

Johansen, Gayle [Gaia Lamb], and Shinan Naom Barclay. 1987. *The Sedona Vortex Experience*. Sedona: Sunlight Productions.

Johnson, Hoyt. 1992a. "The Busiest Business in Town!" *Sedona Magazine*, Spring: 50–53.

——. 1992b. "'This Really Is Enchantment!'" *Sedona Magazine*, Spring: 38–44.

Johnson, Paul. 1995. "Shamanism from Ecuador to Chicago: A Case Study in New Age Ritual Appropriation." *Religion* 25: 163–78.

Jones, Kathy. 1990. *The Goddess in Glastonbury*. Glastonbury: Ariadne.

——. 1991. *The Ancient British Goddess: Her Myths, Legends, and Scared Sites*. Glastonbury: Ariadne.

——. 1994. *Spinning the Wheel of Ana: A Spiritual Quest to Find the British Primal Ancestors*. Glastonbury: Ariadne.

Jorstad, Erling. 1990. *Holding Fast/Pressing On: Religion in America in the 1980s*. New York: Greenwood Press.

Joseph, Frank, ed. 1992. *Sacred Sites: A Guidebook to Sacred Centers and Mysterious Places in the United States*. St. Paul, Minn.: Llewellyn.

Joseph, Greg. 1991. "'48 Hours' Bashes Sedona's New Agers." *Arizona Republic*, March 27: E6.

Joseph, Lawrence. 1990. *Gaia: The Growth of an Idea*. New York: St. Martin's Press.

Judah, J. Stillson. 1967. *The History and Philosophy of the Metaphysical Movements in America*. Philadelphia: Westminster Press.

Kalman, Matthew, and John Murray. 1995a. "Icke and the Nazis." *Open Eye* 3: 7.

——. 1995b. "New Age Nazism?" *New Statesman and Society*, June 23: 18–20.

Keeley, Lawrence. 1996. *War before Civilization: The Myth of the Pacific Past*. Oxford: Oxford University Press.

Keith, Michael, and Steve Pile, eds. 1993. *Place and the Politics of Identity*. New York: Routledge.

Keller, Mary Lou. 1991. "Introduction: Echoes of the Past." In *Sedona Vortex Guide Book*, ed. P. Bryant et al. Sedona: Light Technology Publishing.

Kelley, Klara Bonsack, and Harris Francis. 1994. *Navajo Sacred Places*. Bloomington: Indiana University Press.

Kelly, Aidan. 1992. "An Update on Neopagan Witchcraft in America." In *Perspectives on the New Age*, ed. J. R. Lewis and J. G. Melton, 136–51. Albany: State University of New York Press.

Khalsa, Parmatma Singh. 1974. *A Pilgrim's Guide to Planet Earth: Traveler's Handbook and Spiritual Directory*. San Rafael, Calif.: Spiritual Community Publications.

——. 1982. *The New Consciousness Sourcebook: Spiritual Community Guide no. 5*. Berkeley: Spiritual Community Publications.

Khera, Sigrid, ed. 1978. *The Yavapai of Fort McDowell*. Washington, D.C.: U.S. Department of Housing and Urban Development.

Killingsworth, M. Jimmie, and Jacqueline S. Palmer. 1992. *Ecospeak: Rhetoric and Environmental Politics in America*. Carbondale: Southern Illinois University Press.

King, Richard. 1999. *Orientalism and Religion: Post-Colonial Theory, India, and the Mystic East*. New York: Routledge.

Knight, Gareth. 1979. *A History of White Magic*. New York: Samuel Weiser.

Knowles, Joani. 1995. "Many Service Workers Live outside Town." *Sedona Red Rock News*, January 11: 1A.

Korp, Maureen. 1997. *Sacred Art of the Earth: Ancient and Contemporary Earthworks.* New York: Continuum.

Kryder, Rowena Pattee. 1994. *Sacred Ground to Sacred Space: Visionary Ecology, Perennial Wisdom, Environmental Ritual and Art.* Santa Fe: Bear.

Kubiak, Anna. 1999. "Le Nouvel Age, conspiration postmoderne." *Social Compass* 46 (2): 135–43.

Kuletz, Valerie. 1998. *The Tainted Desert: Environmental Ruin in the American West.* New York: Routledge.

Kurtz, Paul. 1985a. "CSICOP after Ten Years: Reflections on the 'Transcendental Temptation.'" *Skeptical Inquirer* 10 (2): 229–32.

———, ed. 1985b. *A Skeptic's Handbook of Parapsychology.* Buffalo, NY: Prometheus Books.

LaChappelle, Dolores. 1988. *Sacred Land, Sacred Sex, Rapture of the Deep: Concerning Deep Ecology—and Celebrating Life.* Silverton, Colo.: Finn Hill Arts.

Lane, Belden C. 1988. *Landscapes of the Sacred: Geography and Narrative in American Spirituality.* New York: Paulist Press.

Lash, Scott, and John Urry. 1994. *Economies of Signs and Space.* London: Sage.

Latour, Bruno. 1987. *Science in Action: How to Follow Scientists and Engineers through Society.* Cambridge, Mass.: Harvard University Press.

———. 1990. "Postmodern? No, Simply Amodern! Steps towards an Anthropology of Science." *Studies in the History and Philosophy of Science* 21 (1): 145–71.

———. 1993. *We Have Never Been Modern.* Translated by Catherine Porter. Cambridge, Mass.: Harvard University Press.

Laughlin, Charles. 1989. "Transpersonal Anthropology: Some Methodological Issues." *Western Canadian Anthropologist* 5: 29–60.

Laughlin, Charles, John McManus, and Eugene d'Aquili. 1990. *Brain, Symbol, and Experience: Toward a Neurophenomenology of Human Consciousness.* Boston: Shambhala/New Science Library.

Laughlin, Charles, John McManus, and Jon Shearer. 1983. "Dreams, Trance and Visions: What a Transpersonal Anthropology Might Look Like." *Phoenix: The Journal of Transpersonal Anthropology* 7 (1–2): 141–59.

Law, John, and John Hassard. 1999. *Actor Network Theory and After.* Oxford: Blackwell/Sociological Review.

Lawlor, Michael. 1982. *Sacred Geometry.* London: Thames and Hudson.

Lefebvre, Henri. 1991 [1974]. *The Production of Space.* Translated by D. Nicholson-Smith. Oxford: Blackwell.

LeFevre, Camille. 1992. "Will Change Mar Sacred Trust in Sedona?" *Minneapolis Sunday Star-Tribune*, November 22: 1G, 5–6G.

Lévi-Strauss, Claude. 1966. *The Savage Mind (La pensée sauvage).* London: Weidenfeld and Nicolson.

Leviton, Richard. 1991. "The Ley Hunters." In *The Power of Place: Sacred Ground in Natural and Human Environments*, ed. J. Swan, 245–56. Wheaton, Ill.: Quest Books/Theosophical Publishing House.

Lewis, James R. 1996a. "Works of Darkness: Occult Fascination in the Novels of Frank E. Peretti." In *Magical Religion and Modern Witchcraft*, ed. J. R. Lewis, 339–50. Albany: State University of New York Press.

———, ed. 1996b. *Magical Religion and Modern Witchcraft.* Albany: State University of New York Press.

Lewis, James R., and J. Gordon Melton, eds. 1992. *Perspectives on the New Age.* Albany: State University of New York Press.

Light, Andrew, ed. 1998. *Social Ecology after Bookchin.* New York: Guilford Press.

Lippard, Lucy R. 1983. *Overlay: Contemporary Art and the Art of Prehistory.* New York: Pantheon Books.

Lonegren, Sig. 1986. *Spiritual Dowsing.* Glastonbury: Gothic Image.

Lopez, Donald S., Jr. 1995. "Foreigners at the Lama's Feet." In *Curators of the Buddha:*

The Study of Buddhism under Colonialism, ed. D. Lopez. Chicago: University of Chicago Press.

Lovelock, James E. 1979. *Gaia: A New Look at Life on Earth*. New York: Oxford University Press.

———. 1988. *The Ages of Gaia: A Biography of Our Living Earth*. New York: Norton.

———. 1992. "Living With Gaia." *Edges* 5 (2): 14–5, 20.

Lovelock, James E., and Sidny Epton. 1975. "The Quest for Gaia." *New Scientist* 65 (6) (February): 304–6.

Lowe, Richard, and William Shaw. 1993. *Travellers: Voices of the New Age Nomads*. London: Fourth Estate.

Luhrmann, T. M. 1989. *Persuasions of the Witch's Craft: Ritual Magic in Contemporary England*. Cambridge, Mass.: Harvard University Press.

Lukács, György. 1971. *The Theory of the Novel*. Cambridge, Mass.: MIT Press.

Luke, Timothy W. 1995. "On Environmentality: Geo-Power and Eco-Knowledge in the Discourses of Contemporary Environmentalism." *Cultural Critique*, Fall: 57–81.

———. 1997. *Ecocritique: Contesting the Politics of Nature, Economy, and Culture*. Minneapolis: University of Minnesota Press.

———. 1999. *Capitalism, Democracy, and Ecology: Departing from Marx*. Urbana: University of Illinois Press.

Lummis, Charles F. 1952 [1893]. *The Land of Poco Tiempo*. Albuquerque: University of New Mexico Press.

Lyon, David. 1993. "A Bit of a Circus: Notes on Postmodernity and New Age." *Religion* 23: 117–25.

Lyotard, Jean-François. 1993. "Answering the Question: What Is Postmodernism?" In *Postmodernism: A Reader*, ed. T. Docherty. New York: Columbia University Press.

MacCannell, Dean. 1976. *The Tourist: A New Theory of the Leisure Class*. New York: Schocken Books.

———. 1992. *Empty Meeting Grounds: The Tourist Papers*. New York: Routledge.

MacColl, Alan. 1999. "King Arthur and the Making of an English Britain." *History Today* 49 (3) (March).

Maclean, Dorothy. 1990 [1980]. *To Hear the Angels Sing*. Hudson, N.Y.: Lindisfarne Press.

Macnaghten, Phil, and John Urry. 1998. *Contested Natures*. London: Sage.

Magnum, Richard, and Sherry Magnum. 1994. *Sedona Hikes: One Hundred Twenty-One Day Hikes and Five Vortex Sites around Sedona, Arizona*. Flagstaff: Hexagon.

Mallory, James. 1989. *In Search of the Indo-Europeans*. London: Thames and Hudson.

Maltwood, Katherine E. 1982 [1929]. *A Guide to Glastonbury's Temple of the Stars*. Cambridge: James Clarke.

Malyon, Tim. 1994. "Criminal Injustice." *New Statesman and Society*, June 24 (Criminal Justice and Public Order Bill Supplement): iv–vii.

Mann, Dean. 1963. *The Politics of Water in Arizona*. Tuscon: University of Arizona Press.

Mann, Nicholas. 1985. *The Cauldron and the Grail: An Exploration into Myth and Landscape*. Glastonbury: Annenterprise.

———. 1991. *Sedona—Sacred Earth: Ancient Lore, Modern Myths: A Guide to the Red Rock Country*. Prescott, Ariz.: ZIVAH.

———. 1993. *Glastonbury Tor: A Guide to the History and Legends*. Butleigh, Somerset: Triskele.

———. 1996. *The Isle of Avalon: Sacred Mysteries of Arthur and Glastonbury Tor*. St. Paul, Minn.: Llewellyn.

Marciniak, Barbara. 1992. *Bringers of the Dawn: Teachings from the Pleiadians*. Santa Fe: Bear.

———. 1995. *Earth: Pleiadian Keys to the Living Library*. Santa Fe: Bear.

Marcus, Clare Cooper. 1987. "Alternative Landscapes: Ley-Lines, Feng-Shui, and the Gaia Hypothesis." *Landscape* 29 (3): 1–10.

Marler, Joan. 1999. "A Response to Brian Hayden's Article: 'An Archaeological Evalua-
tion of the Gimbutas Paradigm'." *Pomegranate* 10: 37–46.
Marrs, Texe. 1987. *Dark Secrets of the New Age: Satan's Plan for a One World Religion.*
Westchester, Ill.: Crossway Books.
———. 1988. *Mystery Mark of the New Age: Satan's Design for World Domination.* West-
chester, Ill.: Crossway Books.
Martin, Greg. 1998. "Generational Differences among New Age Travellers." *Sociologi-
cal Review,* November.
Martin, Walter. 1989. *The New Age Cult.* Minneapolis: Bethany House.
Marx Hubbard, Barbara. 1994. "Conscious Evolution: A Meta-Religion for the Twenty-
First Century." In *A Sourcebook for Earth's Community of Religions,* ed. Joel Bev-
ersluis. Grand Rapids, Mich.: CoNexus Press/SourceBook Project.
Marzano, Robert J. 1993. "When Two Worldviews Collide: Education and Christian-
ity." *Educational Leadership* 51 (4): 6.
Mathias, Michael, and Derek Hector. 1979. *Glastonbury.* London: David and Charles.
Matthews, Caitlin. 1987. *Mabon and the Mysteries of Britain: An Exploration of the
Mabinogion.* London: Arkana.
———. 1995. *Singing the Soul Back Home: Shamanism in Daily Life.* Rockport, Mass.:
Element.
Matthews, Caitlin, and John Matthews. 1994. *The Encyclopedia of Celtic Wisdom: A
Celtic Shaman's Sourcebook.* Shaftesbury, Dorset: Element.
Matthews, John. 1981. *The Grail: Quest for the Eternal.* London: Thames and Hudson.
———. 1991a. *The Celtic Shaman: A Handbook.* London: Element.
———. 1991b. *Taliesin: Shamanism and the Bardic Mysteries in Britain and Ireland.*
London: Aquarian Press/HarperCollins.
———, ed. 1987. *At the Table of the Grail: Magic and the Use of the Imagination.* Lon-
don: Arkana/Routledge and Kegan Paul.
———. 1991c. *A Glastonbury Reader: Selections from the Myths, Legends, and Stories of
Ancient Avalon.* London: Aquarian Press.
Matthews, John, and Caitlin Matthews. 1985–86. *The Western Way.* 2 vols. London:
Arkana.
Matthews, John, and R. J. Stewart. 1989. *Legendary Britain: An Illustrated Journey.* Lon-
don: Blandford.
Maturana, Humberto, and Francisco Varela. 1980. *Autopoiesis and Cognition: The Re-
alization of the Living.* Edited by R. S. Cohen and M. W. Wartofsky. Boston Stud-
ies in the Philosophy of Science. Dordrecht: Reidel.
———. 1987. *The Tree of Knowledge: The Biological Roots of Human Understanding.*
Boston: Shambhala.
Mavor, James W., Jr., and Byron E. Dix. 1989. *Manitou: The Sacred Landscape of New
England's Native Civilization.* Rochester, Vt.: Inner Traditions International.
McClenon, James. 1984. *Deviant Science: The Case of Parapsychology.* Philadelphia:
University of Philadelphia Press.
McCrickard, Janet. 1990. *Eclipse of the Sun: An Investigation into Sun and Moon
Myths.* Glastonbury: Gothic Image.
McGaa, Ed "Eagle Man." 1992. *Rainbow Tribe: Ordinary People Journeying on the Red
Road.* San Francisco: HarperSanFrancisco.
McGinnis, Michael V., ed. 1999. *Bioregionalism.* New York: Routledge.
McGuigan, Jim. 1999. *Modernity and Postmodern Culture.* Open University Press.
McIlwain, John, ed. 1992. *Glastonbury Abbey: The Isle of Avalon.* A Pitkin Guide. East-
leigh, Hampshire: Pitkin Pictorials.
McKay, George. 1996. *Senseless Acts of Beauty: Cultures of Resistance since the 1960s.*
London: Verso.
———, ed. 1998. *DiY Culture: Party and Protest in Nineties Britain.* London: Verso.
McKenna, Terence. 1991. *The Archaic Revival: Speculations on Psychedelic Mush-
rooms, the Amazon, Virtual Reality, UFOs, Evolution, Shamanism, the Rebirth of
the Goddess, and the End of History.* San Francisco: HarperSanFrancisco.

McLaughlin, Andrew. 1993. *Regarding Nature: Industrialism and Deep Ecology.* Albany: State University of New York Press.

McLaughlin, Corinne, and Gordon Davidson. 1986. *Builders of the Dawn: Community Lifestyles in a Changing World.* Shutesbury, Mass.: Sirius.

———. 1994. *Spiritual Politics: Changing the World from the Inside Out.* New York: Ballantine.

McLuhan, T. C. 1996. *Cathedrals of the Spirit: The Message of Sacred Places.* Toronto: HarperCollins.

Meaden, George Terence. 1991. *The Goddess of the Stones: The Language of the Megaliths.* London: Souvenir Press.

Means, Andrew. 1989. "Sedona in a Spin: 'Vortexes' Whirling City into New Age Debate." *Arizona Republic*, August 5: C1, C3.

Mehta, Gita. 1991. *Karma Cola: Marketing the Mystical East.* New York: Ballantine.

Meinig, D. W. 1971. *Southwest: Three Peoples in Geographical Change, 1600–1970.* New York: Oxford University Press.

Mellor, Philip A., and Chris Schilling. 1994. "Reflexive Modernity and the Religious Body." *Religion* 24: 23–42.

Melton, J. Gordon. 1988. "A History of the New Age Movement." In *Not Necessarily the New Age: Critical Essays*, ed. R. Basil, 35–53. Buffalo, N.Y.: Prometheus Books.

———. 1993. *Encyclopedia of American Religions.* Detroit: Gale Research.

Melton, J. Gordon, Jerome Clark, and Aidan Kelly. 1990a. *New Age Encyclopedia.* Detroit: Gale Research.

———. 1990b. "An Overview of the New Age Movement." In *New Age Encyclopedia.* Detroit: Gale Research.

———. 1991. *New Age Almanac.* New York: Visible Ink Press.

Mendip District Council. 1994. *Glastonbury and Street Area Local Plan.* Mendip District Council.

Merleau-Ponty, Maurice. 1962. *The Phenomenology of Perception.* London: Routledge and Kegan Paul.

Meskell, Lynn. 1995. "Goddesses, Gimbutas, and 'New Age' Archaeology." *Antiquity* 69: 74–86.

Messenger, Stanley. 1991. "A Preparation for the Next Impact." In *Crop Circles: Harbingers of World Change*, ed. A. Bartholomew 1991. Pp. 176–89. Bath: Gateway Books.

Michael, Mike. 1996. *Constructing Identities: The Social, the Nonhuman, and Change.* London: Sage.

Michaelson, Robert S. 1986. "Sacred Land in America: What Is It? How Can It Be Protected?" *Religion* 16: 249–68.

———. 1995. "Dirt in the Court Room: Indian Land Claims and American Property Rights." In *American Sacred Space*, ed. D. Chidester and E. Linenthal, 43–96. Bloomington: Indiana University Press.

Michell, John. 1969. *The View over Atlantis.* New York: Ballantine.

———. 1972. *City of Revelation.* London: Garnstone.

———. 1974. *The Old Stones of Land's End.* London: Garnstone.

———. 1975. *The Earth Spirit: Its Ways, Shrines, and Mysteries.* New York: Avon.

———. 1978. "Glastonbury-Jerusalem, Paradise on Earth: A Revelation Examined." In *Glastonbury: Ancient Avalon, New Jerusalem*, ed. A. Roberts. London: Rider.

———. 1982. *Megalithomania: Artists, Antiquarians, and Archaeologists at Old Stone Monuments.* Ithaca, N.Y.: Cornell University Press.

———. 1983. *A New View over Atlantis.* London: Thames and Hudson.

———. 1985. *Stonehenge: Its Druids, Custodians, Festival, and Future.* London: Radical-Traditionalist Press.

———. 1989. *Secrets of the Stones: New Revelations of Astro-Archaeology and the Mystical Sciences of Antiquity.* Rochester, Vt.: Inner Traditions.

———. 1990. *New Light on the Ancient Mystery of Glastonbury.* Glastonbury: Gothic Image.

Miles, Iain. n.d. ". . . Bogs and Inundations. . . ." Somerset Industrial Archaeological Society and Westonzoyland Engine Trust, with the assistance of the National Rivers Authority.

Miller, Ben. 1993. Community Report. *Sedona Magazine*, Fall: 34.

Miller, Elliot. 1989. *A Crash Course on the New Age Movement: Describing and Evaluating a Growing Social Force*. Grand Rapids, Mich.: Baker Book House.

Miller, Hamish, and Paul Broadhurst. 1989. *The Sun and the Serpent*. Launceton, Cornwall: Pendragon Press.

Miller, Sherrill. 1991. *The Pilgrim's Guide to the Sacred Earth*. Saskatoon: Western Producer Prairie Books.

Mills, Colin Ivor. 1994. "The Social Geography of New Age Spirituality in Vancouver." Master's thesis, University of British Columbia.

Milne, Courtney. 1991a. *The Sacred Earth*. Saskatoon: Western Producer Prairie Books.

———. 1991b. "Sacred Earth: Pilgrim's Portfolio: Five Years among the World's Holy Places." *Equinox* 58 (July/August): 38–47.

Mingay, G. E., ed. 1989. *The Rural Idyll*. London: Routledge.

Mitchell, W. J. T., ed. 1994. *Landscape and Power*. Chicago: University of Chicago Press.

Moir, Jan. 1993. "Summer Lives: The Heal Thing." *Guardian*, August 4: 8 (G2T).

Molyneaux, Brian Leigh. 1995. *The Sacred Earth*. Living Wisdom. Boston: Little, Brown.

Moon, Adrian. 1978. *The First Ground of God: A History of the Glastonbury Abbey Estates*. Glastonbury: Gothic Image.

Moore, Alanna. 1994. *Divining Earth Spirit*. Lismore, Australia: A. Moore, P.O. Box 1263, Lismore 2480.

Morgan, Ann, ed. 1989. *The 1989 Avalonian Guide to Glastonbury*. Glastonbury: Unique Publications.

———. 1990. "Space in Town for Travellers." *Glastonbury Times*, Summer: 9.

Morgan, Ann, and Bruce Garrard, eds. 1989. *Travellers in Glastonbury (A series of articles written during the summer of 1989)*. Glastonbury: Glastonbury Gazette/Unique Publications.

Morinis, E. Alan, ed. 1992. *Sacred Journeys: The Anthropology of Pilgrimage*. London: Greenwood Press.

Mugerauer, Robert. 1985. "Language and Environment." In *Dwelling, Place, and Environment: Towards a Phenomenology of Person and World*, ed. D. Seamon and R. Mugerauer. Boston: Martinus Nijhoff.

Murphy, Michael. 1994. "State's History Trampled: Southwest Ruins under Attack by New Agers, Others." *Phoenix Gazette*, May 9: A1.

Murphy, Patrick. 1995. *Literature, Nature, and Other: Ecofeminist Critiques*. Albany: State University of New York Press.

Muscolino, Michael. 1992. *Little Town Blues: Voices from the Changing West*. Salt Lake City: Peregrine Smith.

Myers, Norman, ed. 1984. *Gaia: An Atlas of Planet Management*. Garden City, N.J.: Anchor Press/Doubleday.

Nasta, Cynthia V. 1981. "On Location in Red Rock Country." *Arizona Highways*, September: 39–44.

National Trust. 1992. *The National Trust Handbook: A Guide for Members and Visitors*. London: National Trust.

———. n.d. *Glastonbury Tor*. Archaeology in the National Trust. Somerset: National Trust.

Nicholson. John. 1992 [1978]. Foreword ("Landscapes in a figure") to *Glastonbury: Ancient Avalon, New Jerusalem*, ed. A. Roberts. London: Rider.

Norris, Scott, ed. 1994. *Discovered Country: Tourism and Survival in the American West*. Albuquerque: Stone Letter Press.

Oates, David. 1989. *Earth Rising: Ecological Beliefs in an Age of Science*. Corvallis: Oregon State University Press.

Oelschlaeger, Max, ed. 1995. *Postmodern Environmental Ethics.* Albany: State University of New York Press.

O'Keefe, Daniel Lawrence. 1983. *Stolen Lightning: The Social Theory of Magic.* New York: Vintage Books/Random House.

Orenstein, Gloria F. 1990. *The Reflowering of the Goddess.* New York: Pergamon Press.

Orion, Loretta. 1995. *Never Again the Burning Times: Paganism Revived.* Prospect Heights, Ill.: Waveland Press.

Oulton, Charles, and Alexander Garrett. 1996. "Down on Their Uppers in Street." *Observer,* July 7: 17.

Ovid. 1955. *Metamorphoses.* Translated by M. Innes. New York: Penguin.

Parish of Glastonbury. n.d. *Local Studies Pack for the Parish of Glastonbury.* Somerset County Council Library Service.

Park, Chris C. 1994. *Sacred Worlds: An Introduction to Geography and Religion.* New York: Routledge.

Pearson, Joanne. 1998. "Assumed Affinities: Wicca and the New Age." In *Nature Religion Today,* ed. J. Pearson, R. Roberts, and J. Samuel, eds., 1998, 45–56.

Pearson, Joanne, Richard H. Roberts, and Jeffrey Samuel, eds. 1998. *Nature Religion Today: Paganism in the Modern World.* Edinburgh: Edinburgh University Press.

Peet, Richard, and Michael Watts, eds. 1996. *Liberation Ecologies: Environment, Development, Social Movements.* New York: Routledge.

Penfield, Wilder. 1975. *The Mystery of the Mind: A Critical Study of Consciousness and the Human Brain.* Princeton, N.J.: Princeton University Press.

Pennick, Nigel. 1979. *The Ancient Science of Geomancy: Living in Harmony with the Earth.* London: Thames and Hudson.

———. 1980. *Sacred Geometry: Symbolism and Purpose in Religious Structures.* Wellingborough, Northamptonshire: Turnstone Press.

Pennick, Nigel, and Paul Devereux. 1989. *Lines on the Landscape: Leys and Other Enigmas.* London: Hale.

Peplow, Edward H., Jr. 1966. "The Call of Oak Creek Canyon." *Arizona Highways* 42 (June): 1–40.

Persinger, Michael A. 1987. *Neuropsychological Bases of God Beliefs.* New York: Praeger.

———. 1989. "Geophysical Variables and Behavior: 55. Predicting the Details of Visitor Experiences and the Personality of Experients: The Temporal Lobe Factor." *Perceptual and Motor Skills* 68: 55–65.

Persinger, Michael, and John Derr. 1985. "Relations between UFO Reports within the Uinta Basin and Local Seismicity." *Perceptual and Motor Skills* 60.

———. 1986. "Luminous Phenomena and Earthquakes in Southern Washington." *Experienta* 42.

Pile, Steve, and Michael Keith, eds. 1997. *Geographies of Resistance.* New York: Routledge.

Pilles, Peter J., Jr. 1981. "A Review of Yavapai Archaeology." In *The Protohistoric Period in the North American Southwest, A.D. 1450–1700,* ed. D. R. Wilcox and W. B. Masse, 163–82. Tempe: Arizona State University.

———. 1989. "Public Education and the Management of Rock Art Sites on the Coconino National Forest." In *Preserving Our Rock Art Heritage,* ed. H. K. Crotty. San Miguel, Calif.: American Rock Art Research Association.

Pisani, Donald. 1989. "The Irrigation District and the Federal Relationship: Neglected Aspects of Water History in the Twentieth Century." In *The Twentieth-Century West: Historical Interpretations,* ed. G. Nash and R. Etulain, 257–92. Albuquerque: University of New Mexico Press.

Plumwood, Val. 1993. *Feminism and the Mastery of Nature.* London: Routledge.

Popenoe, Oliver, and Cris Popenoe. 1984. *Seeds of Tomorrow: New Age Communities That Work.* San Francisco: Harper and Row.

Porter, Eliot, Wallace Stegner, and Page Stegner. 1981. *American Places.* Edited by John Macrae III. New York: Dutton.

Powell, Peggy. 1979. "The Public Controversy behind Secret Mountain: Politics, Conservation, or a Socialistic Confrontation?" *Sedona Life* 4 (3): 16–17, 46–48.

Powys, John Cowper. 1933 [1955]. *A Glastonbury Romance.* London: Macdonald.

Preston, James J. 1992. "Spiritual Magnetism: An Organizing Principle for the Study of Pilgrimage." In *Sacred Journeys: The Anthropology of Pilgrimage,* ed. A. Morinis, 31–46. London: Greenwood Press.

Prigogine, Ilya, and Isabelle Stengers. 1984. *Order Out of Chaos: Man's New Dialogue with Nature.* New York: Bantam.

Prince, Ruth. 1991. "An Anthropology of the 'New Age,' with Special Reference to Glastonbury, Somerset." M.A. thesis, University of St. Andrews, Scotland.

Prokop, Carolyn V. 1997. "Becoming a Place of Pilgrimage: An Eliadean Interpretation of the Miracle at Ambridge, Pennsylvania." In *Sacred Places, Sacred Spaces: The Geography of Pilgrimages,* ed. R. H. Stoddard and A. Morinis, 117–39. Baton Rouge: Geoscience Publications/Louisiana State University.

Rahtz, Philip. 1988. Review of Bailey et al., *Dowsing and Church Archaeology. Antiquity* 62: 808–9.

———. 1991. *Invitation to Archaeology.* Oxford: Blackwell.

———. 1993. *Glastonbury.* London: Batsford/English Heritage.

Raschke, Carl. 1992. "Fire and Roses, or the Problem of Postmodern Religious Thinking." In *Shadow of Spirit: Postmodernism and Religion,* ed. P. Berry and A. Wernick, 93–108. London: Routledge.

Reader, Ian, and Tony Walter, eds. 1993. *Pilgrimage in Popular Culture.* London: Macmillan.

Redfield, James. 1993. *The Celestine Prophecy.* Hoover, Ala.: Satori.

Redpath Communications. 1987. *Harmonic Convergence: A Time of Empowerment.* Glastonbury: Redpath Communications.

Reed, Edward S. 1986. "An Ecological Approach to Cognition." In *Against Cognitivism,* ed. A. Costall and A. Still. Brighton: Harvester Press.

———. 1988. "The Affordances of the Animate Environment: Social Science from the Ecological Point of View." In *What Is an Animal?* ed. T. Ingold. London: Unwin Hyman.

Regush, Nicholas. 1995. "Brain Storms and Angels." *Equinox* 82: 62–73.

Reiser, Oliver L. 1974. *This Holyest Erthe: The Glastonbury Zodiac and King Arthur's Camelot.* London: Perennial.

Reisner, Marc. 1986. *Cadillac Desert: The American West and Its Disappearing Water.* New York: Penguin.

Relph, Edward C. 1991. "Post-Modern Geographies." *Canadian Geographer* 35: 98–105.

Renfrew, Colin, and Ezra B. W. Zubrow, eds. 1994. *The Ancient Mind: Elements of Cognitive Archaeology.* Cambridge: Cambridge University Press.

Rennie, Bryan, ed. 2000. *Changing Religious Worlds: The Meaning and End of Mircea Eliade.* Albany: State University of New York Press.

Restivo, Sal. 1985. *The Social Relations of Physics, Mysticism, and Mathematics: Studies in Social Structure, Interests, and Ideas.* Dordrecht: Reidel.

Riddell, Carol. 1990. *The Findhorn Community: Creating a Human Identity for the Twenty-First Century.* Forres, Scotland: Findhorn Press.

Rigby, Elizabeth. 1979. "Forest Service Working to Stabilize Local Indian Ruin." *Red Rock News,* March 28: 8.

———. 1986. "Oak Creek Canyon, Red Rock, Sedona—Then and Now." *Plateau* 57 (1): 24–31.

Riley, Michael J. 1994. "Constituting the Southwest—Contesting the Southwest—Re-Inventing the Southwest." *Journal of the Southwest* 36 (3) (Autumn): 221–41.

Ring, Kenneth. 1976. "Mapping the Regions of Consciousness: A Conceptual Reformulation." *Journal of Transpersonal Psychology* 8 (2): 77–88.

Riordan, Suzanne. 1992. "Channeling: A New Revelation?" In *Perspectives on the New*

Age, ed. J. R. Lewis and J. G. Melton, 105–28. Albany: State University of New York Press.

Rivenburg, Roy. 1994. "Apocalypse Now? Ted Daniels Chronicles a Host of Predictions of Doomsday in His Newsletter." *Los Angeles Times*, September 9, Life and Style.

Roberts, Anthony, ed. 1992 [1978]. *Glastonbury: Ancient Avalon, New Jerusalem*. London: Rider.

Robertson, Roland. 1995. "Glocalization: Time-Space and Homogeneity-Heterogeneity." In *Global Modernities*, ed. M. Featherstone, S. Lash, and R. Robertson, 25–44. London: Sage.

Roney-Dougal, Serena. 1993. *Where Science and Magic Meet*. Shaftesbury, Dorset: Element.

Root, Deborah. 1996. *Cannibal Culture: Art, Appropriation, and the Commodification of Difference*. Boulder, Colo.: Westview Press/HarperCollins.

Rose, Wendy. 1992. "The Great Pretenders: Further Reflections on Whiteshamanism." In *The State of Native America: Genocide, Colonization, and Resistance*, ed. M. A. Jaimes, 403–21. Boston: South End Press.

Ross, Andrew. 1991. *Strange Weather: Culture, Science, and Technology in the Age of Limits*. London: Verso.

———. 1992. "New Age Technoculture." In *Cultural Studies*, ed. L. Grossberg, C. Nelson, and P. Treichler, 531–55. New York: Routledge.

———. 1994. *The Chicago Gangster Theory of Life: Nature's Debt to Society*. New York: Verso.

Roszak, Theodore. 1977. *Unfinished Animal: The Aquarian Frontier and the Evolution of Consciousness*. New York: Harper and Row.

———. 1978. *Person/Planet: The Creative Disintegration of Industrial Society*. Garden City, N.Y.: Anchor/Doubleday.

———. 1992. *The Voice of the Earth: An Exploration of Ecopsychology*. New York: Simon and Schuster.

Royal Commission on the Future of the Toronto Waterfront. 1992. *Regeneration. Toronto's Waterfront and the Sustainable City: Final Report*. Toronto: Royal Commission.

Rufus, Anneli S., and Kristan Lawson. 1991. *Goddess Sites: Europe*. San Francisco: HarperSanFrancisco.

Ruggles, Clive L. N. 1993. "Archaeoastronomy in the 1990s." Papers derived from the third Oxford International Symposium on Archaeoastronomy, St. Andrew's, U.K., September, 1990. Loughborough, Leicestershire: Group D.

Ruland-Thorne, Kate. 1990. *Experience Sedona: Legends and Legacies*. Sedona: Thorne Enterprises.

———. 1993. *Yavapai: The People of the Red Rocks, The People of the Sun*. Sedona: Thorne Enterprises.

Russell, Peter. 1984. *The Awakening Earth: The Global Brain*. London: Ark Paperbacks.

Said, Edward. 1979. *Orientalism*. London: Routledge and Kegan Paul.

St. Mary's Church. n.d. *The Tapestry and Shrine of Our Lady of Glastonbury*. Glastonbury: St. Mary's Church.

Sanday, Peggy. 1981. *Female Power and Male Dominance: On the Origins of Sexual Inequality*. New York: Cambridge University Press.

Sanders, Pete A., Jr. 1992. *Scientific Vortex Information: An M.I.T.-Trained Scientist's Program: How to Easily Understand, Find, and Tap Vortex Energy in Sedona and Wherever You Travel*. Sedona: Free Soul Publishing.

Sandilands, Catriona. 1999. *The Good-Natured Feminist: Ecofeminism and the Quest for Democracy*. Minneapolis: University of Minnesota Press.

Satin, Mark. 1979. *New Age Politics: Healing Self and Society*. New York: Dell/Delta.

Schill, Karin. 1994. "'Something in This Picture Isn't Right': Popularity Overwhelming Sedona." *Arizona Republic*, October 12: B1.

Schneider, Stephen H., and Penelope J. Boston. 1991. *Scientists on Gaia*. Cambridge: MIT Press.

Scott, Barbara, and Carrie Younce. 1994. *Sedona Storm*. Nashville: Thomas Nelson Publications.

Scott, Jamie, and Paul Simpson-Housley, eds. 1991. *Sacred Places and Profane Spaces: Essays in the Geographics of Judaism, Christianity, and Islam*. New York: Greenwood Press.

Screeton, Paul. 1974. *Quicksilver Heritage—The Mystic Leys: Their Legacy of Ancient Wisdom*. London: Thorsons.

———. 1993. *Seekers of the Linear Vision*. Santa Barbara, Calif.: Stonehenge Viewpoint.

Seager, Joni. 1993. *Earth Follies: Coming to Feminist Terms with the Global Environmental Crisis*. New York: Routledge.

Seamon, David, and Robert Mugerauer, eds. 1985. *Dwelling, Place and Environment: Towards a Phenomenology of Person and World*. Boston: Martinus Nijhoff.

Sedona Forum. 1994. *Building Partnerships with the Forest Service: Developing Positive Roles for the Greater Sedona/Oak Creek Community in Local USFS Planning Processes and Management Strategies*. Edited by William Vannette et al. Flagstaff: Northern Arizona University/Sedona Academy.

Sedona Oak Creek Canyon Chamber of Commerce. n.d. "Experience Sedona: Arizona's Scenic Sensation." Advertisement, *Sedona Magazine* (c. 1994).

Sedona Westerners. 1975. *Those Early Days . . . Old Timers' Memoirs: Oak Creek-Sedona and the Verde Valley Region of Northern Arizona*. Sedona: Sedona Westerners.

Seronde, Jacques. 1989. "Water Report: New Plan Threatens Northern Arizona Forests." *Northern Arizona Environmental Newsletter* 2 (1) (Winter Solstice 1989–90): 5–8.

Sessions, George. 1995a. "Deep Ecology and the New Age Movement." In *Deep Ecology for the 21st Century*, ed. G. Sessions. Boston and London: Shambhala.

———, ed. 1995b. *Deep Ecology for the Twenty-First Century*. Boston: Shambhala.

Shaffer, Mark. 1990. "Fighting for 'Paradise': Sedona Residents, U.S. at Odds on Oak Creek Site." *Arizona Republic*, February 2: B1.

———. 1991a. "Christmas amid the Vortexes: Glory to the New Agers' Thing." *Arizona Republic*, December 23: B1.

———. 1991b. "Group Plans to Buy, Protect Indian Ruins." March 14.

———. 1992. "Oak Creek Canyon Hurt by Popularity: Ways Sought to Protect Sedona Site." *Arizona Republic*, May 26: B1.

Shambhala Healing Centre. 1992. "11:11 Opening the Star Gate at Glastonbury" Produced by Kathy and Michael Jones; "anchored by Tara of the Elohim." Glastonbury, videocassette.

Shanks, Michael, and Christopher Tilley. 1994. *Re-Constructing Archaeology: Theory and Practice*. 2d ed. New York: Routledge.

Sheeran, Patrick F. 1990. "The Ideology of Earth Mysteries." *Journal of Popular Culture* 23 (4): 67–73.

Sheldrake, Rupert. 1988. *The Presence of the Past: Morphic Resonance and the Habits of Nature*. New York: Random House/Vintage.

———. 1991. *The Rebirth of Nature: The Greening of Science and God*. New York: Bantam.

Sheldrake, Rupert, Ralph Abraham, and Terence McKenna. 1992. *Trialogues at the Edge of the West: Chaos, Creativity, and the Resacralization of the World*. Santa Fe: Bear.

Sheridan, Thomas E. 1995a. *Arizona: A History*. Tucson: University of Arizona Press.

———. 1995b. "Arizona: The Political Ecology of a Desert State." *Journal of Political Ecology* 2: 41–57.

Shields, Rob. 1991. *Places on the Margin: Alternative Geographies of Modernity*. New York: Routledge.

Shimazono, Susumu. 1999. "'New Age Movement' or 'New Spirituality Movements and Culture'?" *Social Compass* 46 (2): 121–33.

Sidener, Jonathan. 1991. "Troubled Forest: New Agers versus Old-Age Splendor." *Arizona Republic*, January 24: B1.

Simmons, I. G. 1993. *Interpreting Nature: Cultural Constructions of the Environment*. New York: Routledge.

Sismondo, Sergio. 1996. *Science without Myth: On Constructions, Reality, and Social Knowledge*. Albany: State University of New York Press.

Sjöö, Monica. 1992. *New Age and Armageddon: The Goddess or the Gurus? Towards a Feminist Vision of the Future*. London: Women's Press.

———. 1994. "New Age and Patriarchy." *Religion Today* 9 (3) (Summer): 22–28.

Sjöö, Monica, and Barbara Mor. 1987. *The Great Cosmic Mother: Rediscovering the Religion of the Earth*. San Francisco: Harper and Row.

Slack, Jennifer Daryl, and Jody Berland, eds. 1994. *Cultural Studies* 8 (1). Special issue: Cultural Studies and the Environment.

Smith, Andy. 1991. "For All Those Who Were Indian in a Former Life." *Ms.* (November-December): 44–45.

Smith, Jonathan Z. 1972. "The Wobbling Pivot." *Journal of Religion* 52: 134–49.

———. 1987. *To Take Place: Toward Theory in Ritual*. Chicago: University of Chicago Press.

Smith, Judy. 1990. "Behind the Facade: Fear and Loathing in Sedona's Resort Industry." *Tab*, February 22: 1, 5.

Smith, Neil. 1990. *Uneven Development: Nature, Capital, and the Production of Space*. Oxford: Blackwell.

Soja, Edward. 1989. *Postmodern Geographies: The Reassertion of Space in Critical Social Theory*. London: Verso.

———. 1996. *Thirdspace: Journeys to Los Angeles and Other Real-and-Imagined Places*. Oxford: Blackwell.

Solstice Trust. n.d. *The World Garden Site Plan*. Warminster, Wiltshire: Unique Publications.

Somerset County Council Peat Local Plan. 1992. Somerset County Council Environment Department.

Soper, Kate. 1995. *What Is Nature?* Oxford: Blackwell.

Spangle, Michael, and David Knapp. 1996. "Ways We Talk about the Earth: An Exploration of Persuasive Tactics and Appeals in Environmental Discourse." In *Earthtalk: Communication Empowerment for Environmental Action*, ed. S. A. Muir and T. L. Veenendall. Westport, Conn.: Praeger.

Spangler, David. 1977. *Towards a Planetary Vision*. Forres, Scotland: Findhorn Publications.

———. 1980. *Revelation: The Birth of a New Age*. Elgin, Ill.: Lorian Press.

———. 1984. *Emergence: The Rebirth of the Sacred*. New York: Dell.

———. 1988. "Defining the New Age." In *The New Age Catalogue: Access to Information and Sources*. New York: Doubleday.

———. 1994. "Conversation with Pan and the Nature Spirits." In *The Kingdom Within: A Guide to the Spiritual Work of the Findhorn Community*, ed. A. Walker, 103–11. Forres, Scotland: Findhorn Press.

Spink, Canon Peter. 1991. *A Christian in the New Age*. London: Darton, Longman, and Todd.

Spretnak, Charlene. 1978. *Lost Goddesses of Early Greece: A Collection of Pre-Hellenic Myths*. Berkeley: Moon Books.

———. 1991. *States of Grace: The Recovery of Meaning in the Postmodern Age*. San Francisco: HarperSanFrancisco.

———, ed. 1982. *The Politics of Women's Spirituality: Essays on the Rise of Spiritual Power within the Feminist Movement*. Garden City, N.Y.: Anchor/Doubleday.

Sprinkle, Alsgoud. 1985. *Vortexes??? An Overview of the Geophysical Aspects of Vortexes*. Sedona: RMA Light Press.

Stangroome, Vicki. 1993. *Health Education and Primary Health Care Provision for New Age Travellers: Investigation into Policies, Priorities, and Resources Available to New Age Travellers (the Hippy Convoy)*. Self-published.

Starhawk [Miriam Simos]. 1979. *The Spiral Dance: The Rebirth of the Ancient Religion of the Great Goddess.* San Francisco: Harper and Row.

——. 1982. *Dreaming the Dark: Magic, Sex, and Politics.* San Francisco: Harper and Row.

——. 1987. *Truth or Dare: Encounters with Power, Authority, and Mystery.* San Francisco: Harper and Row.

Stein, Pat. 1981. "The Yavapai and Tonto Apache." *Plateau* 53 (1): 18–23.

Steiner, Dieter, and Markus Nauser, ed. 1993. *Human Ecology: Fragments of Anti-Fragmentary Views of the World.* New York: Routledge.

Stengel, Marc K. 2000. "The Diffusionists Have Landed." *Atlantic* 285 (January): 1.

Steward, Vicki, ed. n.d. *Glastonbury Alternative Visitors Guide.* Glastonbury.

Stoddard, Robert H., and E. Alan Morinis, eds. 1997. *Sacred Places, Sacred Spaces: The Geography of Pilgrimages.* Geoscience and Man, no. 34. Baton Rouge: Geoscience Publications/Louisiana State University.

Stone, Merlin. 1976. *When God Was a Woman.* New York: Harcourt Brace Jovanovich.

Straffon, Cheryl. 1993. *Pagan Cornwall: Land of the Goddess.* Penzance: Meyn Mamvro.

Stubbs, Tony. 1992. *An Ascension Handbook: Channeled Material by Serapis.* Livermore, Calif.: Oughten House.

Summer, Naomi. 1992. "A Study of the Myths and Literature of the 'Women's Spirituality' Movement." M.A. dissertation, Lancaster University, U.K.

Sun Bear and Wabun. 1992 [1980]. *The Medicine Wheel: Earth Astrology.* New York: Fireside.

Sundberg, N., and C. Keutzer. 1984. "Transpersonal Psychology (1)." In *Encyclopedia of Psychology,* ed. Raymond Corsini, 3:441–42. New York: Wiley.

Sunregion Associates. *Sedona Community Plan—Economic Base Study.* 1990. Phoenix: Sunregion Associates.

Sutcliffe, Steven, and Marion Bowman, eds. 2000. *Beyond New Age: Exploring Alternative Spirituality.* Edinburgh: Edinburgh University Press.

Sutphen, Dick. 1988. *Dick Sutphen Presents Sedona: Psychic Energy Vortexes.* Malibu, Calif.: Valley of the Sun Publishing.

Swan, James A. 1990. *Sacred Places: How the Living Earth Seeks Our Friendship.* Santa Fe: Bear.

——. 1992. *Nature as Teacher and Healer: How to Reawaken Your Connection to Nature.* New York: Villard Books.

——, ed. 1991. *The Power of Place: Sacred Ground in Natural and Human Environments.* Wheaton, Ill.: Quest/Theosophical Publishing House.

Swimme, Brian, and Thomas Berry. 1992. *The Universe Story: From the Primordial Flaring Forth to the Ecozoic Era—A Celebration of the Unfolding of the Cosmos:* San Francisco: HarperSanFrancisco.

Talbot, Michael. 1986. *Beyond the Quantum.* New York: Macmillan.

Tambiah, Stanley Jeyaraja. 1990. *Magic, Science, Religion, and the Scope of Rationality.* Cambridge: Cambridge University Press.

Tarbat, Alan. 1988. "Let's Walk around Glastonbury with Alan Tarbat." Glastonbury: Glastonbury Advertising Association.

Tart, Charles T. 1975a. *States of Consciousness.* New York: Dutton.

——. 1975b. *Transpersonal Psychologies.* New York: Harper and Row.

——, ed. 1990. *Altered States of Consciousness:* San Francisco: HarperSanFrancisco.

Tauxe, Caroline S. 1996. "Mystics, Modernists, and Constructions of Brasilia." *Ecumene* 3 (1): 43–61.

Taylor, Bron R. 1995a. "Resacralizing Earth: Pagan Environmentalism and the Restoration of Turtle Island." In *American Sacred Space,* ed. D. Chidester and E. Linenthal, 97–151. Bloomington: Indiana University Press.

——, ed. 1995b. *Ecological Resistance Movements: The Global Emergence of Radical and Popular Environmentalism.* Albany: State University of New York Press.

Teilhard de Chardin, Pierre. 1955. *The Phenomenon of Man.* London: Collins.

——. 1964. *The Future of Man.* London: Collins.

Thomas, Julian. 1996. *Time, Culture, and Identity: An Interpretative Archaeology.* London: Routledge.

Thompson, Keith. 1991. *Angels and Aliens: UFOs and the Mythic Imagination.* New York: Fawcett Columbine.

Thompson, William I. 1974. *Passages about Earth: An Exploration of the New Planetary Culture.* New York: Harper and Row.

———. 1978. "The Future as Image of the Past." *Quest* 2: 54–58.

———, ed. 1987. *Gaia: A Way of Knowing: Political Implications of the New Biology.* Great Barrington, Mass.: Lindisfarne Press.

———. 1991. *Gaia 2: Emergence: The New Science of Becoming.* New York: Lindisfarne Press.

Thrift, Nigel. 1994. "Inhuman Geographies: Landscapes of Speed, Light and Power." In *Writing the Rural: Five Cultural Geographies,* ed. P. Cloke, M. Doel, D. Matless, M. Phillips, and N. Thrift, 191–248. London: Paul Chapman.

Tilley, Christopher. 1994. *A Phenomenology of Landscape: Places, Paths and Monuments.* Oxford: Berg.

Tilley, Terence, and Craig Westman. 1995. "David Ray Griffin and Constructive Postmodern Communalism." In *Postmodern Theologies: The Challenge of Religious Diversity,* ed. T. Tilley, 17–27. Maryknoll, N.Y.: Orbis Books.

Todorov, Tzvetan. 1984. *Mikhail Bakhtin: The Dialogical Principle.* Translated by W. Godzich. Theory and History of Literature, vol. 13. Minneapolis: University of Minnesota Press.

Torgovnick, Marianna. 1990. *Gone Primitive: Savage Intellects, Modern Lives.* Chicago: University of Chicago Press.

Trevelyan, Sir George. 1986. *Summons to a High Crusade.* Forres, Scotland: Findhorn Press.

Trimble, Stephen. 1993. *The People: Indians of the American Southwest.* Santa Fe: Santa Fe School of American Research.

Turnbull, James. 1988. "An Interview with James Turnbull." Interview by Ali McKay. *Glastonbury Communicator* 15: 17.

Turner, Edith. 1987. "Pilgrimage: An Overview." In *The Encyclopedia of Religion,* ed.-in-chief M. Eliade, 328–30. New York: Macmillan.

Turner, Victor. 1969. *The Ritual Process: Structure and Anti-Structure.* Ithaca, N.Y.: Cornell University Press.

———. 1974. "Pilgrimages as Social Processes." In *Dramas, Fields, and Metaphors: Symbolic Action in Human Society.* Ithaca, N.Y.: Cornell University Press.

Turner, Victor, and Edith Turner. 1978. *Image and Pilgrimage in Christian Culture: Anthropological Perspectives.* New York: Columbia University Press.

Turvey, M. T., and Claudia Carello. 1981. "Cognition: The View from Ecological Realism." *Cognition* 10: 313–21.

Ucko, P. J., M. Hunter, A. J. Clark, and A. David. 1990. *Avebury Reconsidered: From the 1660s to the 1990s.* London: Unwin Hyman.

Unique Publications. 1839. *Avalonian Guide to the Town of Glastonbury and Its Environs.* Reprint, 1987. Glastonbury: Unique Publications.

University of Avalon. *Prospectus,* various editions.

Urry, John. 1992. *The Tourist Gaze: Leisure and Travel in Contemporary Societies.* London: Sage.

———. 1995. *Consuming Places.* New York: Routledge.

Vallee, Jacques. 1969. *Passport to Magonia.* Chicago: Regnery.

———. 1988. *Dimensions: A Casebook of Alien Contact.* Chicago: Contemporary Books.

Valverde, Maya. 1989. "Nobody's Right If Everybody's Wrong: One Region, or Separate Communities—The Townspeople of the Area." *Tab,* January 26: 1, 14–15.

van Buren, John. 1995. "Critical Environmental Hermeneutics." *Environmental Ethics* 17 (Fall): 259–75.

van Leusen, Martijn. 1999. "Dowsing and Archaeology: Is There Something There?" *Skeptical Inquirer* 23 (2) (March-April): 33–41.

van Wyck, Peter C. 1997. *Primitives in the Wilderness: Deep Ecology and the Missing Human Subject.* Albany: State University of New York Press.

Varela, Francisco. 1986. "Laying Down a Path in Walking: A Biologist's Look at a New Biology." *ReVision* 9 (1): 93–98.

Varela, Francisco, Evan Thompson, and Eleanor Rosch. 1991. *The Embodied Mind: Cognitive Science and Human Experience.* Cambridge, Mass.: MIT Press.

Vattimo, Gianni. 1988. *The End of Modernity: Nihilism and Hermeneutics in Postmodern Culture.* Translated by J. R. Snyder. Baltimore: Johns Hopkins University Press.

——. 1992. *The Transparent Society.* Translated by D. Webb. Baltimore: Johns Hopkins University Press.

Verde Valley Pioneers Association. 1954. *Pioneer Stories of the Verde Valley of Arizona.* Edited by Bonnie Peplow and Ed Peplow. Camp Verde: Verde Valley Pioneers Association.

VJ Enterprises. 1996. "Spirits of the Earth—Adventures for the Soul." <http://www.execpc.com/vjentpr/southwst.html>.

Vogel, Steven. 1997. "Habermas and the Ethics of Nature." In *The Ecological Community,* ed. R. S. Gottlieb. New York: Routledge.

Walker, Alex, ed. 1994. *The Kingdom Within: A Guide to the Spiritual Work of the Findhorn Community.* Forres, Scotland: Findhorn Press.

Walker, Barbara G. 1989. *The Book of Sacred Stones: Fact and Fallacy in the Crystal World.* San Francisco: Harper and Row.

Walsh, Terry. 1993. *Global Sacred Alignments.* Glastonbury: University of Avalon Press.

Walter, E. V. 1988. *Placeways: A Theory of the Human Environment.* Chapel Hill: University of North Carolina Press.

Washburn, Michael. 1988. *The Ego and the Dynamic Ground: A Transpersonal Theory of Human Development.* Albany: State University of New York Press.

——. 1994. *Transpersonal Psychology in Psychoanalytic Perspective.* Albany: State University of New York Press.

Watkins, Alfred. 1984 [1925]. *The Old Straight Track.* London: Sphere Books.

Webb, Albert E. 1929. *Glastonbury Ynyswytryn (Isle of Avalon): Its Story from Celtic Days to the Twentieth Century.* Glastonbury: Avalon Press.

Weigle, Marta. 1989. "From Desert to Disney World: The Santa Fe Railway and the Fred Harvey Company Display the Indian Southwest." *Journal of Anthropological Research* 45 (1) (Spring).

——. 1990. "Southwest Lures: Innocents Detoured, Incensed Determined." *Journal of the Southwest* 32 (4) (Winter): 499–540.

Weigle, Marta, and Barbara A. Babcock, eds. 1996. *The Great Southwest of the Fred Harvey Company and the Santa Fe Railway.* Phoenix: Heard Museum.

West, Bill. 1975. *Battle at Oak Creek.* Sedona: Pronto Press.

Western, Ken. 1994. "Plugging Holes in Arizona's Tourist Season," *Arizona Republic,* July 17: H1 (Business).

Weston, Anthony. 1995. "Before Environmental Ethics." In *Postmodern Environmental Ethics,* ed. M. Oelschlaeger, 223–32. Albany: State University of New York Press.

White, Rob. 1994. "Sacred Places: The West's New, Booming Extractive Industry." *High Country News,* March 7: 16.

Whitfield, Martin. 1994. "Historic Town Split on Passing Traffic: Different Visions of Life and the Future of the High Street Have Led Glastonbury to the Polls." *Independent,* March 10: 6 (Home News).

Wiener, Paul J., and John D. Eastwood. 1994. *The Impact of Visitors on the Sedona Economy.* Flagstaff: College of Business Administration, Northern Arizona University.

Wilber, Ken. 1977. *The Spectrum of Consciousness.* Wheaton, Ill.: Theosophical Publishing House.

——. 1983. *Up From Eden: A Transpersonal View of Human Evolution.* Boulder, Colo.: Shambhala.

——. 1985a. "Reflections on the New-Age Paradigm: A Conversation with Ken Wilber." In *The Holographic Paradigm and Other Paradoxes*. ed. Ken Wilber. New York: Shambhala, 249–94.

———. 1990. *Eye to Eye: The Quest for the New Paradigm*. Expanded ed. Boston: Shambhala.

———. 1995. *Sex, Ecology, Spirituality: The Spirit of Evolution*. Boston: Shambhala.

———, ed. 1985b. *The Holographic Paradigm and Other Paradoxes: Exploring the Leading Edge of Science*. New York: Shambhala.

Wilber, Ken, Jack Engler, and Daniel P. Brown, eds. 1986. *Transformations of Consciousness: Conventional and Contemplative Perspectives on Development*. Boston: Shambhala.

Wiley, Peter, and Robert Gottlieb. 1982. *Empires in the Sun: The Rise of the New American West*. Tucson: University of Arizona Press.

Willeford, Lynn M. 1993. "Who Will Rule the Schools?" *New Age Journal*. November-December 1993, 19.

Williams, Brian. 1970. *How the Gospel Came to Britain*. Birmingham: Brian Williams Evangelistic Association.

Williams, Mary, ed. 1990. *Glastonbury and Britain: A Study in Patterns*. London: Research into Lost Knowledge Organisation.

Williams, Raymond. 1977. *Marxism and Literature*. Oxford: Oxford University Press.

———. 1980. *Problems in Materialism and Culture*. London: Verso.

———. 1985. *The Country and the City*. London: Hogarth Press.

Williams, Robin, and Romey Williams. 1992. *The Somerset Levels*. West Country Landscapes. Bradford-on-Avon, Wiltshire: Ex Libris Press.

Williams, Stephen. 1991. *Fantastic Archaeology: The Wild Side of North American Prehistory*. Philadelphia: University of Pennsylvania Press.

Williamson, Tom, and Liz Bellamy. 1983. *Ley Lines in Question*. Kingswood, Surrey: World's Work.

Wilson, Alexander. 1991. *The Culture of Nature: North American Landscape from Disney to the Exxon Valdez*. Toronto: Between the Lines.

Winton, Ben. 1990a. "Group Access to Sedona Sites Limited." *Phoenix Gazette*, June 30: B1.

———. 1990b. "Sedona's New Agers: Red Rock Country Draws Believers in Astrology, Psychic Powers." *Phoenix Gazette*, March 31: A12.

Wolf, Fred Alan. 1981. *Taking the Quantum Leap: The New Physics for Nonscientists*. San Francisco: Harper and Row.

———. 1986. *The Body Quantum: The New Physics of Body, Mind, and Health*. New York: Macmillan.

———. 1991. *The Eagle's Quest: A Physicist's Search for Truth at the Heart of the Shamanic World*. New York: Simon and Schuster/Touchstone.

Wolfe, Cary. 1998. *Critical Environments: Postmodern Theory and the Pragmatics of the "Outside."* Minneapolis: University of Minnesota Press.

Woodhead, Linda. 1993. "Post-Christian Spiritualities." *Religion* 23: 167–81.

World Survival Foundation. n.d. "Save Long Canyon," and related documents. <www.savelongcanyon.org> and <www.savelongcanyon.com>. Accessed August 2000.

Worster, Donald. 1985. *Rivers of Empire: Water, Aridity, and the Growth of the American West*. New York: Pantheon Books.

———. 1994. *Nature's Economy: A History of Ecological Ideas*. 2d ed. New York: Cambridge University Press.

York, Michael. 1994. "New Age in Britain: An Overview." *Religion Today* 9 (3) (Summer): 14–22.

———. 1995. *The Emerging Network: A Sociology of the New Age and Neo-Pagan Movements*. London: Rowan and Littlefield.

Young, David E., and Jean-Guy Goulet, eds. 1994. *Being Changed by Cross-Cultural Encounters: The Anthropology of Extraordinary Experience*. Peterborough, Ont.: Broadview Press.

Zablocki, Benjamin. 1980. *Alienation and Charisma: A Study of Contemporary American Communes.* New York: Free Press.

Zell, Tim. 1971. "Theagenesis: The Birth of the Goddess." *Green Egg* 4 (40).

Zell, Otter [Tim], and Morning Glory Zell. 1990. "Who on Earth Is the Goddess?" Church of All Worlds Web site, 11.6.94., lynsared@teleport.com.

Zimmerman, Michael E. 1994. *Contesting Earth's Future: Radical Ecology and Postmodernity.* Berkeley: University of California Press.

Zimmerman, Michael E., J. Baird Callicott, et al., eds. 1998. *Environmental Philosophy: From Animal Rights to Radical Ecology,* 2d ed. Upper Saddle River, N.J.: Prentice-Hall.

Zukav, Gary. 1980. *The Dancing Wu Li Masters.* New York: William Morrow and Company.

NEWS PUBLICATIONS AND LOCAL PERIODICALS
(WITH ABBREVIATIONS AS USED IN TEXT)

Glastonbury

Alternative News Digest: Stonehenge Special Issue
Central Somerset Gazette (CSG)
Festival Eye
Free State
Glastonbury Communicator (GC)
Glastonbury Conservation Society Newsletter (GCSN)
Glastonbury Gazette (GG)
Glastonbury Thorn
Glastonbury Times (GT)
Glastonbury Zodiac Companion (GZC)
Ley Hunter, The Journal of Geomancy and Earth Mysteries
Oracle
Squall
Torc
Western Gazette (WG)
Women for Life on Earth

Sedona

Arizona Republic (Ariz. Rep.)
Call of the Canyon
Canyon Caller
Canyon Echo
4R Newsletter (4RN)
Let the Good Times Roll
Phoenix Gazette
Red Rock Guardian
Sedona: Journal of Emergence (SJE)
Sedona Excentric
Sedona Life
Sedona Magazine
Sedona Red Rock News (SRRN)
Sedona Spectrum
Sedona Times (ST)
Tab
Trail Mix (Newsletter of the Trail Resource Access Coalition of Sedona)

INTERVIEWS

Names or initials are used in text with permission. All interviews were conducted at the respective sites unless otherwise indicated.

Glastonbury: Bruce Garrard, Palden Jenkins, Kathy Jones, Taras Kosikowsky, Keith Mitchell, Ann Morgan, Jan Preece, Rev. James Turnbull, and one anonymous participant.

Sedona: Terry Adams, John Armbruster, Jim Bishop Jr., Bennie Blake, Mike Consol and Holly Consol (interviewed in California), Warren Cremer, Richard Dannelley, Dove Danu, Marietta Davenport, Darryl David, Lhesli Dove, Paul Fried, Charles Ehrton Hinckley and Naomi Niles, Christopher Jelm, Mary Lou Keller, Gaia Lamb, Maury Lamb, Max Licher, Sheri Richards, Pete A. Sanders Jr., Ted Smith Jr., and one anonymous participant.

INDEX

Page numbers in italics refer to illustrations.

ADRIAN J. IVAKHIV is Assistant Professor in the Department of Religious Studies and Anthropology and the Program in Environmental Studies at the University of Wisconsin, Oshkosh. His writing on environment and culture has appeared in *Social Compass, Topia, Ethnic Forum, Gnosis, The Trumpeter,* and *Musicworks.*